U0060226

A Self-Made Man

Osman C.H. Tseng
曾慶祥

A Self-Made Man
Copyright © Osman C.H. Tseng（曾慶祥）(2023/01).
Published by Elephant White Cultural Enterprise Co., Ltd.

Printed in Taiwan, Republic of China
For information address:
Elephant White Cultural Enterprise Ltd. Press,
8F.-2, No.1, Keji Rd., Dali Dist., Taichung City 41264, Taiwan (R.O.C.)
Distributed by Elephant White Cultural Enterprise Co., Ltd.

ISBN: 978-626-7189-43-6 **(精裝)**
Suggested Price: **NT$600**

Osman C.H. Tseng

曾慶祥

A Self-Made Man

For my other half

Lei Yen-ming

雷燕鳴

To the memory of my mother,

Ay Jin-shiang 艾金香

And my father,

Tseng Shiau-huai 曾憲槐

Acknowledgments

I am extremely grateful to Mr. William Kazer for writing the jacket blurb for my autobiography and proofreading the manuscript in its typeset version.

My thanks also go to my daughter Tseng Wen-yi 曾文儀 and son Tseng Wen-chieh 曾文傑. They were always on hand to help me fix my temperamental computer and solve countless technical problems so that I could complete my writing.

Note from an Old Friend

Veteran journalist Osman C.H. Tseng has had a front-row seat to many of the crucial events that have shaped modern Taiwan and thrust it into the global spotlight. Over the years, he has been a sharp-eyed observer of Taiwan's economic coming of age and its transformation from authoritarian rule to a vibrant democracy. In his autobiography A Self-Made Man, he traces the compelling story of his own journalistic career and offers his keen observations of key political figures and the policies they put in place.

His personal story is an unlikely one. Born into a poor farming family in China's Hubei province, he joined Chiang Kai-shek's Nationalist (Kuomintang) army as a teenager, following it to Taiwan as the mainland fell to advancing Communist forces. He arrived at the port of Kaohsiung with only a straw mattress and two sets of worn-out army fatigues.

During his nearly two decades in the army, he taught himself English starting with the ABCs and aided by little more than a battered Chinese-English dictionary and a deep well of determination. That ultimately paid off as he qualified as an army interpreter and later, after the conclusion of his military service, landed an entry-level reporting job with the English language daily newspaper, the China Post.

This is where he began to acquire the fundamental journalistic skills of gathering facts, ensuring accuracy, and making careful observations of events. His career path led him to the helm of one of

Taiwan's foremost business news organizations, the China Economic News Service, where he also crafted editorials and commentaries.

Fittingly, his career took him back to the China Post once again, where he continued to hone his skills as an opinion writer. His widely read commentaries for these two media organizations ranged from the ambitious democratic reforms of Lee Teng-hui, Taiwan's first popularly elected president, to the policy chaos under his successor, Chen Shui-bian, eventually jailed for corruption.

A Self-Made Man will be of interest to journalists and non-journalists alike. Its publication is particularly timely in an era of pervasive accusations of "fake news" that have undermined the traditional respect for the profession of journalism in the public eye. Hopefully, this account of how a persistent individual overcame considerable odds to follow a passion for journalism will contribute to restoring some of that public trust.

William Kazer

Contents

Introduction

I was a little bit hesitant at first to choose the term A Self-Made Man for the title of this book--my autobiography. A self-made man generally refers to an individual who rises to success from humble origins through his efforts. I was hesitant because I was not sure how to define success. Nor was I sure about how much success was required to deem someone a successful person. In my case, I wondered whether my modest accomplishments could be considered a successful life. I am still unsure about that. On reflection, I chose to call my autobiography the story of A Self-Made Man, leaving the above question to the readers to judge after they finish my account.

I think I do meet the other element of being a self-made man: rising from humble origins. I was born in 1933 into a farming family in a small Chinese village beside the Yangtze River. My parents owned a small farm that allowed them to grow just enough to feed our family members. Both of my parents were uneducated. They could not read or write.

I received only six years of village school education in my life. Unlike primary schools in the educational system in the bigger cities, those village institutions taught only Chinese. No other subjects, like math or a foreign language, were part of the curriculum. But even this limited formal education was disrupted by the disastrous Yangtze River floods in 1947. Due to the significant damage from the flooding, my parents could no longer afford to continue funding my schooling. Without their financial support, I finally chose to join the army despite my young age. Although soldiers were poorly paid at the time, they at least had enough to eat.

I was only 16 years old when I came to Taiwan with the military in mid-1949. This was about the time Chiang Kai-shek and his government and military forces retreated to the island following the fall of the mainland to the communists. I remember when I disembarked from a ship in the southern port of Kaohsiung, my only personal belongings were a straw mattress and two sets of worn-out army fatigues.

In Taiwan, I served the next 18 years in grassroots infantry companies, rising from private to captain. I used my free time in the military to study English, which is not my native tongue. I started learning the ABCs at the age of 20.

I studied English the hard way. In the first 10 years or so of my studies, I pressed ahead with my task in army bunkers, barracks, or in the field. I spent weekends and all other available time studying this difficult language. The only learning aid I had was a Chinese-English dictionary.

Yet I had never anticipated that my rudimentary style of learning would be so fruitful that it enabled me to pass a crucial test 13 years later, allowing me to join an English-language newspaper as a reporter. At this point, I was 33 years old.

What I also never imagined was that English would become a language tool for me to practice journalism for the next half-century. I wrote news reports, features, commentaries, and editorials in English. And after I retired from the journalism profession, I also used this acquired language to write my autobiography as well as a book about former President Chen Shui-bian during his eight years in office.

Furthermore, I never expected that I would be able to achieve the status of a professional journalist, given my lack of formal education and journalism training. It was very fortunate for me that I was able to climb up the ladder of journalism. During my decades-long career in this field, I played various key roles from reporter to city editor, editor-in-chief, and editorial writer.

The successes of my effort to study English and my striving to become a professional journalist and writer were made possible, simply put, by hard work, perseverance, and a strong passion for journalism and English writing.

The story of A Self-Made Man, Osman C.H. Tseng, is a chronicle of my life and career. It recounts important events in my life. The story consists of 10 chapters, as set out below.

Chapter 1
Falling Leaves Return to Their Roots

Paying Tribute to My Late Parents

In 2017, I brought my family to visit my hometown Liubutou -- a small village sitting beside the Yangtze River in Hong City in the Chinese province of Hubei. This was the second time I had visited my birthplace since I left for Taiwan as a teenage soldier more than six decades ago. My previous visit was in 1992, without my family accompanying me. Political and personal reasons prevented me from visiting my birthplace more often all of those years.

The main purpose of this trip was to honor my late mother and father, using the occasion of an extended Tomb-Sweeping Day, a traditional Chinese holiday that fell on April 4 that year.

The visit allowed me to glean more information about my ancestral roots and recall the days of my youth. It also gave me a chance to personally view some of the mainland's dramatic economic development at the local and national levels. In this chapter "Falling Leaves Return to Their Roots," I will describe these and other related events.

My wife Lei Yen-ming, daughter Wen-yi, and I left Taipei for Liubutou on March 30, four days ahead of the holiday. We took a morning China Eastern Airlines flight from Taipei Taoyuan International Airport to Hong Kong. By the time we arrived in the city--a former British colony and now a special administrative region of China -- it was well into the afternoon. We made only a brief stopover there, before riding a bus to the neighboring city of Shenzhen for the night, as scheduled.

Regrettably, our schedule was tight, and we couldn't stay in Shenzhen for a longer look around this modern Chinese city. Shenzhen owed its present-day prosperity to its status as one of China's first Special Economic Zones--a bold social experiment launched in 1979, with the blessing of reformist leader Deng Xiaoping.

The next day we three took a high-speed rail from Shenzhen to Wuhan, where we met with my son Tseng Wen-chieh, as previously planned. Wen-chieh, a software engineer at a Taiwan technology company, had to go to work on weekdays. So he came to join us in Wuhan two days later on April 1 at the start of the Tomb Sweeping Festival. Also known as the Qingming Festival, the holiday is observed in both Taiwan and the Chinese mainland.

Traditionally, people on this occasion visit gravesites to pay tribute to their ancestors or their dead relatives. There, they sweep the tomb, offer sacrifices and burn "spirit banknotes" in the hope that the dead are not lacking food and money. They also kowtow and say prayers before the tablets that are set up for the deceased.

Nowadays, with cremation more common than burial, however, many of the above-cited traditional rituals have been simplified, especially in cities. Tomb sweepers now mostly only present flowers at the resting place of their deceased relatives in performing the tomb-sweeping day ceremony.

The tomb-sweeping day rituals we followed in remembering my parents on that trip were a combination of both old and new. We offered flowers and burned "banknotes" and incense at the gravesite of my parents.

As mentioned above, we made a brief stopover in Wuhan. During the stay, my family and I visited a number of scenic spots, including Wuhan University, East Lake, and the Wuhan Yangtze River Bridge. This bridge became a tourist attraction because it was where China's revolutionary leader Mao Zedong staged his historic swim in the mighty Yangtze River in July 1966.

Besides Wuhan, we also took time out to travel to Beijing to see the massive capital, rich in historic attractions. The Beijing leg of our hometown journey came after we visited our Liubutou relatives and paid respects to our ancestors. Regrettably, Wen-chieh, my son, was unable to join us for that leg. He flew back to Taipei in the afternoon of April 4, because he had to get back to work the following day.

In Beijing, my wife, my daughter, and I made visits to the famous Great Wall, Forbidden City, Tiananmen Square, and the Temple of Heaven. We would have stayed in Beijing longer to see more famous places if only we had time.

Now I must return to our trip to Liubutou. The Liubutou journey and my reflections on it are the main subjects that I am going to discuss in more detail in this chapter: Falling Leaves Return to Their Roots.

Liubutou is a small farm village situated on the northwest bank of the Yangtze River, about 80 miles south of Wuhan. It is very close to the historically important Red Cliffs across the river. The Red Cliffs are the battlefield where Cao Cao, one of China's most controversial politicians, was humiliatingly defeated in the year 208 AD by a coalition of his arch-rivals Liu Bei and Sun Quan. Liu and Sun later founded the states of Shu Han and Eastern Wu respectively, heralding the tumultuous Three Kingdoms period of ancient China.

Liubutou now is under the jurisdiction of Honghu, a county-level city in Hubei province. The city took its name from the adjacent Hong Lake. Honghu is known for frequent flooding. This occurs during the summer months of the year when the Yangtze River often overflows its banks.

Years before Mao Zedong took control of the entire mainland and founded the People's Republic of China in 1949, Honghu City and its surrounding areas were a communist stronghold. The communists came to power after they toppled the beleaguered Nationalist government of Chiang Kai-shek. Chiang and his armies retreated to Taiwan.

It is easy to see why Honghu became a communist stronghold. Left behind economically as a result of the frequent flooding, people in these areas were easily convinced by a catchy slogan of the communists: "help the poor turn rich."

Leaving Home in My Mid-Teens

I cited the above two events, the Yangtze River flooding and the communist revolution because they combined to play a role in my departure from home at such an early age.

Why was this the case? To begin with, the swollen Yangtze River in the summer of 1948 caused floods in my hometown and many other places along the river, resulting in extensive crop and property damage.

As a result of the floods, the neighborhood village school I was attending had to be relocated further south to Xindi town, now the seat of the Honghu City government. But that school soon closed as well, because its lone teacher, Mr. Tseng Ching-chang, was enlisted by his county magistrate friend, Mr. Tseng Chien-wu, to serve as his chief of staff.

These developments plunged me into great difficulty. On one hand, I now had no school to attend. But even if I could find a new one to attend, my parents, struggling with the effect of the floods on their livelihood, might have been unable to afford further schooling for me. On the other hand, I couldn't return home and live with my parents either, because that would certainly have added to their financial burden. This was the last thing that I wanted to do.

So I turned to my teacher, Mr. Tseng Ching-chang, for help, and he arranged for me to join the Mianyang county government's self-defense forces as an orderly. From a practical point of view, this military job went a long way toward eliminating my need to continue to rely on my family for financial support. But it also meant a sad disruption of my formal education. At the time, I was only 15 years old.

By this time I had received only a little more than six years of village school education, which amounted to no more than primary school in the normal educational system.

Unlike a primary school, however, the village school I attended, besides having only one teacher, taught only the Confucian classics, comprising the Four Books (The Great Learning, the Doctrine of the Mean, the Analects, and the Book of Mencius) and the Five Classics

(The Book of Changes, the Book of Odes, the Book of History, the Book of Rites, and the Spring and Autumn Annals).

Beyond those courses, there was nothing like mathematics, geography, history, or science, as typically taught in primary schools. The village school system had a long history in China and remained the only institution for fundamental learning in the nation's rural areas during my childhood years. The established elementary education was available only in big towns and cities.

The flooding impact aside, an intensifying Chinese civil war also played a part in my departure from home in my teenage years. Mao's communist forces continued to gain momentum on the battlefield, and this forced Chiang Kai-shek to move his government and military forces to Taiwan. Many civilians loyal to Chiang and his government followed.

At this juncture, some Mianyang county government officials, including my teacher Mr. Tseng, and their dependents quietly retreated to Wuchang city, some 80 miles northeast of my hometown. I was encouraged by my teacher to come along. Our retreat was made in late 1948. Wuchang now is part of Wuhan, the capital of Hubei province in central China.

Soon after our arrival in Wuchang, I privately planned to leave my superiors without their knowledge and look for new job opportunities. On a December 1948 morning, I came across a news item on the back page of a Wuchang municipal newspaper. That piece of news reported that the Artillery School of the ROC Army was recruiting candidates for non-commissioned officers. All who were admitted would need to undergo six months of military training. I was admitted after passing a brief academic test, taken in a Wuchang senior high school, and was welcomed into their ranks.

Many young people like me were recruited from several other Chinese cities. They included Nanjing in Jiangsu province, Jiujiang in Jiangxi province, and Changsha in Hunan, in addition to Wuchang. In total, some 600 such recruits--about the size of two infantry battalions--were sent by train to Hengyang in Hunan in January 1949 to undergo training there.

But things changed fast amid intensifying military conflict between Mao Zedong and Chiang Kai-shek's forces. Our training class was suddenly ordered to transfer from Hengyang to Guizhou province in southwest China, to join our parent Army Artillery School. The military academy had just been relocated there from Nanjing in East China. At this time, we had barely finished half of our six-month training program.

Coming to Taiwan as a Young Soldier

Even more frustrating, as we were heading to Guizhou, mostly on foot, we received a new order to head southeast to Taiwan instead. This order was final, and the entire training class changed direction. We took a commercial ship from Guangzhou city in Guangdong province to Kaohsiung, a port in southern Taiwan. I can't remember the exact time we arrived, but it was in the autumn of 1949, not long before the entire Chinese mainland came under the control of the communists.

In Taiwan, I spent my first 18 years serving in the army, rising from private to captain. After leaving the military, I entered the journalism profession and spent more than four decades practicing English journalism. My longtime career gave me opportunities to perform a range of key journalistic roles, including that of reporter, city editor, editor-in-chief, and editorial writer. Put together, I have been living and working in Taiwan for nearly 70 years to date.

Yet during these long, long years in Taiwan, I returned to the Chinese mainland to visit my birthplace only two times, including the trip in 2017. The previous time I visited my hometown was 25 years earlier in 1992. I made that trip alone without the company of my family members. I did not go to visit my hometown more often for political and practical reasons.

During the first three decades after my arrival in Taiwan in 1949, travel to the mainland was absolutely banned under then President Chiang Kai-shek's "three no's" mainland policy: "no negotiation, no contact, and no compromise." Under this same policy, correspondence with the communist-controlled mainland was also restricted.

So during this period, I could neither go to visit my mainland family members nor correspond with them. I had completely lost touch with my parents and other relatives. In the summer of 1983, as I vaguely recollect, I surprisingly got a letter from one of my nephews via an acquaintance, who had lately managed to visit his relatives living near my hometown. My nephew in the letter asked me to return home for a visit. Through further indirect correspondence, I learned some sad news: my father and mother both had already died. The death of my parents somehow made going back to the mainland to visit my hometown feel less urgent.

In the next couple of years, however, I continued to correspond with my mainland relatives, though indirectly. Sometimes I did so by using my travel to Europe and the United States to circumvent ongoing mail censorship. Occasionally, I also remitted some money to my relatives just as a token of my regard.

The ban on travel to the Chinese mainland was relaxed by Chiang Kai-shek's son President Chiang Ching-kuo in the late 1980s. The younger Chiang decided to allow Taiwan's numerous retired servicemen, who had come to Taiwan along with the armed forces led by his father, to return to the mainland for a reunion with their family members for humanitarian reasons.

As a former army captain or a veteran, now I could legally travel to the mainland to visit my Liubutou home, without being subject to political restrictions. However, I did not quickly take advantage of the relaxation of the travel ban until 1992.

The reason was a practical one. Although travel controls had been relaxed, I myself remained tied up in my work. I was still working on a tight schedule, despite the fact that by this time I had already retired from China Economic News Service as vice president (I retired in 1989 at the age of 55). I still had to work on a tight schedule, because I now was engaged in an almost full-time contributing job since my retirement from CENS. First, I was invited back to the China Post by its publisher Nancy Yu-Huang to write editorials for her newspaper -- two to three opinion pieces a week. Nancy Yu-Huang was my journalism mentor. It was she who offered me my first journalistic job after I left the army.

At the same time, I was asked by CENS publisher Wang Bi-li (who concurrently served as the CEO of the entire United Daily News' Group) to continue writing a column for the Economic News' Monday Edition— an economic tabloid printed in English. The Monday Edition was my brainchild when I was CENS editor-in-chief, a position that I held for nearly eight years.

Contributing at least three to four commentaries and analyses a week to the two media outlets kept me busy indeed. This was so because I had to do a lot of reading and research to make my writing knowledgeable and readable. Of course, I was paid for my contributions. I needed the income to help support my family.

I finally decided to make the 1992 mainland trip—my first since I left home more than four decades earlier—because there was an especially long Chinese New Year holiday that year. Traditionally, Chinese news outlets suspend publication during this long holiday to allow their employees to be reunited with their family members and relatives.

I took an early morning flight to Wuchang city, Hubei province, by way of Hong Kong, a midway transit point required under bilateral Taiwan-mainland transport service rules in effect at that time. I still vividly remember that hours before I dashed off to Taiwan's Chiang Kai-shek International Airport, I submitted my pre-holiday editorial to the China Post.

And I also recollect clearly the title of that editorial was about then communist Chinese paramount leader Deng Xiaoping's surprise visit to southern China. I selected this particular topic because I believed the Deng visit, his first public appearance in more than a year, could have far-reaching effects on China's ongoing economic reforms.

As it was later known, Deng Xiaoping's south China trip lasted for four weeks, from January 8 to February 21, 1992, taking him to Shenzhen, Zhuhai, and Shanghai's Pudong New Area--places designated by the PRC government as special economic zones offering attractive incentives to encourage foreign investment.

Initially, Deng's south China trip was ignored by the Beijing government and national media, which at the time were under the control of some conservatives of the Communist Party. Jiang Zemin, general secretary of the Chinese Communist Party since 1989, for example, showed little support for Deng's tour of the south.

Deng's inspection tour of the above-mentioned high-profile economic development projects came amid such a background: A new round of ideological debate had been heating up within the communist party for a year or so over the issue of what development route China should follow: socialism or capitalism. By this time, Deng Xiaoping had already retired from the powerful role as the chairman of the Central Military Commission and other important positions.

But Deng used his personal prestige and influence to continue to push for China's economic modernization and opening up to the world. In speeches Deng delivered on the trip, he made no secret of his support for the market economy and entrepreneurship. For example, he told his audience that "getting rich is glorious." At the same time, he made scathing attacks on the leftists. "The leftist elements of Chinese society were more dangerous than the rightist ones," he said.

Against the background of such ideological disputes, I felt Deng Xiaoping's south China visit carried two particular meanings. One, he wanted to use his public appearance to let the leftists know he was pro-market and that he did not want anyone to derail his reform agenda. Two, Deng's inspection of the various special economic zones represented his recognition that these development programs, if successfully carried out, could play a significant role in China's overall economic growth and expansion.

Subsequent developments proved Deng Xiaoping was right in giving particular support to China's promotion of special economic zones in those early years. Researchers looking for reasons behind China's sustained phenomenal economic growth over the years all cited the country's policy support for the various special economic zones early on as a key contributing factor.

Douglas Zhihua Zeng, a senior World Bank economist, said in a 2011 article that the SEZs played an important role in bringing new technologies to China and in adopting modern management practices. Overall, he wrote in the article "It is estimated that as of 2007, SEZs (including all types of industrial parks and zones) accounted for about 22% of national GDP, 46% of FDI (foreign direct investment), and 60% of exports.

Setting Foot in Communist-Ruled Mainland--40 Years on

I have deviated a little too far and must go back to my 1992 hometown trip. I flew from Taipei in the early morning of January 31. It was in the late afternoon when I arrived at the Nanhu Airport in Wuhan that day. This was the first time I had set foot on the mainland in more than four decades since I left home for Taiwan, along with Chiang Kai-shek's army. Technically, Taiwan and the mainland at the time were, and still are, in a state of war.

So I felt somewhat excited at the moment of arrival--a complex sentiment hard to describe in words. I soon relaxed, however, after I went through the customs area smoothly without being asked any particular questions by airport authorities. And as I moved on to the exit gate, I quickly spotted a placard welcoming home Tseng Ching-hsiang, my Chinese name.

All the people present to welcome me were my relatives, but I couldn't identify any of them. This was natural. Almost all of them were born after I left home in the late 1940s. And since then I had never returned home. This meant we never had a chance to see each other before. But as we got closer, greeting and talking to each other face to face, I soon came to know they were all my nephews, nieces, and other relatives. They drove more than 80 miles away from their homes to the Wuchang airport to meet me and pick me up.

It's about a three-hour drive back to Liubutou. So when we arrived, it was late into the night. I was surprised to see a crowd of people gathered outside a small brick house to welcome me. I was told it was my eldest nephew's house. And I was going to live with him and his family during my stay. Fireworks were also set off to celebrate my homecoming. Not all the people on hand to greet me were my relatives. Some were neighbors and villagers who presumably came to see me out of curiosity.

I spent three days in Liubutou. By this time, my father and mother had long passed away, as mentioned previously. My two half-bothers, who were from my father's first marriage, had also died. My eldest brother left his wife and five sons and one daughter. My second eldest brother left only one son.

During my 1992 home journey, I also visited my dearly beloved half-sister, who was from my mother's first marriage, and her husband and their family. They both died years later after my visit.

On the 1992 visit, I also learned more about the death of my parents. To my great sorrow, both my father and mother died tragically. On the first night of my arrival, Tseng Fan-wen, my eldest nephew, came to my bedside to quietly inform me how my father died. "Grandfather hung himself to death with a rope tied to a beam" during the Great Leap Forward movement. In subsequent conversations with him and other relatives, I further learned my father committed suicide under extreme pressure from commune cadres.

My father was overwhelmed by hardships in communal life. He, like numerous other Chinese peasants, was victimized by Mao Zedong's enforcement of the commune system. According to reports from that time, everything was shared in the commune. Private cooking was banned and replaced by communal dining. The communes exercised management and control of all rural resources such as labor and land. Everybody in the commune was assigned jobs by their commune leaders. Strict commune rules and restrictions were enforced through public struggle sessions and social pressure. The management method adopted in the commune system was a sort of terror rule.

The people's communes were formed in support of the Great Leap Forward campaign--an economic and social movement that was launched by Mao Zedong in 1958, with the aim of transforming China from an agrarian economy into a socialist society through rapid industrialization and collectivization. However, the Great Leap Forward campaign was viewed by some Chinese and foreign historians as the main cause of the following 1959-1961 Great Chinese Famine.

Reportedly, deaths from the commune system, the Great Leap Forward Campaign, and the resulting Great Famine ran into tens of millions. But ironically, many decades have passed, and the communist authorities are still reluctant to objectively revisit those historic, tragic events and candidly acknowledge any policy mistakes that were made.

My father's early death left my mother, who was in poor health, struggling. One of my nephews told me in a letter written around 1982 and mailed to me through Hong Kong that my mother had just died. She was in her late 70s at the time. My mother, I was also told, had lost her sight in both eyes way before she passed away.

I feel a sense of deep sympathy for her each time I think of the profound impact that her eyesight loss must have had on her life. I also always feel guilty about my failure to fulfill my filial duty toward her. Had I returned home way ahead of her death by trying to circumvent travel restrictions, I might have been able to render some help to ease her plight.

In a conversation with my half-sister and her husband on my 1992 hometown visit, I also learned that my mother was virtually abandoned in her later years, as few of my relatives were willing to care for her. Obviously, this was a very sad and difficult situation for my mother. However, you could hardly blame my brothers or other relatives for their reluctance to provide care for my mother. They themselves, I feel, were in a state of helplessness, given the depressing political and economic conditions prevailing in mainland China during those early times.

Politically, in the nearly first three decades since Mao Zedong defeated the KMT and founded the People's Republic of China in 1949, the "Great Helmsman" kept launching political campaigns, one after another. After his Great Leap Forward and Collectivization policies failed and resulted in the subsequent 1959-1961 Great Chinese Famine, Mao initiated a new and devastating movement, the Great Proletarian Cultural Revolution, in May 1966.

According to The New York Times, the Cultural Revolution was a decade-long upheaval that had dramatic, often violent effects across China. In a May 2016 article entitled China's Cultural Revolution, Explained, its author Austin Ramzy commented "The movement was fundamentally about elite politics, as Mao tried to reassert control by setting radical youths against the Communist Party hierarchy. But it had widespread consequences at all levels of society."

The British newspaper, the Guardian, in May 2016 also printed an article examining China's Cultural Revolution 50 years on. Tom Phillips, the author of the Guardian article, wrote "In fact, the cultural revolution crippled the economy, ruined millions of lives and thrust China into 10 years of turmoil, bloodshed, hunger, and stagnation." After violence had run its bloody course, the country's rulers conceded it had been a catastrophe that had brought nothing but "grave disorder, damage, and retrogression."

Yet the long series of campaigns pushed by Mao Zedong not only created nationwide turmoil, characterized by unrelenting political persecution and class struggle. The campaigns also caused serious economic stagnation, so serious that 30 years after the PRC's founding, the mainland remained a backwater, lagging far behind the rest of the world.

One indication of mainland China's serious economic stagnation, caused by the various damaging political campaigns, was its lagging level of GDP per capita. In 1980, the year that marked the start of Deng Xiaoping's historic economic reform and opening-up policy, China's GDP per capita was US$309. In the same year, the comparable figure was US$9,418 in Japan, US$11,070 in Germany, and US$12,576 in the United States. The GDP per capita figure for Taiwan, where I have been living since 1949, for that same year, was US$2,367. (Source: the IMF estimates between 1980 and 1989)

The PRC's extremely low GDP per capita, if reflected in people's real economic life, would mean that the vast majority of its citizens still had to struggle hard to make ends meet 30 years after its founding. Those less fortunate, might even have to constantly live on a starvation diet.

So in a society where people even had difficulty feeding themselves, it's hard to blame anyone for lack of compassion because they could not afford to help others. In fact, people living in a place where rulers had to resort to enforcing persecution and political struggle to stay in power tended to become indifferent toward one another.

In my mother's case, she, fortunately, had a filial daughter, my half-sister. From time to time, she took my mother to her home and cared for her. But she did so not without some difficulties. She had her own parents-in-law to look after at the time, as her husband explained to me during our conversations. In other words, my sister had to take her parents-in-law's feelings into account whenever she invited my mother to her home and to live with them.

The Hometown I Saw on Return

How did I see the economic developments in my hometown and its surrounding areas on the 1992 trip? Before telling my observations, I must admit that my stay there was brief, and I was unable to see more places to gain a more representative picture. But my brief stay there did give me chances to see the most visible things or general situation, which I think could reflect the development levels of the mainland's rural areas as a whole.

From what I saw, things did not seem to have changed much from the late 1940s, when the Chinese Communist Party took control of the entire mainland after ousting the KMT-led government. Nearly half a century had passed, and people in the rural areas were not better off under communist rule. Many still lived in mud-brick houses without paved roads. There was no running water and no regular supply of electricity. Hygiene and sanitation conditions were terribly poor. Such living environments and conditions were also prevalent in neighboring villages and towns where I either also visited or passed through.

The aforementioned living and environmental situations, however, were what I saw in Liubutou and its neighboring places back in 1992. On my second, 2017 hometown visit -- a trip with which I began this chapter -- I witnessed firsthand a lot of big changes in Liubutou and elsewhere in mainland China.

In my hometown, for example, mud-brick houses were gone. In their place were concrete homes. All the villages I saw had access to the supply of electricity and running water. Roads linking to neighborhoods and highways were paved. Gravel and dirt roads were things of the past.

My 2017 hometown return, unlike the previous one in 1992, took me to more places beyond Liubutou and its neighboring villages and towns. I traveled to some big mainland cities, such as Wuhan and Beijing. And as my family and I rode the Shenzhen-Wuhan high-speed rail, which covered Guangdong, Hunan, and Hubei provinces, we saw high-rise housing, office towers, and sprawling industrial complexes along both sides of the routes.

Obviously, the high-speed bullet train, the high-rise housing, and the industrial complexes that we saw on our train ride from Shenzhen to Wuhan were just part of a testament to China's fast and sustained economic growth and development over the years.

The World Bank, in an overview (last updated March 28, 2017) made such comments about the economy and development in the People's Republic of China: "Since initiating market reforms in 1978, China has transformed from a centrally-planned to a market-based economy and has experienced rapid economic and social development. GDP growth has averaged nearly 10 percent a year—the fastest sustained expansion by a major economy in history—and has lifted more than 800 million people out of poverty…With a population of 1.3 billion, China is the second largest economy and is increasingly playing an important role in the global economy."

It's true that the Chinese mainland's growth and development attained in the last few decades have been a phenomenal success. Many economists often praise such success as China's economic miracle, citing many contributing factors. But, in my view, the most fundamental factors are as follows:

First and foremost is China's landmark "economic reform and opening-up" policy launched in 1978 under the leadership of then paramount leader Deng Xiaoping. Under the former part of this policy, Beijing adopted a series of critical economic reform measures. They included de-collectivization of agriculture, permitting entrepreneurs to start businesses, selling some of the shares of giant state-run corporations, and reopening the Shanghai Stock Exchange.

The latter part of the 1978 economic reform policy obliged Beijing to open up the mainland to foreign investment for the first time since the Kuomintang (KMT) era. A most prominent opening-up measure was the creation by Deng Xiaoping of a long series of special economic zones, such as Shenzhen and Zhuhai.

To attract foreign investment, companies operating in such economic zones were given tax privileges and, more importantly, less burdened with red tape and political interference, problems that tended to scare away investors. These special zones brought in not only huge amounts of foreign investments but also the technology and managerial skills that came with them. These special development projects soon proved to be a key growth engine in the economy of China.

Another significant factor contributing to the mainland's economic growth miracle, as I observed, is China's decision to join the World Trade Organization. To achieve this goal, the mainland spent 10 long years negotiating with WTO member countries and enacting painful market-liberalizing steps to win admission in 2001.

After joining the WTO, China moved to cut tariffs and phase out non-tariff trade barriers. And, as agreed on, China also opened up a variety of its markets from finance to insurance, telecommunications, commerce, transportation, construction, and tourism. Besides, the service sector also was considerably liberalized. Major restrictions on retail, wholesale, and distribution operations were removed.

These market-opening moves paid off considerably. China saw a new surge in foreign investment following its WTO admission, as foreign investors, already eyeing China's cheap labor and lower land cost, flocked to the country in large numbers to cash in on easier market access and reduced tariffs -- all made possible by its newly enacted liberal policies. It can be said that the painful efforts made by China to win entry into the WTO that sparked a growing inflow of capital and technology played an important part in the mainland's emergence as the manufacturing center of the world.

Additionally, by dismantling the various deep-rooted protectionist practices, China went a long way toward improving the competitiveness of its economy. Without market-protecting policies, companies have had to work hard to improve efficiency so that they could compete favorably, not just in the domestic market but also in the entire world. That China has now climbed to the position as the world's largest exporter is a vivid reflection of how competitive the Chinese economy has become.

One more fundamental factor, yet which was rarely cited in examining China's sustained fast economic growth, is that the country has succeeded in maintaining political stability after the death of Mao Zedong in late 1976. Had China continued to carry out various destabilizing political campaigns, as it had in the Mao era, it would never have been possible for the Chinese mainland to become the world's biggest magnet for investment.

Yet despite its sustained economic growth, the World Bank in the previously cited overview pointed out, "China remains a developing country (its per capita income is still a fraction of that in advanced countries)." According to China's current poverty standard (per capita rural net income of RMB 2,300 per year in 2010 constant prices), the World Bank noted, "there were 55 million poor [people living below that poverty standard] in rural areas in 2015."

Because of the time limit, I was unable to acquire credible information showing the level of "per capita rural net income" in my hometown. I mean I found no available data to tell me where the village of Liubutou and the wider Honghu City area stood in the mainland's average living standard -- above or below the poverty line, as defined in the World Bank overview.

But the remarks made by the village's leader and party secretary, Mr. Tseng Feng-yuh, should suffice to give me a general idea about what I was interested in knowing.

The two hats that Mr. Tseng wore gave him the responsibility to distribute public resources allocated by higher government authorities and to take care of infrastructural construction and economic development in his jurisdiction. It was very kind of him to receive and treat me and my family during our visit to Liubutou. He acted as our tour guide. He also arranged for a car with a driver to bring us to and from nearby scenic spots and, in addition, places where I attended schools during my childhood years.

In my conversations with him, I made a lot of inquiries about Liubutou, past, and present. The essence of his reply to my questions about Liubtou's economic well-being is given below: "Relatively speaking, the Honghu area, Liubutou included, is lagging behind other regional places in economic progress. One main problem we face is that we don't have developed transportation systems that can link us to major commercial hubs, such as Guangzhou to the south and Shanghai to the east. Because of this, companies have been reluctant to invest in our area."

The people in Liubutou and its neighboring areas, he added, "are now pinning their hopes on finishing the construction of a new cross-Yangtze River bridge near the historic Red Cliffs." The bridge in discussion is a joint venture project funded by local and foreign investors, as I was told. If completed, the cross-river bridge would greatly improve the area's communications with the outside world. But construction work has been suspended for some two years after the project's foreign investors allegedly failed to keep up the remaining installments.

Besides the inability to attract business investment, many villages in the Honghu area also have been suffering from a common problem: a steady outflow of labor. As I learned, many of my nephews and other relatives' children are working in faraway places. They are not alone in finding jobs outside Liubutou. Many other young locals do the same. While working in places away from home, they remit their savings back to their families to support their parents and relatives. But for Liubutou as a whole, there is a side effect: As young people in growing numbers move to bigger cities or industrial regions in search of better jobs, they leave behind their fields lying fallow, adding to the decline of the local economy.

Relatives Are Friendly and Hospitable

One other thing that impressed me deeply on this trip is that the people in my hometown are very friendly, hospitable, and generous to visitors, more so than most of their urban cousins, even though they are not as affluent.

Take my Liubutou relatives and friends for example. I had not given them prior notice that I was coming for a visit. I was not unaware that this was an impolite omission. But I had a reason: I did not want them to make preparations for my visit that I feared would add to their inconveniences and take up too much of their time.

So I called Tseng Fan-wen, my eldest nephew, only after we checked into our hotel, the Yuexi Peninsula Resort, located miles away from Liubutou. But to my surprise, Fan-wen and several other relatives and friends reached our hotel within half an hour or so of my call. Fan-wen phoned my room through the front desk and told me they were waiting in the lobby to receive and welcome us. So my wife, my children, and I swiftly raced to the hotel lobby to meet them. They all wore warm smiles on their faces. Their facial expressions immediately dispelled my fears that they might have felt unhappy because of my failure to notify them well in advance.

It was late in the afternoon after we checked into the hotel. So we were taken out for dinner at a nearby farm restaurant, and soon after we introduced ourselves to one another and exchanged brief greetings. I did not notice how many people attended that first night's dinner party, but I do remember we sat at a big table that was full. Those present included my nephews, other relatives, and village representatives, in addition to my wife, my daughter, my son, and myself.

It was a big dinner featuring fish and lotus dishes. Honghu City, named after its huge neighboring lake, produces some forty sorts of fish and an abundance of lotus, as I was told. The fish and lotus dishes were very delicious. My wife, son, daughter, and I all enjoyed the food very much. But regrettably, I did not eat enough, because I was busy doing the talking and fielding all kinds of questions raised by participating relatives and friends. They showed great interest in current events in Taiwan, including public sentiment toward the mainland.

It was late into the night when we got back to our hotel. On the way, I felt quite excited and grateful, as I recalled the warm receptions and treatment that my family and I had received since our arrival.

Despite the fact that we did not get much sleep that night, we rose early the next morning. By eight o'clock, we had eaten our breakfast. By that time, Fan-wen and the village party secretary Mr. Tseng Feng-yue, had already reached our hotel to pick us up, as arranged the previous night. We were driven to Liubutou, first, to visit each of my six nephews' homes. As we did so, I chatted with them and their children and, in some cases, their children's children. Because our schedule was so tight, we had to keep our conversations brief.

After visiting the homes of my nephews, we then proceeded to the grave site of my mother and father to pay tribute to them. Accompanied by my wife and children, I stayed there for about an hour, as I reflected on my childhood memories and relationships with my parents. As I did so, a sense of guilt resurged in me about my failure to fulfill filial obligations to them as their son.

From my parents' resting place, we moved on to the tombs of my late sister-in-law, my half-brother, and my half-sister to pay our respects to them. While making all these tomb visits, we were accompanied by my nephews and their family members.

It was exactly twelve noon when we finished all the grave visits and tomb-sweeping ceremonies. This was lunchtime, so we were taken for a meal at a restaurant, the same as the one where we ate our dinner the previous evening. What was different from the previous evening was that for the lunch today, as many as four tables each seating 12 persons were set. The vast majority of a party of about 50 attending the lunch were my relatives. By organizing such a big lunch party, I assumed, Tseng Fan-wen and his brothers also intended to use such a reunion to introduce their children and their grandchildren to me and my family. They did so in the apparent hope that their families and mine could get acquainted with each other and would keep in touch in the future.

Time really flies. My eldest nephew Tseng Fan-wen, who is more than 10 years younger than me, is now in his early 70s. Fan-wen has four younger brothers and one sister. His youngest brother, Tseng Fan-wei, is 55 years old. The five brothers and their sister all have grandchildren and, in many cases, great-grandchildren.

Visiting a Three Kingdoms Era Battlefield

After lunch, my family and I did some sightseeing. We visited the historically important battlefield where a decisive campaign was fought in 208/9 AD between the allied forces of the southern warlords Liu Bei and Sun Quan and the numerically superior forces of the northern warlord Cao Cao.

According to literature, the battle started as Cao Cao sought to take the Red Cliffs, south of the Yangtze River, in his attempt to reunite the territory of the Eastern Han dynasty. But he was repelled by the allied forces of Liu Bei and Sun Quan. As a result, Cao Cao was forced to retreat to Wulin on the northwestern bank of the Yangtze. Wulin is adjacent to my hometown.

The southern allied forces gave chase, throwing Cao Cao's army into chaos, and forcing it to retreat further along Huarong Road. A humiliatingly defeated Cao Cao finally decided to withdraw to his home base of Ye (in present-day Handan, Hebei). In the battle, large numbers of soldiers and horses were killed, and ships destroyed.

The campaign was decisive, because the allied victory at the Red Cliffs, near present-day Chibi City in Hubei, ensured the survival of the Liu Bei and Sun Quan regimes, giving them control of the Yangtze and thus providing them a line of defense. This in turn led to the subsequent creation of the Three Kingdoms in ancient China: Wei (north of the Yangtze), Shu (in the southwest), and Wu (in the southeast).

We didn't actually go to visit the site of the Red Cliffs, because if we did it would have involved us crossing the Yangtze by taking a ferry. We had not enough time to make it. Instead, we just took a look at it across from the north bank of the river. Even so, we could still vividly see the two big Chinese characters Red Cliffs engraved on a cliff side facing the Yangtze River.

We did visit the northern part of the battlefield, Wulin, where Cao Cao initially retreated to. The battle inflicted serious damage on Wulin. It occurred when a huge fleet of warships sent by Cao Cao to attack the Red Cliffs was set afire at the midpoint of the river by an alliance general-led squadron feigning surrender. The fire, carried by a strong southeastern wind, rapidly spread to the shore of Wulin and into its coastal villages.

One terrifying historic spot related to the Red Cliffs battle that we saw in Wulin was a mass grave. On our way to the Temple of Xiangshan, a noted Buddhist shrine in the area, we were shown a stone tablet that has three Chinese characters written on it. In English, the three characters mean this is a mass grave with 10,000 human bodies buried in it. The mass grave which the stone tablet refers to is a deep pit, which still can be seen on the nearby ground. According to the village head, Mr. Tseng Feng-yue, those buried in the pit were soldiers -- from both the Cao Cao camp and the Sun-Liu united forces-- who were killed in the Battle of the Red Cliffs.

There, of course, is no way to check the accuracy of the number of the dead buried in the mass grave, as written on the stone tablet, given the lack of credible studies on a battle that took place so long ago -- about one thousand and eight hundred years ago. But just that rough figure can lead visitors to imagine how fierce the Red Cliffs Battle was.

My family and I were also driven to Sunlin and Xinti, the latter of which is the seat of the Honghu City government, for a visit. Sunlin and Xinti are two of the places where I attended a village school in 1947-48. Those were the last two years in which I received my tutorial-type elementary education, which lasted for six and a half years in total. This was the only schooling I ever received in my life. In other words, when I left school for Taiwan with the military in 1949, my academic level was equivalent to that of an elementary education at best.

By revisiting Xinti and Sunlin, as I just mentioned above, I hoped to find something that might bring back some memories of my teenage years. But to my disappointment, I discovered no traces whatsoever of the old Xinti and Sunlin that I could recall. But there was little wonder that things had changed greatly. It had been about 70 years since I last saw the two places in the late 1940s.

We concluded our afternoon sightseeing at around 6 o'clock. It had to be so because we were supposed to attend another dinner in the evening. It was held at a plush restaurant in Honghu City, where we were going to stay for the night. We had checked out of our rooms in the Wulin hotel early in the morning before we started the day's activities.

The Honghu dinner party was thrown by a relatively distant nephew of mine, Tseng Fan-sui. He retired from the Honghu City government years earlier as its civil affairs director. It also was Fan-sui who, along with Tseng Fan-wen and others, drove 80 miles to the Wuchang airport to receive me in 1992 when I made my first hometown visit.

Like the previous two dinners, the one in the Honghu restaurant consisted mainly of fish courses, which we particularly enjoyed. I do not have any idea how many people were invited to the party that evening. But I do remember the table we sat at for the meal was an extraordinarily large one that was fully occupied. From my observation, some of those invited to dine with us appeared to be figures of note in their respective professions or fields in the city.

During the dinner, which lasted almost two hours, we talked a lot about a wide range of subjects. I had tried to refrain from touching on cross-strait politics. But it proved hard to avoid talking about relations between Taiwan and the Chinese mainland in conversations involving people from the two sides. The reason is simple: Cross-strait relations, whether they are moving forward or backward, can matter to people on both sides of the Taiwan Strait.

A Shifting Tone on Ties with Taiwan

Somehow the sensitive issue of cross-strait unification finally was brought up. But the tone taken by my friends from the host side seemed to have gotten tougher than what I heard and noted on my previous 1992 trip. This tone change seemed to me to have something to do with the mainland's fast-growing economy and its rapidly expanding military power over the past more than two decades

The tone of voice I heard on my last, 1992 return to Liubutou was somewhat softer. At that time whenever Taiwan and mainland relations became a subject of discussion, my mainland relatives and friends would invariably push a sensitive point: the need for the unification of China. But they did so mostly by appealing to "patriotism." One schoolteacher, Chang Wen-zhi, who happened to be my childhood schoolmate, for example, handed me a note at one point in our conversations. To this day, I still keep that note with me. It reads in part: "I hope you, Mr. Tseng, will use your commentaries to promote the unification of the motherland for the rest of your life for the good of the entire Chinese people."

I could call the mainland's "appeal to patriotism" a soft approach, as it truly was indeed. Yet this soft approach was not adopted without some reason behind it. What that reason was could be seen from just a brief look at the comparative economic and military conditions between Taiwan and the mainland at that time.

In the early 1990s, Taiwan backed by sustained rapid growth as a newly developing economy had ample resources to invest in its military and strengthen its defense capabilities. Because of such investments, Taiwan, in general terms, was able to secure its air and naval spaces and defend itself against any possible hostile attack.

However, things have changed over the last two decades. Taiwan's economic growth has slowed down. This was an inevitable development though for an economy that has matured or become fully developed. Yet a slow economy meant that Taiwan could no longer afford to raise huge amounts of funds to buy more advanced weapons necessary to meet its growing defense needs.

By contrast, the mainland or the PRC has over the years become the world's second-largest economy, after the United States. And at the same time, the PRC has attained the status of a military superpower, not just regionally but also globally.

As a result of the shifting economic and military powers, the mainland has now gained the upper hand in addressing cross-strait issues, emboldening it to get tougher with Taiwan, and reversing its past soft posture.

How much tougher the PRC has become could be sensed in the remarks made by a mainland friend attending the above-mentioned Xinti restaurant dinner given us during my most recent (2017) hometown visit.

"The mainland of course would avoid using force to unify Taiwan... For if we choose to do that, the island would become a scorched land...within perhaps just tens of minutes," the friend said. His remarks came after we chatted about Taiwan's newly elected

President Tsai Ying-wen and her uncompromising stance on the one-China issue. Tsai is supportive of Taiwan's independence and has been reluctant to accept a long-established "1992 consensus" since she took office in mid-2016. The "1992 consensus" refers to a tacit agreement reached between Taiwan and the mainland to address the thorny "one-China" dispute.

Since what my friend aired above was just casual talk, I would rather not identify him by name on that subject. After all, his aforementioned remarks in no way represented government policy. But they did reflect, in my view, a public mainland attitude that the issue of cross-strait unification could be resolved by force readily if the PRC decided to do so.

As someone who comes from Taiwan, which has become his second home, I felt somewhat embarrassed by my friend's somewhat coercive words. So I had to say something in response. But at the same time, I did not want to say anything that could spoil the friendly dinner party atmosphere. Otherwise, I would have responded with the following comments:

"The differences between Taiwan and the mainland are so complicated that they cannot be resolved unilaterally by either side without provoking concerns in the region and beyond. In fact, past experience has proved that there is no quick fix for the long-running political divide between Taiwan and the mainland. After all, Taiwan following long years of military investment and training has built a credible deterrent force aimed at protecting itself against unprovoked attacks."

Of course, I did not actually express those views as put in the above quotation marks, because as I just said I did not want to prompt hard feelings in my mainland friends. Instead, I responded at the dinner party with a soft warning, which I believe would be mutually agreeable but less confrontational. "Should a war, unfortunately, break out between Taiwan and the mainland, both sides would be losers. No real winners," I said.

The impact of the long-standing political differences spread beyond the issue of cross-strait unification. They also had an influence on public attitudes in Taiwan. For example, many mainland citizens, who came to Taiwan with the Chiang Kai-shek-led government in the late 1940s, were asked the following question in a recent survey: Where would they choose to spend their later years, Taiwan or the mainland, if and when such a choice comes up for them to make? The answer given by most of the respondents was such: They preferred to live in Taiwan during the final years of their lives, citing different political systems and other reasons.

Emotional Connection with Liubutou.

If I were surveyed in the same poll, my answer would be the same. But I would cite some different reasons. I mentioned this public sentiment because I actually faced a similar question of where I would prefer to spend my final years during my most recent stay in Liubutou.

I remember when our two-day visit came to an end, I felt a strong emotional connection with this small farm village, where I was born and grew up. I still do as of this writing.

But does this indicate that someday I will return to my old hometown and spend my remaining years there? Or would it mean that I might finally decide to have my remains buried in Liubutou, as in the ancient Chinese saying: "Falling Leaves Return to Their Roots"? This question has frequently come to my mind these days since my return from the 2017 visit. Yet the more I thought about the question, the more unlikely it felt.

In conversations with my Liubutou relatives, several of them suggested that we relocate to the mainland to live and work. They asked me, in particular, to return home and make that the last leg of my life journey. One relative even advised my daughter Tseng Wen-yi that I should be buried in Liubutou alongside my father and mother, once I am gone.

Their suggestions, in essence, echoed traditional thinking about home and ethics. According to such thinking, people who are getting old after having worked and lived in distant places for long years should return home and die in their place of birth. The Chinese saying of "Falling Leaves Return to Their Roots" embodies that traditional concept. More specifically, people who have spent the best part of their lives abroad tend to feel homesick for their birthplace and thus want to return to that place for permanent settlement, just like falling leaves drawn back to the ground.

Change in the Traditional Meaning of Home

In my case, however, the traditional definition of home--or the falling leaves adage--has become somewhat irrelevant. First, my old home in

Liubutou, Honghu City, virtually no longer exists: My parents are gone and my brothers and sister also are gone. As for the younger generation -- those who were born to my sister and brothers -- they for the most part were born after I left home for Taiwan in 1949. So actually, I am not familiar with them, let alone their children and children's children.

So my old Liubutou home practically was nonexistent. Having said that, I must emphasize that there is one thing that has not changed and will never change. That is, Liubutou is my hometown and my roots are in that remote Chinese village. I will always bear this in mind for the rest of my life. I also hope that my daughter and son will do the same -- keeping in mind that their ancestral roots are in mainland China or, to be specific, Liubutou, Honghu City of Hubei province.

To me, the traditional definition of home is no longer applicable in another way. First, I built my own home in Taiwan. And Taiwan has become my second "hometown." Consider, that I have spent the vast majority of my life in Taiwan,

Actually, I have become connected with this island closely. I got married here in 1967. Lei Yen-ming, my wife, and I have our own family with a grown-up daughter Tseng Wen-yi and a grown-up son Tseng Wen-chieh. We have been living in Taipei for more than a half-century. Because of this, whenever anyone asks about my home place, I would instinctively say Taipei. I named Liubutou only when I was asked about my birthplace or old hometown.

Regarding my Liubutou relatives' suggestion that my family relocate to the mainland and settle there, I see there is a little possibility we will do so. Take my son and my daughter. They were born in Taiwan and received education in Taiwan--from kindergarten to graduate school. They both have decent jobs, which they were trained for. Along the way, they both have built a network of good friends, including colleagues and schoolmates.

All this suggests that there appears to be no reason whatsoever why my daughter or son should leave Taiwan in favor of moving to the mainland to live and work in an entirely unfamiliar environment. Therefore, it is unlikely for my children to relocate to the mainland, at least not in the foreseeable future.

What reaction would my wife have if I asked her to leave Taiwan and take up residence in mainland China? Her reply I am sure would not be positive. Yen-ming is 12 years younger than me. She was born in Guizhou province, China, and brought to Taiwan by her parents at the age of five. So she, too, grew up and received her education in Taiwan. She has a big circle of close friends and schoolmates here. If put in a new location, like the mainland, she would likely have problems adapting. After all, she too is in her advanced years now.

How about myself? The question I might face in any plan to move to the mainland for settlement would be more of an emotional one: I have a great affection for Taiwan. I owe it a lot.

From my own personal experience, Taiwan is a place where hiring, for the most part, is based on merit rather than academic diplomas. Were it not the case, I would never have had the opportunity to carve out a career in journalism, a profession I have always felt proud of in my life.

I didn't have any academic credentials, not even a primary school diploma. In my 18 years in the military ending December 1965, I rose from a teenage private to an army captain, not because I had had a military academy degree, as normally required.

After retiring from the military, I joined the Taipei-based, English-language newspaper China Post in January 1966. That was the start of my journalism career, which spanned more than four decades and involved me serving in various key journalistic positions.

During my decades-long journalism career, I worked for several different news outlets, but none of my employers had ever enquired about my academic credentials. There was only one time that my education background came up as a subject of discussion. But it was raised by me.

In late 1964, I wrote to the China Post publisher Nancy Yu-Huang, my journalism mentor, telling her that I was interested in her reporter-recruiting ad. I explained to the publisher that I didn't receive any formal education and asked her if she could allow me to attend her recruitment test.

With her permission, I took part in a test on English proficiency and passed it. Thus, I was admitted to the China Post and started my career in English journalism. Over the years, I have often thought that had I been denied the opportunity to participate in that exam because I didn't have a university diploma, I might never have had the chance to enter the journalism profession.

Work is another factor in any decision on whether to go back to my old hometown Liubutou to stay there permanently. Although I now have fully retired from the journalistic profession, I am still doing some research, currently for my second book--a story about myself.

Doing my kind of research in Taiwan, I feel, is more convenient than in my hometown. This means that the need to research for my current or any future writing project will be another factor that I would have to take into account in deciding whether or not to return to Liubutou for a permanent stay. Writing is the most important thing in my life.

If I could not take up permanent residence in my mainland hometown while I was alive, would it be possible for me to do so after my death? In this instance, I would leave a will requesting my children have my body or ashes buried beside the graves of my father and mother. From the viewpoint of traditional Chinese filial ethics, it would be the right thing for me to do. For if I could arrange my burial in a place next to my deceased father and mother, it would allow me to fulfill a most important ethical obligation: To accompany the souls of my parents to the other world.

However, such a burial arrangement might be seen by my own children as unrealistic. They might conclude this would require them to fly across the Taiwan Strait to Liubutou annually to sweep my tomb. That would cause them considerable inconvenience. What is more, taking a long-haul tomb-sweeping trip to Liubutou annually would be a lingering burden, not a one-shot problem.

They might even complain that while I seek to sort of solve an old problem, a new one or an artificial one would be created. In their view, my longstanding separation from my parents, caused by cross-strait politics, is indeed a tragedy. But if I were to have myself buried in Liubutou far away from our Taiwan home, that would amount to an extension of that tragedy with them being the victims this time.

All this indicates that any attempt by me to have my body buried in Liubutou after my death might have to be abandoned in the end as being unrealistic. But if I am going to be buried in Taiwan, as is most likely to be the case, a new concern may come up: My burial in this land would inevitably lead to a further eroding of my Taiwan family's relationships with my ancestral residence or roots in mainland China.

If and when it becomes apparent that I will have to be buried in Taiwan, I would pray to my parents that I be forgiven for failing to choose my final resting place next to them. And I would promise to meet them and accompany them in the next world forever.

That said, I am not sure whether there is truly an afterlife or a life beyond this life. Some researchers believe that humans have souls which can live on after death. About two thousand and three hundred years ago, the Greek philosopher Socrates was quoted by Plato and his other students as believing that "even after death, the soul exists and is able to think."

In more pragmatic terms, I hope to use my final years in this life to visit Liubutou more often to pay tribute to my parents at their burial sites. I had planned to make another visit two years after my return from the 2017 trip. But the outbreak of the Covid-19 pandemic forced us to abort that plan. Now I can only pin my hopes on an early end to the Covid-19 pandemic so that cross-strait travel returns to normal.

I am in my late 80s now. There is no way for me to know how many more years I will be able to live. On a recent clinic visit, my cardiologist C.E. Chiang once again said this to me: "I can guarantee that there will be no question for you to live to the age of 100." His reassurance, while welcome, certainly needs to be discounted as a morale-boosting remark. But I do believe that as long as I keep my daily exercise routine (I normally walk 14,000 to 15,000 steps daily on a mountain trail. It takes me 2 hours and 25 minutes to cover this distance), heed what I eat and lead a healthy lifestyle, I am sure I will be around for some more years.

Chapter 2
Revisiting a Wartime Fort 60 Years On

Serving as a Teenage Soldier

In March 2014, I revisited a defense fortification built in the early post-WWII years. The fortress is perched high on the cliffs at the western edge of Shou Mountain in Kaohsiung, overlooking the Taiwan Strait. But everything there has changed beyond recognition. I couldn't believe that this was the place where I had been stationed six decades ago as a teenage private.

During those times Taiwan was still in a state of war with the Chinses mainland. Relations between the two sides were extremely tense. Mao Zedong had just founded the People's Republic of China in Beijing in 1949. Mao threatened to liberate Taiwan after Chiang Kai-shek and his military forces retreated to this island.

On the other hand, Chiang Kai-shek, as president of the Republic of China, invested heavily in building Taiwan into a strong anti-communist base. Chiang made recovering the Chinese mainland from the communists a sacred mission for the ROC.

My experience in being stationed at that fort on Shou Mountain in the port city of Kaohsiung, therefore, needs to be set in the context of the dangerous political and military tensions between Taiwan and mainland China during the late 1940s and the early 1950s.

I spent nearly four years (1950-1953) in that fort as a young soldier of the ROC army. During those years I was serving in a searchlight contingent, part of a garrison force responsible for defending Kaohsiung Harbor and its surrounding areas against possible invasion by the People's Liberation Army.

The Mt. Shou defense post, a name inherited from the era of Japanese occupation, was situated next to a small village. Residents of this village made a living by gathering firewood and catching fish. The military-civilian community was reliant on a sole rocky shoreline trail to link it with its nearest towns: Sizihwan Bay to the south and the Zuoying navy base to the north.

The contingent which I worked with consisted of more than 10 young soldiers, almost all of them of my age. We were equipped with a giant searchlight. Our primary mission was to use a powerful beam of light produced by the said huge searchlight to help friendly artillery troops spot approaching enemy planes or navy ships aiming to enter our defense areas under the cover of darkness.

On my recent visit to this hillside, however, I found everything there had changed through and through. I wondered whether the entire old military defense post was still fully functional. The giant searchlight, which as I recall was on a big concrete base, for example, could not be found anywhere around.

My wife, Yen-ming, and I stopped by a barbed wire fence and peered into the camp. We noticed some barracks inside it seemed to be standing idle, without being occupied by military personnel. I did find a guard standing at the gate of the camp, however. I walked up to him enquiring about that giant searchlight's whereabouts.

I explained to him that the searchlight that I was talking about was previously deployed somewhere nearby. The guard replied that he knew nothing about what I was referring to. He was too young to answer my question. After all, the tactic of using searchlights to spot approaching enemy airplanes has long been something of the past with the advent of the jet age.

Nor could I find the whereabouts of a small Buddhist temple. This temple is still on my mind now because it played such an important part in our daily lives while we stayed there. The more than 10 young soldiers of our group used the temple as living quarters. We not only slept in the building, but also dined and spent our leisure time therein.

Yen-ming and I, in our brief visit to the defense post and its surrounding areas, did see a much bigger Buddhist temple standing close to the now seemingly deserted military camp. I talked to several residents and asked them if they knew anything about the older temple I was looking for. After I minutely described to them what it looked like, one of them told me with certainty that the present temple standing before us was rebuilt on the site of the early one, which had been dismantled.

My Earliest Memory of Taiwan

I felt deep regret that I didn't have a chance to see once again the temple where I had lived for so long and grew up from a late teenager to an adult. The experiences combined to form an important part of my earliest memory of Taiwan.

As with the military defense post, the old fishing village next door also had changed so much that I could no longer recognize it. The two dozen or so wooden houses that I could vividly recall could not be found in the area anymore. In their place were seafood restaurants, coffee shops, traditional Taiwanese eateries as well as private residences.

We were told that many of the above commercial businesses were set up only in the last 10 years or so, as investors responded to the government's policy of opening Taiwan's tourism industry to its former rival, mainland China. This opening-up policy was understandable. The mainland had become the world's largest source of tourists, backed by its newfound wealth.

Unlike in my years when I was deployed there, people living or doing business in this mountainside area these days have the good fortune to enjoy better public services. On my latest visit, I found that, whether households or business establishments, they all had electricity and running water. Previously, such public services were completely unavailable.

A similarly important change is that the main shoreline trail as well as all secondary access roads on the hillside area have been covered with an asphalt surface. The improvements in road conditions and the availability of electricity and running water, I believe, must have made life for people living in this place much easier than in my time there.

Another important government policy change was also noted. In the old days, the whole defense post area was strictly off-limits to the general public, as were many other garrison sites on Mt. Shou.

Nowadays, the mountain, with a peak elevation of 363 meters and a length of 10 kilometers from north to south, is fully open to visitors, local and foreign alike.

Regrettably, Yen-ming and I were unable to see more of the mountain on the trip because of limited time. Mt. Shou now has been designated as a nature reserve by the government to preserve its rich ecosystem, which includes more than 1,000 Formosan rock macaques--a species unique to Taiwan. As a lover of jogging and hiking, I also regretted my inability to visit and trek across the middle eastern section of the mountain, which features an extensive network of beautiful boardwalk hiking trails.

I had long hoped to come back to visit the Mt. Shou fort. But for one reason or another, I failed to fulfill this wish. Finally, a good opportunity came up. I was invited by my old military colleagues to take part in a dinner party reunion, scheduled for late March of 2014 at Zuoying -- a district of Kaohsiung City and home to Taiwan's largest navy base.

The dinner was organized to celebrate the anniversary of our arrival in Taiwan. We, about two battalions of young men newly enlisted from the Chinese mainland, took a ship from Guangzhou and disembarked at Kaohsiung port in June 1949. Zuoying was chosen as the site for the reunion party because this was the place where we trained for the next six months shortly after we landed in Kaohsiung.

So I used the opportunity of attending the party to visit Kaohsiung and the Mt. Shou defense post in particular. In the previous pages, I have said that that military fortification and its surroundings had changed beyond recognition.

Below I will cite several other things that may also explain why the military post on Mt. Shou is the most memorable place for me, and why I decided to go back there for a visit.

First, this is the place where I spent most of my youth, besides my hometown in Hubei province. A lot of scenes and events which I experienced on that mountain area were indelibly imprinted on my mind.

Take for example the small mountain spring pool located near our defense post which was something I could never forget. It played an indispensable role in our life there. We and the nearby villagers all relied on it for the supply of water. My associates and I had to walk hundreds of meters from our residential site to the spring pool to take water daily for drinking, cooking, and washing. In the eyes of the present-day world, this would be something unthinkable. But in those old days on that hillside, we all took such daily chores for granted without any complaints at all.

Also still deep in my memory was a particular cliff situated closer to us. This cliff provided a better position to watch the sea from our place. I often liked to stand on it to look at the beautiful rock and sand beach below. In fine weather, the scene of the setting sun disappearing into the clear blue sea was especially beautiful.

The mountain trail connecting our defense post to the Bay of Sizihwan, as I previously mentioned, was also something unforgettable for me. I enjoyed walking along that trail in the evenings. I often used the time to think. One thing I frequently contemplated was what I would do once I left the military. I knew I would not continue to serve in the military until I was old enough to retire.

One other thing enabling me to remember that particular wartime defense post is that it is a place where I made some lifetime friends. The ten or so of us served together in the searchlight contingent of the Kaohsiung Garrison Command for a couple of years until we were transferred to infantry units in other places in Taiwan. But we have since remained good friends, unaffected by subsequent geographic separation and by our pursuits of different careers. Our shared experience and history, I believe, have played an important part in our enduring friendships.

Sadly, a few of these good friends, including Mr. Kuo You-bing and Mr. Tang Zheng-shi, have left us. But their memories live on. Their words and deeds often come up as subjects in conversations with their wives during our regular bimonthly dinner gathering. Mrs. Kuo and Mrs. Tang remain my good friends.

The Place Where I Began Learning English

The third reason for me to revisit the military post on the western hillside of Mt. Shou was that I began studying English there. Choosing to begin studying English, as I later discovered, was a life-changing decision for me. I remember it was sometime around 1952 when I started learning English spelling and pronunciation. At that time, I was 20 years old.

In a normal education system, people at that age should have been in their second year at a college or university. For them, spelling and pronunciation were basic English courses that they were taught while attending junior high school. So little wonder when some of my colleagues and friends heard I was starting to learn the ABCs at the age of 20, they reacted with skepticism. They were skeptical about my chances of success.

It's true I was a real late starter. But my friends failed to recognize a widely shared view: Zeal, hard work, and dedication combined could remedy the shortcoming of starting late. I am not claiming and never did, that I possess all of the three qualities. But my life seems to have demonstrated that I owe what I have achieved in my pursuit of English studies to those three attributes.

My teenage learning experience was rather special. I never received any formal education. Before I came to Taiwan in 1949, I received only some six years of village school education, as I recounted in the previous chapter. The kind of village school which I attended taught only the Four Books and Five Classics. (The Four Books are comprised of the Doctrine of the Mean, the Great Learning, Mencius, and the Analects. The Five Classics consist of the Book of Odes, Book of Documents, Book of Changes, Book of Rites, and the Spring and Autumn Annals).

After my arrival in Taiwan, I continued serving in the army as part of my mandatory military obligation, and thus had no chance to attend school and receive formal education. I would have been entitled to attend a middle school at the time if my village school experience was taken as an equivalent of Taiwan's elementary education.

But even if I were so admitted, I would have been unable to afford it, unless I could get a part-time job earning a living and covering education fees. Yet finding an adequate job would have been something out of my reach at the time, given my young age and my lack of work experience.

In those early days, military personnel intending to increase their academic or intellectual capabilities could do so only by educating themselves in the barracks and by using their spare time. In the first two years or so of my coming to Taiwan, I did read a variety of Chinese language books, including literary works and works dealing with contemporary issues, in addition to newspaper columns.

Such readings surely benefited me a lot. They increased my general knowledge, broadened my vision, and provided me opportunities to learn how to enhance my Chinese writing skills. However, continuing to do general readings as I mentioned above could not improve the prospect of me entering a military academy. In the military, if one wanted to move up the career ladder, one had to hold a minimum academy degree. This I believe has become even more so in the present-day armed forces. Yet to enter a military officer training school, you had to pass entrance examinations. Chinese, mathematics, and English were mandatory test subjects.

For me, this meant that I also had to spend time learning mathematics and English, in addition to Chinese. For a time, I did work hard preparing for the exams. But it did not last long. I soon found I was more interested in English than mathematics. Sometimes, I even fancied that if someday my English became good enough to read newspapers and publications in this foreign language, it would be a great pleasure for me. So I came to focus more on English at the expense of learning mathematics.

Yet studying English in a society whose mother tongue is Chinese was quite a challenging task. You could hardly find people in your neighborhood who spoke or wrote English. This was especially true with the small fishing village situated next to our defense post. People in this civilian community, as I remember, were mostly illiterate and they spoke only Fukienese, knowing nothing about English. What I am trying to describe here is that when living in an environment where no one uses a language that you're learning, you would have no one to turn to for help, in case you had difficulty understanding a certain new word or some grammar rules, for example.

In modern times, the above-cited circumstances no longer pose any problem for an English learner, even if those situations still exist. The reason is that people now have the advantage of learning English from radio or television broadcasting, no matter where they are located. These days, people who want to study English also can conveniently do so by using the service of the Internet.

During my years at the Mt. Shou defense post, I had access to neither radio nor a TV broadcasting service, let alone the use of the Internet, which was still well in the future.

But I was lucky to acquaint myself with a navy petty officer, Mr. Wang Ke-ming. Mr. Wang and several other senior sailors of the ROC Navy had just been deployed in our defense area as our next-door neighbors. They were charged with the responsibility of communicating with warships passing by via signals.

Learning the ABCs from a Navy Petty Officer

Mr. Wang Ke-ming, who graduated from a Shanghai missionary school before he came to Taiwan, had a good command of English. One summer day in 1952, we had a chance to meet and talk with each other. After learning of my desire to study English, Mr. Wang offered to teach me for free. He was so generous that he said he would welcome participation by any of my colleagues if they were willing to learn the language too.

Following my conversations with Mr. Wang, I moved quickly to sound out my colleagues about the English-learning idea. Approximately half a dozen of my colleagues I discussed this with responded positively. We thus formed an English-learning class with me acting as a natural "student leader." I was responsible for taking care of all teaching-related matters and also served as a link between Mr. Wang and us, the students.

We started virtually with learning the letters of the alphabet. Mr. Wang taught us how to spell, read and pronounce English words. In the early weeks, we spent time learning and memorizing new words. Shortly after, we started studying texts, using standard English textbooks compiled for junior high students.

We, the English learners, were allowed by our military unit superiors to hold classes -- occasions where we met to be taught by Mr. Wang -- normally once a week. We had to do exercises and read texts and memorize new words in our spare time available during early mornings and late evenings.

Although Mr. Wang was not a trained teacher, he proved to be a very good one in our eyes. He was always trying to do his best to help us with homework. He was patient with us, but he was also firm in what he required of us. What also impressed me was that Mr. Wang, from the beginning to the very end, never called to suspend a class because he was otherwise engaged.

Our English-learning class, regrettably, lasted for only a little more than one year until the autumn of 1953. At this time, we -- the entire searchlight contingent members -- were reassigned to a field infantry division deployed outside Kaohsiung, and hence had to leave the Mt Shou defense post.

After I left Kaohsiung, I saw Mr. Wang Ke-ming only twice. The last time was in the early 1970s when I paid a visit to him at his home in Tainan city. At that time, he had long since retired from the ROC Navy and was preaching the gospel as a pastor. I am not a churchgoer. But I believe I understand one thing: Church leaders must lead by example. They therefore must possess a range of important moral virtues, including strength of character, love, caring, grace, and humility. In my view, my friend Mr. Wang Ke-ming embodies all such essential qualities.

By the time I left Mt. Shou in late 1953 following my reassignment to a field infantry division, we, the entire English-learning class, had finished the first two of a series of three volumes of a junior high school English textbook. On the eve of my departure, I went to a Kaohsiung book-store and bought the third and last volume of the same English textbook, which I had not yet studied at that time.

Always Carrying My Three Learning Tools

In addition to buying a copy of the third part of that textbook, I also bought a pocket English-Chinese dictionary. I decided to purchase such a mini-dictionary because it could fit into my military uniform pockets and be conveniently carried around. After leaving the searchlight contingent of the Kaohsiung Garrison Command, I served in combat companies for the next 10 years. During this period, I got into the habit of carrying three learning tools in my pockets: a dictionary, a vocabulary notebook, and a textbook or some other reading materials.

Bringing these three things with me, I could study English wherever or whenever convenient. In short, it enabled me to spend every moment of my spare time learning this foreign language. This time-conscious learning method worked well for me. I finished the third volume of the said junior high school English textbook within a year's time of my departure from Kaohsiung, despite tough combat troops' lives characterized by constant field training and exercises, as well as periodic movements from one location to another.

My ability to complete the third part of English courses for junior high students within a year only with the aid of a pocket English-Chinese dictionary told me two things. One was that the previous nearly two-year learning experience I acquired at the Mt. Shou defense post provided a foundation for me to continue studying English on my own.

Two, the Mt. Shou English-learning experience stimulated in me a passion for English that drove me to continuously study this foreign language, undaunted by difficult learning environments. This ardent affection for English has never faded in the rest of my life.

To people having received a formal education, my attainment of a junior high school level of English certainly was nothing in particular. But for me, it was of great significance. This achievement proved to be only the beginning of what was going to be a long, challenging but rewarding learning experience in my life.

After leaving the military post at Mt. Shou in 1953, I spent the next 10 years (referring to non-work hours only) continuously studying English, mostly in military bunkers on the frontline island of Kinmen (Quemoy), off the southeastern coast of communist-controlled mainland China. I used the first two years of that period to complete the study of senior high school English courses. After this, I then began reading non-textbook publications. My favorite reading materials during those years were the English-language China Post and the American magazine Reader's Digest. In the meantime, I began practicing English writing.

The most challenging thing I faced in the course of my English study during those early years remained the same: You had no one to turn to for help when you had difficulty understanding the definition of a certain English word or the meaning of a complex sentence. What was also frustrating was that you could hardly find someone who was able or willing to correct my English writing.

My hard work and perseverance in English learning began to bear fruit a decade later. In mid-1963, I passed an army-wide English test that earned me the chance of being transferred from a grassroots combat company to the Army General Headquarters in Taipei. In the highest command of the army, I worked along with the U.S. military assistance advisors, both as an English interpreter and as a translator. This new job considerably improved my life and learning environment in the military.

Then in December 1965, two and a half years after my transfer to the Army General Headquarters, I passed another examination of greater importance to me. This one was given by Taiwan's then sole English-language daily, the China Post. The newspaper gave an examination to recruit reporters. I passed the test, leading two dozen or so fellow candidates, some of them English majors graduating from universities.

Interestingly, when I first began studying the English alphabet at the age of 20 as a soldier stationed in the above-cited Mt. Shou military defense post, I had never anticipated that this brief learning experience would pave the way for me to take up English journalism as my life career path.

I am straying a little bit from the topic of revisiting Mt. Shou. I now must pick up where I left off. After fulfilling my long-held wish of going back to see that memorable place in my life, Yen-ming and I left for downtown Kaohsiung. On the way, we stopped by the Bay of Sizihwan--a scenic spot noted for its popular swimming beach and being home to a leading higher education institution, National Sun Yat-sen University. As previously planned, we made a brief stopover there, but not just for sightseeing. Yen-ming and I each have some experiences worth recalling in this place.

For me, Sizihwan was the place where I spent the first night after disembarking at the neighboring Kaohsiung port in mid-1949 from a ship, which carried some 600 of our young soldiers from Guangzhou, Guangdong province.

My first impression of Sizihwan was a woman who, with her face covered with a piece of clothing, was selling bananas. I was curious about why she wanted to wear face-covering clothing. In my hometown, I never saw a woman dressed in such a way. My attention quickly shifted to her business. I intended to buy bananas from that Sizihwan woman. But embarrassingly, I found no money in my pockets.

What also was imprinted on my mind was that Sizihwan was a place where some 10 Searchlight Contingent colleagues and I often spent our Sundays and holidays swimming at the beach and playing basketball at a concrete court located not far from the sea. I remember it took us about an hour's walk to get to Sizihwan from our hillside defense post. During those days, feet were our only means of transport in the absence of public transport service.

Yen-ming, like me, has a vivid memory of this bay area. She started her elementary education at a seaside primary school there. I myself also knew that school, which was located at a roadside. Each time when we went to the city of Kaohsiung, we had to pass right by its front door.

Disappointedly, Yen-ming and I could not find that primary school. The old basketball court and the adjacent path leading to the swimming beach, which I was familiar with, were no longer present. Their disappearance, however, was not surprising. Just consider this: It had been more than half a century since I left Kaohsiung.

Drastic changes were also noticed in the surrounding areas. A lot of fine Japanese-style wooden houses, for example, had gone. In their place was National Sun Yat-sen University, which was founded in the early 1980s. So obviously, those wooden houses as well as the aforementioned primary school had been either dismantled or relocated elsewhere to make room for the construction of buildings housing the university's various colleges and departments.

Yen-ming is 12 years younger than me. But we have similar backgrounds, in addition to the common experience that we had -- a delightful time in the bay of Sizihwan when we were young. Like me, she came from the Chinese mainland. She came to Kaohsiung with her parents in the the1940s. Her father, also like me, had a military background. He was serving in an artillery unit in Hainan province as a lieutenant colonel then. As my wife recalled, she and her parents, along with the artillery unit, took one of the last three warships of the ROC Navy as they withdrew to Kaohsiung, just before the fall of the island to the Chinese communists. At the time Yen-ming was only five years old. Her father soon found a job with the Kaohsiung Harbor Bureau. The family has since taken up residence in this southern port city.

After receiving her primary and secondary education in Kaohsiung, Yen-ming left for Taipei to attend a private girls' college, Ming Chuan. She later got a job at the China Post's color printing department working as a fine arts designer. At the time, I was working as a reporter in the editorial department of the same English-language newspaper. It was at the China Post where we met each other and became good friends. We married in Taipei in 1967. Since then, Yen-ming seldom went back to Kaohsiung city to visit the places where she grew up.

Visiting Yen-ming's Alma Mater

After winding up our tour of the Sizihwan Bay area, we then proceeded to downtown Kaohsiung. There she and I made a visit to her alma mater, Kaohsiung Municipal Girls' Senior High School. Walking inside this nearly century-old school, she quickly spotted many striking changes from her days there. The auditorium where she and her schoolmates often met to listen to lectures and take part in entertainment activities, for example, was replaced with a high-rise building. She was also unable to find the classrooms where she used to take courses. A senior school official explained to her that many "new" classrooms had been built successively in the last few decades to replace order ones. So she said "I guess the classrooms you referred to must be the ones long dismantled and replaced."

Yen-ming also asked an interesting question: Where has the Girls' Senior High School's landmark -- the "White House" -- gone? She was referring to a building that contained the student toilets. It once stood on the girls' school campus, and its eye-catching exterior walls, covered in white paint, earned it's a memorable nickname -- the White House -- the official residence of the president of the United States.

The female school official responded with a smile. "I know what you mean, but it was rebuilt a long time ago." In case "you have an urgent need for the toilet," she suggested, "you may pay a visit to the one in a more ordinary color," pointing to a structure straight ahead of us.

In general, our 22-23 March 2014 trip to Kaohsiung city and its suburbs Mt. Shou and Zuoying was smooth and quite enjoyable, thanks to well-conceived arrangements made by our daughter Tseng Wen-yi. She arranged everything for us, from reserving two round-trip high-speed rail tickets to booking a spacious room in a newly inaugurated villa-type hotel. This was a well-located hotel providing good sea views, with Kaohsiung Harbor on its left and the Sizihwan scenic spot on its right.

My daughter also worked out an itinerary, with a Kaohsiung city map attached to it. For our convenience, she uploaded the itinerary and the map to both my iPad and mobile phone. So it was very easy for us to find information such as where to go, what to eat, and even when, just by clicking a button on my mobile phone or iPad.

Our two-day Kaohsiung visit culminated at an age-old restaurant in the city, which serves Shanghai food. We decided to dine at this restaurant because it features a rare specialty -- a moray eel dish. Even before we started out on our Kaohsiung trip, we had set moray eel high on a list of food that we would like to eat in this southern city of Taiwan.

We chose moray eel as a "must eat" dish on our Kaohsiung visit this time for a special reason. Nearly half a century ago on a spring day, I took a train down to Kaohsiung from Taipei to see Yen-ming at her parents' home. At that time, we were still dating each other. I invited her out to dine at a restaurant in a bustling market area. One dish I ordered was moray eel cooked with chives. This dish was special also because boiling oil was poured over it at the very moment it was served. The food tasted so good that Yen-ming and I immediately made a wish to eat it again someday. The moray eel which we ate at the age-old Kaohsiung restaurant this time was cooked in the same way, and it was just as delicious as the food we had been served 47 years ago.

The tale of my return to a post-WWII-era defense post will end here. In the following chapter, I will narrate how I persisted in studying English in infantry companies during the next decade, without being impeded by difficult army life and constant troop movements.

Chapter 3
A Decade of Change

Using Every Available Moment for Study

In the previous chapter, I mentioned I started learning the English ABCs in a Kaohsiung military garrison post in 1953 at the age of 20 and that my tutor was an ROC Navy petty officer, Mr. Wang Ke-ming. Under his tutelage, I finished the first and second volumes of a junior high school English textbook. In terms of duration, my English learning experience lasted for about one and a half years until the fall of 1954.

Serving as an army officer with the rank of captain.

At this time, two difficult challenges arose, threatening to impede my continuation of English study. The first challenge stemmed from my transfer, along with my garrison searchlight contingent colleagues, to infantry companies. This resulted in my departure from the Mt. Shou defense post, where I had been stationed for nearly four years.

Life in infantry units was expected to be much tougher than in my Mt. Shou garrison post. This was true, as I soon personally experienced. In infantry units, you always faced long work hours. You underwent endless training programs, from basic to advanced, and from field exercises to war games. All this meant that infantry soldiers were always left with little time to pursue personal interests, such as self-development, as in my case.

A second challenge arising from my mandated transfer was a fear that I might be unable to find someone in my new unit, who would be willing to teach English to me, like Mr. Wang. Although I now had finished the study of the first and second parts of a junior high school English textbook, I was still a complete beginner. At this stage of learning, it was vitally important for me to be taught some basics, such as English concepts and grammar rules.

Nevertheless, I was undaunted by the potential challenges lying ahead. I was determined to keep learning English. On the eve of my departure from Mt. Shou, I went to a Kaohsiung book-store to buy the third and last part of the said English textbook--the part which I hadn't yet studied in my Mt. Shou unit.

In addition to the third volume of the junior high school textbook, I also bought a pocket-size English-Chinese dictionary. I decided to purchase such a mini-dictionary because it could fit in my military uniform pocket and be carried around. This would make it convenient for me to look up new words, whenever such a need arose.

After my transfer to an infantry unit, I adjusted the way I learned English to suit the conditions of my new work environment. I had to. Infantry troops invariably worked long hours. This meant that the time I could use to pursue my study was even less. Hence, I needed to make use of every available moment to memorize new words and study texts.

During my years in the various infantry companies, I often got up earlier and went to sleep later than my colleagues. Before dawn, I would quietly walk out of our barracks to read English texts under an electric light pole. When on night duty, I would take a vocabulary notebook out of my pocket to review new words, whenever the circumstance permitted.

Besides getting up early and sleeping late, I also did my studying on weekends and holidays. I often used such times to review the words and texts which I had learned in the past weeks or months. Holidays allowed me plenty of free time to utilize and thus were more suitable for me to do total reviews of new words and new texts. Also, during days off from work when everyone went out on the town to visit relatives and friends or places of entertainment, the whole camp became quieter. A noise-free environment was favorable to concentrating on my studies.

In line with field infantry life, I also got into the habit of putting three learning materials -- a vocabulary notebook, a textbook, and a dictionary -- in my pockets, while moving around or participating in military exercises. By bringing these materials along, I could keep learning by using intervals or breaks.

Learning English in such a way was truly hard. But it produced encouraging results for me. In the more than one-year period, from the time I left the Mt. Shou defense post to the latter half of 1954, I finished the last of a series of three volumes of a junior high school English textbook -- the one designated by Mr. Wang at the start of our English learning class.

Unlike the first two volumes, which I studied under the tutelage of Mr. Wang, as I related earlier, I completed the study of the third volume only with the aid of an English-Chinese dictionary. This gave me a great boost, strengthening my belief that I now could learn English on my own without the help of a teacher.

Reading has always been my favorite leisure activity.

English Learning Interrupted Briefly

Upon my completion of the entire junior high English textbook, however, I suspended my study of the language for nearly one year. I did so with the aim of improving my learning environment. In September 1955, I applied to attend a six-month communications training program in a narrow field. I was admitted after passing an entrance exam. The training program, sponsored by the intelligence bureau of the Defense Ministry of the ROC, was conducted at the Political Warfare College in Fuxin-gang, Taipei.

The cadets of the training class were taught skills, among other things, to encrypt and decrypt confidential documents and messages. Such translation processes were implemented to enhance communications security. Precisely, when a document or data was encrypted, even if intercepted during the course of transmission by an unauthorized person or an enemy, it could not be read.

The six-month training program was an intensive one. In addition to being taught eight hours of regular lessons each workday, students were also required to attend morning and evening sessions. On top of that, students were from time to time given written assignments. Such extra tasks always involved students reading designated books and then writing their own views and comments on them.

To work on such assignments, I often visited the college's library to borrow books and reference materials. The library had a rich collection of books and journals. It also featured a wide choice of individual seating in quiet and silent areas. So quickly I was attracted by that study place. Besides doing my assignments at the library, I also spent my Sundays and holidays there doing some general reading, while I was not otherwise engaged.

Rarely did I run through a whole book or volume because of a time limit. I did only selective reading. I read some of the works authored by internationally known Chinese scholars such as Liang Qichao and Hu Shih. These works broadened my horizon and inspired me a lot.

Dr. Hu Shih (1891-1962) was a Chinese philosopher, essayist, and diplomat. He was widely recognized as a key contributor to Chinese liberalism and language reform. He passionately campaigned for replacing scholarly classical Chinese writing with a written style closer to the spoken language.

One day as I was reading a collection of Hu Shih's writings, I came across an interesting piece. In it, he used an age-old fable of the race between a tortoise and a hare to teach a lesson to the reader. That piece of writing inspired me greatly. I since have used the tortoise spirit as my motto in improving my English skills: reading, listening, writing, and speaking.

The fable concerns a hare that makes fun of the slow-moving tortoise. The tortoise, unhappy with the arrogance of the fast-moving hare, challenges it to a race. The hare gets off to a fast start. Believing that it can win easily, the hare stops running and decides to take a nap before finishing the race. The tortoise, however, continues to move slowly but without stopping. The tortoise finally wins the race.

After telling the story, Dr. Hu Shih advised his readers that "if you don't have the natural abilities of the hare, you must learn the spirit of the tortoise and be willing to make the effort."

Like the Tortoise - Willing to Make the Effort

Over the years I was frequently asked by friends and others the question "how could you make it?" They were referring to my longtime career as a journalist and English writer, while I have never received any formal education or training in such fields. My reply has always been the same: I "am willing to make the effort, as was the tortoise" in its race with the hare.

During my time at the Political Warfare College, I also read some of Liang Qichao's writings collected in his Yinbingshi heji (The Ice-Drinker's Studio). I chose to read this book in part because I admired Liang's political reform ideas.

Liang Qichao (1873-1929) became a widely known figure when he was still young. In 1898 Liang was granted an audience with the Chinese Emperor Guangxi -- the second to last ruler of the Qing Dynasty. At the time, Liang was in his mid-20s.

The emperor had earlier accepted Liang's mentor Kang Youwei's proposal to transform China into a constitutional monarchy. The proposal, called "Reform and Self-Strengthening," however, was short-lived, after the Empress Dowager Cixi intervened. The intervention resulted in the emperor's house arrest and Liang Qichao's flight to Japan. The Kang- and Liang-led reform program came to be known as Hundred Days' Reform in recent Chinese history.

In Japan, Liang continued writing articles during his 14-year stay there. He used his writings, mostly published in his "New Citizen" journal, to call for political and democratic changes back home in China. He believed that promoting democracy was the surest route to strengthening the country.

It was in the early 1950s when I read Liang Qichao's Yinbingshi heji. During those times, Taiwan was still under martial law. Publication or open discussion of pro-democracy issues was discouraged. So Liang Qichao's reform ideas were informative and resonated well with me.

Another reason for me to spend my limited time reading Liang's writings was that he had been widely known for his new style of

Chinese writing. Many observed that Liang Qichao's style combined both traditional literary Chinese and contemporary spoken Chinese.

It was ironic that when I read Liang's essays I had only a desire to learn the style of his Chinese writing--the terms and skills he used in presenting his ideas. I had never anticipated that some 10 years later I would retire from the military and take English journalism as a career. And that this life-changing event would prompt me to place greater emphasis on strengthening my English writing capabilities rather than on how to improve my Chinese writing.

Also interestingly, when I read Liang's works where he stressed the importance of journalism to national strength, I only thought that I couldn't agree with him more on that point. Beyond that, I did not have any particular feelings about it. I never imagined that someday in the future I myself would become a member of the media industry and spend the rest of my life working as a career journalist and writer.

In sum, my effort at learning English was completely disrupted during the six-month period, as I received communications training at the Political Warfare College. That was so, not just because of an extremely tight training schedule but also because I devoted almost all of my free time to reading Chinese language books--such as the two which I cited above--leaving me no time at all to continue studying English.

My six-month training program ended in early 1955. Upon graduation, I was assigned to a logistics company under the 93rd infantry division of the ROC as a communications warrant officer. For me, this was a significant promotion. Before I was admitted to the Political Warfare College, I was an infantry private.

The ninety-third division at the time was deployed in Kinmen --
an outlying island facing mainland China's coastal province of Fukien.
Then – as now – the communist-held mainland was a political rival to
the ROC or Taiwan. In compliance with the assignment, I took a naval
passenger and cargo ship from Keelung Harbor to Kinmen.
Immediately after my arrival, I reported to my new unit -- the logistics
company. I served in that same company for the next two years before
we (the entire division) moved back to Taiwan.

The Learning Environment Improves Greatly

Once I settled in Kinmen, I resumed my English study during non-
work hours. By this time, my learning environment had improved in
several ways. First, I was elevated to the rank of a warrant officer from
that of a private, as a result of my graduating from the training
program of the Political Warfare College. In the ROC army then, a
warrant officer was not a formally commissioned officer, yet the
holder of this rank could receive the same treatment as a
commissioned officer. This meant in a sense I now had greater
freedom of managing my non-work time to the benefit of my study.
Previously as a private, I didn't have such an advantage.

Second, I now served as a crypto officer with the responsibility
to encipher and decipher classified military documents and messages.
This was a job I was trained for at the Political Warfare College. In
my role as a crypto officer, I had one sergeant working under me as
my assistant.

This picture shows a U.S. military advisor to Taiwan addressing a group of ROC army translators. Sitting immediately to the left of the speaker is me.

All this meant that I did not have to perform the various leadership duties, as required of a platoon leader. A platoon leader, like me, was a junior officer in an army company. But unlike me, they had to plan, organize and lead troops under their command to carry out the missions assigned by the higher authority. Since I did not have these various leadership duties to fulfill, I naturally had more time to spend on my private studies.

And thirdly, I was assigned by my company commander to live separately in a bunker. This further improved my learning environment. The bunker, situated atop a hill, was small, just providing enough space for a bed and a desk. Yet I really enjoyed living in such a small space, as it allowed me to be myself without being influenced by other people. The availability of such a quiet environment enabled me to concentrate on my studies. I would not have had such an advantage if I were assigned to live in a bigger bunker or a camp where I would have to share living quarters with others.

I lived in that Kinmen bunker for the following two years until late 1957 when our infantry division was transferred back to Taiwan. During this two-year period, I completed a senior high school English textbook, which consisted of three parts. The completion was significant in two important ways. One, my English capabilities now measured up to the standards of senior high school, as defined in the formal education system. Two, my English vocabulary and comprehension skills had reached a level that allowed me to do non-textbook, general readings such as English magazines and newspapers.

From my learning experience, I found senior high school English courses were much harder than those for junior high students in terms of text complexity. The way I studied my senior high textbook was such: I always learned its lessons one at a time and according to their arranged sequence.

I was in the habit of first highlighting a lesson's words that I did not understand, then finding their Chinese meanings in a desktop English-Chinese dictionary, and finally writing down those new English words in the margin of a related page, together with their Chinese translations.

After this job was done, I then proceeded to study the text. But even so, I still often met with difficulties fully understanding the meanings of the text. The reason was that each English word has multiple meanings, thus it was very difficult for me to determine what it meant in the context of the text.

In addition, a lot of phrases and idioms could not be found in ordinary dictionaries. Often, for the sake of some words or sentences, I walked a very long way to ask someone for help. During those days few had a good command of English in the military, especially at the company level.

In the two-year stay in Kinmen, besides finishing the senior high school English textbook, I also listened to Dr. Lilian Chao's English lesson, The Student Digest, on the air in the final six months of our deployment there. It was a popular English-learning course taught through radio broadcasting in the early morning Monday through Friday.

This half-year learning experience was especially nerve-wracking for me. For instance, I didn't have a watch or clock at the time. Without such a timepiece, I often didn't have any idea what time it was when I woke up in the middle of the night. Or whether the broadcasting program had come on air. From time to time, I'd awaken with a start several times a night. In such situations, I would dare not go back to sleep, just waiting beside the radio.

After returning to Taiwan proper, our division was ordered to move into army bases to undergo a new cycle of intensive basic and combat training. We now worked on a schedule much tighter than in Kinmen, where we performed only garrison duties. For me, life on training bases meant I had less available time to do my studies than when I was stationed in Kinmen. And I could no longer live alone in a small but quiet bunker as previously.

But all this did little to dampen my enthusiasm for learning English. Then, in mid-1958, I began subscribing to an English-language newspaper, the China Post. This marked the beginning of a new phase in my English studies -- from reviewing textbooks to reading a daily newspaper.

Reading My First English Newspaper

Now as I look back on the difficulty I encountered when I first read the China Post, I realized it was truly too hard for me to do this kind of reading at that point in time. I had just finished senior high school English courses, plus a half-year lesson learned from radio broadcasting. According to some expert research, the average English-language newspaper requires a 6,000 to 8,000-word vocabulary, while a high school graduate is expected to have a vocabulary size of only around 5,000 English words.

The extent of the difficulty I faced in reading the China Post early on can be seen from the account given below: I delighted in reading the newspaper on Sundays and holidays. This was so because, on such days, we usually had no official work to do. Thus, I had time to read more news items. I also liked to use Sundays and holidays to catch up on my reading.

Yet despite the increase in my reading time, I moved forward slowly. For example, it always took me a whole Sunday just to finish page 1 of the Post, a page devoted to reporting international news. By the time I went through the entire page, all of its available empty spaces were filled with my notes: new English words and their Chinese translations.

To help facilitate my comprehension, I worked out a reading method. Namely, I kept reading a certain page of the Post, page 1 for instance, for a fixed period of time, until it became relatively easy for me to catch the news articles on that page. Only after experiencing such a reading period, did I then proceed to study a new or another page.

The logic behind such a reading method was an assumption that each newspaper page specialized in features of different nature. And each page had its own editor. They too tended to have different coverage policies and preferences in selecting news stories. When news stories printed on a given page were consistently of similar kinds, they would naturally become easier for the regular reader to understand. This was especially so for someone like me, who was still studying English as a beginner.

The method I devised to promote my comprehension by exclusively reading a certain page for a fixed period of time was beneficial in another way. Some of the articles appearing in a newspaper were just news updates. Such follow-ups were mostly printed on the same page, on which they first appeared. This being the case, when you read a story that reported the latest developments in a news event, which you had read about previously, it would certainly be much easier to understand.

My English reading ability increased steadily, as I kept up reading the China Post. I cannot clearly remember when I could finish all the major stories of the paper in a day's time. The Post was available mostly in 12 pages during those days--times when martial law placed strict limits on the number of newspapers. I normally went through all of the pages with the exception of those carrying sports news and cartoons. I have had a bad habit of skipping those pages whenever I read a newspaper, whether English or Chinese.

With my reading speed and comprehension continuing to improve, I gradually expanded the scope of my English reading materials to include magazines, novels, biographies, as well as speeches by contemporary and historical figures. Strictly speaking, I started reading such publications only after I returned to the offshore island of Kinmen in 1960 for a second two-year stint.

In that year, our division was redeployed to Kinmen from Taiwan to assume a new two-year defense mission. From an individual point of view, my stint in Kinmen this time was less favorable, in terms of the learning environment, than my first two-year stay there two years earlier.

By "less favorable," I mean I myself experienced multiple job transfers in the new two-year span, causing instability and inconveniences in my private life. Firstly, I was transferred from my original logistics company to a communications company on the eve of our departure for Kinmen. In the new company, I served as an officer supervising the operations of a communications center. Along with the transfer, I was promoted to the rank of second lieutenant, up from a warrant officer, a position which I had held for the previous four years.

Then more than a year later, I was ordered to return to Taiwan to receive six months of training in an army communications school located in the northeast county of Ilan. Upon graduation, I went back to my communications company in Kinmen. But soon after, I was transferred to a 4.2-inch mortar company to serve as a communications officer. In this position, I headed the wire and wireless communications sections. The new assignment involved me being promoted to the rank of first lieutenant.

The series of job transfers caused interruptions to my efforts at learning English. With each transfer, for instance, I had to spend extra time getting to know my new colleagues and familiarizing myself with my new work environment.

What's more, both of my new job assignments involved me performing leadership responsibilities and duties. In the case of my role at the 4.2-inch mortar company, for example, I had to take care of the men under me and supervise them in carrying out their work on wire and wireless communications. During my first two years in Kinmen, I was not obliged to assume leadership roles at all as an encrypting officer. In short, my assumptions of leadership roles left less time for me to study English.

Before leaving Taiwan for my second two-year combat mission in Kinmen, I paid a visit to Taipei's Kuling Street, known for selling back issues of magazines and used books. There I bought a large number of Reader's Digest (American edition) magazines, in addition to some English novels. Back issues of magazines or old novels were sold at prices considerably lower than at ordinary bookstores.

Reading Back Issues of Magazines and Books

During my second two years in Kinmen, minus the six months when I was away for communications training in Taiwan, these old books and magazine back issues became my mainstream reading in my spare time. I read them mostly in the mornings when my colleagues had yet to get up, and in the evenings after they went to sleep.

Of the various publications I brought from Taiwan, I liked Reader's Digest most. The general-interest Digest targeting the average American family was one of the most popular magazines in the United States then, with a global circulation of more than 10 million. My favorite Digest articles were the regularly appearing column "My Most Unforgettable Character" and a condensed version of a published book contained at the end of the magazine. But oftentimes, I failed to read through the condensed but still lengthy book pieces either because of a time limit or because they were too difficult for me to fully understand.

After arriving in Kinmen this time, I tried in vain to renew my subscription to the China Post, which I had subscribed to in Taiwan for the past two years. The English paper's Kinmen municipal agent was unwilling to accept my subscription order, citing delivery inconveniences.

The failure to have the Post delivered to my camp prompted me to walk some 40 minutes to the municipal library to read the Post on Sundays and holidays. Yet I was so eager to read the paper at the time not entirely for the reason to learn English. I also hoped to know through the Post the latest developments in political affairs in Taipei-

-kinds of news which sometimes were not fully covered in the Chinese language newspapers. This was because Taiwan during those early times was under martial law. Government authorities decided what the media could and could not print.

As the only English daily in Taiwan at the time, the China Post, as I saw, was allowed to enjoy greater freedom in printing political news. By doing so, the then KMT government hoped to ease international criticism that the ROC imposed strict restrictions on press freedom in Taiwan. A striking example of this is given below:

On a late summer Sunday in 1960 I routinely went to the Kinmen library to read the China Post. Soon after I picked up the paper, a front-page headline grabbed my attention: Lei Chen Arrested on Sedition Charges. The Post reported that the arrest came days after the Free China Fortnightly, a political journal that he edited, was shut down. Lei Chen was a leading political activist in Taiwan at the time.

On several following holidays I continued to go to that library to read the Post, and some Chinese language newspapers as well, to see how things developed about the Lei Chen case. News stories all reported Lei Chen's arrest and pointed to his increasingly vehement criticism of then President Chiang Kai-shek and his KMT government.

Lei Chen in his journal challenged Chiang's policy of retaking the mainland from the communists as unrealistic. He called instead for the government to slash military spending in favor of concentrating on economic developments in Taiwan. His overt promotion in 1960 of forming a new political party to oppose the KMT's one-party rule eventually led to a shutdown of the Free China journal and his own arrest in September that year. In the following October, he was sentenced to 10 years in prison after a military tribunal convicted him of sedition.

As I carefully followed the developments of the Lei Chen case in the local press, I got the impression that the China Post offered relatively bolder and more detailed coverage of the politically sensitive event, compared to the treatment of the same news by the Chinese language newspapers.

Many years later, I had a casual conversation with Nancy Yu-Huang, co-founder, and publisher of the Post. In it, I brought up the Lei Chen case. I told her my observations of the way the Taipei press covered the story of Lei Chen's alleged sedition crime. I said, "I felt the China Post appeared to enjoy greater freedom in treating the politically sensitive news." She nodded in agreement and with a smile. My casual conversations with the publisher took place at a time after I joined the Post as a staff reporter.

Not long after I started reading the China Post, I began trying to write things in English. This trial marked my English learning effort entering what I called a new or third phase. Previously, I had finished the first phase, in which I learned the ABCs with emphasis on memorizing new words. In the second phase, I expanded the scope of my reading materials to include periodicals and books.

I started my third phase of English study by writing simple sentences. After a time, I then began to translate Chinese-language news items into English. During my second stint in Kinmen, I went further to keep a diary, but not on a daily basis. This was, in part because I did not have enough time to do it regularly and in part, because there were not many new things that warranted being written down.

A Chance to Test My English Capabilities

In mid-1963, about a half year after our division was relocated back to Taiwan from Kinmen, a chance came up for me to put my English capabilities to the test. By this time I had spent about 10 years of non-work hours learning this foreign language. One day in May that year, I learned from my company commander that the Army General Headquarters Command of the ROC was recruiting candidates for English translators and interpreters.

I would have missed the chance had Mr. Sun Liao-fu failed to pass on to me the recruitment document in time. The document had reached our home barracks for some time, but I didn't see it because we were out for weeks on combat exercises at a training base dozens of miles away.

During the drills period, officers and men were not permitted to leave the training base to visit our home barracks. Mr. Sun was an exception, because he, as a company commander, had the responsibility to do so to see how things were going back "home."

By the time when Commander Sun handed me the recruitment paper of the ROC Army General Headquarter Command, there was barely time enough for me to make preparations to register my application for the test. The paper required that whoever intended to participate in the competition had to submit an autobiography written in English, along with their application. The autobiography needed to be typed. A handwritten version was unacceptable.

The time was short for me to file my registration. But luckily, not so long ago, I had written a brief story about my life just to practice English. This meant that I only needed to make some changes to it. Upon completion of the changes, I took a one-hour-and-a-half bus ride to downtown Taipei city to look for an English typist to type my manuscript. I had to go that far to find a typing service because I couldn't find one in the vicinity of our training base.

I barely met the deadline. About one month after the submission of my application, I received a notice from the Liaison Office of the Army General Headquarters Command. The Liaison Office, a unit that operated directly under the General Headquarters, provided interpretation and translation service between the ROC army and the then Military Assistance Advisory Group of the United States.

The notice informed me that my application had been accepted and I needed to come up to Taipei to sit for an exam. I could not recall the time when the exam was conducted, but I do vividly remember it was held at a Taipei primary school just across from where the Chiang Kai-shek Memorial Hall stands today. The Memorial Hall grounds formerly were the site of the Army General Headquarters Command, before it was relocated to Lungtan in Taoyuan county.

The exam included four sets of questions: multiple choices, true or false, fill-ins, and an essay. They, as I recall, were designed to test the applicant's English vocabulary, common sense, translation ability, and reading comprehension.

Chapter 3
A Decade of Change

I vaguely remember I answered almost all of the questions printed on the exam sheets. When I left the exam site, I felt confident of success.

On a Sunday evening--a couple of weeks after I took the Taipei test--as I was taking a walk on the grounds of our camp, I heard someone call me from behind. I turned back and found it was a sergeant friend of mine. He was working in our regiment command with the responsibility of handling incoming and outgoing documents of the entire regiment. He said to me: "Lieutenant Tseng, I congratulate you on 'having crossed the bitter sea.'" At the first moment, I was completely bewildered by his congratulatory remarks. But he quickly explained, "We've just received a letter from the Army General Command headquarters, saying you have passed the recent interpretation/translation test. The letter ordered you to report to the Liaison Office to take up a liaison job there, effective June 1, 1963."

I thanked my friend very much for letting me learn of this great news early. Otherwise, the news would become known to me only after the letter reached my company, a journey that could take at least two more days.

Here a few words are needed to explain what my sergeant friend meant by saying that I "have crossed the bitter sea." He meant, in brief, that with my transfer to the Army General Command from a grassroots level combat company, I had rid myself of hard field infantry life, no longer being subject to never-ending drills and movements from one location to another.

Upon receiving the said letter, my company commander Mr. Sun Liao-fu happily agreed to let me leave and go to Taipei to take up my new assignment. He told me he was so glad that he was able to pass the recruitment document to me in time. I too felt I owed him a debt of gratitude. The news that I was going to leave our unit, the 4.2-inch mortar company, swiftly reached the ears of everyone. In the days leading to my actual departure, I was thrown one dinner party after another. Regrettably, I always got drunk in the end, almost without exception. Most embarrassing was that at one time I was so drunk that I could go to my bed only with the help of my company commander.

Transfer to Army Command Headquarters

Being able to pass the Taipei recruitment test and the resulting reassignment to the Army General Command as a liaison officer was the most important change in my life. First, it represented that my past 10 years of persistent efforts to study English were rewarded in a meaningful way. This was quite encouraging.

Second, my transfer to the Army General Command marked a milestone in my military life. In the vast majority of the past 15 years since I enlisted in the military in 1949, I had led a tough infantry life, characterized by cycles of "life in the barracks" and "life in the field." In the barracks, while there was no need to go through harsh war game exercises, you faced endless training and equipment maintenance inspections by the various higher authorities, meaning that you were always busy making preparations.

After reporting for duty to the Liaison Office of the Army General Command, I found my living and working conditions had changed considerably overnight. There, I acted as a military office worker, following a regular nine-to-five work schedule. After work, I was totally free, managing my own time and choosing my own lifestyle. Your superiors would never interfere in your private life.

The above-cited improvements in my military and personal life marked the realization of my long-time desire to attain a stable environment that would be conducive to my pursuit of self-development, including the study of English.

Working for the Liaison Office, I was luckily designated to live in a bachelor's dormitory situated right in the expansive Army General Command Headquarters complex. One major advantage of living in the headquarters complex was that you could avoid suffering from Taipei's notorious traffic congestion. Many of my colleagues who lived in the suburbs had to spend extra time traveling to and from work every day.

In my new unit, I still stuck to a daily habit that I had acquired during my time serving in infantry companies. I always got up early every morning. After washing my face and brushing my teeth, I then rushed to the Liaison Office to read the China Post, which the office subscribed to. I did so until the time for breakfast. I made reading the English language newspaper my regular morning session. While doing so, however, I always made sure that I went to report for work on time.

On duty, I generally did two kinds of work. One was to perform the role of an interpreter bridging the communication gap between U.S. military advisors and ROC military personnel, who did not speak the same language. The need for such interpretation service arose when

U.S advisors went out to the countryside to inspect training and exercises by ROC troops.

I had two designated U.S. advisory counterparts--one first lieutenant and one chief sergeant. They were working for the Army Section of the U.S. Military Assistance and Advisory Group (MAAG). The office of the U.S. Army Section was right next door to that of the highest commander of the ROC Army. During those times, the Republic of China and the United States still maintained both diplomatic and military relations.

At times I also did some paperwork, while I had no interpretation duty to perform. I translated letters and documents from Chinese into English or vice versa. I loved my job at the Liaison Office very much, as it provided me with opportunities to improve my spoken and written English.

Another important advantage of my coming to work and live in Taipei was that it gave me a chance to witness life in this metropolis. Taipei, like many other capital cities, was a diverse society politically, culturally, and linguistically. Had I continued to stay in an infantry company isolated from the outside world, I would never have had this valuable eye-opening experience.

Taipei then had a huge American diplomatic and military presence, in addition to the existence of a large number of foreign business and cultural communities. The U.S. government provided both economic and military assistance to the ROC. In the respect of military ties, Taipei and Washington were bonded by a mutual defense treaty. Under this treaty, Washington set up a defense command in Taiwan to help protect this island against invasion. It also maintained a large military advisory group on this island with the mission to help train the ROC Armed Forces.

Living and working in such a diverse and dynamic society, I came to realize one important thing: This metropolis was full of opportunities, but unless you were well prepared, you would never be able to avail yourself of them.

On a certain December morning in 1965, an opportunity came up. I spotted a reporter-recruiting advertisement in the China Post, while reading the paper that morning. The ad attracted me so much that I hoped to give it a try. But at the same time, I was hesitant to do that for some reason. First, I worried that my lack of a college degree might disqualify me from taking part in the paper's recruitment examination. Also, I was concerned that my English knowledge might not measure up to the standards set by the paper.

Nevertheless, I summoned up the courage to write a letter to the newspaper telling them that I had neither a college diploma nor journalistic experience. But that I hoped to be given a fair chance to participate in the exam. To my surprise, the Post replied positively to my letter, allowing me to take the test. Yet what surprised me even more was that I became the sole successful applicant, surpassing about a dozen others.

On reflection, I found that I could perform relatively well on the exam due in part to my previous years of experience in reading the China Post. Some of the exam questions were derived from the latest current affairs which had appeared in the English-language newspaper in the past. One of the questions, for instance, asked the participants to give the name of the highest U.S. commanding officer in the

Vietnam war (from 1964 to 1968). Without any hesitation, I wrote down on my test sheet General William C. Westmoreland.

From Military Service to English Journalism

This was truly a life-changing examination. A week or so after the test, I was asked to go to the China Post for an interview with the paper's publisher Nancy Yu-Huang. Obviously, I also passed the oral test. The publisher at the end of the oral test invited me to join her paper as a reporter, beginning on January 5, 1966.

After being formally employed by the Post to serve as a staff reporter, I applied for retirement from my military unit--the Liaison Office of the Army Command Headquarters. My application was accepted. I thus ended my 18 years of service in the military. At the time I was 33 and held the rank of an army captain.

I never imagined that I would spend the next 46 years working as a journalist and a writer using English, a language which I began to learn in the army at the age of 20.

In my long career in journalism, I worked for several different news media outlets besides the China Post. In the process, I performed various key journalistic roles, including city editor, editor-in-chief, and editorial writer, as well as a reporter covering news on the ground for more than 10 years.

Looking back, I found that my lack of formal education and journalism training was never a barrier, either in my employment or in the workplace. In fact, all of the journalistic jobs I assumed were offered by my employers on their own initiative. Perhaps my first reporting job at the Post was an exception. But this was not entirely true. Admittedly, I actively looked for that reporting job but was granted it only after passing an entry test.

In the previous pages, I told how I started learning English and how persisting in this endeavor helped me transform my career from military service to journalism. And I related how my steady devotion to this occupation turned me into a professional journalist and English writer.

In the following segment, chapter 4, I will recollect how I started my English journalism career.

Chapter 4
Starting a Career in Journalism at 33

Striving to Make up for a Lack of Journalistic Training

I reported to the China Post for work on January 5, 1966, as agreed on. I gained admission to the English-language newspaper after I passed both a written exam and a face-to-face interview. At the time I was still in the military. But I agreed with publisher Nancy Yu-Huang in the interview that I would apply for retirement if I passed a six-month training period and my employment with the newspaper became official.

In the end, I went through the training program, and the China Post formally hired me. I thus applied to my military unit for retirement. My application was granted. So I left the army, ending my nearly two decades of military service. This was truly a life-altering moment: Making a career change in my early 30s, from nearly

The picture shows me working on a typewriter, while serving at the China Post in the early 1970s.

two decades of military service to journalism, a profession which I was never trained for.

From day one, I constantly faced two big challenges. One was how to gather news worth reporting. The other was how to write English news stories that were readable. As I said earlier, English is not my native tongue, and I began to learn it at the age of 20.

In all, I gathered news and wrote news articles for around a dozen years, accounting for one-fourth of my total journalism career. After leaving the reporting job, I served in several other positions that involved me editing news stories and writing commentaries until my retirement. Performing well in the roles of editing and commentary writing was no less challenging. It demanded profound English knowledge and high-level writing skills.

In other words, the challenges I faced in this latter stage of my journalism career remained strong. I had to continuously work hard and put in long hours to improve my capabilities to ensure that I could measure up to my editing and commentary writing responsibilities.

It can be said that working hard and continuing to learn were the hallmarks of my decades of journalism life.

My trial employment period at the China Post began with the start of a six-month "reserve reporters" training seminar, sponsored by the newspaper. The purpose of the seminar was manifest in its name. Classes were offered twice a week. I was an obligatory attendee. During the six-month period, I came to work for the Post daily, from 6:30 p.m. to midnight, while continuing to work for my military unit in the daytime.

I was assigned to assist in the running of the seminar. Besides me, there were five other attendees. Among them was Alice Sun, who like me was formally accepted and offered a job. Miss Sun, however, was designated as an assistant to the publisher, not working in the editorial department as I was. The remaining four candidates all had participated in the same reporter-recruitment test but failed to pass it. However, they were put on the waiting list. But somehow they were never formally employed.

Attendees to the seminar were taught news-gathering and news-writing skills, as well as journalistic duties and ethics. Lecturers included Taipei bureau chiefs stationed by major international news agencies, such as UPI (United Press International), AP (Associated Press), AFP (Agence France-Press), and Reuters. These veteran journalists and writers were invited to lecture on journalism and share their practical experiences with us.

Among other lecturers was Nancy Yu-Huang, the Post publisher. Nancy Yu-Huang held journalism degrees from Yenching University in Beijing, China, and Columbia University in the City of New York, United States. She taught us the value of the classic "Five W's and One H" of Journalism. They stand for six questions: What happened? Who was involved? Where did it take place? When did it occur? Why did that happen? And How did it happen? Answers to these questions are considered basic in gathering news or writing news stories. A news story failing to address any of these questions was viewed as incomplete. So the "Five W's and One H" were held as the basic guidance for journalism practitioners.

Standing in the middle is the publisher of the China Post. The others are reporters, with me standing on the far left. We came to the northern Keelung Harbor to see Alice Sun off (standing on the right of the publisher) who was taking a ship to the United States for advanced studies.

At the end of her course, Nancy always gave us assignments to collect news and write stories in accordance with the formula she raised above. But according to my memory, in the beginning, none of us six trainees scored better than 60 out of 100 on the news stories that we wrote and turned in.

George Chu, the China Post's city editor at the time and executive officer of the training program, gave us a piece of advice on how to conduct interviews. His advice impressed me deeply and proved helpful for me to do my own interviews during my subsequent 10-odd years of gathering news. I will summarize below what George Chu told us at the seminar on that particular course:

"...Make preparations for an interview in advance. First of all, do homework on the subject and the person that you are going to interview. Then list the questions you want to ask...Identify yourself at the outset of the interview and state what information you intend to obtain...Do not hesitate to ask any tough or embarrassing questions. Try to drag things out of an unwilling interviewee...Check with the interviewee when you have doubt about certain remarks or terms. Ask the interviewee if he or she has anything to add in the end. And remind him or her that you might call back for clarification or some additional information when such a need arises in the process of writing the interview story."

Every major trade has its professional standards, duties, and ethics that its members are expected to follow and fulfill. Shortly after I came to work for the China Post, I successively bought three English-language books at Taipei's Caves Book Store and Rainbow-Bridge Book Store, all of them dealing with the practice of journalism. The titles of the three books are The Professional Journalist, An Introduction to Journalism, and An Introduction to Mass Communications.

The first one, by John Hohenberg of Columbia University, deals with a variety of news principles and practices. But I remember I gave priority to reading two particular sections of that book. One was a discussion of what is news and what is news writing. The other section "deals primarily with the reporter--a key figure in all forms of journalism, and discusses his or her responsibilities, as well as ethical considerations."

Aspiring to Become a Professional Journalist

As I recall, when I decided to buy this book -- The Professional Journalist -- I had a big wish: I aspired to become a professional journalist ultimately, as in the book title. Many years later when I was performing the directing roles as city editor and editor-in-chief, I often told my reporters about that episode of my early journalistic experience.

"An Introduction to Journalism" was authored by F. Fraser Bond, who once taught journalism courses at Columbia University and New York University. In the preface, the author said the book was written to serve as a textbook either for a whole year's course or for the work of one intensive term.

From this book, I learned two basic journalistic concepts: One, the nature of journalism. Bond said the term "journalism" embraces all the forms in which and through which the news and the comments on the news reach the public. He further quoted Eric Hodgins of Time magazine as defining journalism as "the conveying of information from here to there with accuracy, insight, and dispatch, and in such a manner that the truth is served, and the rightness of things is made slowly, even if not immediately, and more evident."

Two, the purposes of journalism: Journalism has four main reasons for being: to inform, to interpret, to serve (the community, the reader, and the advertiser), and to entertain.

The third journalism-related book I bought shortly after I joined the news profession was: An Introduction to Mass Communications, co-authored by Edwin Emery, professor of journalism at the

University of Minnesota; Phillip H. Ault, associate editor of South Bend Tribune, Indiana; and Warren K. Agee, dean of Henry W. Grady School of Journalism, the University of Georgia.

At the time I purchased this book, I just hoped to gain some general knowledge about what mass communications were. I was so ignorant that I could not even distinguish between mass communications and journalism. That book essentially provided answers to my questions. In its first chapter about the impact of mass communications, the authors said in the opening paragraph: "Men today learn almost everything they know through some medium of mass communications -- television, radio, newspapers, magazines, books, and film." So from the third book, I learned that newspapers and magazines, or print journalism, are just part of the diverse mass communications sector.

While getting to know the basic knowledge and principles of journalism is of great importance to anyone who aimed to become a good reporter, the key to success lay in practicing. So from the very beginning, I realized that if I wanted to become a successful reporter, I had to go out to cover news and write news stories. This is just like swimming. If anyone wanted to learn swimming, he or she had to actually practice it. Learning only some swimming rules and skills would never be possible for you to become a good swimmer.

In the first more than half a year at the China Post, I had very few chances to go outside to cover news and write stories. Only occasionally did my city editor, George Chu, send me out to attend press conferences, interview some influential figures or investigate an emerging scandal.

For the most part of this period, I was requested to do mainly two things in the newsroom. One was to cut articles or stories from the day's Chinese-language newspapers, which the Post for some reason failed to cover the previous day. But they were still worth reporting by us after they were rewritten or translated into English.

In such cases, we often first checked the contents of the clippings to see if they were accurate. If not, we would seek to correct them by calling the original sources and getting the right information. Sometimes, when we found the content of a certain clipping was incomplete, we would also make telephone inquiries with the relevant sources to obtain some additional information before that story was reprinted in our paper.

Since I was responsible for doing the clippings, I usually was the one who did those above-cited tasks. But in some situations, I only needed to mark any questionable areas in the clippings, which I thought had to be checked out, and then passed the clipped items on to relevant reporters, letting them do the checking once they came to the office.

Besides making newspaper clippings, I was also charged with the task of selecting Chinese-language news stories from among dispatches supplied by local wire agencies, mainly the state-run Central News Agency. These selected stories were then distributed to reporters or writers, who then rewrote or translated them into English before they were finally edited, checked, and sent to the printer for publication in the Post's next-day edition.

Oftentimes, the editor-in-chief did the bulk of such rewriting or translations. The Post had a long tradition that its editor-in-chief did quite a lot of the rewriting work. But perhaps because of that reason, the chief editor performed no other duties normally required of that role in a newspaper. During my early years at the Post, the holder of this position was Joe Hung, who was known as a fast writer.

In the beginning, I was doing the job of selecting and distributing news under the guidance of my city editor, George Chu. Chu quit his job and went to the United States to pursue advanced studies more than a year and a half after I joined the Post. In the U.S, he obtained a Ph.D. from Southern Illinois University. He later gained a teaching position at a certain U.S. university.

One other thing worth mentioning is that the China Post at the time ran just 12 pages—the upper limit of the number of pages that a newspaper, whether Chinese or English language, could print during those times when Taiwan was under martial law. The Post's editorial contents were divided into domestic and international news sections. Traditionally, the Post's international news came mainly from major international news agencies, such as AP, AFP, UPI, and Reuters. Namely, the Post sourced all the foreign news stories it printed from those wire services by subscription.

As for the Post's domestic news, it stemmed primarily from three sources: Reports submitted by its own reporters; dispatches supplied by the Central News Agency and several other local news service outlets; and items cut from the Chinese-language newspapers.

I mentioned a moment ago that the second part of my duty during my early days of work at the China Post was to select news. By "selecting news," I meant a job involving me choosing news from among the above-cited latter two sources: Central News Agency-supplied dispatches and articles cut from Taiwan's major Chinese-language newspapers.

News Selections a Challenging Task

Even now, at the time of this writing, I still see that sensibly selecting news from among a wide variety of news stories is no easy task. It's true there have been many widely accepted rules and principles governing news selection, and addressing the more fundamental issue of "what is news?"

But the catch is that when it comes to actually selecting news, those rules and principles sometimes are simply inapplicable. For example, everyone can see that events such as disasters, murders, accidents, and scandals are newsworthy and should be selected and reported as news. But the point is that such events do not happen every day.

In other words, there are often times when there are no big happenings. On such occasions, all available news stories are ones about day-to-day events, giving the news selector no choice but to choose items from among such stuff, based on his or her subjective viewpoint.

Additionally, reader preferences are widely thought to be a good criterion for news selection. However, such a policy is not without controversy. Some argue that relying on reader or viewer preferences to select news tends to conflict with professional norms. After all, the primary responsibility of journalism is to "guide the reader," if this long-held journalism value holds.

Normally, selecting news in a newspaper was a job usually assumed by senior journalists. They made news selection decisions on the basis of their experience and intuition as well as their paper's overall editorial policy.

In my case, the reason that I was charged with the task of selecting news despite my lack of journalistic experience was that I needed to undergo such on-the-job training, as I was told. The Post authorities believed that assigning me this kind of work at the start of my employment was the most effective way to cultivate my news sense and judgment. Further, they said, the training could help better promote my understanding of the China Post's unique editorial policy and preferences as an English-language newspaper. "They were different from those of the native Chinese language newspapers in many ways," my city editor told me.

While I did benefit from such training, I also paid a "price" for it: I was often sarcastically criticized by my editor and colleagues for "selecting news without news sense." But I felt no resentment towards my critics. I believed that I shouldn't be blamed, given the fact that I never received any journalism education and training before joining the Post. What I did amid those harsh comments was to console myself that my news judgment capability would improve with my accumulation of experience.

During my early days as a reporter trainee at the China Post, as I recall, I always seized the time to write English. This was so because my primary duty at this point was to cut items from Chinese-language newspapers and choose news stories from among wire dispatches that were suitable for use by the Post.

I usually did my writing after supper--around 6:30 p.m.--and before everyone else in the editorial department came in for the night shift--about 8 p.m. This meant there were only one and a half hours left for me to practice writing. At the time, I had not yet formally begun covering news. Hence, I had nothing of my own to write about. I could only translate articles clipped from Chinese-language newspapers or those supplied by various news agencies. But I chose only materials that best suited my writing capability. By that, I meant stories that were short in length and simple in content.

But even so, my copy often faced the fate of being thrown into the wastepaper basket by the editor. While some of my copy was used and published, this came only after it underwent substantial revision. Occasionally, I felt discouraged by the way my copy was handled. But I never allowed such frustrations to dampen my enthusiasm to write English. I was fully aware that unless I could write English well, I would never be able to become a professional English journalist and writer.

Encouraging Comments from the Publisher

An encouraging moment came for me at last, about eight months or so after I joined the China Post. The publisher, during a monthly editorial department staff meeting, made very favorable comments on my performance. This surprised me. She praised me for having "in-depth" understanding and good "news judgment," citing her months of observation of my work. This was the first time that I had ever heard anyone commenting on my work in such an encouraging manner since I joined the paper.

The publisher's comments were a great boost to me and my morale. Before then, I, frankly, had sometimes asked myself whether it was wise for me to have taken English journalism as a career path. My reflection was not without a foundation. I often felt demoralized by the harsh way my copy was treated and the negative remarks that my colleagues made about me. In short, I was called a layman.

After commending my performance, Nancy Yu-Huang went further to instruct that I be released from office work so that I could have more time to go out to cover news and write reports. "Continuing to keep Osman doing office work," she said, "would be a waste of manpower."

From that day on, I no longer had to cut newspaper articles and file them. That part of my duty was transferred to a colleague who held a university degree in journalism. But I still had to continue carrying out the other part of my responsibility: selecting wire dispatches and newspaper clippings and distributing them to fellow reporters and the rewriting staff. This job still occupied a considerable amount of my night shift time.

Even so, I felt very excited about the new developments. First, the publisher's positive comments on my performance signaled that I had passed the six-month trial period and become a formal staff reporter of the Post. Obviously, the publisher had consulted with my bosses, City Editor George Chu and Editor-in-Chief Joe Hung, before she reached the decision to readjust my work. Second, her instruction to reassign me to covering news and writing news stories meant that I now could work on the front line of journalism.

After all, I had decided to respond to the Post's latest reporter recruitment test primarily because I was attracted by the prospect of being hired as a reporter, as the paper promised in its ad. So if I were continuously tied up in the office for whatever reason without being able to cover and write news, it would certainly fall short of my expectations.

Acting on the publisher's instructions, my city editor immediately relieved me of my newspaper clipping work so that I could have more time to gather news. In another move, George Chu assigned me to cover a number of government and private institutions. They included the Legislative Yuan (the central lawmaking body) and the ministries of National Defense, Economic Affairs, and Finance in the executive branch. The list of my assigned coverage areas also included a number of U.S. and other foreign missions. These delegations were stationed in Taiwan, the Republic of China, to promote diplomatic or economic relations with this country.

After assigning me the above-mentioned coverage areas, also called beats in journalistic jargon, George Chu then brought me to visit each of those organizations and introduced me to their PR persons and relevant department heads.

He liked to stress to me the importance of getting to know these people and establishing good relations with them. He said this was so because they might prove to be my valuable sources once something of significance happened. "In case a major scandal breaks out in a certain organization, which you are assigned to cover and report about, you need to have some helpful internal contacts who are knowledgeable and willing to provide you inside information," he said.

"A good reporter must be able to develop friendly sources and win their trust so that they are willing to alert him or her to a breaking event before it becomes known to the general public," he continued.

My city editor also advised me on how to maintain contacts with the various organizations assigned to me as my lines of coverage. "While I assigned you to cover so many organizations, I didn't mean you get to make personal visits to them every day." He explained this to me one day on our way back from a visit to the then U.S. Taiwan Defense Command, as I recollect. (Note: Taiwan and the United States had maintained formal defense relations until January 1, 1979, when U.S. President Jimmy Carter announced a switch of diplomatic recognition from the Republic of China to the People's Republic of China.)

"Unless you sense that something significant is likely to happen in a certain organization, you only need to contact your sources by telephone to check whether there is anything new. Such telephone checks also could allow you to keep in touch with them," he continued.

The China Post was unlike the Chinese-language newspapers, which followed a strict beat reporter system in covering news. Under this system, as I later learned firsthand, reporters visited their designated coverage organizations on a daily basis. One major advantage of this system was that the reporters could develop knowledge in their coverage areas and get to know related people and make friends with them. Such specialized knowledge and good personal relationships in turn could help the reporters do in-depth reporting with authority, once a complicated scandal broke.

My city editor further illustrated to me why the China Post did not want to follow the news-gathering pattern of the Chinese-language newspapers. "To begin with, we are a small newspaper with a limited number of reporters. Thus it's simply impossible for us to adopt a beat reporter system even if we intended to. What we should do, instead, is how to make the best use of our limited manpower."

As a matter of fact, he went further to analyze, "it's not necessary for us to regularly visit each and every government agency, as do the Chinese-language newspapers. For one thing, many events which they gathered as news from their daily visits were mostly judged so from a domestic perspective. As an English-language newspaper, we've got to have a global vision. We need to gather and print news that is of interest to our international readers. In other words, we must not gather and evaluate what is news merely from a domestic point of view."

The China Post at the time, as I remember, was printing 12 pages regularly—the maximum number of pages that a newspaper, be it in Chinese or English, could run during those years—a time when Taiwan was under martial law. For the Post, the vast majority of the pages were devoted to carrying international news. The purpose of allocating a greater portion of space to carrying international news was to help expatriates in Taiwan keep in touch with events happening back in their homeland or elsewhere around the globe. During those times, television was not as developed as today, and there was no Internet news. International travelers, therefore, had to rely on print media to learn news breaking around the world. World news which the China Post carried was supplied by major international wire services.

Only three to four of the total pages of the China Post were set aside to carry domestic news then. The domestic news that the Post printed came mainly from three sources, with its own reporting staff providing exclusives and news stories targeting the expatriate communities in Taiwan and international visitors.

The second source of domestic news the Post printed was Taiwan's state-run Central News Agency and a couple of smaller agencies providing domestic news. The Central News Agency had reporters stationed all over Taiwan responsible for covering local news. It sold news articles in the form of dispatches to various local newspapers and electronic news media on the basis of subscriptions.

The third source of domestic news was clippings cut from Chinese-language newspapers, as mentioned earlier. But these clippings were used by us only after they were double-checked and updated by our own reporting staff.

Some might wonder whether such practices posed any competitive concerns for the Chinese-language newspapers involved or for the China Post itself. Actually, this was rarely the case. The reason was that the Post and the Chinese newspapers attended to sharply different audiences. The former was read mostly by expatriates, international visitors, and local intellectual elites, while the latter catered to domestic readers. Another reason was that we always gave credit to sources for each and every story we used.

In reporting domestic news, the China Post adhered strictly to a founding principle laid down by its chairman Y. P. Huang: "As an English-language newspaper published in a Chinese land for a foreign readership, the China Post should report more positive things." Under this policy, the Post was never known for its coverage of crime stories. Seldom did it devote more space to reporting a murder, robbery, corruption, or sex scandal story than was needed to print the facts.

The logic behind such self-imposed restraints was a belief that for an English-language newspaper, carrying too much news about criminal activities or unlawful behavior runs the risk of overplaying the negative side of society before the eyes of foreign nationals. This, Y.P. said, could mislead them about Taiwan.

Y.P. Huang and his wife Nancy Yu, both of them trained journalists, spent their entire lives promoting English journalism in Taiwan. The two held a strong conviction that as an English-language newspaper, the Post had an inherent obligation to help build communication bridges with the international community through the focused collection and reporting of news.

It was under this conviction that the Post always concentrated its efforts on coverage of news and events--such as law and policy changes--that concerned the foreign communities in Taiwan and matters that impacted the island's diplomatic and economic relations with the rest of the world.

I took the China Post's founding principle and its longstanding policy on treating domestic news, as well as my city editor George Chu's suggestions about how best to gather news, as my reporting guidelines, while working for the paper.

As advised by George Chu, I did not make daily visits to all of my designated coverage organizations. In fact, it was simply impossible for me to do that, given the fact that I was assigned so many institutions to cover. I paid daily visits to a certain institution only when I had felt that something meaningful was likely to happen there, or when something of importance had already broken there and follow-up visits were necessary to track its subsequent developments.

Spending More Time Covering the Legislature

However, there was one particular organization -- the Legislative Yuan -- which I visited almost daily. I paid visits to the lawmaking body so frequently because this was a very important source of news and information. The legislature, as always being the case, not only made laws, it also heard reports by the heads of ministries and the various other executive departments about their business and performance.

The lawmaking body normally held full sessions on Tuesdays and Fridays. On other workdays, it held committee meetings to screen bills. More often than not, lawmakers also convened committee hearings, with relevant government officials and influential public figures invited to report on issues of national concern.

I rarely skipped such hearing and reporting sessions, because I saw them as opportunities for me to gather interesting news, or just to learn new things. Some testimony or speeches delivered on such occasions might not be worth reporting as news but could be something new to me. Spending time learning new things was helpful for me to broaden the scope of my knowledge.

This policy paid off. It was from the legislature that I came to understand how the lawmaking body deliberated bills and passed them into laws, and how the legislative branch exercised its oversight duties. From there, I also learned how key government policies were formulated and how they could impact the performance of the economy, for better or worse.

During my years covering the Legislative Yuan for the China Post, I also got into the habit of staying until the end, whenever I attended a high-profile session, be it held at the full Yuan or the individual committee level. I wanted to stay from the beginning to the end, just to make sure that I would not miss anything special that happened in the process.

In the culture of legislative interpellation in Taiwan, there were often cases in which administration officials, grilled by exacting legislators, inadvertently revealed the government's position on a certain politically sensitive issue, or deliberately made some ambiguous comments that could be read in more than one way. And such situations often happened amid a lengthy, heated debate.

For a case in point, I will give an episode in my early days of covering the legislature. It was on a fall Tuesday or Friday morning of 1966 when the legislature was holding a full session listening to then Premier C. K. Yen deliver his twice-a-year work report. I was sitting in the press gallery of the lawmaking body to cover the event.

Premier Yen in his work report gave a detailed account of what his Cabinet had done in the past half a year and outlined his work plans for the next half. Yet throughout his lengthy report, the premier revealed nothing exciting beyond routine business. Nor did Premier Yen say anything special in the subsequent interpellation session. Seeing nothing interesting, my fellow media reporters covering the lawmaking body left the site in succession.

But I chose to remain in my seat, even as the legislative session was drawing to a close. Things did not disappoint me. All of a sudden, a legislator (whose name I can no longer remember now) proceeded to the rostrum and raised a highly politically sensitive question for Premier Yen. The legislator asked C.K. Yen whether it would be possible for the ROC government to reach an alliance with the former Soviet Union to bomb communist China's fledgling nuclear facility. (Note: Communist China set off its first nuclear device in 1964 and two years later launched a live nuclear warhead atop a missile to demonstrate the capabilities of its program. And the Chinese communists' push for the development of nuclear weapons sparked concerns in Taiwan and elsewhere in the world.)

The ROC legislator floated the controversial alliance idea against a background of a deteriorating rift between the Soviet Union and the People's Republic of China. The squabble resulted from the two communist superpowers continuing to engage in a bitter ideological war about how to advance the cause of communism worldwide.

The PRC was becoming increasingly vocal about Moscow's advocacy of seeking "peaceful co-existence" with the "forces of capitalism" and its policy of promoting cooperation with the Western nations. PRC leaders, however, branded such Soviet policies as "counterrevolutionary." They contended that a much more "militant and aggressive" policy should be adopted to spread the communist revolution around the world.

The ROC legislator, in calling for a military alliance with Moscow against Beijing, apparently was of the belief that the deepening PRC-Soviet rivalry, which had escalated to the boiling point toward the mid-1960s, should be exploited to Taiwan's advantage. But the legislator failed to realize the various potential implications that his USSR alliance proposal, if accepted, would have for Taiwan and its relations with the United States, the strongest ally of this island.

First, the proposal could prompt a political storm in Taiwan itself, not to mention the question of how this idea would be accepted in the USSR (the Union of Soviet Socialist Republics). For decades, the ROC government had treated the USSR as an arch-adversary, along with the PRC, under its anti-communist policies. Now if the ROC decided to bring about a rapprochement with the USSR, the government could immediately face a logical question from the public of why this country had to continue to antagonize the PRC, while both of them were equally evil, in terms of their ambitions to communize the world.

Second, if Taiwan was discovered seeking a military alliance with the USSR with the aim of destroying the PRC's nuclear programs, Beijing would inevitably vehemently respond. This could mean an escalation in cross-strait tensions, endangering the stability of Taiwan. Such an outcome would be just like the old proverb: "Go out for wool but come home shorn."

And third, any move by the ROC government to develop political relations with the USSR would likely upset the United States, which at the time still maintained diplomatic and defense relations with Taipei. Washington could be upset because if the ROC should seriously move toward allying with the USSR, it would run counter to the American government's lately adopted "divide and rule" strategy for handling its relations with Moscow and Beijing.

Under this strategy, the U.S. government would be delighted to see the ideological battle between the two giant communist powers continuing to intensify, as this would be advantageous to Washington in putting the PRC against the Soviet Union.

From the above analysis, the legislator's call for a USSR alliance was truly a very complicated question for C.K. Yen. The premier, as I could perceive from the press gallery, seemed to be put in a difficult position, unable to answer the legislator's proposal in an explicit manner. He could not give a positive reply, as this might be seen as reflecting ongoing government thinking on a possible union with Moscow. Nor could he give a negative one, for that would indicate a lack of ideas on what to do in the face of a rising nuclear threat from the Chinese mainland. Nor could the premier keep mum about the question, as this would be taken by the legislator as a snub. Premier Yen had a long reputation for avoiding making any enemies in the legislature.

After a brief pause, Yen came up with presumably what he thought to be a politically safe answer to the legislator's call for an alliance with the Soviet Union to jointly counter the PRC's nuclear programs. His answer was short, just a few words: "The government would study the possibility of your suggestion."

The reply indeed was short, but, to me as a junior reporter, it was quite meaningful and newsworthy. I took the premier's reply to the legislator as a willingness of the ROC government to explore the feasibility of establishing political relations with the USSR, with the ultimate aim of forming a united front against the PRC.

In fact, there had been some voices among the public for the ROC government to review its long-established anti-Russia policy. Proponents pointed out that an increasing rivalry between the USSR and the PRC provided a golden opportunity for Taipei to improve relations with Moscow.

Premier Yen Denies My Story

Shortly after I returned to the Post from the legislative session, I wrote an article containing something like this: Premier C.K. Yen said at the Legislative Yuan that the ROC government would "study the possibility of uniting with the Soviet Union to bomb communist China's nuclear facility." The premier made the above remarks yesterday during an interpellation session as he replied to a legislator's proposal to that effect, I explained in the article.

My news report was not only accepted by the editor but was even put at the top of the front page of the China Post's next-day edition. Regrettably, my reporting prompted a strong and immediate protest from the premier.

A Cabinet press officer explained to me afterward that the premier upon reading what I reported the following morning, reacted angrily. He immediately instructed his office to issue a denial of my report. The denial was broadcast by all television and radio stations in their mid-day news of that day and was carried by all evening newspapers.

Yet for me at the time, the main concern was how my publisher and editors would treat the matter after reading the premier's denial of my report. Would they blame me for incorrectly quoting the premier's remarks? But that was not the case, because the premier did say things like that. I was also concerned that I might be criticized for getting into a bit of sensationalism by presenting the premier's remarks in a way that attempted to attract the attention of the reader.

To my relief, my editors made no complaints about me. After all, the report in question was used and published with their approval.

As for the publisher, she was unaware of my news story being denied by Premier Yen until I briefed her face-to-face on the case. She had just returned to Taipei in the afternoon from an overseas trip, not having time yet to watch TV news or read the evening newspapers.

After listening to my explanations, the publisher did not appear upset, aside from advising me to be more careful in the future in handling sensitive news stories. In an apparent attempt to dispel any unease that I might feel at my article being denied, she said "Take it easy. Don't worry." Nancy added that she never fired a reporter just because his or her news story was denied or corrected. "As a publisher, I frequently received complaints from readers about the contents of The China Post. Some were justifiable, some were not. The key was that we must always work hard to make improvements and progress," she admonished me.

Did I learn anything from that controversial report which I wrote? I did. I shouldn't have picked Premier Yen's remarks "to study the feasibility of...." for my story lead, which attracted my editors, prompting them to play up the news. In Chinese political culture, such words were often used by government officials and politicians merely as a polite way to turn down a suggestion viewed as unacceptable or unfeasible.

For Premier Yen, he might have never anticipated that his "diplomatic answer" to a legislator should have been treated by a paper as big news and put on its front page. Perhaps what concerned him, even more, was that the newspaper that printed his "diplomatic" remarks was an English-language newspaper -- The China Post. The premier might worry that many people in the Post's foreign audience, after reading the report, could be led to believe that the ROC government was considering allying with Moscow against Beijing.

Besides the ROC Legislative Yuan, I also covered a number of executive agencies, and foreign representative offices in Taiwan, as I briefly mentioned earlier. Since I could not visit all of them at one time, I was selective about which organizations to visit. I made such selections according to actual needs. Generally, my coverage focused on news about Taiwan's economic developments, foreign trade, and its international relations.

Among the executive agencies, I covered was the Council for International Economic Cooperation and Development (abbreviated as CIECD). It was a new Cabinet agency created to adjust to the termination in 1964 of U.S. economic aid to Taiwan (Note: Normally, the United States would terminate its economic aid to a certain country once that aid program was viewed as having achieved its intended aims. According to U.S. Department of State sources, American development assistance to Taiwan, from the 1950s to the mid-1960s, helped Taiwan create a prosperous economy. It was such success that prompted Washington to decide to terminate its economic aid to Taiwan in the mid-1960s).

The primary mission of CIECD was to encourage the inflow of foreign investment, loans, and technology into Taiwan as an effort to sustain the island's economic growth in the absence of U.S. economic aid. I was interested in covering CIECD because this was a place where news about local and foreign technical cooperation projects frequently emanated and was most suitable for publication in the English China Post.

Another government agency to which I gave priority in gathering economic news was the Ministry of Economic Affairs. I focused my coverage on the ministry's efforts to promote exports and industrial development. During those times, Taiwan relied heavily on exports to earn the foreign exchange needed to import machinery, raw materials, and technology to develop its industry and export-oriented businesses.

One of the most noticeable export-promoting measures at the time was the establishment of a series of export processing zones. The first one was located in the southern city of Kaohsiung and opened in 1966. I can still remember I was invited, along with other media reporters, to attend the zone's opening ceremony and cover its processing facilities and assembly operations. To attract investors to this and other such zones to set up assembly factories, the government enacted a series of special laws, including the "Statute for Investment by Foreign Nationals" and the "Statute for Investment by Overseas Chinese."

One other high-profile policy pursued by the Economics Ministry at the time was an effort to promote industrial upgrading, from labor-intensive to capital- and technology-intensive industries. To that end, the Economics Ministry passed special legislation to encourage big local and foreign companies to transfer technology to Taiwan's small and medium businesses. Small-sized companies then accounted for more than 90 percent of all businesses on this island. This was the situation despite the fact that the overall economy had, for more than a decade, continued to grow at double-digit rates.

So whenever a local company entered into a joint venture with a Japanese or U.S. company, for instance, I would carefully examine one particular matter: What technology the foreign partner would bring in and how it could contribute to the upgrading of Taiwan's industry. Or whether that foreign investor just sent in the capital to set up assembly facilities, taking advantage of Taiwan's cheap labor. During those times Japan led all other foreign countries as the largest investor in Taiwan. Yet Japanese investors were the constant target of criticism for being reluctant to transfer to Taiwan their core technologies needed for the production of key parts and components, making Taiwan continue to rely on Japan for the supply of such crucial goods. This resulted in this island suffering chronic trade deficits with Japan.

A third government institution that I often visited to gather news was the National Science Council. The NSC at the time was a young government agency created to advise the ROC president on science policy and planning. Its primary aims were to promote basic scientific and industrial research, and manpower training, and invite noted scientists and scholars, mainly from the United States, to Taiwan to give lectures and help local juniors do research work.

Precisely speaking, the NSC was an outgrowth of the then Sino-American Science Cooperation Committee. This committee itself was formed jointly by the National Academy of Sciences of the United States and the Academia Sinica of the Republic of China in 1964. This was a time when AID (The U.S. Agency for International Development) was phasing out its program in Taiwan. One main task of the committee was to recommend programs in areas of science relevant to Taiwan's socioeconomic development.

The NSC's first chairman was T. Y. Wu, an internationally known physicist who had been teaching at the State University of New York at Buffalo before he was invited to Taiwan by President Chiang Kai-shek to assume that position. Wu was a very kind and helpful person. I often went to his office when he was not occupied with meetings in the hope of getting something new from him or the NSC.

Learning to Be 'Faceless'

Kind and helpful as he was, the scholar had an explosive temper. One time when I came to visit the NSC, it happened the chairman was about to leave his office. He hurried toward a limousine waiting outside while tying his tie. Since I had come to get him to comment on something urgent, I called out to him "Chairman Wu, where are you going?" To my embarrassment, he turned back and said loudly "None of your business." At that moment, I quickly reminded myself of a piece of advice given to me by an American professor of journalism, when I started to work for the China Post. "A news reporter must learn to be faceless," he said.

At times when I could not find anything worth reporting from the Chinese government agencies assigned to me to cover, I would turn to some foreign representative offices in Taipei by either visiting or phoning them, in hopes of getting something new. Note: During those years, the Republic of China still had its legitimate representation in the United Nations, with a seat in the General Assembly and as a permanent member of the Security Council. Hence, some U.N. affiliated agencies, such as the World Health Organization and the U.N. Development Program, all had stationed representatives in Taipei.

On many occasions I was lucky enough to obtain some exciting news on my visits to such international representative offices. In an interview with a senior resident WHO official one day, for example, I obtained an exclusive: A copy of a WHO-supported project to help Taipei improve its sewage system by installing more pipes and treatment plants. The project was aimed at enabling Taipei to eventually fully eliminate its primitive practices of dumping raw sewage in rivers and at sea.

In addition to covering the legislature, executive branch agencies, and the local representative offices of international organizations on workdays, I sometimes also made myself available for doing special coverage and interviews on weekends and holidays.

On a fall Sunday in 1967, I remember, I took a morning bus to Taipei Songshan International Airport to cover the arrival of U.S. President Lyndon B. Johnson's Science Advisor Donald Hornig. The top U.S. scientist was on a visit to learn the status firsthand of the ROC's science and technology development. Hornig and his delegation members intended to discuss with their ROC counterparts what improvements should be made and what areas in which U.S. assistance was needed the most.

Hornig held a news conference at the airport, discussing his purpose of coming to visit Taipei and answering questions from reporters. At the end of the event I rushed back to the Post to write a report on the Hornig visit and put it on the desk of Joe Hung, the editor-in-chief. On the way home that day—it was in the late afternoon, I felt very happy that I could cover the visit by such an American dignitary and wrote a story about it, completely forgetting that I had sacrificed another holiday, that otherwise could be spent with my family, to do reporting.

In the following evening shortly after my fellow reporters and everyone else in the editorial department came in, Joe Hung, the editor-in-chief, openly praised me in front of them for "working hard and doing a good reporting job." He was referring to the story that I did the previous day about the press conference given by the U.S. presidential science advisor at Songshan Airport.

Read Between the Lines to Find Story Ideas

Oftentimes there was nothing worth reporting. In such situations, I would try to find and develop story ideas from news articles appearing in Chinese-language newspapers. Such efforts often brought rewarding results for me. One day in late 1966 or early 1967, for instance, I read a brief news item in a Chinese-language daily, which reported something like the following: Songshan International Airport in Taipei needed to be expanded to meet the advent of the jumbo jet Boeing 747, but its limited space and the strong opposition offered by anti-noise neighborhood residents and activists made any meaningful expansion unlikely.

The news item immediately caught my attention. I thought it could be developed into a good story for our newspaper by asking relevant officials to discuss in more detail the reported difficulties and what they were trying to do to solve them.

I thus went to a nearby pay phone booth to make a call to the Civil Aeronautics Administration deputy director, whose name I can still remember was Hua Chih. I introduced myself and said I hoped to talk to him about Songshan Airport's air traffic handling capacities. I then asked whether he would be available for an interview that day. He accepted my request without hesitation.

Some explanations need to be given here. That I had to go to a public phone booth to make a call would certainly be seen as unimaginable in modern days. People blessed with the availability of smartphones nowadays can make a phone call anywhere: at home, in the office, or while traveling. But back in my early journalistic life in

1966 as a junior reporter, I did not have the luxury of installing a fixed line telephone in my home. This was simply because I couldn't afford to install one. A phone applicant at the time had to provide a prohibitive deposit of NT$16,000 (The exchange rate then was 40 Taiwan dollars to one US dollar), about five times the amount of my monthly salary. In addition to the deposit, a user had to pay a costly monthly fee. Moreover, there was a long, long wait for an applicant to get a telephone installed. Just this lengthy process of getting a phone set up was enough to discourage many people from renting a telephone.

Yet without a wire-connected phone of my own, it was quite inconvenient for me to make appointments or conduct telephone interviews from my home. Hence, I often had to rely on a neighborhood pay phone or those installed on the roadside.

After Hua Chih received my interview request, I immediately took a taxi to the Civil Aeronautics Administration located right beside Songshan airport, Taiwan's sole international airport then. By the time I arrived, the deputy director had already stood at the administration building entrance to greet me. Instantly, he escorted me to his office. I got down to business as soon as we were seated. I raised two broad questions for him. One, with the advent of the super-giant Boeing 747 aircraft, was Taiwan ready for it? Two, if not, what was the Civil Aeronautics Administration going to do about it?

Before answering my questions, Hua first briefed me on the latest developments in the race by major international airlines to buy and use the 747s to provide air transport services for passengers and freight. This past April [1966], he pointed out, Pan Am World Airways had already ordered 25 747-100 aircraft for US$525 million.

On the other hand, Boeing Company, the U.S. manufacturer of the 747, Hua noted, had agreed to deliver the first such plane to Pan Am by the end of 1969. And the U.S. airline had stated it would launch its first commercial flight with the 747 in early 1970.

In addition to Pan Am, Hua went on to say, 26 other major airlines around the world had also announced plans to buy the giant airliner.

With so many international airlines going to purchase 747s and use them to provide air transport services, would Taiwan's Songshan airport be big enough to accommodate the jumbo jet--characterized by a wide-body, dual-aisle interior and an unprecedentedly large capacity to carry well over 400 passengers in first, business and economy cabins? I asked.

"No, Songshan airport cannot handle that job currently. We need to act fast to address the question," Hua replied, noting that Pan Am, which was currently serving Taipei among other destinations in the region, was scheduled to operate the 747s within about three years from now. "The problem with us is that Songshan airport is becoming overcrowded and cannot be expanded because of limited space. To accept the Boeing 747s, we must have wider runways and larger terminals to load and unload the double-decker plane easily," he explained to me.

Therefore, he said, the Civil Aeronautics Administration, an agency operating under the Ministry of Transportation and Communications, "is planning to build a new and bigger international airport in Taoyuan, about 80 miles south of Taipei. "The process of procuring the land on which to build the airport has been underway," he revealed. Before we concluded the interview, the deputy director handed me a copy of a blueprint for the construction of the new international airport.

After leaving the Civil Aeronautics Administration, I went directly back to the Post. When I arrived at the editorial department, I can still remember, it was in the early afternoon and the publisher was presiding at a special news-gathering meeting. She noticed me as soon as I got in and signaled me to take a seat. "Is there any news?" she asked.

"Yes, indeed," I replied. I then briefed her on my interview in the morning with the Civil Aeronautics Administration deputy director and the news and information which I obtained from him. After completing my briefing, I suggested that the interview be used as a top story for the Post's following-day edition.

The publisher, as I noticed, kept nodding and smiling as she listened to my briefing. "Osman, you did a good job." She then turned to the editor and said "The interview contains a lot of interesting information worth being split into two installments, one for tomorrow and one for the day after tomorrow."

"One installment," she went further, "reveals that the government plans to build a new international airport to accommodate the Boeing 747 and other jumbo jets. A new international airport would also help ease the traffic congestion at the existing Songshan airport." The other installment, the publisher continued, "will tell how actively airlines worldwide are moving to embrace the wide-body aircraft." By dividing the interview contents into two installments, she added "It will allow us to make better use of a newsworthy exclusive."

Always Find Time to Pursue Self-Improvement

With so many subject areas to cover and an unrelenting passion for getting exclusive interviews and news stories, as I mentioned in the previous pages, how could I find the time to meet such job requirements, while at the same time pursuing self-improvement goals?

One primary way I adopted to meet the various demands on my time was to work on Saturdays, Sundays, or other holidays. Sometimes, for example, I arranged for important interviews to be conducted on holidays with the consent of my interviewees. My willingness to work on holidays also allowed me to cover events, such as press conferences, public hearings, and speeches that were conducted on off days.

Often there were such cases when several news events took place at the same time. In such situations, I would choose to cover the one that was most newsworthy, leaving the ones of less importance to be checked over the phone afterward with the relevant spokesperson. Oftentimes, I also phoned for help from fellow media reporters who attended a certain event which I failed to.

In the event that I had neither interviews to conduct nor news to cover at the weekends, I would use such time to write special reports which I did not have time to do or complete in the office. I was willing to make such extra efforts because I saw them as necessary to enhance my English writing skills.

Holidays were also my English reading time, whenever I was not otherwise engaged. News publications I read most often during those early years of my journalism life were The Reader's Digest, The U.S. News and World Report, as well as our own newspaper, the China Post. I liked to read these publications in part because they were relatively easy for me to understand.

I was not a casual reader -- reading for pleasure. In fact, I have never been that kind of reader. Shortly after entering the profession of English journalism, I developed such a reading habit: Whenever I read a news column or a special report, I paid close attention to its style and structure as well as the language and phrases used. By reading so carefully, I intended not just to advance my English comprehension skills, but also to learn how to write this second language better myself.

Believe it or not, I still do my reading that way even to this day— more than a half-century on, calculated from the time when I began to serve as a junior reporter. Whenever I read an interesting section in a New York Times, Washington Post, TIME, or NPR article online, for example, I would do it repeatedly to memorize some special English usages, which I didn't understand previously.

In previous pages, I have mentioned that I, while being a junior reporter, frequently worked on weekends and holidays. Now I will recount how I managed my workdays. A reporter at the time was unlike an office worker who generally worked nine to five -- going to the office at 9 a.m. and leaving for home at 5 p. m. Reporters, however, had to arrange their working hours according to their actual needs.

Normally, I got up at around eight in the morning. I could not rise earlier because I routinely worked late into the night in line with the deadlines. During those years, newspaper deadlines all were set at midnight.

Luckily, it took me only about a 15-minute bike ride to get back to my place of residence after work. In the first nearly two years of my working for the China Post, I lived in its bachelor dormitory on Xinsheng North Road in Taipei, just a few blocks away from the paper's offices. I moved out of the Post-operated dormitory only after I got married.

My workday started with reading the day's major Chinese-language newspapers. I always did so while eating breakfast. Reading newspapers early in the morning was a must for me. First, it allowed me to check whether I missed any important news the day before in my coverage areas. Second, by reading the morning newspapers early, I hoped to find some good story ideas in any of them that I could develop into an in-depth report for our paper, using the rest of the day.

After scanning the newspapers of the day, I then went out to cover the news. My first destination of coverage was mostly the Legislative Yuan located on Zhongshan South Road in downtown Taipei. While there I would either attend a regular full legislative session, which usually fell on Tuesday and Friday, or cover a committee meeting or a public hearing.

If there was nothing I felt was worth staying longer at the legislature for, I would go elsewhere to visit other coverage areas, a government department, or a foreign representative office.

Sometimes I was lucky enough to have a field day with many news events happening on the same day—a special press conference, an economic seminar, and a visit to Taiwan by a foreign dignitary, for example.

With the exception of special cases, my morning coverage activities always ended at around 12 noon in line with Taiwan's now-defunct lengthy "lunch-rest break" custom, which lasted for two and a half hours. During this period, all government agencies and private businesses ceased to operate until 2:30 p.m.

Having nowhere to go to collect news during the two-and-a-half hours breaks, I always spent the period mostly at a food and beverage store on Taipei's Zhonghua Road, where I usually did three things: One was to have a light lunch, which mostly consisted of a large glass of milk, a boiled egg, some bread and a glass of juice.

The second thing I did there was to go over papers, documents, or notes that I made while attending morning events. As I was doing so, I often highlighted places that I thought might be suitable for use in tomorrow's edition of the Post.

The third thing I did at the food store was to read our own newspaper, the China Post. I focused on international news-- dispatches supplied by UPI, AP, Reuters, AFP, and other world news agencies. I gave priority to reading such news dispatches for two major reasons. One, it allowed me to learn more about what's going on around the world, information which I could not rely on the local Chinese-language newspapers to supply. These media traditionally devoted quite limited space to printing foreign news.

Two, reading more wire service news provided me with more opportunities to observe how the journalists of the international news agencies practiced journalism. Specifically, how they covered a news event and turned it into a readable news story, using plain English. Learning their news gathering and English writing skills was of vital importance to me--someone who never received any journalistic education and had to write news stories in English, a language which he began to learn just a decade earlier.

Normally I left the food and beverage shop that I frequented about half an hour or so before government offices and private institutions reopened for the afternoon shifts. After leaving the shop the first thing I did was to buy a copy of each of the day's major evening newspapers to check if there was any significant event breaking in the morning before I started my afternoon newsgathering activities.

Reading evening newspapers in the early afternoon was a necessary and useful routine for me. Evening newspapers often could not carry out fuller coverage of big news, especially a complicated development, that happened in the morning, because of the time limit. So each time when I found an interesting evening newspaper article that I saw as lacking some essential ingredients, I would spend the rest of the afternoon digging up more information and turning that article into a comprehensive news story of our own.

My afternoon news covering activities used to include stops at entities that I failed to visit in the morning, or which I sensed might have something happening that was worth reporting. Alternatively, I might go to meet with someone for a previously arranged interview or attend a press conference to listen to an influential figure saying something that might be of interest to our readers.

Usually, by around 6 p.m., I would be on my way back to the Post to begin working the night shift. Occasionally I arrived in the office a little late because of attending a social engagement, such as a dinner party. Usually, I tried my best to avoid participating in such activities for fear of wasting my time.

But sometimes you had difficulty turning down an event. For instance, you received an invitation co-signed by a fellow journalist who happened to be a good friend. This friend even followed the invitation card up with a phone call explaining that his co-host, so-and-so, hoped to have a chance to chat with some media representatives and that your presence would be greatly appreciated. In such a situation, you simply could not decline the invitation without offending a media colleague. But even so, I always sought to leave early by finding an excuse.

Normally I came to the office early, about one and a half hours before the start of the night shift at 8 p.m. By this time, the first of a series of three batches of news dispatches, supplied by the Central News Agency and several other local news services, had already come in.

As soon as I got in, I began to select articles from those Chinese language news dispatches for possible use by the Post. News selection was my main responsibility on the night shift. I distributed all of the articles I selected to relevant reporters and writers, who in turn translated them into journalistic-style English texts. Such texts were then edited or rewritten mostly by the editor-in-chief, before they were laid out for printing, usually at around 1 a.m. every night.

Since the Central News Agency dispatches came in several batches, I could use only the intervals to handle the news material I myself gathered in the daytime.

At the beginning of my work for the China Post, I wrote only short and brief stories, leaving longer and more complicated material to my city editor, the copywriter, or the editor-in-chief to do the writing or translation. That I wrote only simple news stories was in part because the time I could use to do writing was quite limited and in part because my English capability at the time was far below the level of writing difficult stories.

Still, from time to time I managed to write some special reports or features mostly using the weekends or holidays. I cannot remember how many such articles I had written in the several years since I first joined the China Post as a junior reporter at the beginning of 1966.

But I did find some worn-out clippings in my book cabinet with my byline on them. They dealt with a variety of topics, most of them issues and problems which Taiwan faced in the decades after WWII.

One such article, dated September 1, 1968, discussed Taiwan's then chronic exodus of talent. In it, I interviewed Allen Lau, executive director of the American Bureau for Medical Aid to the Republic of China, and several other experts about their views on how to relieve the severity of the brain drain problem in Taiwan.

Allen Lau suggested that Taiwan's industry "should join the government in tackling the issue of brain drain by undertaking research and development." By any standard, he said, the local industry's investment in R&D was lagging behind. He believed that "If the private sector could significantly increase its share in R&D, it will automatically lead to the solution of Taiwan's outflow of talented people."

The views offered by other interviewees were essentially the same: Taiwan's continued talent outflow was caused in part by the lack of graduate training facilities. Therefore, one of the interviewees said, "The government or higher education institutes should establish well-equipped and competitively staffed research centers in Taiwan. Also, developing closer collaboration between research institutes and industries are equally important."

"How to Eliminate Cramming Sessions" in Taiwan was another special report, which I wrote and was published in March 1967. In this interview, I used the opening paragraph to describe how badly the cramming session was judged in the broad society: "Sports leaders blamed cramming sessions on the country's failure to train outstanding athletes. Poorer parents blamed them as a continuous drain on their hard-earned income. Public health officials blamed cramming sessions for damaging the health of school children. Even educators themselves blasted cramming sessions for affecting the integrity of schoolteachers."

The cramming session was widely defined as one "which is conducted outside school and aimed at preparing school children for entrance examinations for the school of higher education." All the experts I interviewed were unanimous in pointing to two far-reaching negative effects. One, cramming sessions were harmful to students because they stressed memorizing rather than independent thinking. Two, cramming sessions were often carried out at the expense of athletic and other officially stipulated courses.

One other old article I found in my book cabinet carries the title "Tsou Mei Recovering Slowly." I did this one in May 1966, just five months after I joined the China Post at the start of my English journalism career--fresh from my retirement as an army captain.

Tsou Mei, 44, was a Taiwan agricultural specialist, who suffered serious head injuries after his car crashed in Togo three years earlier in 1963. He was working in this West African country as chief of a ROC farming demonstration team. The incident happened when his car hit a roadside tree. He was riding with two fellow team members, who were killed outright. Initially, Tsou was treated at a U.S. Army field hospital in Madrid, Spain, before he was flown back to Taipei a year later in 1964 to receive further treatment at the Taipei Veterans General Hospital.

I interviewed Tsou Mei's presiding doctor Shang Chung-kwei, asking him what progress his patient had made in the past two years since his admission into the hospital. Dr. Shang said, "His chronic high fever was gone. Also gone were his recurring cramps and jerks. Tsou is now in a state of semi-coma. Sometimes, he is entirely unconscious but at other times he seems to know what is going on around him... His progress is very slow, and I cannot say exactly how much more time it will take for him to recover."

Tsou Mei's case received widespread attention in part because he was among the first ROC agricultural specialists dispatched to Africa by Taipei to demonstrate how to improve farming methods and increase food production. Before going to Togo, Tsou Mei had led a 14-member team to Liberia to help local people grow rice. Tsou's pioneering farming demonstration work in Africa won him a reputation as Taiwan's first agricultural ambassador to Africa.

Sending specialists to various African countries to teach and spread Taiwan's agricultural development experiences and technical know-how was a new form of economic aid, which the ROC rendered on that continent during the 1960s to win friends and diplomatic allies.

Among other articles which I wrote in my early China Post years with my byline on them and still keep to this day were three special reports on a five-day visit to Tokyo. I made the visit in August 1968 at the invitation of Air Vietnam as a China Post reporter. The Vietnamese airline invited a group of journalists from the Taipei press to join its inaugural flight to Tokyo, marking the extension of its Saigon-Taipei service to the Japanese capital.

I used the brief visit, which was supposed to be a simple Air Vietnam-sponsored travel activity in Tokyo and its suburbs, to conduct research on this Japanese metropolis. It was just a quick study featuring interviews with relevant Tokyo municipal officials. This had to be the case because the time I could spend doing it was quite limited. A fellow Taipei journalist traveling on the same flight called me a workaholic. "No, I am not. I merely wanted to take advantage of the trip to do some reporting," I responded.

After my return from Tokyo, I wrote three series of reports. The first one, entitled "Tokyo Is an Orderly City," told the reader that, in the eyes of a foreign tourist like me, this Japanese metropolis was truly orderly. "You can hardly hear a driver honk the horn. Motorists stop at zebra lines to allow pedestrians to have the right of way. On the other hand, you could see no pedestrian jaywalk across a street illegally, or cross against the red light." The report attributed Tokyo's orderly traffic partially to its law-abiding citizens. Also attributable was a municipal policy of monitoring and broadcasting the city's changing road conditions to motorists around the clock.

The second of the three articles I wrote on my Tokyo visit described measures taken by the city government to tackle the problems of air pollution, delinquency and poverty. In the third and final survey, I detailed how the Tokyo metropolitan government communicated policy and programs to its 11 million citizens and how it listened to public views and complaints and then had them reflected in its administrative reforms.

Time passed so fast. I had worked for the China Post for three full years by December 1968. I mention this particular time because it was then that I resigned from the Post. Two growing personal concerns explained why I decided to leave the newspaper.

One of the two concerns I referred to was about my career future: Increasingly, I worried that it might be impossible for me to realize my goal of becoming a professional journalist, using English as a writing tool, if I continued to work for the China Post. The other concern of mine was a matter of bread and butter.

Unhelpful Copy Processing System

To begin with my first concern, for the past three years since I joined the China Post, I always worked hard to collect news, so hard that it often earned me high praise from my bosses. I myself also felt my news-collecting performances were not too bad.

But what was of concern to me was the writing aspect of my job as a reporter. I could only, for most of the time, write straight news. More exactly, I could only turn into English texts less complicated Chinese-language news materials, which I gathered in the daytime.

I rarely wrote longer or more complicated English news stories. Part of the reason was that I simply did not have time enough to do that. During the night shift, I had to spend a considerable amount of my time doing non-writing jobs. First, I had to select Chinese-language news articles, which could be used by the Post, from among the dispatches supplied by the Central News Agency and other local sources. Second, I often had to do fact-checks over the phone. So it was almost always the case when there was little time left for me to write anything other than brief news stories.

Besides the problem of not having much time to do writing, I was also concerned about the way the editorial department processed news stories. I felt the copy processing system of the Post did not favor cultivating reporters' English writing capabilities. Normally, in an English-language newspaper, there were copy editors or rewrite persons, who were responsible for editing and rewriting stories submitted by their staff reporters.

Having people exclusively responsible for performing those jobs was especially important in the case of the China Post. This was an English-language newspaper operating in a society where everyone spoke and wrote Chinese--the native language. This meant that all kinds of original news materials, be they gathered by the Post's own staff or supplied by outside sources, were expressed in Chinese. Hence, these news materials had to be turned into journalistic-style English for publication in the China Post. Yet few of the Post's reporters -- all of them like me native Chinese speakers--were able to write fluent English. Much of their copy thus needed to be edited heavily or even rewritten by a rewriting staffer.

But regrettably, the editorial department rarely hired enough personnel responsible for rewriting reporters' news articles. Because of the rewriting manpower shortage, many of the reporters' stories were submitted directly to the editor-in-chief and piled up on his desk, waiting for him to process. This resulted in a situation where the chief editor had to single-handedly do all the editing and rewriting work.

Yet the editor-in-chief had his own deadline to meet. Because of the deadline pressure, he more often than not put aside difficult-to-rewrite copy or copy that required more of his time to handle. He instead preferred to use Central News Agency-supplied dispatches or newspaper clippings that he felt were easier for him to process--translating them from Chinese into English.

But the editor-in-chief's preference for using Central News Agency dispatches hurt the Post's own reporters dearly. I, for one, often felt frustrated at seeing my articles rejected, without being able to appear in the following day's edition of the Post. So frustrated that I sometimes got the feeling that there was no point in continuing to work for the newspaper.

Things could be greatly improved if there was a regular staff member charged with rewriting copy turned in by the reporters. A regular rewriting staffer could speed up the process of copy-editing. This in turn could increase the chance that the news stories submitted by the Post's own reporters would be published. This increase would give more opportunities for reporters to learn how their English text was changed and what improvements they needed to make in their writing in the future.

Failing to get their news articles printed could hurt the reporters in another way. As I recall, several times I felt acute embarrassment at my reports failing to be used by the editor. Such cases were damaging because they could undermine the confidence in you of your interviewees and others involved. These sources might become doubtful about your capability as a news reporter. Consequently, they could refuse to grant any further interview requests, in that they thought whatever they said to you wouldn't get published in your newspaper.

Then why was the China Post unwilling to hire regular rewrite persons, a step that not only raised operating efficiency but could also help improve the quality of copy? The answer to this question, as I observed, was not entirely because of any unwillingness of the Post authorities to make the necessary investment.

As I saw, it had more to do with the policy of the editor-in-chief. To me and some of my colleagues, he was reluctant to get people to do the rewrite job. He seemed to be of the belief that hiring unqualified people to perform the rewrite job could do little to reduce his workload. On the contrary, it could even add to his burden, because he in the end would still have to extensively change the copy done by the rewrite person.

But the fact was that there often were native English speakers with a college education and writing experience, who came in to apply for a rewrite job but were rejected outright for being incapable of playing that role. In some other cases, the applicants were accepted for a trial period of one to two months, but few of them were finally hired due to the same reason.

While it was true that not every college-educated native English speaker could write a readable news story, it was also true that the China Post had never established a set of realistic criteria that could be used to evaluate the qualifications required of a rewrite person or copy editor.

In the above pages, I have narrated the first of my two growing concerns. Now I will summarize what I said on those pages in a few sentences: I felt increasingly concerned about my continued lack of time to do more writing, as my employment with the Post entered well into its third year. That was the case because I was also charged with the task of selecting the news and checking facts on the night shift. In the daytime, I had to go out to cover news and do interviews, making it impossible for me to write anything. Additionally, I also felt frustrated at the Post's then inadequate copy processing system which was unfavorable for the cultivation of reporters' English writing capabilities.

A Bread-and-Butter Matter

My second growing concern was about bread and butter. I began to feel that my salary was insufficient to meet the needs of my family after I married Lei Yen-ming in late 1967. By this time, I had worked at the China Post for nearly two years. Bread-and-butter issues might be mundane, but few people could afford to ignore them. I was no exception.

When I first joined the Post in January 1966, I earned a monthly salary of NT$2,100, or a little more than US$50. This salary was more than twice as much as what a public high school teacher earned. So the entry pay the Post offered me was relatively good. Specifically, it was enough to meet my living needs as a bachelor.

As a bachelor, I was entitled to live in the Post-run dormitory free of charge. The newspaper also provided free meals at the dormitory, a multi-story building which was located miles away from the Post's official residence on Fu Shun Street in Taipei's then most prosperous Zhongshan District.

But I lost my eligibility to live in the dormitory after I got married. My wife Lei Yen-ming was my Post colleague. She was working in the color-printing department as an art designer, but she resigned from the paper shortly after we agreed to marry. She wanted to be a full-time housewife.

At the beginning of our marriage, we lived in a small brick house, which we rented from a good friend. Yet the house was so small that it consisted of only a living room, a bedroom, and a kitchen. So we soon moved out of my friend's house, after we found and rented a top-floor apartment in a newly completed two-story building. This apartment was more spacious, but it cost us an expensive NT$850 a month in rent.

For me, the rent was truly expensive, as it accounted for more than one-third of my monthly salary. By this time, I had got a pay increase of NT$300, bringing my total monthly salary to NT$2,400.

In other words, my rent now constituted a considerable proportion of my income. According to one credible housing-cost study, I read at the time, for salaried people, affordable rentals needed to be within the range of one-fifth to one-fourth of their incomes.

In my case, I had to spend one-third of my salary on housing. Naturally, I now felt the pressure of increasing living costs after marriage. The financial pressure was even more keenly felt after my wife gave birth in October 1968 to our daughter Wen-yi, our first child. To relieve the financial pressure, it was necessary for me to get a significant pay increase at this point. But gaining permission for such a raise was no easy thing under the Post's existing payment system.

An Offer to Report News in Chinese

In the above paragraphs, I have recollected my concern about increasing living costs after I got married and my growing frustration with a lack of time to do more English writing during my time at the China Post. The concern and the frustration were so serious that they prompted me to consider leaving the newspaper. But it was a third factor--an external one--that precipitated my eventual departure from the Post.

The external factor will be given below. On a certain day in early December of 1968, Mr. Chang Pyng-feng, a senior journalist from the Chinese-language China Times, approached me. He invited me to join his newspaper with the offer of pay much higher than what I earned at the China Post.

Mr. Chang at the time was directing the operations of the Taipei -based China Times's "Central Government News" section. The section was responsible for covering parliament and the executive branch, the latter of which included the Cabinet and its various ministries and departments.

Mr. Chang told me that they needed someone with news collecting experience and good English knowledge to cover diplomatic affairs. "From what I have learned about you, you are the kind of person we are looking for. I sincerely invite you to join us."

Mr. Chang and I got acquainted with each other while covering the Legislative Yuan. Owing to covering the same beat, we often met at the legislature. We regularly visited the lawmaking body to either cover its twice-a-week full sessions or committee meetings. On such occasions, we sometimes exchanged views on current news events or made some casual talk.

"If you could come to work for our newspaper, you will be offered NT$3,000 a month, the same as we paid our experienced reporters," he told me. "On top of regular salaries," he continued, "our reporters are also paid for bylined stories. Such payments normally could add up to NT$300 a month."

From the way the China Times paid its reporters, as Mr. Chang analyzed, I would be able to earn around NT$3,300 a month, if I joined them. The income figure he promised me was 30% higher than the amount I made at the China Post. At the end of our conversation that day, I thanked Mr. Chang very much for his job offer, but I told him I needed time to consider it.

Days later, Mr. Chang called me, urging me to make a quick decision. On the phone, he also pointed to some intangible benefits that reporters working for the China Times could enjoy—things that he failed to mention in our previous face-to-face conversations.

I rephrase below what he said to me over the phone: The China Times was a leading Chinese-language newspaper in Taiwan, commanding wide influence and enjoying a high level of social status. Hence, reporters working for the paper could boost their professional standing in society. On the other hand, he said the China Post as a small, foreign-language newspaper might be even unknown to the vast majority of people in Taiwan.

While I had some reservations about Mr. Chang's characterization of the China Post with respect to its social influence, I did agree with him on the point that working for the China Times could reap the kind of intangible benefits he described to me, in addition to financial incentives.

Yet what really made me hesitant to quit the China Post in favor of going to join the China Times were two more basic questions that made it difficult for me to reply to Mr. Chang promptly: The first of the two questions should I continue to stay at the Post to practice English journalism? If so, the challenge was that there would be a long, long way to go before I could write English news stories as a professional writer. This was especially true, given the unfavorable copy handling system of the China Post. Or should I switch to practicing journalism in Chinese? If so, would be I up to the job, considering that previously I had never written Chinese as a journalist?

Still, I finally decided to leave the China Post and go to join the China Times. But at this point, I faced the difficult problem of how to discuss my resignation with the publisher Nancy Yu-Huang in person. Look, this was a woman executive who was not just my boss but also my journalism mentor. It was she who opened the journalism door for me. She allowed me to take part in her recruitment test despite my lack of a university diploma, an educational qualification required of all applicants. Further, she provided me with on-the-job training for gathering news and writing news stories. Also, she personally instructed me on how to be a good journalist.

After reading my resignation letter, Nancy drove directly from her home on Yangming Mountain to the Post in downtown Taipei to meet and talk with me, in an attempt to persuade me to cancel my resignation.

Sitting in front of an employer and a veteran newspaper person, whom I owed so much for bringing me into the journalism profession, it was really hard for me to politely but firmly resist her effort to retain me. But in the end, I prevailed, thanks to a piece of advice given to me in advance by a colleague and close friend, Mr. Louis Chiou. He told me that "regardless of whatever the publisher would say to you, you just reply to her with a firm no." I truly did as Mr. Chiou advised.

As a matter of fact, it was very difficult for me to withdraw my letter and not resign by now. Before I tendered my resignation letter to Nancy, I had already formally informed Mr. Chang of the China Times of my decision to accept his job offer and come to work for them.

When I reported to the China Times for work and how I exercised my news gathering duties in one of Taiwan's two largest Chinese-language newspapers will be recounted in Chapter 5.

Chapter 5
A Brief Foray into Chinese-language Journalism

An Arrangement to Avoid Criticism of Poaching Me

Officially, my employment with the Chinese-language newspaper China Times became effective on January 1, 1969--the day right after I left the English China Post, where I had worked as a staff reporter for the past three years. But in reality, I did not come to work for the Times until the start of the following month. But the Times still generously paid me a full month's salary for January.

The one-month gap between my resignation from the China Post and my actual start to work for the China Times was deliberately arranged by the Times authorities. More exactly, it was arranged by Chang Pyng-feng, the senior journalist with the responsibility of directing the paper's central government news-gathering operations. It was he who recommended and invited me to the China Times. As to the question of why Mr. Chang wanted to get me to work for the Times has already been discussed at the end of the preceding chapter. To put it simply, the Times needed a person like me with news-gathering experience and had English-language skills good enough to cover diplomacy.

Mr. Chang explained to me why he made the one-month-gap arrangement: "Mr. Tseng, although your employment with us will become effective from January 1, 1969, we prefer you to start working for us from the following month or the beginning of February. This time gap was intended to avoid giving the impression that we, the China Times, are poaching people from the China Post. Should that be the case it would hurt our relations with the Post. That's the last thing we'd want to see."

But just why did the Times care so much about its relations with the Post? "Please note," Mr. Chang elaborated on the reason, "our Chairman Yu Ji-zhong and the China Post's Publisher Nancy Yu-Huang are relatives in the first place. Besides that, they also are sort of allies within the Taipei media circles. With such high-level inter-relationships in mind, your' coming to work for us has to be handled very carefully."

Mr. Chang continued, "but if you came over to work for us directly after your resignation from the China Post, it could easily be taken by others as we were poaching people from the China Post. Such a view would put Chairman Yu in an embarrassing position. What is worse, it could even work to damage the traditionally friendly relations of our two newspapers."

So what did I do in a month for which I got paid fully, but without being given any assignment? Certainly, I did not allow the month to go by idly. I spent every day reading the China Times carefully to see what news events it printed, from page one to the last page. I paid particular attention to the paper's coverage of central government news and the ROC's diplomatic and international relations--areas in which I was expected to play a reporting role.

The other thing I did daily during that month was to practice writing news-style stories in Chinese. In so doing, I often used some well-written newspaper articles as models to study how the authors wrote news reports and features, including the way they structured their contents and the words and skills they used to present them.

The Chinese-language newspapers which I read daily also included Taiwan's two other leading morning newspapers: the United Daily News and the state-run Central Daily News, in addition to the China Times.

That I wanted to use the month to practice writing news stories because previously, as I mentioned earlier, I had never written anything Chinese in a particular style or a professional manner, despite the fact that this language is my mother tongue. I hoped one month of practice would help me do my news reporting job in Chinese.

Awed at the Size of the Times's Editorial Department.

As previously designated, I went to the editorial department of the China Times to report for work in early February of 1969. During those early years, the Times was still located on Tali Street in Taipei's Wanhua District. Instantly, I was brought by Mr. Chang Pyng-feng, now my immediate superior, to visit Chairman Yu Ji-zhong. "It is a long tradition that Chairman Yu must see every newly recruited reporter before he or she starts working for us," Mr. Chang told me on the way. He went further to explain: The chairman sees reporters as the backbone of a newspaper. So he attaches great importance to the recruitment of such workers, insisting on personally receiving each and every new recruit, who comes to join the reporting team of the China Times."

Chairman Yu was a gentle and kind elder. He was an intellectual-turned newspaperman. He came to Taiwan shortly before the fall of the Chinese mainland to the communists in 1949. He launched the China Times and started his journalism business in the year that followed. During the brief meeting with him, I remember, the chairman gave me no particular instructions, except to make some encouraging remarks.

Back at the editorial department, I was introduced to the editor-in-chief, city editor, the news selecting and distributing editor, and the editors of various pages. These editors sat at a cluster of desks set at the center of the newsroom. I was also brought to meet the many section editors, who were responsible for overseeing the coverage of various kinds of news, from parliamentary and Cabinet news to the police and crime news, sports news, entertainment news, and economic, financial, and market news.

These section news directors supervised a combined total of more than 40 reporters. To give an example, the central legislative and executive news section, which operated under the direction of Chang Pyng-feng and with which I was going to work, was composed of seven to eight reporters. The above-mentioned combined total of 40-odd reporters did not even include the newspaper's numerous correspondents stationed in Taiwan's various counties and cities, as well as in foreign capitals, such as Washington and Tokyo.

After looking at the sheer size of the entire editorial department and the way it operated, a general impression immediately formed in my mind: The China Post--the English-language newspaper where I had spent the past three years -- was no match for the China Times in manpower and operating scale.

Beyond that first impression, a feeling of excitement also emerged in my mind. I felt proud to have joined such a big Chinese-language newspaper, becoming a part of its most important news-gathering and reporting team. On my way back home that night, I thought to myself: The China Times might be the paper that could provide a favorable environment, in which I could work steadily toward my newly reset goal of becoming a professional in Chinese-language journalism.

But my goal was never achieved. The failure was not because I was deterred by any challenges I faced in the process of carrying out my reporting duties. Nor was it because the China Times gave me no opportunity to pursue my goal -- it did. Rather it was an unexpected twist that prompted me to quit the China Times and return to the China Post more than a year later. To this day I still have no word for this dramatic turn. I can only call it destiny. An account of this episode will be given in more detail toward the end of this chapter.

Crows Are Black the World Over

The above quotation was a well-known Chinese proverb. It was cited to me by China Post Publisher Nancy Yu-Huang during a one-on-one conversation on the eve of my departure to join the China Times. Nancy was responding to a farewell comment I made in our conversations. I told her that the way the Post's editorial department processed news articles did not favor the cultivation of reporters' writing skills.

I felt a little bit disappointed that she took my comment as entirely targeting the Post's editorial department for playing something like office politics. Actually, my remark also included an indirect suggestion that the newsroom of the Post lacked a sound copy-handling process and that this problem needed to be corrected by increasing investment in manpower.

"Office politics existed in the workplace everywhere," she went on to explain. "It is just like the old saying 'crows are black the world over.'" Although the publisher failed to catch my main point, intentionally or not, the saying she quoted to me soon proved to be true, as I saw with my own eyes.

Almost immediately after starting work for the China Times, I personally experienced the play of office politics and felt keenly the impact such a political game had on me and the exercising of my duties.

To begin with, I was assigned to cover diplomacy and foreign news, as agreed early on, succeeding Mr. Hu (whose full name has been withheld here for the sake of politeness). But neither my predecessor nor anyone else from the editorial department brought me to the Ministry of Foreign Affairs--the primary source of diplomatic and foreign news--to meet relevant officials there and show them my credentials, as customarily required.

With no such assistance, I had to help myself. At the time I already had three years of news covering experience (at the China Post) behind me. So I was bold enough to go directly to the Foreign

Ministry's Information and Cultural Department to introduce myself. The information department was responsible for, among other things, handling relations with the press. I called on several officials of the department, telling them who I was and the purpose of my visit. The officials I visited included the department's director, a sub-section chief, and a junior diplomat named Chen Chien-jen.

Fifty years on, I can no longer recall the names of the department director and the section chief. I do not even have any impression of them. However, I can still remember Mr. Chen Chien-jen, an entry-level diplomat then. This can be attributed to a number of factors. First, Chen was in charge of issuing news releases and receiving reporters from the news media. For that reason, I had frequent associations with him. Each time when I visited the Foreign Ministry, then located on Taipei's Boai Road, next to the Presidential Office, I would drop into his office to say hello to him, while checking with him whether there was any news. One thing I often enquired about was if there was any prominent foreign figure currently on a visit to this country or planning to pay a visit.

Another reason that enabled me to remember Mr. Chen Chien-jen is that this junior diplomat soon became a rising star in the ROC diplomatic service. He rose rapidly through the ranks to prominent positions. He served as foreign minister under former KMT President Lee Teng-hui during the final years of his administration (1988-2000). Then after Chen Shui-bian came to power in mid-2000, he was appointed as Taipei's representative to the United States. And he was reassigned to head Taipei's EU representative office in Brussels, Belgium, after the pro-independence president won a second four-year term in 2004. (Note, Taipei has maintained representative offices in the U.S., the EU, and many other countries to promote bilateral relations in the absence of diplomatic links. These representatives are treated as de facto ambassadors.)

Mr. Chen Chien-jen's rapid rise and the various high-profile diplomatic roles he played continued to draw my attention. That was so because I myself happened to become a career journalist, covering a wide range of subject matters over the course of the next few decades. Diplomacy and international relations were among my main concerns. So each time I saw him in the news, I would pay particular attention to what he was saying or doing, hoping to get something from his activities to write about.

Yet, to be honest, I must say what impressed me most deeply about Mr. Chen was the way he received me when I first called on the press room of the Ministry of Foreign Affairs. I told him that I was from the China Times and that from now on I "will be responsible for covering the Ministry of Foreign Affairs, representing that newspaper."

But Mr. Chen did not respond with any remark like welcoming me. Rather he seemed to be doubtful about my claim to represent the China Times. The expression in his eyes told me that. So the cold and unfriendly reception Mr. Chen gave me made an impression on me. But I did not blame him for distrusting me.

He had a reason. First, the China Times did not present any document notifying the Foreign Ministry that I had taken over the role as its new diplomacy reporter to cover the agency. Second, my predecessor Mr. Hu, as I noticed, continued to maintain his presence in some Foreign Ministry offices. Initially, I thought he was there to say goodbye to his sources. But I soon found I was wrong because he did not at the same time let them know who I was and why I was there, even when we came across each other on such visits.

The embarrassing situation I encountered at the Foreign Ministry stemmed, as I later learned, from a power game being played back at the editorial department of the Times. This needs to go back to the circumstances under which Mr. Chang Pyng-feng, the Times' "central government news desk" director, wanted to invite me to join the paper. At that time, he anticipated he would soon be promoted to the position of city editor. If that was the case, he thought he would need a reporter having a good command of English to help him take care of diplomatic and international news. But in the end that job unexpectedly and disappointedly went to a contending candidate, Mr. Lin Shui-tong.

Yet Mr. Chang's failure to get promoted also had an impact on me: The new city editor, Mr. Lin, saw me as Chang Pyng-feng's man. I was so classified because I was hired by him before Mr. Lin's nomination became public. This obviously meant my recruitment was made without prior consultation with the incoming city editor, Mr. Lin. This, as a consequence, led him to cast doubt on my loyalty to him.

That perception and emotion, in turn, prompted Mr. Lin to become sympathetic to the previous diplomatic reporter, Mr. Hu, whom I replaced. The new city editor's sympathy somehow evolved into his unspoken support for my predecessor. This chain reaction, I presumed, explained the reluctance of Mr. Hu to hand over his duty of covering the Foreign Ministry to me without provoking intervention from the new city editor.

Chapter 5
A Brief Foray into Chinese-language Journalism

During my nearly year and a half stint at the China Times, Mr. Lin rarely spoke to me. Whenever he did, it was when he assigned me special tasks directly--without going through my immediate superior Mr. Chang Pyng-feng. Even in such cases, our exchanges were brief, limited to business conversations. Our only closer interactions happened a day or two before I left the Times. He gave me a farewell dinner on Taipei's Zhonghua Road. It was attended only by him and me. No one else was present or invited. I can no longer recall exactly what we talked about over dinner. But I do remember I told him I would always treasure my association with the China Times because it provided me a great opportunity to learn and practice Chinese journalism. By Chinese journalism, I meant using Chinese to write news reports and stories. This was in sharp contrast to my previous job in the China Post, where news reports had to be written in English.

Looking back on my days at the China Times as a reporter, I found it hard for me to tell exactly how well I performed there. For one thing, this was a reporting job that I carried out nearly six decades ago. So it's naturally impossible for me to fully remember how I covered news and wrote news stories then, and how my work was judged by my superiors and others.

However, I do remember a comment made by Mr. Chang Pyng-feng about my Chinese writing. As I mentioned earlier, Mr. Chang supervised the operations of the central government news section, and it was he who invited me to join the Times. He said: "Your Chinese writing ability is above average. However, you might have some way to go, if you wanted to compare yourself with Guo Jen-chieh." (Note:

Mr. Guo at the time was widely recognized in the newspaper as the "star" reporter of our central government news gathering team).

From Mr. Chang's comment, I knew where I stood in that team. He made the remark during a private conversation I had with him shortly after I came to work for the Times. He was responding to my concern as to whether my Chinese writing capability was up to the standard set by the China Times. I was so concerned about my writing skills because previously I rarely had had the chance to write about professional matters in Chinese.

In addition to commenting on my writing, Mr. Chang also gave me a piece of advice during the conversations: "Whenever you write a special report or an analysis be sure you focus on a subject of discussion or something special to talk about if you want to attract the reader." It was very useful advice. Many years later, in fact, I often liked to cite it to my younger colleagues for their reference.

Another reason that I cannot fully recall how I carried out my reporting work in the China Times goes beyond the time factor. Chinese journalism, as the other factor, formed only a small fraction of my entire journalism career. After leaving the China Times, I worked for the China Post and later for several other news organizations. All of such organizations were dedicated to the printing of English-language publications, rendering my China Times experience almost irrelevant. In other words, I seldom had a chance to revisit my days thereafter my departure.

Luckily, I still keep with me some 50 short and long articles, which I wrote while working for the China Times. All these clippings bore my name as bylined stories. The chances were that I had written some more bylined stories than the above-cited ones, but somehow I did not cut them out, or I did but failed to keep them to this day. Note that I did not keep, at all, any non-bylined news reports that I wrote during that period. (Some explanation here: A bylined article is unlike a straight news report which normally covers only daily happenings and mostly comes out without bearing the reporter's name. On the other hand, a bylined article, roughly speaking, could be one accompanying a news report giving some additional or in-depth information related to the news event reported. Of course, it could also be an exclusive or a scoop.)

Some five dozen or so of the bylined articles that I kept helped me recall a number of interesting things from the long ago past. First, I noticed one of those clippings was dated February 25, 1970. A further examination of those clippings showed this piece was the most recent one. This suggested that my tenure at the China Times lasted for at least one year and two to three months. Note, at the beginning of this chapter I had already explained that my employment with the newspaper became effective from January 1, 1969.

Second, those clippings give some indications of what news I covered and wrote about at the China Times some six decades earlier. Also, these old news stories could provide present-day people with some interesting insights into what the people in Taiwan were most concerned about in the early post-World War II decades.

And third, from those clippings, I realize that I often served as both a beat and general assignment reporter while working with the Times. Roughly speaking, a beat reporter covers the same subject or organization all the time, while a general assignment reporter covers any story assigned to him or her by the city editor.

As a general assignment reporter, I was frequently given instructions by my city editor to do interviews that often had little to do with my regular beat. Surely I oftentimes also did interviews based on my own story ideas. The people I interviewed included noted foreign and local figures. They were asked to comment on current issues, ranging from the Vietnam War to the ROC's foreign relations, as well as economic and social reforms being pushed domestically.

Interview of a Leading Anti-Vietnam War Activist

In one instance, as showed in one of my China Times clippings dated April 5, 1969, I interviewed a noted U.S. Roman Catholic priest and peace activist Daniel Berrigan during his brief stay in Taipei. Before coming to visit the ROC capital city, Berrigan had spent one week in South Vietnam, where he met with then South Vietnamese President Nguyen Van Thieu (1965 to 1975) and top American military commanders stationed there to help fight communist aggression from the North.

In that exclusive interview, Berrigan told me he firmly believed that then newly inaugurated Republican President Richard Nixon -- the 37th U.S. president who served from 1969 until his resignation in 1974 over the Watergate scandal -- "should thoroughly overhaul American policy on the Vietnam War," which he said had dragged on for so long and at such high cost.

(According to literature on the subject, U.S. involvement in the Vietnam War traced back to almost the immediate post-World War II years. Its aim was to prevent a takeover of South Vietnam by the communist North under a broader containment policy to check the spread of communism. The war was prolonged and escalated through most of the 1960s. At one point. U.S. military personnel in Vietnam had reached some 530,000. Long years of U.S. air bombings and ground attacks, however, failed to defeat the Viet Cong and the regular North Vietnamese Army. As the war became bogged down and U.S. casualties soared, a large angry anti-Vietnam War movement erupted across the United States.)

Daniel Berrigan was a high-profile leader of the anti-war movement. He said "The way the Vietnam War was being waged did not look like we were fighting the enemy. Rather it appeared like we were there to just invite attacks by the communist North." He suggested that Richard Nixon "should help South Vietnam to build its own military strength, especially its air force. "Such a policy could not only reduce the number of U.S. forces in South Vietnam but also help win the support of the liberals back at home," he said.

It needs to be noted here that soon after taking over from Democratic President Lyndon Johnson, Nixon instituted a Vietnamization program that called for a gradual reduction of American forces in Vietnam, while at the same time working to increase the combat capabilities of the South Vietnamese armed forces.

Berrigan, in that interview, also took strong exception to ongoing Paris peace talks supported by Nixon's predecessor. In his view, North Vietnam was willing to participate in the peace negotiations only because it wanted "to use such talks as delaying tactics to expand its infiltrations into the South."

It's worth noting that the Paris talks proceeded on and off, lasting for years. It was not until 1973 when a peace treaty, officially titled the Agreement on Ending the War and Restoring Peace in Vietnam, was finally reached between the relevant parties. The conclusion of the peace accord ended direct U.S. military involvement in the same year. But the war was prolonged until the loss of Saigon to the North Vietnamese Army in 1975. Saigon's fall marked the end of the Vietnam War and the resultant reunification of North and South Vietnam.

President Nixon's program to gradually reduce the U.S. military presence in South Vietnam was welcomed by anti-war and peace activists at home. But it caused serious concerns not just in South Vietnam, but also in other anti-communist countries in Asia, such as the Republic of China on Taiwan. Politicians and civil leaders in the region were worried whether Nixon's military withdrawal move represented a shifting of America's long-established anti-communist policy and, if so, what impact it would have on their efforts to resist communist aggression.

I brought up the above-mentioned concerns in a separate interview with a senior U.S. journalist and syndicated columnist Willard Shelton and asked him for comment. Shelton was on a 10-day visit to Taiwan and I was assigned by my city editor to interview him about America's Vietnam policy and his observations about this island.

Before answering my question as to why President Nixon wanted to withdraw from South Vietnam, he made a brief mention of Nixon's predecessor Lyndon Johnson (1963 to 1969): The Democratic president during his final years in office steadily escalated U.S. military interventions in South Vietnam. But in spite of that, Johnson failed to decisively win the war, causing his popularity to plummet and forcing him to eventually decide not to seek a second term. "Still, I strongly supported Johnson's Asia policy, admiring his courage and determination to resist communist invasion in particular," said Willard Shelton.

Returning to my question about why Richard Nixon wanted to withdraw American military forces from South Vietnam, Shelton cited three major factors, which he said had contributed to Nixon's withdrawal decision. One, there was a growing tendency toward isolationism in the United States and many European countries. One main indication of such isolationism was that the United States and many of its European allies were all endeavoring to develop their own economies, unwilling to get involved in world affairs.

Two, Americans had grown extremely weary of war, after fighting the Second World War, the Korean War and, more recently, the conflict in South Vietnam. So they were becoming reluctant to support a seemingly endless Vietnam War with their hard-earned money, which they would rather spend on raising their living standards. As a third factor, an increasingly strong anti-war movement across the United States also had a bearing on President Nixon in his decision to retreat from South Vietnam.

Although Shelton believed that Nixon had his reasons to pull combat troops out of South Vietnam, he still felt the need for the United States to increase military and economic aid to the Republic of

China and other Asian countries facing the threat of communist aggression. The ROC, in particular, he said, was the outpost of the free world countering the expansion of communism. So if the security of the ROC was threatened, he said, it would have an impact on the Asian region and even the entire free world.

Interviewing Intellectuals on Political and Economic Reforms

Aside from doing interviews with visiting prominent foreign figures on current world affairs and their potential impact on the ROC, I was also frequently dispatched to talk to intellectuals and civil leaders of the country, and asked them questions on ongoing domestic issues, such as political and economic reforms.

In one such interview, to give an example, I asked two Taiwan-born intellectuals about their views on the island's political and social norms. Chen Ding-cheng and Li Xiang-jen, who currently were residing in the United States and Britain, respectively, returned to Taipei to attend a forum sponsored by the ruling Kuomintang.

Chen Ding-cheng called for the ROC government to vigorously enforce "clean politics," and wipe out political corruption. He said many ROC citizens living abroad were very concerned about Taiwan's political norms, a reference to rampant corruption in government. "Widespread government corruption could not only impede crucial reforms but also damage the ROC's international image, detrimental to developing relations with other countries," Mr. Chen said.

Li Xiang-jen, the other forum attendee who came from Britain, said that enacting severe penalties for officials engaged in corrupt activities alone "won't be enough." He said "It is also important to encourage the public to expose irregularities that exist in the government. When more and more people are willing or daring to act as whistleblowers, it would increase the risk of unethical officials being caught and charged with corruption or wrongdoing. This, in turn, would have a deterrent effect on potential offenders."

Yet to encourage public scrutiny of government policy and exposure of unethical behavior, Mr. Li continued, it required the willingness of the government to protect freedom of speech and, more fundamentally, freedom of the press. "Only (when) such freedoms are protected, will whistleblowers not be afraid of reprisal." (Note: Press freedom in Taiwan then was greatly restrained under martial law).

In another bylined piece, which I cut from the China Times, I interviewed Hong Dong-xiang, a leader of the trade union in a big government-owned wines and spirits plant located in Taipei. His discussion with me provided a general view of the inadequate working conditions that prevailed in Taiwan during those years.

Mr. Hong told me that Taiwan had to continue to improve blue-collar workers' conditions--from working hours to wages, safety standards, and health care. He noted that people in many small businesses often worked more than eight hours a day and that wages in no small number of cases were not even enough to support a family of three.

In some private companies, he said, employers did not even provide labor insurance coverage and gave no employee benefits at all. According to the labor leader, most private employers were unwilling to see their workers organize trade unions. Without a trade union to exercise collective bargaining power, Hong pointed out, workers could hardly expect their employers to voluntarily improve the conditions of their employment.

From the dozens of China Times articles which I wrote while working for the paper, I get the impression that my city editor liked to give me extra tasks to do. I guess he might be motivated by either of the following three reasons or a combination of the three, as I now try to figure out why that was the case.

One, by giving me more extra assignments, he could obtain greater flexibility in using the reporting staff. This in turn could allow him to get more work done. Years later, I found truth in that point after I myself assumed the roles of city editor and editor-in-chief while working for other news organizations.

Surely my English knowledge might also play a part in why I was frequently given extra assignments. For example, there were often cases in which coverage of an English-speaking foreign personality coming to visit Taiwan had to be conducted in that language. In a Chinese-language newspaper, not many reporters were capable of conducting interviews in English. This was at least the situation in the China Times that I saw during my time there.

A third possible reason was that Mr. Lin might think the amount of my work was too light and that it did not match the level of the pay

I drew. Because of this consideration, he might feel it was necessary for him to add more tasks to my workload to ensure fair play.

The Difficulty Covering the Foreign Ministry

One other possible reason why my China Times city editor often gave me extra work presumably was his recognition of the difficulty in covering diplomacy. This news beat normally did not generate large numbers of stories. Thus covering diplomacy alone could affect my performance in terms of news-reporting output.

Truly, the Ministry of Foreign Affairs, my first news beat in the China Times, did not produce much news. But what was even worse for a reporter was those ministry officials were difficult to approach whenever you had something to ask them for comment. A widely shared view in the media circles was that seeking to arrange an interview with a diplomat was much more difficult than getting one with any of the other department officials.

You certainly had free access to some routine events that took place in the Ministry of Foreign Affairs. But this was limited only to what they preferred you would print. Most freely available were press releases issued by the ministry to inform the arrivals of foreign VIPs, or departures of those who had traveled to Taiwan, after meeting with government officials or attending economic conferences, for example. There were also cases in which foreign ministry officials were quite generous. They sent some kinds of materials to the newsrooms in person for publication. But most of such materials had little news value. Yet the reporters still had to persuade their editor to use them for the sake of public relations.

No aggressive reporters would allow themselves to be satisfied with getting routine event news. I believe I was among the aggressive. I always sought to gather something special or exclusive. During those times Taipei and Beijing were engaged in a bitter struggle for diplomatic recognition in the United Nations and elsewhere around the world. So I always watched closely for any signs of new developments in such a recognition fight.

The fight for diplomatic recognition was a long-running one. It came into being shortly after the communists led by Mao Zedong took over the mainland and established the People's Republic of China in Beijing in 1949. After the defeat, Chiang Kai-shek and his Republic of China government retreated to Taiwan. This outcome has since resulted in two rival governments simultaneously existing in China.

Ever since, Beijing has claimed to be the "sole legitimate government of China." It continued to insist that any foreign country intending to establish diplomatic relations with the PRC had to sever ties with the ROC in Taipei. By the late 1960s, the PRC had succeeded in winning an increasing number of countries switching recognition from Taipei to Beijing.

To counter Beijing's diplomatic offensive, Taipei adopted a two-pronged strategy. One was to try by all means to retain its existing political allies. The other was to solicit support from many newly independent countries--those which declared independence since the end of World War Two—by rendering them economic aid in return.

In addition to engaging in the struggle with Beijing to win diplomatic recognition by third countries, Taipei at the time also faced an uphill battle to defend its representation right in the United Nations. The PRC government and its allies, most notably Albania, introduced an annual vote at the U.N. General Assembly in the latter part of the 1960s aiming to replace the ROC with the PRC. On 25 October 1971, Albania's motion to recognize Beijing as the sole legitimate government representing China was finally passed as General Assembly Resolution 2758.

Theoretically speaking, for a reporter like me working on a diplomatic beat in Taiwan during such a time, there should have been a lot of newsworthy events to cover. But the reality was that almost all of the activities involved in the contest for diplomatic recognition were carried out behind the scenes. For example, information about any foreign country attempting to switch recognition to Beijing, or about how Taipei was acting to counter a potential adverse diplomatic change were all shrouded in top secrecy.

Similarly, if you attempted to find out what countermeasures Taipei was likely to take in the event that a new motion seeking to replace its U.N. seat with Beijing was brought up for debate in the annual General Assembly session, your efforts would certainly have proved futile. This was so because ministry officials were always tight-lipped on whatever efforts the government might make to safeguard its representation right in the United Nations.

Some key diplomatic officials even refused to meet journalists. I will give below an example from my personal experience. One morning in the summer of 1969, I called the residence of George

Kung-chao Yeh for an interview with him. Yeh was a veteran diplomat who was the ROC's first minister of foreign affairs after Chiang Kai-shek and his KMT government withdrew to Taiwan from the mainland in the late 1940s. During his tenure, he signed the Sino-Japanese Peace Treaty in 1952 and the Sino-American Mutual Defense Treaty in 1954. He later served as ROC ambassador to the United States but was recalled to Taiwan in 1961 by Chiang for his perceived failure to elicit greater support for blocking the admission of Mongolia to the United Nations in that year.

At the time I made the above-mentioned phone call, George Kung-chao Yeh was serving as minister without portfolio. Yeh did not personally take my call. It was his secretary who answered it. I explained to the secretary, a female, that I was a reporter from the China Times and hoped to have a chance to see the minister that day. I would like to ask him, I said, a few questions. A central one, I continued, would be about what Taipei was planning or going to do in the face of Beijing's increasingly strong campaign to expel the ROC government from the United Nations.

My decision to ask for an interview with George Yeh was based on two reasons. One, the U.N. was going to convene its 1969 General Assembly session in the coming fall. By then, the PRC and its allies would certainly push for a new vote to expel the ROC from the world body as it did in the past few years. Two, Minister Yeh was the most qualified diplomat with whom to discuss the ROC representation right issue, given his profound experience in handling the country's diplomatic and international relations.

Yeh's secretary replied to me on the phone: "You can come over, but I am not sure whether the minister would have time to receive you and take your questions." I hung up and told myself: "I should try my luck." So I took a taxi to Minister Yeh's residence, as the secretary described to me. It was a big one-story house, which I now can only vaguely remember was located somewhere on Taipei's Songjiang Road.

I rang the doorbell. Moments later, a woman opened the door and looked at me, sizing me up. I soon learned she was the secretary who answered my phone call. I quickly introduced myself, telling her I was the China Times reporter who had just phoned to ask to interview Minister Yeh. She replied, "Sorry, Minister Yeh is doing his daily workout, unable to receive you now." At first, I did not take or was just unwilling to take, those remarks as a veiled refusal to accept my interview request. Anyway, she gave no signs of letting me in at the end of her remarks.

Facing such a situation, I responded: "Okay, I would like to wait outside until Minister Yeh finishes his workout." About an hour or so later, I rang the doorbell again. This time the same woman emerged before me, telling me that Minister Yeh was very busy today with his work, having no time to meet you. Unwilling to give up easily, a while later I rang the doorbell the third time. Coming to answer the door still was that female secretary, who appeared to have got somewhat annoyed with me. She said "Minister Yeh has just left home," then shut the door." If Yeh had really gone out as she said, then the minister most likely left through the back door. I was so certain, in that I had been moving back and forth in front of the house all the time since my arrival and had not seen any person or a car leaving the house from the front door.

Needless to say I felt very frustrated at being unable to do what otherwise would be a good exclusive story by getting a senior official to talk about Taiwan's diplomatic predicament. In the next few days, I repeatedly asked myself a question why the minister was loath to receive me for an interview. Finally, I came up with the following assumption. He was afraid of bringing himself trouble by discussing sensitive diplomatic issues with a mass-circulation newspaper. Things could become even more troublesome for him in the event that he said anything that would contradict the views of higher government authorities.

Not so long earlier, Yeh had got his fingers burned, as he dissented from the official government position in handling the Mongolia issue. That resulted in him being removed from his position as ambassador to the U.S. and recalled to Taipei by then President Chiang Kai-shek. It's worth noting that the ROC had effectively blocked the Mongolian People's Republic from entering the U.N. throughout the 1950s by using its veto power as a permanent member of the U.N. Security Council. But things began to change in 1960 when the then Soviet Union announced that unless Mongolia was admitted, it would block the admission of all of the newly independent African states. Faced with pressure from the Soviet Union as well as the ROC's own allies, including the U.S., Taipei finally relented under protest. Mongolia thus was finally admitted into the U.N. in 1961. Minister Yeh, however, was reportedly blamed for playing a part in the shifting of the ROC position on the Mongolia issue.

Chapter 5
A Brief Foray into Chinese-language Journalism

A 'Consolation Prize' from Times Chairman Yu

Unexpectedly but encouragingly, I got a "consolation prize" from China Times Chairman Yu Ji-Zhong a few days later for the frustrations, I endured in my failed attempt to interview George Kung-chao Yeh. "Mr. Tseng Ching-hsiang (my Chinese name) showed great courage and perseverance in performing his journalistic duties. Such spirit deserves to be commended," said the chairman. He made the commending remarks at a monthly meeting of editors and department chiefs. My boss Mr. Chang Pyng-feng attended that meeting and reported my story of trying in vain to obtain an interview with Ambassador George Yeh.

The case of George Yeh refusing to receive me for an interview illustrated just one of the many difficulties I encountered in covering diplomacy while working for the China Times. From that job, I got the impression that ROC diplomatic officials were almost invariably reluctant to receive journalists and share their opinions, especially when it came to something politically sensitive.

If you were fortunate enough, you got someone to receive you. But they agreed to talk to you only on the condition of anonymity. They refused to have their names printed in whatever you wrote. Being able to get someone to tell you something worthy of writing about was of course lucky enough. But the problem was that using unnamed sources could raise doubts among the readers about the authenticity of your sources and, therefore, the credibility of what you reported.

There were also cases in which diplomatic officials were relatively more cooperative. They granted me exclusive interviews after I convinced them of my needs. But they only agreed to speak off the record, meaning the information provided to you could not be used in any manner or attributed to the sources.

Beyond the above experiences, I also met some officials who only agreed to talk to me on background. In journalism jargon, "on background" means that you cannot even quote the information you are provided by your interviewees, but you can rephrase what they told you in your articles.

Some of the diplomatic stories which I covered during my days at the China Times were written under the "on background" arrangements, reached with my interviewees. Below is a classic example of this. In or around May 1969, I interviewed a senior ROC Foreign Ministry official to examine the status of the country's diplomatic relations with Italy.

I now can only remember the official by his family name, Sun. He was chief secretary of the Ministry of Foreign Affairs at the time. Mr. Sun had previously held senior positions in the ROC embassies in Rome and the Vatican.

Mr. Sun was willing to accept my interview only because I cited my work associated with his daughter Alice Sun. I told him on the phone I was Alice's former China Post colleague. Alice, a graduate of National Taiwan University, worked for the China Post only briefly before she left for the U.S. to pursue advanced studies there. Ms. Sun and I joined the Post at the same time after we both passed a reporter-recruiting test given by the English-language newspaper.

Chapter 5
A Brief Foray into Chinese-language Journalism

My interview with the chief secretary was conducted at his home on Taipei's Hangzhou South Road, near what now is Chiang Kai-shek Memorial Hall. Mr. Sun and his wife were so kind and generous that they treated me to coffee and cake. Yet once we got down to business, Mr. Sun turned solemn, reiterating a previously agreed-on condition that I "must not disclose in any way his identity and must not directly quote any statements he made to me. However, I could rephrase whatever he said in my story."

Based on the background information given to me by the chief secretary, combined with my own knowledge, I wrote a piece of analysis titled "Italy's Attempt to Recognize Beijing Has Been Brewing for Quite Some Time, " which appeared in a China Times column called "Watchtower." To comply with the "on background" rule set by him before he agreed to talk with me, my analysis was written in a way that none of the statements in it were directly taken from Mr. Sun and that no attributions were made at all.

Major contents of that analysis are quoted below: "Italy's attempt to establish diplomatic relations with the People's Republic of China has been brewing for a long time. In 1966, the Italian government came up with a Beijing-leaning resolution in the U.N. General Assembly calling for the world body to create a committee to explore the possibility of admitting communist China. Although that proposal was defeated due to a lack of majority support, Rome has never given up its efforts to befriend the PRC...

"Despite the 1966 defeat, the Italian U.N. mission made two further attempts at the General Assembly in the following two years of 1967 and 1968. But the Italian resolution was defeated again on both occasions, also as a result of failing to win a majority."

Note: The Italian draft resolution, co-sponsored by Belgium, Brazil, Chile, and Trinidad and Tobago, called for the General Assembly to establish a research committee. This committee would consist of a small number of eminent and experienced persons tasked with the mission to find facts, draw their conclusions, and make proposals for an equitable and practical solution to the China issue. This proposal was regarded by many observers as a way to gain formal consideration of the so-called "two-China" solution, which would allow membership for both Taipei and Beijing, with the latter presumably in the Security Council seat as well. This formula, however, again failed to gain majority support, mainly because both Chinese governments, especially Beijing, rejected any such solution. (Source: United Nations Voting on Chinese Representation: An Analysis of General Assembly Roll-Calls, 1950-1971--A doctoral dissertation by John Kuo-Chang Wang).

I continued in my analysis "Italy's repeated defeats of its moves to bring the PRC into the United Nations appear to have discouraged the southern European country from pressing ahead with its plan to switch diplomatic recognition from Taipei to Beijing, at least for the present. Therefore, Taipei's diplomatic relations with Rome can be expected to maintain their present status for some time...."

"Although the ROC and Italy have maintained diplomatic ties, Rome has never opened an embassy in Taiwan after the ROC government moved to this island from the mainland in 1949. This is despite the fact that Taipei has stationed a permanent diplomatic mission in that country.... Rome's intentions of keeping its distance from Taipei could be seen also in its delay more than a year ago in giving confirmation of the ROC's newly appointed ambassador, Hsu Shao-chang. Confirmation was finally ascertained only after Vice Foreign Minister H.K. Yang paid a visit to Rome and held talks with higher Italian government authorities...

"Bilateral relations got tense further since late last year (1968) following Italian Prime Minister Aldo Moro's success in forming a new government. Moro, who was the chief architect of Italy's proposal to create U.N. committee to study the possibility of admitting the PRC, has reportedly decided to recognize Beijing at the expense of Taipei. Intelligence reports from the ROC's diplomatic missions in Italy and other relevant allied countries continued to pour in lately, all alerting the government to that possibility...

"It is learned that the Ministry of Foreign Affairs is trying all possible means to persuade Rome to give up its plan to switch recognition. Efforts so made included appealing to the U.S., Japan, and other influential allies of the ROC to jointly exert pressure on the Moro government. But up to this point, such efforts appear to have proved futile...Some observers thus have concluded that Italy's recognition of the People's Republic of China is only a matter of time. They urged the government to prepare for the worst."

Note, more than a year later in November 1970, Italy finally switched recognition from Taipei to Beijing. This unfriendly move led the Republic of China to close at the same time its embassy in Rome and a consulate-general in Milan.

Covering Visit by South Vietnamese President Nguyen Van Thieu

A big event occurred on my diplomatic beat in May 1969: South Vietnamese President Nguyen Van Thieu (1965 to 1975) paid a five-day visit to the Republic of China in Taiwan starting late that month. This was the first time I covered such an important diplomatic event as a foreign affairs reporter since I joined the China Times early that year. By any measure, a visit by a foreign chief of state was big news. It would be even more so when that leader came from a crucial political ally of the ROC. At the time, both the ROC and South Vietnam were engaged in bitter struggles against communist aggression. For South Vietnam, the aggression came from the communist forces in North Vietnam. For the ROC, on the other hand, the communist aggression came from the People's Republic of China on the mainland.

I wrote a series of three bylined articles on the visit by the South Vietnamese president. The first one, titled 'Nguyen Van Thieu Visit: Symbolizing Regional Cooperation in Asia,' was published three days ahead of his arrival. Covered in this first piece were two major subjects. One was an account of preparations being made by the ROC government to receive the South Vietnamese leader and his entourage of more than 70 people, including senior Vietnamese government officials. Responsible for making the preparations was a big receiving team consisting of 50 people from various ROC government departments. This team, led by a ranking diplomat, Vice Foreign

Minister Tsai Wei-ping, was responsible for arranging everything from accommodation to security, meetings, and visiting activities.

The other subject raised in this article was a look at bilateral cooperation issues likely to be discussed by senior officials from the two countries. They included topics worked out by the two sides to promote cooperation in the political, military, and economic fields. During his stay, I pointed out in my report, President Nguyen Van Thieu was expected to meet with his host country counterpart Chiang Kai-shek, and exchange views on a range of issues of mutual concern, including the going-on war in Vietnam and peace and security in the broader Asian and Pacific region.

My second bylined article on the visit was published on the very day the South Vietnamese president arrived in Taipei. This one was aimed at introducing to the ROC audience what progress Nguyen Van Thieu had made in rebuilding his war-torn country in the last few years since he became an elected leader, and what challenges he was confronting ahead.

Among the progress, I wrote: Enacting South Vietnam's first Constitution, launching a nationwide campaign to root out corruption and incompetence at all levels of government, and passing a national mobilization law that authorized him and his government to mobilize all resources needed to support a war against communist aggression, while at the same time endeavoring to develop the South Vietnamese economy.

The biggest challenge the Vietnamese president was facing was how to bring a fast end to a prolonged war in his country. It should be noted here that the Vietnam War was a prolonged military conflict that started as an anti-colonial war against the French and evolved into a Cold War confrontation between international communism and free-market democracy. The Democratic Republic of Vietnam in the north was supported by the Soviet Union, the PRC, and other communist countries, while the U.S. and its anti-communist allies backed the Republic of Vietnam in the south. The need to bring a fast end to the Vietnam War was evident: An anti-Vietnam War movement was rapidly spreading throughout the U.S., increasing pressure for Washington to withdraw American troops from South Vietnam.

Yet Saigon's military efforts to repel North Vietnam's invading troops and stop its infiltration of the South to date showed no sign of any significant success. This was so even one year after Nguyen Van Thieu ordered enlisting an additional 135,000 men into the South Vietnamese military, bringing its troops to a total of more than 800,000. The above figures were quoted from U.S. President Lyndon John's nationwide television address on April 1, 1968, about the Vietnam War.

My third and last piece about the visit to Taipei by the South Vietnamese president came in the form of anecdotes. This piece recorded the soft aspect of how President and Mrs. Thieu spent their first day in Taipei. During their five-day visit, the Vietnamese first couple stayed at the luxury Grand Hotel Taipei. Due to the strict protocol of presidential visits, there was no way for me to interview either the president or the first lady in person.

However, I came to the Grand Hotel and managed to penetrate layers of security guards to reach Thieu's provisional presidential office on an upper floor, where I interviewed two of his senior aides, including a press official. Based on my conversations with them, I wrote a series of anecdotes about Thieu's first-day experiences in Taipei, with emphasis placed on how he started his day, what foods he liked most, and how he kept himself informed of the military and political situations back in his war-torn home country. Note: The ROC government authorities set up a hotline in Thieu's provisional presidential office in the Grand to ensure that the Vietnamese leader and his top aides traveling along with him could maintain 24-hour communications with Saigon during their five-day stay in Taiwan. I was told the dedicated point-to-point communications link was put into good use almost immediately after President Thieu and his entourage arrived in Taipei.

The above anecdote contained nothing extraordinary, but I liked that piece very much. Look, to cover this story--titled 'An Account of State Guest's First Day in Town'--I ventured to penetrate "layers of security guards" at the risk of being caught by security services and expelled from the press corps covering the Thieu visit. Incidentally, I am not sure whether or not my story about how South Vietnamese President Thieu spent his first day in Taipei was seen as a news scoop. But I now do remember that no other Taiwan newspapers printed similar stories that same day.

An Interview Under 'Unlikely Circumstances'

One other special bylined piece that I wrote while covering diplomatic news for the China Times was also an exclusive interview, this time with Rev. Paul Adenauer, son of former West German Chancellor

Konrad Adenauer. His father, Adenauer senior, stayed in power for 14 years beginning in 1949. As the first chancellor, he led West Germany from the ruins of World War II to a prosperous nation that forged and maintained full alignment with NATO and the United States during the Cold War era.

That I decided to interview Rev. Adenauer certainly had much to do with his family background. But what made me still vividly remember that interview a half-century later is another reason. It was an "unlikely circumstance," in which I met the younger Adenauer and got him to talk with me. I will describe this particular news reporting experience below.

Rev. Adenauer's visit to Taiwan was brief, lasting only three days. But somehow I learned of his arrival only on the eve of his departure. By the time I was finally connected to him at his Grand Hotel room, it was around 8 p.m. that evening. So if I asked for an interview at such a late time, it would not only be impolite but could also cause inconveniences to him. So I told him that I hoped to have a chance to interview him sometime the following day. "Sorry, my schedule for tomorrow will be particularly tight as I am going to leave Taipei in the afternoon. So I won't be able to take time out to receive you," he replied to me on the phone.

I quickly responded before he hung up: "I know you are quite busy. But please listen to me. I attach great importance to covering you as a distinguished visitor so far away from West Germany. I would like to obtain your views on how to promote closer relations between our two countries."

"But the question is that I simply cannot fit you in tomorrow," he said. I refused to take no for an answer. "But I know you are going to visit the suburban National Palace Museum tomorrow morning. So how about letting me ride with you in your car? This would allow me to ask you questions on the way to the museum." He reluctantly agreed.

I reached the entrance of the main Grand Hotel building at 09:00 a.m. the following day, as appointed. By this time, a tall Western man, appearing to be in his mid-30s, had already been standing there. Immediately, we recognized each other. But just as we were in the middle of exchanging greetings, a car dispatched by the ROC Government Information Office to pick him up stopped in front of us. Mr. and Mrs. Paul Adenauer got in the car and I followed. I sat in the front passenger seat.

I got down to business as soon as the car engine started, asking him questions and listening to his comments. It was about a 30-minute drive from the Grand Hotel to the National Palace Museum. By the time we arrived at the museum, I had not yet finished all the questions I intended to raise for him. So I could not help but ask two more questions while standing in the museum lobby. Thanks to his kindness and cooperation, I was able to do a good exclusive interview with him, which otherwise would have been impossible.

On relations between the Republic of China and West Germany, Rev. Adenauer pointed out in the interview that the two countries had much in common. West Germany and the ROC both were politically divided, all due to communist aggression. Both governments were endeavoring to achieve national unification. But for West Germany, he said, the primary effort was to build economic prosperity and raise living standards as incentives for all Germans to support its unification policy.

In the economic area, he said both West Germany and the ROC were following similar development models: Both countries owed their early post-war year's economic successes to American aid. Their continued prosperity thereafter, however, relied on wise government policy, such as encouraging exports and developing overseas markets, as well as hard work by the people.

As an economist specializing in small businesses, Rev. Adenauer pointed out that rapid economic expansion in his country in the period since the end of World War Two had favored big enterprises at the expense of small businesses. Such imbalances needed to be addressed by government policy, the younger Adenauer said.

Reassigned to Covering Transportation News

According to my old China Times clippings, I was assigned a new beat covering transportation news beginning from mid-July 1969. I replaced Mr. Ko Jen-chief, who was viewed as a star reporter in the China Times, as I mentioned earlier.

My reassignment to this new beat came six months after I joined the Times as a reporter responsible for gathering diplomatic news. As I now look back on the news beat reassignment, I find it hard for me to precisely tell whether or not the job transfer was a reflection of my boss's dissatisfaction with my performance on the previous diplomatic news route.

Normally, when a reporter is taken off a certain beat, it means that he or she might not have performed well in that news territory by, for example, missing major stories. But this example did not suit me. According to my memory, I never missed any diplomatic stories of importance. In fact, I feel I performed fairly well on the diplomatic beat, judging by the various special and exclusive stories I did from time to time, as I described in the previous pages.

Then why was I reassigned to cover transportation events? One plausible reason, as I now recollect, was that the China Times had lately adopted a new editorial approach placing greater emphasis on transportation news. By this time the government had just launched a number of big-ticket projects to expand the infrastructural facilities needed to sustain Taiwan's rapid industrial development and economic growth.

Following nearly two decades of fast growth in foreign trade and manufacturing businesses, Taiwan now ran into serious infrastructure bottlenecks threatening to impede further development, due to lagging investment in basic facilities, such as highways, railroads, harbors, and airports. These development bottlenecks led then Premier Chiang Ching-kuo to initiate "10 high-profile construction projects" in the early 1970s. Six of them were transportation projects.

They included plans for the construction of a North-South Freeway (now known as National Highway No. 1), Electrification of the West Line Railway, the building of a Northbound Railway, Chiang Kai-shek International Airport (later renamed Taiwan Taoyuan International Airport), and Taichung Harbor (originally called Wuxi International Harbor).

Feasibility studies on some of the projects had already got underway, as I took up the transportation beat. Normally undertaking a major utility project, like the ones I just cited, had to go through a long and challenging process before actual construction began. It ranged from feasibility studies to engineering designs, raising funds, and land procurements. As each of these processes moved forward, it tended to encounter difficulties of varying degrees. Such challenges were almost always newsworthy and deserved to be reported as news.

Take for example the multibillion-dollar 374-kilometer North-South Freeway project. One big challenge the government faced was where the money, needed to fund the construction of the new highway system, would come from. Initially, the Ministry of Transportation and Communications planned to increase vehicle fuel taxes as a primary source of such funding. But the ministry was finally forced to drop that plan after opponents and many members of the general public offered resistance for fear of triggering a round of high inflation.

On the other hand, the ROC's application to apply for loans from the Asian Development Bank did not go smoothly either. Its project feasibility study, conducted by a U.S. consulting firm, De Leuw, Cather & Co., failed to pass the evaluation by the Manlia-based development bank for lack of some essential information. Until such additional information was submitted, the Asian Development Bank would not approve Taiwan's loan application.

Fund-raising difficulties aside, the measures taken by government authorities to purchase land continued to make headlines, as many landowners along the proposed route of the 374-kilometer freeway persistently refused to sell their land to the government, citing "unreasonable compensation payments." Additionally, there were some who did not want their land to be bought by the government in anticipation of higher prices that might come with the development of the freeway (Note: The actual work on the construction of the north-south freeway began in 1971 and the entire length of the road was opened to traffic in 1978).

To keep track of the landowner protests and other problems encountered in the freeway's planning and design stages, I paid regular visits to the Taiwan Provincial Highway Bureau, which was designated to oversee the building of the north-south freeway and render administrative support for the American consulting company. Because of my frequent visits to the bureau, I got acquainted with its chief engineer Hu Mei-huang. The chief engineer was so cooperative and helpful that he from time to time gave me news leads and ideas. It was, for example, from him that I got the news about the failure of De Leuw, Cather's preliminary feasibility study to gain approval by the Asian Development Bank--the project's main lender.

Unlike the construction of the north-south freeway, the government confronted no land procurement problems in building Taiwan's third international harbor. But rather, the authorities presiding over the new port building project faced strong lobbying from conflicting local interest groups, like governmental city councils and business associations.

The ROC government formally announced its decision to build a new international seaport in the summer of 1968, as it moved to invite a group of Japanese port experts to Taiwan to conduct an on-the-spot survey with the aim of finding the most suitable site for the proposed port. The announcement immediately sparked speculation among the public as to where the new harbor was likely to be located. The public discussion focused on two potential candidate sites. One was Tamsui, a small fishing town located on Taiwan's northwest coast. The other was Wuxi, a fishing port situated in central Taiwan.

So soon after the government announced its port-building decision, interest groups from the two regions of Tamsui and Wuxi launched a fierce propaganda battle touting the advantages of their respective regions' geographic and economic position and lobbying to get the proposed new harbor constructed in their location. The Japanese port experts sent their final survey report to Taipei one year after they were commissioned to undertake the job. The contents of the report were classified as secret.

Thus until the Cabinet announced its acceptance of the Japanese experts' recommendation to build Taiwan's third international harbor in Wuxi in central Taiwan, few had known the port site suggestion, except a few who had had access to the confidential report.

Misled or not, some of my fellow media journalists reported days ahead of the scheduled announcement of the new port location, claiming that Tamsui had been chosen as the site for the construction of the new port. But they all got it wrong.

My report on the same event came out a day or two later than theirs. But I got it right. I quoted an anonymous Transportation Ministry source as saying that the government "will soon announce its decision to build the new harbor in Wuxi on the recommendation of the Japanese port experts."

Within about two days of my news report, the government formally announced its choice of Wuxi as the site on which to build Taiwan's third international harbor. The announcement thus ended weeks of speculation and tense lobbying by the competing political and interest groups.

Wuxi and Tamsui both are situated on Taiwan's west coast, with the former in the mid-west and the latter in the northwest. Wuxi, however, is centrally located, 110 nautical miles from Keelung Port in the north and 120 nautical miles from Kaohsiung Port in the south. Both of the two existing ports had become congested following nearly two decades of continued fast growth in exports and imports. This necessitated the construction of a third international port to ease increasing port congestion.

In addition to the need of helping ease port jams, the building of a new international harbor also had to consider two other important factors: promoting balanced regional development and reducing inland transportation costs. These were the two primary considerations that were taken into account by the Japanese experts when they recommended that Taiwan's third international harbor needed to be constructed in Wuxi rather than Tamsui. First, Wuxi, the central Taiwan town, and its nearby cities and counties were lagging behind those in the north in industrial and economic development. So if a new seaport was constructed in Wuxi, it would stimulate business and industrial growth in the central areas, while contributing to balanced regional development for all of Taiwan.

Second, as the Japanese expert survey reported, a new port built in central Taiwan could also reduce transportation costs for import goods, with final destinations in either the south or the north, and export goods that are produced in those two areas (Note: Actual construction on the Wuxi harbor began in 1973, with the first vessel launched from the new international port in 1976).

In addition to reporting the above-cited two construction projects of the north-south freeway and Taichung harbor, as more commonly known, I also covered two other big transportation events, as shown in my bylined China Times articles. One was on the government's initiative to build what is now Taiwan Taoyuan International Airport. The other was about how to eliminate the numerous railway level crossings in Taipei that caused serious daily traffic congestion in many parts of this metropolis. The situation was so serious that these level crossings were criticized by many as cancer on Taipei traffic.

There were 37 railway level crossings in this capital city then, 28 of which were run by the western trunk line of the Taiwan Railway Administration (TRA) and nine by its Tamsui line. Put together, trains of the two lines passed those level crossings around 250 times a day. Each time when a train approached and passed the level crossing, bars were lowered to stop passage by motorists and pedestrians for at least five minutes, bringing nearby traffic to a standstill.

Yet despite their cancerous impact, the several dozen level crossings were left stifling the city's traffic flow without being improved. That was the case because policymakers allowed themselves to be mired in a nagging policy dispute about whether to elevate the rail tracks that passed Taipei City above street level or move them underground, as a way to eliminate the many level crossings for good.

After years of debate, those advocating elevating the railroads that passed Taipei gained the upper hand. So government authorities finally decided in January 1969 to have the rail tracks crossing Taipei City elevated.

But another thorny problem emerged: Who should foot the bill, Taipei City or the government of then Taiwan province? Neither party was willing to pay an estimated NT$1.3 billion (The Taiwan dollar-US dollar exchange rate was 40 to 1 then) amid elevating costs. Failing to raise the necessary funds, the railway elevation project was shelved indefinitely. (Note: Years later these level crossings were eventually eliminated as the two main railroads passing the city were moved underground under two separate development projects).

My assignment as a transportation news reporter at the China Times lasted for only about five months from July to November 1969, according to my clippings. During this short period, I twice interviewed then Communications Minister Sun Yun-suan, a rising political star. In one such interview, I asked about the feasibility of his plans to levy a slew of vehicle-related taxes to raise funds to support the expansion of highways and other infrastructural systems.

In the other interview, I talked with the minister about his new plan to launch an annual one-month, island-wide campaign to improve road safety. I asked why he believed that such a yearly event could help reduce Taiwan's high traffic accidents without becoming a formality in the end. At the time Taiwan registered an average of five traffic-related deaths each day. The high traffic fatality rate provoked growing public calls for the government to take effective measures to improve the situation.

(Note: My second interview with Minister Sun was conducted in the middle of August 1996, about two months or so before he was transferred to the Ministry of Economic Affairs to preside over Taiwan's industrial and economic developments. He headed the Economics Ministry for the next 10 years until he was named as premier in 1978 by then President Chiang Ching-kuo. Sun Yun-suan was widely credited to be one of the architects of Taiwan's "economic miracle.")

In late November of 1969, I was removed from the transportation beat, five months after I was assigned to cover that news territory. There is a saying "everything happens for a reason." But to this day I am still not sure for what reason I was taken off the transportation beat. Traditionally, as discussed previously, there were two ways to evaluate how well a reporter did his or her job. One was to see if the reporter was diligent in covering and reporting the events happening in his or her designated news territory, without missing anything significant. That was not a problem for me, I dare say. As I recall, I always worked hard trying to improve my performance. Also, I was always willing to spend time keeping track of all events taking place on my beat.

The other broad way to assess a reporter's performance was to examine the special stories he or she did in a given period, in terms of quantity and quality. Since quality is a highly subjective matter, I will avoid touching on it here. Instead, I will talk about the quantity aspect. According to my China Times clippings, I wrote at least 15 special articles--long and short--that bore my name during the five months in which I covered transportation news.

'A Hero Has No Chance of Using His Might'

That figure might not be impressive. But if you took into account the circumstances in which newspapers operated in those days, you may find why I did not write many more bylined stories. During my time working for the China Times, newspapers in Taiwan could only publish a maximum of 12 pages a day under martial law. Such a page number limit posed serious constraints on newspaper editors. With limited space, they had to be highly selective about which news articles would be published and which would be left out of the newspaper's next day edition. As a rule of thumb, the editors always gave priority to the printing of the latest news, often at the expense of bylined stories or stories of less urgency. There was nothing wrong with this policy, but the problem was that oftentimes a reporter worked hard to produce a special story, only to find it squeezed out at the editor's desk.

Limited editorial space aside, there was another factor that placed a check on how many bylined stories a reporter could write and get published in a month. Here is a brief description of what that check was: During my days working for the China Times, reporters were also paid for any bylined stories they wrote. The original meaning of such byline-based payments was to encourage reporters to work harder by doing more research and writing more special or exclusive stories. But gradually they were seen by reporters as a kind of supplement to their income or monthly salaries.

But the reality was that the China Times, constrained by the limited number of pages, like every other Taiwan newspaper, could not provide space sufficient to publish as many special stories as turned in by their reporters. This being the case, if some wrote an unusually high number of special stories in a month it would inevitably reduce the opportunities for others. To ensure fairness, editors thus enforced an unspoken quota system, quietly regulating how many bylined articles could be written and used each month by a reporter.

While the competition for editorial space in the newsroom was a media industry-wide problem, it appeared to be especially keen at the China Times. This was so because the China Times, as one of the two largest newspapers in Taiwan at the time, alongside the United Daily News, hired a particularly large number of reporters totaling well over 40. This meant that for each page there were about four reporters working on it.

This reporter-page ratio was even higher if the pages devoted to the printing of advertisements were excluded. What hurt most was that such limited availability of space worked to curtail opportunities for reporters to gather and write more news stories, even if they were eager to do so. As I was writing this chapter, I happened to have a chance for a casual chat with a veteran China Times journalist, who rose through the ranks of the newspaper to become president. Mr. Lin Sheng-fen used an old Chinese saying to illustrate the restraining effect the disproportionately high reporter-page ratio had on the reporters: "A hero has no chance of using his might." I have no idea of whether my frequent beat transfers had anything to do with the above-stated phenomenon of "competition for editorial space."

From my clippings, I also found that beginning from December 1969, I was covering a new subject area-- the Control Yuan. This indicated that by now I had experienced job transfers three times since I joined the newspaper a year earlier. At the start, I was assigned to cover foreign affairs and then transportation news.

The Control Yuan was a part of the parliament of the ROC government system during those times. The Control Yuan has a role in some ways like U.S. Congressional oversight of the executive branch and its numerous subordinate agencies. Essentially, it exercised the following powers: impeachment, censure, audit, and corrective measures.

So when I was reassigned to cover the Control Yuan, it also meant I was transferred to a job of collecting parliamentary news. In Taiwan in those days, as in many places elsewhere, politics was the most prestigious news beat which was usually assigned to reporters with more experience. Examined from this angle, my latest beat transfer was a positive change for me. It might signal that my performances in the previous two news territories were favorably evaluated by my bosses.

But the problem was that the Control Yuan, whose high-profile business was its two-month, annual year-end plenary session held to review policies and performances of the Cabinet and its subordinate ministries and departments, normally produced little news. From time to time I was also assigned to cover lawmaking events whenever my boss Chang Pyng-feng was otherwise engaged. Mr. Chang was promoted to city editor and editor-in-chief many years later.

On the Control Yuan beat, the first feature story I wrote was a close look at the woes plaguing Taiwan's lagging agricultural sector- -a result of long years of the government focusing on pursuing high growth in industry and exports. This story was based mainly on reports made by members of the Control Yuan's agricultural policy and development committee. These Control members had just wrapped up their annual inspection of local governments and farm businesses. They used the opportunity of the watchdog body's year- end review meetings to share what they had found in their latest field investigation.

Chief among the woes was a chronic outflow of youths to the industrial districts and urban areas, lured by higher pay. Such continued manpower outflow resulted in severe labor shortages in the agricultural economy. During the harvest workers were even harder to come by, no matter how much you were willing to pay them.

Another major difficulty faced by the farmers was that, as labor and fertilizer costs kept increasing, they were unable to reflect such increases in the sale of their own products because of restrictive government regulations in place to ensure the stability of food prices.

The net consequences of the above-cited difficulties were such: Running farm businesses had become unprofitable. The problem of unprofitability, combined with longstanding severe labor shortages, forced many farmers to let their land lie fallow. In their reports, the Control Yuan members urged the government to take effective measures to aid farmers, reviving a declining agricultural sector.

Among the other features which I wrote during my time covering the Control Yuan was a piece exposing how ineffective the country's highest watchdog body itself was in handling complaints and grievances made by ordinary people.

According to a central government law, the people in the country "are empowered to initiate proceedings against public functionaries by filing a written complaint with the Control Yuan." Upon receiving a complaint, Control Yuan members on duty would then have to discuss how to handle the case, launch an investigation into it, or refer it to the government agency concerned for their reference, for example.

The Control Yuan, however, was often blamed for being slow to handle citizen complaints. The watchdog body received close to 20 complaints a day on average. While some of these cases were handled promptly, a lot more were addressed with long delays. Worse, there were also situations in which complainants never received any responses long after they had submitted their cases.

This latter situation meant that the complaints made by some people of economic or political injustice were never investigated and, hence, their grievances were never arbitrated. Overall, the way the Control Yuan handled people's grievances was criticized as highly ineffective. In some specific cases, members were even charged with dereliction of duty. Political analysts attributed the ineffectiveness of the Control Yuan to a number of factors.

One was that most Control Yuan members were not all that enthusiastic about handling public complaints due to a lack of energy and political incentives. Most members were elected on the Chinese mainland more than 20 years earlier or before the Nationalist government retreated to Taiwan in 1949. This suggested that the majority of the members were now in their late 60s or early 70s, meaning they were no longer as active. Politically, these politicians faced no reelection pressure, in those parliamentary organs protected under martial law at the time were not subject to reelection.

Another factor was that Control members lacked the backing of capable research and administrative aides in performing their watchdog duties. I learned from my sources that while the Control Yuan had a total of 29 members, there were fewer than 20 experienced staffers who could assist them in conducting investigations.

This was unlike in the U.S. Congress where senators and representatives have a big army of assistants helping them gather information, do research, and look into cases. Data show that a senator's staff may range in size from fewer than 20 to more than 60, while a representative can have 18 full-time and four part-time staffers.

A lack of a powerful internal ethics committee was blamed as the third factor for the Control Yuan's ineffectiveness in handling public complaints. Even some of the body's own members admitted that the Control Yuan needed to enact a set of stricter rules to regulate fellow members' behavior. The existing Control ethics committee, they said, "must be empowered to take action against any members who repeatedly failed to attend meetings without a convincing reason, or investigate complaints in a timely and effective manner."

Destiny Intervenes

Something unexpected happened, just as I was working to consolidate my journalistic position in the China Times by working harder and honing my Chinese writing skills. On a Sunday evening in the early summer of 1970, Louis Chiou, a former China Post colleague and a close friend of mine, came to my home for a drink. After a few glasses of beer, Mr. Chiou stunned me by informing me that China Post Publisher Nancy Yu-Huang, my previous employer, was trying to get me back to work for her.

"Are you kidding?" I asked. "No, I'm not kidding you. It's true," Mr. Chiou replied, explaining that he came to my home this time "not entirely for drinks." "The main purpose of my coming to see you today is to convey to you as a messenger Nancy's attempt to invite you to rejoin the China Post." After expressing my surprise, I then asked him "What do you think prompted Nancy to come up with the idea of asking me to return to the China Post?" Before Mr. Chiou answered my question, I went on to say, "Listen, I have left the Post to work for a Chinese-language newspaper China Times for nearly one and a half years. During this period, I never had any chance to write anything in English. This is to say that I would not be very helpful to the Post even if I agreed to come back to work for the paper."

I will rephrase what Mr. Chiou said in reply to my question as follows: "Although you left the China Post well over a year ago, Nancy (the publisher) never forgot you. She kept her eye on how you were doing at the China Times. Whenever Nancy opened the Times and found your bylined story, she would take time out to read it through. From your writing, she realized that you covered a wide range of topics. And all the things you reported in your articles were, in general terms, newsworthy, interesting, and relevant. This reinforced her belief in you as a diligent reporter with good news sense. So she thought if the news gathering and reporting experiences you acquired at the China Times could be put to use for her paper by hiring you back, it would be greatly helpful in strengthening the capability of the Post's news collecting team."

Although astonishing, Nancy's intention to get me back to the China Post did not come as a complete surprise to me. In the more than one-year since I resigned from the Post, we had chances from time to time to see each other at public events, where we attended as representatives of our media organizations. On such occasions, she would always take the initiative to greet me and chat with me, giving me the impression that she had put behind whatever hard feelings caused by my resignation from the China Post.

At one high-profile reception held in honor of a senior U.S. diplomat working with the American Embassy in Taipei, while other attendees were exchanging greetings and views, she took me to a corner of the reception hall to update me on changes the China Post had carried out while I was away. The gist of what she told me was that the Post was doing quite well lately in terms of both circulation and advertising revenues. Therefore, she said she now was better able and more willing to invest in the operations of the Post's newsroom. By telling me all this, I speculated, she might be trying to use the promise of a better working environment to motivate me to come back to the Post to work for her.

Aside from explaining to me why Nancy Yu-Huang was trying to hire me back, Mr. Chiou, who by now was serving as deputy editor-in-chief and makeup editor at the China Post, also revealed to me that Nancy "has already expressed her intention of 'inviting you to rejoin us to China Times Chairman Yu Ji-zhong and asked his consent to release you."

When Louis left our home it was late in the evening. Yet despite hours of drinking and conversations, he came away with no promise from me to accept Nancy's go-back-to-the-Post invitation. However, the conversations we carried out that evening did prompt me to do some soul-searching in the subsequent few days.

The first thing that came to mind was that now I had to seriously consider which of the two languages, Chinese or English, I should choose as a permanent writing tool in pursuing my journalism career, so that I would have a better chance of success. If I chose the Chinese language, I'd better stay on with the China Times. But if I selected English, it would be better for me to return to the China Post.

In theory, it's better for me to choose Chinse because this is my mother tongue. But given the level at the time of my Chinese writing skills, there would still be some distance to go before I could become a professional writer in this language. On the other hand, if I chose English, which is a foreign language to me, the distance for me to cover could be even longer if I wanted to reach the level of a skilled English writer.

In short, I now needed to make a sensible choice between practicing Chinese-language or English-language journalism as a lifetime occupation before I decided whether to accept Nancy's invitation to return to the China Post.

Beyond the matter of language choice, I had to compare which of the two newspapers, the China Times or the China Post, provided a more favorable environment for its journalists to operate in. Having worked for the Post for three years before I came to join the Times more than a year earlier, I believed I was better able to make some real comparisons between the two.

The Times, as one of the few large privately-owned newspapers in Taiwan at the time, offered higher pay and better welfare for their employees. But it was not without its problems. The most damaging one was that its personnel management system failed to provide job stability for the paper's journalists. Office politics was a primary source of this problem. Take my personal experience, for example. I was transferred from job to job three times during my more than one year's employment with the paper. This was something quite uncommon. I cannot recall what really prompted my frequent job transfers. But I believe it had much to do with office politics. It's true that my third news beat--covering the parliamentary level Control Yuan--was viewed by some as a promotion of journalistic status for me in the paper. But the truth was that the Control Yuan at the time was, and still is, a low-profile political organization, which normally did not generate a high number of news events.

On the other hand, the China Post, although small, provided some unique advantages. One, its reporters could simultaneously cover several different subject areas. This provided opportunities for them to learn different things and broaden their knowledge. Two, since the Post reporters could cover multiple subject areas, they faced fewer difficult situations when they found no news to gather and write about. Reporters of the bigger newspapers, which strictly stuck to the beat reporting system, were not so lucky, however. It was because they could each cover only one single news line as assigned to them, except in particular circumstances.

But there was a major drawback to the China Post, as I discussed previously. Its newsroom mostly operated without a regular but much-needed rewrite process. This function was especially important for an English-language newspaper, like the China Post. Almost all of the paper's reporters were non-native English speakers; they did not have much English writing experience. Their copy in most cases needed to be heavily edited or even rewritten. Hence, the lack of a dedicated rewriting staff often resulted in their articles being inadequately handled or even discarded sometimes.

While this shortcoming deeply frustrated the reporters, the China Post still proved to be a good place for people who were interested in learning English and eager to improve their writing capabilities, provided of course you were willing to make the effort and with dogged perseverance.

After weighing the pros and cons of each of the two newspapers, I found it was still hard for me to reach a conclusion as to whether I should stay with the China Times or return to the China Post in response to Nancy's invitation.

Events, however, took a new turn a week after Mr. Chiou of the China Post came to visit me at my home. In a subsequent evening as I was writing a news story at my desk, my immediate boss, Mr. Chang Pyng-feng, who invited me to the China Times, approached me saying quietly that the chairman, Yu Ji-zhong, wanted to see me.

As soon as I walked in, Mr. Yu gestured for me to sit down. The opening remark he made to me, as I now recall, was: "That woman repeatedly called me and tried to get you back to the China Post." The chairman was referring to Nancy. From that remark and his facial expressions, I noticed he got a little bit annoyed with Nancy. He then said to me: "So whether you will choose to stay with the Times or go back to the Post is up to you." "Nancy Yu-Huang told me she would offer you the position of city editor if you returned to work for her. But here I must tell you I cannot guarantee you anything if you decide to stay with the Times," he added.

Everything seemed to have been arranged in advance. Days after my meeting with Chairman Yu Ji-zhong, Mr. Chiou of the China Post came to my home again, this time with half a dozen bottles of Taiwan beer. After finishing the beers, together with some spirits, I finally agreed to come back to the Post. Did I make that decision under the influence of alcohol or strong lobbying or both? Even now I cannot tell which was which.

But I do remember one thing for sure: My enduring passion for English journalism and English writing played a significant role in my choosing to rejoin the China Post. That passion has since never faded in me. I would say it was a major driving force in my journalism and writing career, one that spans some six decades. During these long years, I also worked for several other news organizations beyond the China Post and the China Times. My inter-media transfers involved me performing various journalistic roles from covering news to directing news operations, and writing newspaper editorials. After retiring from active journalistic duties in my mid-70s, I branched out into a new field--writing books also in English.

On reflection nowadays, I found my return to the China Post was a decisive turning point in my career. Because of my return to the Post, I was able to get more opportunities to practice English journalism, build my capabilities in this field, and become what I am today. In this I advanced—from a cub reporter to become a career journalist and writer.

Conversely, if I had continued to work for the China Times, were there opportunities for me to carve out a significant career in the Chinese-language media even if I spent the same length of time as I did practicing English journalism? I don't know. No one placed in my situation could. Perhaps that's why Mr. Yu Ji-zhong said to me "…However if you choose to stay with the China Times, I cannot guarantee you anything."

Here I remember someone saying: "I believe there is some force guiding us -- call it God, destiny, or fate." But I myself feel that even though there is an invisible force showing you the path of your life, the key to success is still in your hands. That is, you must be willing to make the effort, take the risks, and have the willpower to overcome whatever difficulties along the way. Believing everything is predetermined by destiny or fate will never help you achieve your goals and realize your dreams.

I left the China Times in late February or early March of 1970, about 15 months after I came to join the paper. On the eve of my departure, I went to the chairman's office to say goodbye to him and thank him for giving me the opportunity to work at his newspaper and acquire valuable experience in the practicing of journalism. At the end of our conversation this time, he generously rewarded me with an extra month of salary. I now have no idea of how much that extra payment was. But I do remember it was enough to help me purchase our home's first TV set, a black and white version. This was a luxury household appliance during those days.

My second stint at the China Post also lasted for about three years, as did my first employment with the paper. During most of the second period, I, as city editor, successfully carried out some major reforms with the support of Publisher Nancy Yu-Huang. But after her husband Chairman Y. P. Huang took over control of the editorial department more than one year later, I soon had clashes with him over management and editorial policy, leading me to ask for a transfer to a writing job. A detailed account of how I performed in the China Post this time will be given in chapter 6.

Chapter 6
My Second China Post Stint

Attending a press conference given by former U.N. Secretary-General U Thant at Taiwan's Songshan Airport. The senior U.N. official was transiting to Japan to visit Expo '70. Standing right behind him is this writer.

Appointed City Editor

In the early summer of 1970, I went back to work for the China Post at the invitation of the publisher after being away for well over one year. The duties and responsibilities I assumed this time were significantly different from that of my first employment with the English-language newspaper.

The first one lasted for three years beginning in January 1966. During that period, I started as a journalism beginner. I executed a variety of non-reporting jobs, including clipping and filing newspaper articles. Then as time went by and I proved myself capable of doing reporting work independently, I was transferred to the job of gathering and writing news. (Note, the details of what work I did in my first tenure at the Post and how well I performed them have been discussed in Chapter 4: 'Starting an English Journalism Career at 33').

Below I will recount what roles I played and what accomplishments I achieved during my second stint in the China Post. Not so long after my coming back, Nancy, the publisher, named me as city editor. This meant I now was responsible for directing a news-gathering team--one which was not so big. It was very small compared with that of the Chinese-language China Times, where I had spent the previous 15 months as a full-time reporter.

Although small in scale, the mission of the Post's news-gathering team was basically the same as the one at the Times: to report and explain the news. The only difference between the two lies in the targeting of readers. The China Post focused on English reading audiences, while the China Times aimed mainly at Chinese-speaking readers.

In launching the China Post in the early 1950s, Mr. and Mrs. Huang, the co-founders, laid out the Post's marketing strategy based on that readership difference. Specifically, they wanted the Post to reach the then large numbers of Americans and other foreign nationals residing in Taiwan, as well as those native Chinese who liked to read news in English for one reason or another.

In essence, Mr. and Mrs. Huang wanted the Post to play the role of bridging the language gap between the local society and the foreign community here in Taiwan. To fulfill this mission, the city desk of the Post always concentrated its efforts on getting local news that was of interest to its expatriate readers.

To enrich its local news content, the Post sometimes also used articles taken from Chinese-language newspapers, after being checked for accuracy, updated, or significantly expanded. The unique foreign audience-oriented nature of the Post made it possible for this newspaper to follow that practice without undermining the interests of either side or posing competition concerns for each other.

Owing to its focused coverage and the advantage of drawing on information from the Chinese-language news media, the Post was able to maintain a relatively small number of staff reporters, usually at around half a dozen, without affecting its ability to deliver accurate and timely news information to its readers. One related thing deserving mention here was that newspapers at the time did not print as many pages as nowadays, because the government then imposed strict controls on the size of the print media under martial law. This meant that the demand for news-gathering manpower, in general, was smaller.

After taking over the China Post city desk, I steadfastly stuck to the above-cited founding principles. As city editor, I regularly performed a range of tasks. Chief among them was to coordinate the effort of reporters, give them special assignments and read the articles they turned in. I sometimes also checked the edited copies when the issues discussed were controversial or politically sensitive, for instance.

Among the other tasks, I regularly undertook were developing story ideas, monitoring information on breaking news, and seeing which news went on to which page and that related news were printed alongside each other so as to gain greater reporting effect. Regarding this latter job, I would always go to consult the foreign news page editor whenever wire service reports were involved.

An example of this was the treatment of the news about the Republic of China's loss in late 1971 of its China seat in the United Nations to the People's Republic of China. On October 25 that year, the United Nations General Assembly passed a resolution to seat the PRC as the sole legitimate representative of China, while at the same time expelling the ROC from the world body (Note: The resolution was passed by a roll-call votes of 76 to 35. It came after a string of such pro-Beijing vote were defeated at the annual plenary sessions of the General Assembly.)

The ROC's forced withdrawal from the United Nations was a devastating blow to Taiwan and was, without question, a big event for the Taiwan print media. The China Post printed four articles relating to the results of the U.N. vote on its front page the following day, all given prominent places.

One was a piece quoting the remarks made by ROC chief delegate to the U.N., Ambassador Liu Chieh. The ambassador and his fellow mission members angrily walked out of an ongoing General Assembly meeting. The delegation did so after seeing two American-sponsored motions, all intended to defend Taipei's representation right, were successively defeated in a series of votes, and Beijing's admission became apparent.

"In view of the frenzy and irrational manner that has been exhibited in this hall, the delegation of the Republic of China has now decided not to take part in any further proceedings of this General Assembly," said Ambassador Liu. He continued, "The ideals upon which the United Nations was founded had been betrayed…It has become a circus, no longer a dignified, rational body for peace."

Next to the article on Ambassador Liu's remarks were three separate wire service stories reporting the reactions of the U.S., the ROC's most important ally, to the results of the October 25 U.N. vote on the China representation right. One of them was entitled "Rogers Stresses ROC Ties." In it, Secretary of State William P. Rogers said the "expulsion of Nationalist China (the ROC) from the United Nations was a regrettable act that could adversely affect the future of the world body."

Rogers was further quoted as saying "The Nixon administration will however respect the majority decision of the United Nations in expelling the Taiwan government…However, Nationalist China will continue to be a respected member of the international community and the ties between us are unaffected by its expulsion from the U.N."

On the top, left-hand side of the same page was a third news story with the headline "Senate Wants Cut in Aid and U.N. Funds." The story said "The expulsion of Nationalist China from the United Nations, branded an 'embarrassing, humiliating' setback for the United States, produced angry demands in the Senate for retaliation against foreign aid clients and a cutback in U.S. payment to the U.N."

According to the same story, Senator William Saxbe, Republican-Ohio, was forced to "return a 3.2 billion dollar aid authorization bill to the Senate foreign relations committee until tempers cool." He warned that "if a vote on the measure comes now, emotions aroused by the defeat of Taiwan would beat the legislation."

A fourth related article carrying U.S. reactions to Taiwan's expulsion from the U.N. contained a call for the United States to strengthen patrols of the Taiwan Strait. The article reported: "Yuan-li Wu, former U.S. assistant secretary of defense, told Congress the United States should increase its 7th Fleet patrols to enhance the credibility to renewed pledges to honor its mutual security treaty with the Republic of China....Wu said this kind of action was needed because there were doubts in Asia about U.S. adherence to its treaty commitments in view of shifting U.S. national interests toward mainland China, with which the Nixon administration was trying to establish a dialogue."

(Note 1. The ROC and the U.S. at the time had maintained mutual defense as well as diplomatic relations. Such links continued until 1979 when the Carter administration switched political recognition from Taipei to Beijing. Yet while the U.S. shifted diplomatic recognition to the PRC, it actually never really abandoned Taiwan. The U.S. has continued to maintain strong unofficial relations with Taipei under a domestic law -- the Taiwan Relations Act. Note 2.: To write this chapter recounting my second tenure in the China Post, I went to Taipei's National Central Library spending a whole day there looking at some old editions of the newspaper. By doing so, I hoped to obtain some information and signs that would show what my news-gathering team and I covered and reported for the Post then. Yet the library no longer kept print editions of the Post from those old days. There are only e-editions available. I randomly scanned through the e-editions for the period from 1970 to 1972 and photocopied with authorization dozens of articles appearing in them. The account given above of how the Post treated the news about the ROC's loss of its U.N. seat, and how the U.S. responded to that event was based on four such e-articles. The remaining e-news stories covered a wide variety of other subjects. They provide a basis on which the rest of this chapter is written.)

Reporting on ROC Reactions to U.N. Seat Loss

Inevitably, the loss of the Chinese representation right in the United Nations was to have far-reaching implications for the ROC's foreign relations. Such implications, I believed, would certainly spur the country on to examine what changes needed to be done to ensure that the ROC could do without the U.N. seat from here on. So in the immediate aftermath of the U.N. debacle, I placed greater emphasis on coverage of reform calls and actions likely to be made by the government and the private sector.

As expected, a wave of public calls erupted throughout Taiwan for the government to launch wide-ranging reforms needed to build national strength from within. Specifically, the aim of such proposed reforms was to achieve self-reliance amid potentially growing diplomatic isolation, likely to result from the loss of the U.N. membership.

The public demands for change got quick responses from government authorities, according to my photocopied China Post articles. The Post printed at least three series of articles reporting government responses in the next two weeks following the ROC's October 25, 1971, U.N. defeat.

The first such article carried an announcement made by the secretary general of the ruling Kuomintang Chang Pao-shu. He announced at a monthly Dr. Sun Yat-sen memorial meeting held in Taipei City Hall that the "government will soon take steps to reform central parliamentary institutions." The institutions Chang referred to were the National Assembly, the Legislative Yuan, and the Control Yuan then. They were often collectively called the parliament of the Republic of China.

At the same Taipei City Hall meeting, Secretary General Chang also declared that the KMT-led government was going to work out concrete measures to help improve governing efficiency by inviting "talented young people into government service."

The second of the three series of articles came in the form of two separate interviews which first appeared in the Chinese-language China Times and United Daily News. We picked the key points in each of the two interviews and translated them into English for publication in our newspaper. In both cases, we gave credit to the original interviewers.

In the China Times interview, Dr. Ku Cheng-kang, vice chairman of the Constitution Research Council, made the following remarks: "Two years ago, the President [Chiang Kai-shek] authorized by the National assembly proclaimed a set of measures to carry out partial parliamentary elections. But there were two deficiencies in this policy: 1. The number of new parliamentarians (referring to those selected under partial parliamentary elections) was too limited, only 27 in all. This represented only one-seventieth of the total members of the National Assembly, Legislative yuan, and Control Yuan. 2. The term of such newly elected parliamentarians was not clearly defined. This fails to meet the general metabolic purpose of the parliamentary bodies. Separately, the National Assembly will adopt new rules at its fifth plenary meeting next year to ensure that the younger generation will have opportunities to take part in government at the central level."

A third article on the ROC's public and private reactions, which we printed in the immediate wake of its forced U.N. withdrawal, carried testimony made by then Foreign Minister S.K. Chow. He told lawmakers "In the future, the Republic of China will promote foreign relations in closer coordination with the country's efforts at developing international trade and economic cooperation." Minister Chow was testifying before a closed-door meeting called by a legislative foreign affairs committee. This was the first time Minister Chow appeared before the legislature since the ROC pulled out of the United Nations about two weeks earlier.

In this China Post article, we also quoted a legislator who attended the legislative committee meeting as echoing Minister Chow's views. The unnamed lawmaker told the China Post that "foreign relations indeed needed to be promoted with the backing of Taiwan's economic strength." It is worth noting that by this time the ROC had already become a leading player in world trade and a major economic aid giver, with aid receivers in many parts of the globe.

Minister Chow in his testimony also revealed that "future foreign policy priority would be given to promoting closer bilateral relations after losing the multilateral U.N. stage." "We will promote bilateral relations not just with our diplomatic allies but also with countries, with which we do not have formal ties," he said. In building better relations with non-diplomatic ties, he continued, "The government will do so by strengthening economic cooperation and trade exchanges." In this regard, Minister Chow reported that the Ministry of Economic Affairs and the agencies in charge of foreign aid and investment were going to play a leading role.

Wearing Two Hats--Covering News and Coordinating Teamwork

In my role as city editor, I myself also covered news as did the rest of my team members. I cannot exactly recall the names of all of the reporters working for the Post during my time as city editor. Those whom I do remember included Thomas Tu, Victor Pai, Su Yu-fen, Kenneth Liu, Yang Hsin-hsin, April Cao, and photographer Sherman Liu. In my memory, they all were wonderful people. The time during which we worked together was not long. But for me, having the privilege of gathering and reporting news alongside them as a team in those early years was a memorable experience in my journalistic career.

There were two reasons why I also went out to cover news, while I was supposed to supervise news-gathering operations: One was that

I believed my joining the reporters in collecting news could allow our team as a whole to carry out more coverage and interviews, thus maximizing our limited reporting staff.

The other reason was that I enjoyed news events and writing news stories myself. I felt doing more such work could train me to get sensible information and write fluent English. I believed this was the only way for me to achieve my goal of becoming a professional journalist and writer. So I always went out to cover or dig for news whenever time permitted me to do so. While I was eager to do coverage, I always reminded myself to avoid overstepping the beats of my colleagues.

In some cases when I decided to attend a certain press conference or to go somewhere to cover a particular news event, it was because either I was more suitable to do so, or because the relevant reporter was unavailable at the time.

An example of this is given below. On a summer weekend morning in 1970, I received a phone call from the Ministry of Foreign Affairs, informing me that then U.N. Secretary-General U Thant was slated to transit Taipei en route to Japan that afternoon. It was suggested that I send a reporter to Songshan International Airport to cover the transit visit of the U.N. secretary-general.

Unable to reach my colleague responsible for gathering diplomatic news, I instead rushed to the airport to cover the story. The top U.N. chief executive was on his way from Manila -- where he addressed an international meeting sponsored by the Press Foundation of Asia -- to Japan to visit Expo '70 in Osaka.

U Thant took a brief rest at Songshan airport, lasting for less than one hour. He did meet the local press at the VIP room, but he did not say anything worth reporting. Throughout the news conference, U Thant dodged questions showered on him.

His refusal to talk to the local reporters was understandable, however. During those days, the battle between rivals Taipei and Beijing for the right to represent China at the U.N. was becoming increasingly fierce. As the chief of the U.N. Secretariat, U Thant presumably did not want to offend either of the two parties by saying anything controversial or politically sensitive.

The event of U Thant's Taipei transit never came back to my mind until many years later when I was handed a file photo by an old media friend of mine. That photo showed U Thant sitting at a Taipei airport VIP room table drinking his coffee, as he faced a crowd of journalists from local media organizations. The reason that my friend gave me this old picture was that it showed me being filmed among the reporter crowd.

Attending a press conference without getting the leading speaker to say anything newsworthy was surely not a matter worth mentioning. But just the fact of being able to attend a media event to meet a U.N. secretary-general transiting Taipei at a diplomatically sensitive time indeed was something special.

From the dozens of news articles taken from the old China Post editions kept electronically in the National Central Library, as I said earlier, I found I covered a wide variety of subjects during the period from 1970 to 1972 in my capacity as city editor. They ranged from political events to health and fitness to human interest stories. One big political event I covered was the March 1972 presidential election of the Republic of China.

Covering Chiang Kai-shek's Reelection

It was not a very exciting presidential election, as I recall. For one thing, there was only one single candidate -- Chiang Kai-shek, the incumbent president. This meant that Chiang ran unopposed. There was no challenger from either within or outside the ruling KMT. Opposition parties were banned then under martial law.

No mass rallies were held by Chiang to solicit support either, as there was no need. At the time, the ROC president was elected indirectly by the National Assembly. The vast majority of the assemblymen were KMT members. They had the obligation to follow the order of the party, meaning that they had to support whoever was nominated by the party. (Note: The National Assembly was elected in mainland China shortly before it moved to Taiwan in 1949, along with the ROC government. In Taiwan, the delegates continued to exercise their duties of electing the president and amending the constitution, despite the fact that their voters were on the Chinese mainland. The assembly was later abolished in the middle of the 1990s. The abolition came after the nation changed its presidential election system from an electoral college vote to a direct popular vote).

The National Assembly, at the end of a two-week plenary session, unanimously re-elected Chiang Kai-shek to a fifth term of six years. He received all but eight of the 1,361 ballots cast. At the time Chiang was 84. Re-electing an 84-year-old political leader for six more years in office might be seen as unimaginable in present-day democratic Taiwan.

But Chiang Kai-shek's March 1972 re-election needs to be examined in the context of the ROC in those early difficult years, particularly in the immediate six months before Election Day. During this pre-election period, the ROC experienced two devastating political blows. First, the ROC was forced to withdraw from the United Nations in October 1971, as the U.N. General Assembly voted to admit Beijing, or the People's Republic of China, as the sole legitimate government of China.

The loss of the U.N. representation right to Beijing was bound to have far-reaching implications for the ROC's international relations in the years ahead. This is to say whoever was elected the next president would have to bear this responsibility. Namely, the next leader had to make sure that Taiwan's diplomatic, trade, and other bilateral relations with foreign countries would not be interrupted as a result of its loss of the U.N. representation right. Beijing without a doubt would do everything possible to tighten the isolation of Taiwan in the international community, using its newfound political power in the U.N.

The second fatal blow was dealt by President Richard Nixon of the United States, the ROC's most important diplomatic and military ally. Nixon in February 1972, one month ahead of Taiwan's presidential election, paid a visit to Beijing with the aim of normalizing relations with the communist government. Initially, Taiwan took Nixon's Beijing visit calmly. But at the end of the trip, Nixon signed a communique with Beijing in Shanghai. In the communique, the United States acknowledged Beijing's one-China policy and agreed to withdraw military installations from Taiwan. Nixon's concessions were made to obtain Beijing's consent to work toward the normalization of bilateral relations.

The Shanghai document shocked the ROC and its citizens in Taiwan and abroad. They worried that should the U.S. sever its ties with the ROC and pull out its military facilities in favor of exchanging diplomatic recognition with Beijing, it could weaken the security of Taiwan, enticing the PRC to invade this island.

Against such a background, Taiwan's immediate concern was, without doubt, to select a leader in the upcoming March 1972 presidential election who could lead the country through the new diplomatic and political difficulties. Note, the incumbent President Chiang Kai-shek had expressed his desire to step down after his fourth term expired the following May.

Truly, there were signs in recent years that Chiang was grooming his son Chiang Ching-kuo to be his successor by giving him opportunities to experience key government positions, including as defense minister and premier. But Chiang Ching-kuo, while capable, had yet to build up his prestige and influence to get the entire populace of the country to rally behind him and his policies. Most believed that the younger Chiang still needed time to build his leadership credibility.

The difficulty in selecting a replacement for Chiang Kai-shek was that the elder Chiang possessed many essential leadership qualities that could hardly be found simultaneously in other current ROC politicians: patriotism, unwavering dedication, longtime anti-communism experience and political prowess.

These qualities earned Chiang respect and support from the vast majority of the ROC citizens. They felt the ROC now needed Chiang Kai-shek's continued leadership more than at any previous time. This could be seen from the fact that letters and cables poured in from ROC citizens living in Taiwan and abroad months before the National Assembly held its March 1972 presidential election, calling for the Electoral College to reelect Chiang to a fifth term.

It was against such a backdrop that the more than 1,300 assemblymen attending the March 1972 plenary session--held at the Chungshan Building up in Mount Yangming in suburban Taipei-- unanimously elected Chiang Kai-shek to another six years in office.

The election result was announced an hour or so later by Paul Cardinal Yupin from the balcony of the downtown Taipei City Hall (near the present-day Ximen MRT Station), the official residence of the National Assembly. Tens of thousands of people had already gathered in front of the assembly building to hear the cardinal announce the news about Chiang's re-election.

The cardinal in his capacity as chairman of the presidium of the National Assembly made a brief but solemn statement after announcing Chiang Kai-shek's re-election. He said: "President Chiang is the prophet of anti-communism. He is not only our national savior but also a world-renowned great statesman...We want to hail him and pray for him. And we must wholeheartedly follow President Chiang for early recovery of the [Chinese] mainland."

Following Cardinal Yupin's remarks, the big crowd, mostly students and workers, split into columns parading through the streets of Taipei, some holding placards of Chiang's portraits and some with

ROC national flags. They were led by dragon and lion dance troupes and brass bands. At the end of their parading, the well-wishers converged on the presidential plaza to offer their congratulations to Chiang and shout slogans "Long Live President Chiang" and "Long Live the Republic of China."

I, from the China Post, covered and wrote the above news story about Chiang's reelection and the subsequent celebration activities. In addition, I also did an exclusive interview on the same day with Wang Yun-wu, a senior assemblyman who presided over the process of voting. In the interview, I asked Wang to analyze the significance of Chiang Kai-shek's reelection. Wang, a prominent scholar, told me that "Mr.

Standing beside Mr. Wang Yun-wu for this photo after I interviewed with the famous Chinese publisher and scholar for a story for the China Post.

Chiang Kai-shek is the most ideal choice at a time when this country is in need of a leader who can give constant inspiration to the people and maintain social and political stability."

Amid the recent series of adverse changes, Wang continued, "there inevitably were some people who began to worry and feel uncertain about the nation's future." But the assemblyman believed the "fear of uncertainty among the public was soon to be dispersed with President Chiang Kai-shek's reelection." The "adverse changes" that Wang referred to were the October 1971 U.N. General Assembly resolution to admit the PRC at the expense of the ROC, and the February 1972 Beijing visit by U.S. President Richard Nixon

(Note: Some extra explanation needs to be made here. The way Chiang Kai-shek's reelection was so enthusiastically greeted and hailed by the people undoubtedly reflected the high degree of respect and support that he commanded in this country. But it also suggested a kind of personality cult surrounding Chiang, a result of longtime authoritarian rule executed in the nation by him and his party, the Kuomintang).

Chiang Kai-shek gave an acceptance speech at the closing meeting of the National Assembly's plenary session on March 25, a few days after his re-election. "It is not without a deep sense of diffidence that I have ventured to answer your call. Instead of pointing out my failures, the National Assembly is continuing to trust me with the duty of suppressing the communist rebellion and accomplishing national recovery," he said.

Chiang pledged that "for the remainder of my life I shall endeavor to do my very best to extinguish the evil sources of Maoist treachery and violence internally, while externally endeavoring to ensure the welfare, peace, and justice in free Asia."

In his address, Chiang also denounced "international appeasers of the Chinese communists." "It is regrettable that some shortsighted and misguided people have mistaken wrong for right and have labeled black as white. They have evaluated the situation of strength or weakness on the basis of counting the number of people," Chiang said.

Interview with an 84-Year-Old Medical Doctor about Longevity

Aside from covering politics and other hard news, I from time to time also did some soft news, or human-interest stories. That was the case only when I had no urgent work to do. From among the articles which I photocopied at random from the e-editions of the China Post kept at the Central National Library, as cited earlier, I found a piece in which I interviewed an octogenarian medical doctor, James Oo-kek Khaw, asking him to discuss his secrets of maintaining health and longevity.

Although the interview was conducted more than half a century ago, the "three rules" that Dr. Khaw followed were helpful for him in maintaining good health. They remain relevant and inspiring. After all, how to live longer or what healthy behavior and attitudes increase lifespan have always been a subject of exploration since ancient times. So I condensed the text of that interview, dated September 3, 1970, into the following.

"Keep yourself occupied, do everything in moderation, and always be happy are the three rules that help maintain the good health of an octogenarian medical doctor. At 84, Dr. James Oo-kek Khaw still puts in a day's work that a young person might envy. He works seven hours a day and seven days a week..."

"He works so hard not for money but for following 'his first rule to keep himself fully occupied.' It was for this reason that Dr. Khaw joined the work of U.S. Naval Medical Research Unit-2 (NAMRU-2) two years ago following his retirement from the Chinese Army Medical Corps as a major general after 21 years of service..."

"His chief work at NAMRU-2 (a former U.S. research laboratory located in Taipei beside the National Taiwan University-affiliated Hospital) is with the study of Clonorchis sinensis, a liver fluke caused by eating raw or poorly cooked freshwater fish. The fluke is widespread and in chronic form may cause cancer of the liver.

Besides his work with NAMRU-2, Dr. Khaw has also been overseeing the operations of the Red Cross Society of China's blood bank as its director for the past more than 10 years. Perhaps because keeping occupied means never being at loss for time, Dr. Khaw is also an advisor to General Loo Chi-teh, director of the National Defense Medical Center (NDMC). In this latter position, he works on microbiology, pathology, and parasitology in the medical biomorphic department, of which he had been the director for over 20 years before he retired in 1968...

"It is just unbelievable that a man of over 80 can perform such a heavy daily workload that would be almost impossible for most young men...Believe it or not, this is what Dr. Khaw is working on." In the interview with the China Post, Dr. Khaw also described his typical work day as follows:

"He gets up at 6:30 a.m. He immediately takes a shower and then proceeds to play with his grandson. After all this, it's 8:30 a.m., time for breakfast. His food for breakfast usually includes a few slices of bread, a glass of milk, and a fried egg.

"When finishing his breakfast, it is 9:00 a.m., time for him to go to the office at NDMC, where he spends two hours usually assisting researchers and students in their studies.

"At 11:00 a.m. Dr. Khaw leaves NDMC for NAMRU-2 to begin five hours of research work there. He naps half an hour at his office after taking a light meal at the snack bar of NAMRU-2.

"If there is no social engagement on his schedule that day, he leaves NAMRU-2 around 5 p.m. for home...Dr. Khaw's typical evening is spent on reading newspapers and scientific magazines and watching TV programs before he retires at midnight for the day.

"Saturday and Sunday are no times of rest for Dr. Khaw. He goes to NDMC's laboratory to see those younger researchers doing their studies while keeping a ready helping hand...Giving a helping hand to anyone who needs it is the retired general's second rule -- and always be happy -- to promote longevity. You can be happy only by helping others.

"Dr. Khaw is a light eater. He believes that if a person wants to have a long life, he or she should always take food in moderation, never in excess. He does not drink except for a few social drinks. He likes to smoke a cigar after each meal but never more than one."

I never heard from Dr. Khaw again after I met him in September 1970 at NAMRU-2 for the above-cited interview. I expected him to live to the age of 100 and beyond, given the many healthy habits he lived by.

Interestingly, when I interviewed Dr. Khaw in 1970 I was 37 years old. In 2018, as I undertook this writing project and recalled my interview with him, I had reached 86. Like him, my working life far exceeded the usual retirement age of 65. When I did my life's last paid work (a one-year full-time job to do translation, from Chinese into English, for a China Times-affiliated newspaper's e-edition), I was 79. Now in my mid-80s, I am still working—this time writing my autobiography. So in some sense, I too have always been doing things to keep me "fully occupied."

Like Dr. Khaw, I get up around 6:30. After taking breakfast, I spend about one and a half hours reading well-written English news articles online. I do such a regular reading for two purposes. One is to keep me informed of current world affairs. The other is to observe how others write their articles. I did so in order to learn their writing skills, thereby improving my own.

Normally, around 9:30 a.m., I begin to do the writing. I would nap 20 to 30 minutes after taking lunch. I resume writing in the afternoon until 4:30 when I start to do my daily exercise. My workout is a combination of walking, jogging, and a steep 137 meters hill climb, lasting two hours and twenty minutes in total. During and after supper—usually around 7:30 p.m.—I watch TV news. Occasionally, I also watch some TV action films or programs featuring power struggles in ancient Chinese royal palaces, for example. I retire normally between 10 and 10: 30 p.m. for the day.

However, there was a striking dissimilarity between Dr. Khaw and me. Dr. Khaw "does not drink except for a few social drinks," but I drank regularly during most of my adult life. Sometimes I even drank heavily. This happened usually during late-night meals with my colleagues after work or when attending some special social occasions. I quit drinking only in my late 60s. I am not quite sure what adverse impact my long drinking history has had on my liver or my brain. Some research shows that alcohol use does hurt people's health in such ways. But to me, it seems that both my brain and my liver are still functioning OK, even though I am in my mid-80s.

I do not know what factors have helped me to live longer than the average person. But I did get some relevant information from some expert studies and will give it below: According to the United Nations World Population Prospects 2015 Revision, the average life expectancy at birth was 71.5 years over the period from 2010 to 2015, worldwide—68 years and 4 months for males and 72 years and 8 months for females.

A separate set of data compiled by the World Health Organization shows "There has been a 10-year rise in life expectancy over the past five decades, thanks to great advances in healthcare across the world."

In an article entitled "How you can increase your longevity," Dr. Mark Stibich said "genetics account for a maximum of 30 percent of your life expectancy. The rest comes from your behaviors, attitudes, environment, and a little luck." (Note: Dr. Stibich, who received his Ph.D. in health behavior from the Johns Hopkins University School of Public Health, is a longevity writer and a behavior change expert.)

My Coverage Policy as City Editor

To give an overall picture of what kinds of domestic news I preferred to use as China Post city editor (from 1970 to 1972), I will condense into the following a couple of items taken at random from the newspaper published during that period.

These condensed news pieces can suggest what domestic news we at the English-language China Post chose to gather or use then. Additionally, they could also reflect on how far Taiwan has progressed or how things have drastically changed during the past half a century -- politically, economically, and socially.

One news item concerned the visit to Taiwan by a high-profile former American defense secretary, Robert S. McNamara. When McNamara made the Taiwan visit in 1970, he had become president of the World Bank.

The World Bank's primary mission at the time was to work closely with the public and private sectors in developing countries to reduce poverty and build shared prosperity. For Taiwan, the World Bank provided a variety of loan programs, aimed at helping improve railroads, construct deep-sea fishing boats, upgrade vocational education and training, as well as a far-reaching family planning program.

McNamara on the trip showed particular interest in Taiwan's family planning program, which was also funded by several U.S. social and educational institutes. At the end of his three-day visit, McNamara told the local press that he was "very impressed" by Taiwan's successes in promoting family planning.

In the same week of the McNamara visit, the China Post also ran a separate but related news article, in which we quoted then Taiwan Provincial Health Commissioner Li Ti-yuan as calling for the reduction of the island's dependent population ratio.

By "dependent population," Commissioner Li meant the citizens being under the age of 15 and over 65. Based on this calculation, Commissioner Li estimated that every 100 working-age citizens in Taiwan at the time had to support 76 dependent persons.

To give some comparative figures, Li pointed out that the working age to dependent population ratio in the United States was 100 to 64 and 100 to 45 in Japan. "So ours is simply too high," Li said. He suggested that Taiwan needed to reduce its productive-dependent population ratio to 33 percent. By reducing the ratio to that level, he said, Taiwan's total population could "be expected to not exceed 20 million by 1990."

Commissioner Li warned, however, "If the ongoing family planning is not widely practiced in Taiwan, our plan to keep the total population from not exceeding 20 million by 1990 would become an unattainable goal." In the worst-case scenario, he added, the total number of people could even soar to 25 million by then. Should that be true, he said, it would add considerably to Taiwan's population density, already among the world's highest.

Family planning at the time was a topical issue in Taiwan and many other places in the region and beyond. Like elsewhere, this island faced fast population growth in the early decades after the end of the Second World War, averaging an annual rate of 3.84 percent. The universal fast population growth rate was attributed in large part to a post-war baby boom. For Taiwan, there was another significant contributing factor: A massive influx into Taiwan of military personnel and government workers in the late 1940s in the wake of the ROC government's loss of the Chinese mainland to communist rule.

The high population growth aroused grave concerns among Taiwan's policymakers and its international aid donors. They worried that the high birth rates, if not checked, could offset the gains of Taiwan's economic growth, impeding post-war reconstruction and long-range development plans.

After long years of public debate and promotion by activists, the first government-backed five-year family planning program was adopted for implementation, starting in the middle of the 1960s. So when Robert McNamara came to Taiwan in 1970 to learn the state of the island's family planning on behalf of the World Bank, he was just in time to see the completion of that pioneer program and what achievements it had attained since its implementation five years earlier.

The five-year program featured educating the public on the value of family planning and providing low-cost contraceptives universally to eligible couples to help them reduce fertility rates.

But initially, the adoption of the program met with strong resistance from society in general and the military in particular. Socially, it ran counter to a long Chinese tradition that was in favor of large families. The big family tradition, in specific terms, meant "the bigger the family you have the happier you are."

Militarily, a program promoting small families with fewer kids, could, as its opponents argued, lead to a dwindling number of young people available for military service over time. If the armed forces had difficulty enlisting the necessary numbers of troops, they warned, it could endanger their ability to achieve their assigned mission of "counterattacking and recapturing the communist-controlled Chinese mainland ultimately."

But public resistance never dampened private and government advocates' enthusiasm for promoting family planning. The government remained determined to bring a fundamental change from the traditional social norm of "The more children you have the happier you are" to a modern one of "Two children are just right."

It was such untiring efforts that finally influenced the Taiwan provincial government to adopt the first five-year family planning program, as mentioned previously. The program was incorporated into the government's economic development plan and implemented initially as a public health measure. Follow-up study and discussion led to the enactment by the central government of a population policy based on the family planning program. A central point of this policy was to reduce fertility rates among women of childbearing ages or eligible young couples.

Textile Quotas a Frequent Coverage Topic

Many people in present-day Taiwan might not have any idea of what textile and garment quotas are about. To put it simply, quotas were enforced in the post-World War II era by major industrially advanced countries, such as the United States and Canada, to restrict imports of textiles and garments from some developing economies, including Taiwan, as a means to protect their domestic businesses.

For Taiwan, textile and garment production and exports all were big economic events then. To the print media, they were almost a constant source of news. I recollect that I as city editor always watched for signs of any new development in the above-mentioned sectors. I paid particular attention to such news because the China Post as an English-language newspaper had an inherent duty to stress coverage of international trade and economic exchanges, the most important parts of Taiwan's foreign relations.

Saying that textile and clothing were a constant source of news was in part because quota-triggered controversies and tensions among manufacturers and traders never ceased. A main problem was that the import quota systems were subject to an annual review carried out through bilateral negotiations with the importing countries at the end of the year. The aim of such review and negotiations was to determine the volumes of textile quotas for the year ahead. Yet such trade talks were not always smooth. Sometimes they even broke down over serious differences, disputes which were always worth reporting.

Once the volumes of textile quotas for a new year were decided through talks with a certain importing country, the ROC government, more exactly the Board of Foreign Trade, would then move quickly to allocate them to domestic manufacturers and suppliers in accordance with their respective export performances registered in the past year. In some special cases, the textile quotas were also allocated through open tender. Such complicated allocating systems often gave rise to complaints among companies. Some were justifiable and some were not. Justifiable or not, the press media had an obligation to help the relevant companies get their voices heard.

The following two short China Post news reports, dated November 1971, can reflect some of the difficulties which Taiwan and its textile and garment manufacturers encountered at the time in exporting their products to the United States, the industry's largest overseas market. One of such reports was entitled "Disputes Delay Agreement with the U.S. on Textile Quotas." The text of this news report is given in part below:

"Agreement on the quotas of non-cotton textiles exported to the U.S. is not expected until the end of this month, H.K. Shao, deputy director of the Board of Foreign Trade, said yesterday upon his return from the United States. Shao had led a ROC delegation to Washington, D.C., a week earlier with the aim of negotiating a new bilateral quota agreement. He suggested that the ROC government would soon dispatch another mission to the U.S. to continue the negotiations. This time, he said the mission would be headed by his boss Wong Yi-ting, the BOFT director...

"Telling reporters at the airport, Deputy BOFT Director Shao explained that a new bilateral agreement got stuck in disputes over whether synthetic silk should be included in any renewed import controls. Shao said differences in setting an annual growth rate of the textile quotas also prevented the two sides from concluding a new trade pact sooner."

The other piece of the above-cited two China Post news articles was about how the BOFT allocated its newly negotiated U.S. textile and garment quotas to domestic manufacturers and traders. The text of that news item, with the title "Trade Board Announces Non-Cotton Quota Measures," is summarized below:

"The Board of Foreign Trade announced on November 19, 1971, measures governing the quota allotments of non-cotton textiles for exports to the U.S. The first-year quota will be 467,500,000 square yards. This consists of the basic quota of 425 million square yards and a 10 percent annual increase or 42.5 million square yards. The first-year allotment will also include 406 million square yards for the manufacturers who have qualified export performances, 25 million square yards for those who have no export performances, and 50 million square yards for allotment through competitive bidding...

"In the second agreement year, 25 percent of the quotas will be reserved for the following uses: About 76 square million yards or 15 percent of the total quotas will be allotted through competitive bidding in the first year. Another 10 percent of the quota will be allotted via competitive bidding in the second year."

Taiwan's early days' textile and apparel industry constantly drew media attention also because of its rapid capacity increase and sales expansion -- from domestic to overseas markets. Such fast capacity increase and market expansion made the textile industry a most important factor in Taiwan's achievement as an economic miracle in the early post-war decades.

The industry was rebuilt from the ruins of the Second World War. With the help of U.S. aid in the form of cotton, the government's tax incentives, as well as Taiwan's cheap labor, the industry quickly achieved self-sufficiency in yarn, synthetic fibers, cloth, and garments.

After satisfying Taiwan's domestic needs, the textile industry began developing exports, first to the U.S. and then to Canada and EU states. The expansion in overseas sales, however, was so successful that it prompted import restrictions in no time by those importing countries.

By late 1971 when we covered the BOFT's negotiations with the U.S. for the renewal of quotas to that country, the textile and garment businesses, along with consumer electronics, had become Taiwan's largest foreign exchange-earners. The textile and garment industry alone exported more than US$1.2 billion worth of products a year. Taiwan was badly in need of foreign exchange during those early years to fund imports of machinery, raw materials, and other essentials. (Note: Some of the data cited in the previous paragraphs was quoted from a paper by Lee-in Chen Choi Chiu, a fellow of Chung-Hua Institution for Economic Research. The paper is entitled "The Policy, Institution, and Market Factors in the Development of Taiwan's Textile and Garment Industry).

Trying to write events that took place half a century ago according to one's memory is not an easy task for anyone. I am no exception. It's hard for me now to recall exactly how I helped improve the quality of the China Post's domestic news pages as city editor during my second stint there in the early 1970s.

But I do remember one thing: I always followed the China Post's two long-established, informal rules on news gathering whether in my capacity as city editor or as a staff reporter.

Rule One: I always gave priority to gathering or selecting news events that suited the particular nature of the China Post--an English-language newspaper published in a non-English speaking, Chinese society. This unique nature meant that the Post inherently needed to assume a bridge-building role between its domestic and expatriate readers.

With that in mind, we always printed whatever international happenings might interest Taiwan's readers or that they needed to know, and domestic news of interest to the foreign community. Over time, this obligation developed into an instinct in me. For instance, I tended to take a particular interest in changes in Taiwan's international relations, be they diplomatic or trade, or cultural.

Rule Two: Never hesitate to use material already printed in Chinese-language publications, if their use could help enrich the content of our news pages. For us, using newsworthy Chinese media materials could also save us a great deal of time. The time so saved could allow us to concentrate our limited reporting manpower on doing exclusives or covering news best suiting our editorial needs.

While making it a policy to allow drawing on Chinese media information, we did set two strict requirements for doing so. One, before adopting any Chinese newspaper article, we had to check its facts and data for accuracy. In the process, trying to put in new information or more recent developments was a must. The other requirement was to never forget to give credit to the original author or media organization which he or she worked for.

Reforming Copy-Processing

In concrete terms, I carried out a long-desired reform in the newsroom's copy-processing system during my tenure as city editor. With the support of Publisher Nancy Yu-Huang, I hired two regular copy editors, and added a third after Mr. Joe Hung, the editor-in-chief, left to work for UPI (United Press International).

In the past, the Post had rarely hired a regular or full-time employee dedicated to editing and rewriting news stories. Insufficient rewriting staff, however, resulted in Mr. Hung having to handle all of the day's copy submitted by reporters.

Relying on any one person to handle such a heavy workload of news article editing and rewriting was not only unreasonable but also unrealistic. Yet unrealistic as it was, the problem had existed for a long time and had not been resolved yet. That was so even though the problem had long proved damaging to the quality of the paper. Several examples of the adverse effects are given below:

One, insufficient rewriting manpower often led to sacrificing copy requiring heavy editing or rewriting. These stories would have to be dropped because correcting them would demand extra time and effort. This in turn would increase the deadline pressure. But for the reporters involved, nothing could disappoint and hurt them more than having their articles abandoned, no matter what the reason was.

Two, oftentimes an article was published leaving some embarrassingly inaccurate figures and data uncorrected. Such mistakes could have been avoided, had there been a dedicated rewrite man or woman to act as a gatekeeper.

Additionally, a shortage of hands to rewrite news stories resulted sometimes in the failure to produce enough print-ready texts. This in turn caused a need to rely on the use of pictures to fill space. Adding to the problem was that many of the pictures should have never been used because they had no news value at all.

After listening to my analyses of the Post's rewrite staff shortage and its damaging effects, the publisher approved my proposal for increasing such manpower. As planned, I first hired two copy editors, one working in the afternoon, the other on the night shift.

The afternoon job virtually was a newly created one. Applicants had to be native English speakers with experience in writing and, also importantly, having a good command of Chinese.

The successful applicant was charged with two tasks. One was to translate into English the news articles or feature stories that I selected and clipped from the day's Chinese-language newspapers, morning or evening. In the process, I would always have these clipped articles checked and updated before they were passed on to the rewrite person. Beyond translating news articles cut from the Chinese-language media, the rewrite person was also responsible for correcting special reports turned in by our own reporters.

I can still remember the name of the person I first hired to do the afternoon rewriting job. Richard Johnston was an American citizen with a master's degree in economics. He worked for us for a year or so and then returned to the U.S. I had no word from Richard until many years later in the mid-1970s when I received a phone call from him. He told me he was in Taipei again, this time serving in Chase Manhattan Bank's Taipei office as vice president.

Chapter 6
My Second China Post Stint

The other copy editor working on the night shift was also a U.S. national. He did not understand Chinese, but his years of experience in news writing made him a good choice for the copy-editing job. He knew what data needed to be checked and what information needed to be added. And more importantly, he worked fast.

He was very helpful and cooperative. We both worked into the middle of the night, the time when everything was finished. I stayed so late to ensure that I would not miss any late-breaking domestic news. A third person in the newsroom who also worked late was Louis Chiou, the deputy editor-in-chief. He had to wait until the last minute when the page proofs went to the printer.

After finishing our work for the day, we three often went for a drink at a nearby roadside food stall (During those times there were few restaurants open around the clock) usually accompanied by a bowl of beef noodles. Peter, the night shift copy editor, worked for the Post for about a year before going back to the U.S. We have not seen each other since then. I feel ashamed that I cannot even remember the full name of this old colleague and friend.

I have no idea when Mr. Hung left the Post for UPI, but I do remember soon after his departure, a third copy editor, also a male and a native English speaker, was employed. He wrote English quite well, and this had to be the case because he was also charged with the responsibility to do final English checks with respect to the titles of all news pages before they were sent to the printer.

I was grateful to the publisher for authorizing me to carry out the copy-processing reform. Without her firm support and her willingness to make the investment, the change would never have been possible.

The investment paid off. After the addition of the copy editors, the newsroom's copy processing became smoother. No longer was there such a phenomenon that news stories were held up at the editor's desk without being used, just because there was not enough time or manpower to edit or rewrite them.

With the addition of new and experienced copy editors, furthermore, the chances of allowing news articles containing embarrassing incorrect data to go unchecked were greatly reduced.

A third benefit resulting from the reform of the copy processing system was that we no longer resorted to overly using photos to fill space, a longstanding problem caused by a short supply of ready-for-print copy.

In fact, we now sometimes turned out more print-ready stories than needed for the day. Hence, we often had to leave out some less pressing but newsworthy stories for use by editors working in the daytime. By this point, the number of the Post's local news pages had been expanded to include one on trade and economic affairs and one on entertainment and the arts. Daytime editors of these pages were happy to use those leftover articles because for them, story nature and copy quality were considerations more important than the factor of timing.

A Beat-based Reporting System Proposal Nixed

As discussed above, I successfully reformed the copy processing system of the Post's newsroom, and this was made possible with the support of the publisher. Nancy, however, turned down my proposal to adopt a near-beat reporting system. Although this latter reform idea was rejected, I feel it is still worth being recounted here.

At a previously arranged meeting at her office one day, I proposed that we needed to increase the depth of our newspaper's editorial content by establishing a beat-based reporting system. I explained to her why I saw such a need: "From time to time, I heard readers criticizing some of our news stories for being superficial, lacking in-depth research."

Although that criticism was not always true, I said, it did point to a potentially damaging weakness in our reporting. We had to pay serious attention to the criticism and take corrective measures. I went further to elaborate on what caused the superficial impression and what improvements needed to be made. My descriptions to her were roughly like this:

"We do not have enough people gathering news. The small numbers of reporters we now have are each required to cover a variety of subject areas simultaneously. This keeps them busy visiting their wide-ranging coverage areas and tracking routine news events. Such busy covering activities denied them time to conduct in-depth research into complex topics."

To reform, I suggested that the China Post "should hire and keep no less than half a dozen reporters each specializing in one particular field, while also responsible for doing general assignments. The "particular fields" which I identified ranged from the government to industry, science and technology, police affairs, entertainment and arts, and health and medicine.

High turnover of reporters, I continued, was another major factor contributing to readers' criticism of our news stories lacking depth. Our reporters generally worked for only one to three years before they left for work elsewhere or advanced studies abroad. The Post's consistently high turnover of reporters became common knowledge in the local media circles, earning it a reputation as an "advanced English training institute."

The high turnover rate meant the China Post faced a constant problem of being unable to keep its reporters working long enough to accumulate experience and specialized knowledge. As a result, the Post's reporters mostly were less experienced, making them less capable of covering complex subjects.

In order to help retain reporters, I also recommended that we raise the level of salaries for our news-gathering people. "The Post's reporters," I pointed out to her, "on average were making less than those working for the Chinese-language media."

"In fact," I reasoned, "our reporters should have been paid relatively higher if just for the extra time and efforts they had to make in writing news stories in English, a second language to them. After all, hiring a reporter with a good command of English was more difficult than hiring someone writing in the native language of Chinese."

The publisher's response to my proposal was candid and straightforward, fully reflecting her personality. She said, "Listen, Osman. With limited financial resources, we simply cannot afford to pay our reporters in a way that the Chinese-language newspapers do." As a non-native language daily, she went on to explain, "Both of our circulation and advertisement revenues were inevitably far smaller than theirs."

She also did not agree with me that a higher salary was an answer to reducing the reporter turnover of the Post. "From our past experience, salary is not the determining factor in a reporter's decision whether or not to keep working for us. What matters most to them are these other two things. One is whether they are willing to accept the difficult challenges faced in practicing journalism in English--not their mother language. The other thing is what they really pursue. If their interest is in pursuing academic or advanced studies abroad, then it would be impossible for us to retain them, no matter how well we are willing to pay them."

Surely, there was some truth in what she said to me, particularly on the latter point. My city editor George Chu and his predecessor George Tsai, for example, both departed the China Post to pursue advanced studies in the United States after working for the paper for a couple of years. Both of them obtained their PhDs and got university teaching jobs in that country, later on, never returning to work for the Post.

Since the publisher rejected my proposal for adopting a beat-based reporting system, I never raised that matter again in front of her. But that did not mean I agreed with her on all of the viewpoints she expressed. Take for instance the "limited financial resources" reason, which she gave for why the Post could not provide better pay for its reporters. I did not fully agree with her on that point.

Truly, there were inherent limitations on circulation and advertisement sales for an English-language daily operating in a non-

English speaking community. But I did believe there was some room for improvement in both areas if only the China Post were willing to change its long tradition of running the paper as a family business, in favor of adopting more modern managerial methods.

Needless to say I felt disappointed by the publisher's rejection of my beat-centric reporting proposal. But overall I was highly grateful to Nancy for allowing me a high degree of freedom in playing my role as city editor. In that role, I mostly reported to her directly. But this seemed to sound like I always bypassed the editor-in-chief. No, that was not the case.

It is fitting to give some explanation here. During most of my early time working for the Post, the editor-in-chief position was held by Mr. Hung. But Mr. Hung was rarely seen performing any managerial or administrative duties, as normally required of a newspaper's chief editor. He was mainly in charge of writing, rewriting, copy editing, and checking print-ready page headlines. That was so perhaps because Mr. Hung was highly skilled in those areas. But what was also true was that the China Post had in the past never hired an editor-in-chief with full powers. So my reporting directly to the publisher did not constitute a violation of work ethics rules at all.

Basically, the publisher adopted a hand-off approach toward my management. She rarely interfered with my work. I decided on my news-gathering policy on my own. She mostly respected my decision to hire or fire a reporter whom I saw unfit for the reporting job.

In general, I reported my work to her through either bilateral face-to-face discussions or regular editorial staff meetings, the latter of which were held twice a month -- if she was not traveling abroad at the time. She traveled overseas a lot, but not always for the Post's own business. She was active in attending international activities, such as the World Press meetings and the women's Zonta International conferences. Sometimes she also went abroad to promote Taiwan's foreign relations as a private citizen, drawing on her English knowledge and experience in international affairs.

Many outside the China Post described Nancy as "a strong woman." But within the newspaper, as I observed firsthand, she was also a demanding boss. She would not listen to you bragging about what you did or what you had achieved. She only wanted to be shown the facts or your actual performance.

Everything Begins to Change

In late 1971, the China Post saw a role swap in its top leadership, the first such role exchange since its 1952 founding. The move, which surprised everyone within the paper, was certain to have an impact on its policy and the way business was conducted.

With the change in leadership, Nancy moved to lead the business department, while her husband chairman Y.P. Huang came to take charge of the editorial department. The position exchange came about one and a half years after I returned from the China Times to work for the Post for the second time. I decided so at the invitation of the publisher.

A week or so before the leadership change was announced, the publisher ran over to the city desk asking me to come to her office where she broke the news to me. Barely after I sat down in front of her desk, the publisher opened the conversation, telling me that she "is going to hand over her task of overseeing the editorial operations to her husband the following week and that she would use the time left to take a rest." Yet just as I was wondering whether she would really be going "to take a rest," she quickly added, "I will be going to supervise the business department."

In that conversation, Nancy did not explain exactly why there would be such a role swap. Or why Mr. Huang wanted to leave his traditional role of running the business department and agreed instead to take over control of the editorial department, which was uncharted territory for him.

But she did reveal something unusual: "Mr. Huang had always worked backstage in the last two decades since the Post's founding…It can be said that he was a real behind-the-scenes hero of the Post." Now with the role change, she said, "Y.P. will have a chance to work frontstage, receiving more public attention."

In the past, Nancy was always the face of the China Post. To the outside world, Nancy and the China Post were one and the same. It was unknown whether or not this longstanding "one and the same" public image of the Post had played a part in their decision to exchange jobs.

During the face-to-face talks I had with Nancy, she also gave me a piece of advice on how to deal with Mr. Huang, my incoming immediate boss. "Osman, you must learn to get along with Mr. Huang. You need to change your past work style, just burying yourself in your job in the editorial department. As city editor, you must always report your work and ideas to him, keeping him informed on the latest events and letting him understand how you are going to handle them. Honestly, Mr. Huang is not a regular reader. So you must always keep him up to date on news events."

She continued, "There is another important thing I feel I should remind you about here: Be more flexible in dealing with different views or opinions. Do you want to know how Mr. Huang sees you? He told me one day that you sometimes 'are as stubborn as a mule.'"

I thanked Nancy for giving me the advice and for pointing to my weakness of being too "stubborn." I took her advice seriously and tried my best to overcome my perceived weakness, whenever I discussed news policy or news event coverage with the chairman. Yet no matter how hard I tried to adapt myself and accommodate Mr. Huang, I still had difficulty working with him. Feeling unable to surmount this difficulty, I finally decided to again quit the China Post, ending my second stint there.

Y.P.'s style of managing the editorial department was sharply different from Nancy's. As I personally observed and experienced, Mr. Huang often went against journalistic norms in running the editorial business. To cite three major examples:

First, Y.P., unlike Nancy who delegated authority to subordinates, concentrated power in his own hands. He gave instructions and assignments to reporters directly. Each day around 3 p.m., everyone, including me, gathered in his office either to report to him on the day's news events or answer his inquiries or take whatever assignments he would give.

At such meetings, Mr. Huang often also made these decisions: What news event was assigned top story, what news item went on to what page--front, back, or inside--and where a photo was to be placed. Additionally, he always designed page makeups. So virtually he acted as editor-in-chief, city editor, and page designer simultaneously, bypassing all those position holders.

Second, Mr. Huang liked to use photos to present news events, accompanied by brief descriptions. This again was a departure from the Post's past editorial tradition. Indeed, there were some noted news publications, like the American news magazine, Life, placing emphasis on the use of photos. But Life, which featured abundant colorful graphics and very brief news, concentrated on sports and celebrities.

In contrast, the China Post was a general interest English-language daily. But if you used an excessive number of photos, as was often the case, it tended to take up too much space at the expense of text. Written material was, and still is, essential and irreplaceable in presenting complex news subjects. The cliché "A picture is worth a thousand words" is applicable only in certain particular circumstances. Even worse, a lot of photos should have never been used, because their poor quality was unable to attract reader attention or convey any meaningful messages.

Third, Y.P. showed a reluctance to use politically sensitive news events. This again was unlike Nancy, who decided whether or not to publish a story only by news value, giving little consideration to the question of sensitivity. The example given below can say much about the reluctance of Y.P. to use news matters, which he viewed as politically sensitive.

In the close wake of the ROC's ousting from the United Nations in October 1971, public calls in Taiwan mounted for the government to carry out broad, deep reforms needed to cope with the adverse impact that the U.N. seat loss would have on this country.

The reforms called for ranged in topics from diplomacy to politics and economy. Some of these reform calls were already reported in the Chinese press. Inspired by such reports, I felt there was a need for us, as an English-language newspaper, to run a series of stories advocating wide-ranging reforms. The reason I proposed to do so was twofold. One was to reflect public reactions to Taiwan's expulsion from the U.N. The other was to express our endorsement of such reform calls by publishing them using our media platform.

But Mr. Huang responded to my proposal with just one brief sentence: "We need to be very cautious and careful in handling such political matters." Beyond that, he did not say anything else, like yes or no. Failing to obtain the green light from him, I thus was forced to drop my story ideas.

Yet what prompted me to feel particularly strongly about working with Mr. Huang was his practice of giving assignments and instructions to reporters directly. Such a management style effectively rendered my position as city editor meaningless. What's more, I also disagreed with him on the way he treated the news. I saw his practices as going against basic journalism norms.

But he was the boss and the investor who had the right to decide how the newspaper was run. So I had only two choices: One was to ask to be transferred to a writing job, eliminating the need for me to work directly under him. The other choice was to quit the China Post altogether.

Thankfully, Mr. Huang accepted my first request to transfer me from my city editor position to a job doing the writing. This was a great gain for me because my main interest was in writing. I believed that only keeping writing could help me to improve my writing skills. After all, my ultimate career goal was to become a professional journalist and English writer.

Previously, I described Mr. Huang's rejection of my proposals to do stories on public reform calls in the aftermath of the ROC's U.N. seat loss as his reluctance to print politically sensitive matters. Now I will cite a separate event, which was not directly related to my work relationship with Mr. Huang but can be cited here to support my above description.

The event in question concerned Mr. Huang's pick for my replacement after I was transferred to the writing position. I will withhold the name of my replacement because the focal point of my discussion here is the way Mr. Huang ran the editorial department. So for reasons of politeness, I will only identify my successor as Mr. A.

Mr. A's appointment at the city desk to replace me was a surprise to everyone at the Post. Mr. A was not chosen from among the people of the editorial department. Nor was he known to have any past journalism experience, like covering news. Mr. A, in a casual conversation, said to me he once authored a hit Chinese action series for Taiwan Television Enterprise. But he never mentioned he had any experience writing English news or doing any journalistic work.

Mr. A was transferred from the Post's business department, but he was not a salesperson either. I seldom visited the business department. But whenever I did, I saw him sitting on the left-hand side of Y.P., making him look like a special aide to the chairman.

Once I overheard someone say Mr. A had a military background and high-level contacts in the Taiwan Garrison Command. The Garrison Command was notorious for serving as a secret police organization with the authority to censor the media as well as try political offenders under martial law.

In those early days, the print media in Taiwan all practiced self-censorship in order to avoid breaking political restraints that could provoke prosecutions and even lead to imprisonment. Self-censorship aside, the media also needed someone like a political fixer to help solve problems in case you broke a certain rule.

Reportedly, it was this kind of background that convinced Mr. Huang to appoint Mr. A as city editor. So the appointment was politically motivated. The chairmen hoped that Mr. A could help him perform as a political gatekeeper. If this speculation was true, it could help prove my perception that Mr. Huang was unwilling to print things thought to be politically sensitive.

A New Job Opportunity Presents Itself

Not long after I took up the writing work, an invisible force or destiny intervened again. I was unexpectedly offered an opportunity by a Hong Kong-based, English-language trade magazine, Asian Sources, to cover industry and product news for the journal as its Taiwan correspondent. This unexpected turn was just like the case I discussed in the previous chapter. In that case, I attributed my going back to work for the China Post from the Chinese-language China Times to the play of destiny.

On a certain afternoon in mid to late 1972, I got a visit from an American I hadn't met before. He showed up in the Post newsroom enquiring as to who was Osman Tseng. I immediately raised my head and turned to him asking: "Is there anything I can do for you?" He quickly responded, "Sorry to disturb you, but can I talk to you for a moment?" I said yes, showing him to a nearby sofa. We had barely sat down before he introduced himself to me and explained the purpose of his coming to see me.

Joe Bendy, the visitor, was the editor of Asian Sources—a trade journal headquartered in Hong Kong with bureaus in neighboring places such as Taiwan, South Korea, and Japan. The journal, now better known as Global Sources, was a monthly publication to facilitate exports from the said areas mostly to the Western markets via editorial content and advertisements.

After introducing himself and his publication, Mr. Bendy said, "Mr. Tseng, I came here to invite you to work for us." To motivate me to accept his offer, he added "I can assure you that working with us will be able to broaden your vision on trade and economic knowledge."

I did not immediately take up his job offer until a day after when we met again. As appointed, I went to see him the following morning in a hotel on Lin Sen North Road in Taipei, where he was temporarily staying while traveling here. He first briefed me on what I was expected to do if I agreed to work for him and how I was going to be paid for the job done. Initially, he said, I could work part-time before I proved myself capable of doing and completing reporting assignments given to me each month.

At the end of the second meeting, I told Mr. Bendy that I was willing to work for him under the terms we both agreed on. I began to cover and report on Taiwan's industry and export products for Asian Sources. The Hong Kong trade media outlet grew and expanded fast. By mid-1975 when I left Asian Sources, the journal had been spun off into two separate monthlies, Hardware and Electronics. My workload and responsibility -- during the three-year period (from mid-1972) when I was working for Asian Sources -- increased too. In the beginning, I performed as Asian Sources' Taiwan correspondent and soon after as its Taiwan bureau chief, aided by two reporters who covered certain product lines.

During my three years of work for Asian Sources, I covered a wide range of export products from processed farm foods to handicrafts, garments and footwear, components and parts, and consumer electronics. This broad coverage responsibility gave me ample opportunity to witness much of Taiwan's post-World War II economic transformation from agricultural businesses to light industries, and its companies shifting sales to overseas markets after meeting domestic needs.

As Asian Sources' Taiwan correspondent, I learned a lot from my editor Mr. Bendy, as he gave me assignments, provided me with story ideas, and corrected my copy. Further details about my work for Asian Sources will be recounted in the following segment, Chapter 7.

Chapter 7
Hired as Asian Sources Taiwan Bureau Chief

Covering Trade and Export Products

In around May 1972, I was employed by Asian Sources, a Hong Kong-based trade journal, to cover Taiwan's export products as its resident correspondent. My agreement to accept the job came a day after Mr. Bendy, editor of the trade monthly, went to visit me at the China Post's editorial department. The editor in our brief conversations expressed his desire to get me to work for his magazine. Mr. Bendy and I had never met before. Until then we did not know each other. So his visit took me by surprise. Obviously, he learned my name and my occupation from a third party.

Yet since I was busy with my work at the time, we did not go into details about his idea of hiring me. But I agreed to go to see him and discuss the matter the following morning at his Lin Sen South Road, Taipei, hotel room, where the editor was staying during his current visit to the city.

As agreed, I went to his hotel to visit him the next day. Mr. Bendy first briefed me on the aim of Asian Sources, which he explained was to report on export products from Taiwan and several other places in the region for buyers in Western countries. He then told me what he would like me to do if I accepted his job offer. Mr. Bendy's descriptions of his magazine's nature and the tasks he expected me to do interested me. So I immediately agreed to work for him. Asian

Sources was a general-interest trade monthly then. It was headquartered in Hong Kong and operated sales offices and editorial bureaus in Taipei, Tokyo, and Seoul at the time.

Under an oral agreement reached with him, I would be paid on a "word count" basis, drawing no fixed salary. Specifically, I would be paid one New Taiwan dollar for each word used, not for every word I wrote and submitted. No formal contract for my service was signed. Nor did I demand one.

Yet despite the lack of a formal employment contract, we developed and maintained good working relationships: I did about six special report-type articles on Taiwan's export products each month initially. The articles were designated by the editor. I airmailed my finished assignments to his Hong Kong office always at the end of the month--the deadline.

Mr. Bendy, on the other hand, accepted and edited my reports. During my entire time working for Asian Sources, as I recount, I never experienced cases in which my articles were rejected, or I failed to get paid. All payments were made by check, which were delivered directly to my mailbox in the first week of every month.

My working relationships with Asian Sources came to an end three years later in the middle of 1975 when I quit. The reason for me to leave that job will be discussed toward the end of this chapter.

During the past more than four decades since my departure from Asian Sources, I have never gone back to exactly what industry products and trade activities I covered and wrote about for the publication. Neither do I have any idea of how that Hong Kong trade media has been faring since I left.

Recently as I began to write this chapter about my years working for Asian Sources, I had to turn to the Internet for any information that could help awaken the memory of my Asian Sources years--an important working period of my journalism career. I soon found, to my surprise, that the Hong Kong-located trade media had undergone extraordinarily rapid growth and expansion over the last few decades.

According to an online article posted by Asian Sources to celebrate its first 40 years from 1970 to 2010, the magazine has changed its name to Global Sources and become a public company with its stock listed on the NASDAQ exchange of the United States. But it still retains the Asian Sources brand.

To give a general idea of just how fast the Asian Sources company has expanded and how widely diversified it has become, I will quote a passage from the online article below: "Today Global Sources is a leading business-to-business media company and a primary facilitator of global trade, helping a community of 967,160 active buyers to source from complex overseas markets and enabling suppliers to sell to buyers in over 240 countries. Fourteen online marketplaces, 13 monthly magazines, over 80 sourcing research reports, and 17 specialized trade shows deliver information on 4.5 million products and 253,000 suppliers per year. In 2010, the company had a team of more than 3,000 people based in over 60 cities around the world."

From the above-cited data and figures, I understood the Asian Sources company had continued to play the role of bridging the gap between sellers in Asia and buyers from the West since its inception in 1970 and had attained incredible achievements in fulfilling its editorial aims.

Asian Sources was co-founded by Mr. Merle A. Hinrichs and Mr. C. Joseph Bendy in November of 1970 -- less than two years before I joined the magazine. I had the privilege of working under both of them. They both are American nationals. Mr. Hinrichs was a graduate of Thunderbird, previously called the American School of International Management. Mr. Bendy was an English literature graduate from Chicago. As I saw, the two had a clear division of labor between them, with Mr. Hinrichs heading the business department and Mr. Bendy in charge of editorial content.

In the 40th anniversary article, the two provided an answer to a self-posed question: "How could the trade media company accomplish what they had achieved today?" One major reason cited in the article was that the company "has grown and adapted in response to changing patterns of trade and world consumption in much the same way the countries in Asia have looked beyond their boundaries to identify markets and grow businesses."

But to me as someone who joined Asian Sources as its Taiwan correspondent at its inception, the trade media's spectacular success also had much to do with its clearly defined founding philosophy and its independent editorial policy.

The founding philosophy, as stated in the same article, was: "Advertisers would obtain the best response from well-prepared advertisements targeting a readership of specialized import merchandisers. In turn, these buyers would come to rely upon the magazine's content for their important buying and sourcing decisions."

Note: The bulk of the magazine's revenue at the time came from advertising sales.

Regarding editorial content, as I noticed, Mr. Bendy and Mr. Hinrichs from the very beginning attached great importance to the magazine maintaining editorial integrity and independence. To give an example, they "strictly avoided promoting a particular product or a trading personality on the front cover of Asian Sources."

From my own experience, as I recall, I had never been requested during my three years with the magazine by either my editor or my colleagues working in the business division to write anything promoting a particular company or its senior executives or their products. "Our editorial content would always present facts, analyze developments and anticipate trends." This was a guiding principle, that Mr. Bendy stressed to me, as he invited me to work for Asian Sources at the Taipei hotel and advised me on how to work on my assignments.

That guiding principle was a most important consideration when I agreed to cover business news for Asian Sources, a publication with the vast majority of its annual revenue coming from advertisement sales. As I now think back, had any of my Asian Sources bosses failed to abide by the avowed policy of maintaining editorial independence and allowed advertisement business interests to interfere in my coverage and reporting, it would have never been possible for me to work on that job as long as three years.

How I Cover Export Products and Write Reports

As Asian Sources' Taiwan correspondent, I covered export products and wrote reports on an assignment basis. Mr. Bendy, my Hong Kong editor, airmailed me six to seven assignments per month. As a rule, I always completed my assigned work and submitted the reports to him at the end of the month. By almost the same time, I would have received my new assignments, which Mr. Bendy wanted me to do for the following month.

For each assignment or product report, I was supposed to interview four manufacturers or more, depending on how well these interviews went. If I failed to get all the information I needed from the four manufacturers already interviewed, I would then go further to interview a fifth business executive. In this situation, I used to select an industry association official, instead of a manufacturer, to talk with. By doing so, I hoped that he or she could provide me with an overall picture of the export product, with regard to production, exports, supply of raw materials, prices, and wages.

To complete an assignment, initially, I spent about four days-- roughly split between the time used to interview companies and the time set for writing reports. But sometimes it took me much more time to accomplish the task of conducting all the necessary interviews, because of the difficulty going to meet certain interviewees who were working or living in a Taipei suburb or a remote rural area.

Unlike at the present time, going out to conduct interviews at those times was not as convenient. There were not well-developed public transport systems which enabled you to move around

271

conveniently and rapidly. Thus I had to take a slow-moving bus to, for example, a neighboring town or a rural area where the manufacturer involved was located. Under such a circumstance, it often took me well over a half day to just interview one single person.

Also, during those days Internet connectivity did not exist. Actually, it was never even heard of. This meant there was no way for me to interview manufacturers via email, which would save me time and make things much easier.

In my first year working for Asian Sources, in fact, I even had yet to install a landline telephone in my home. Therefore, I always had to go to a public phone booth to make a call to an interviewee just asking for some additional information, for example. Worse, oftentimes I had to wait in a long line outside the phone booth for my turn. Conversely, I from time to time had to keep a fellow caller or several callers waiting outside the booth until I completed a lengthy telephone interview.

Doing the writing part of my assignment was not an easy task either. This was in part because my writing speed was slow, especially at the beginning of my work for the magazine. So it always took me a relatively long time to finish an article. To make up for my slow-speed problem, I always spent more time on writing.

What also contributed to my slow writing speed was my lack of English knowledge and industrial technologies. There were often cases in which I could not tell the English name of a certain industrial product or the names of an item's components or accessories in their English equivalents. Thus I had to spend time looking for the correct

English names. Things would have become easier for me if I had some useful reference books on hand.

Apparently aware of my problems, Mr. Bendy suggested in a letter that I buy a Walmart catalog at a second-hand bookstore in Taipei. He said the Walmart catalog was comprehensive covering all kinds of consumer goods, components, and accessories as well as their English names. I bought one as advised. That book indeed was helpful for me to easily find almost all consumer products' English names unknown to me previously.

Inspired by my editor's suggestion of going to get a copy of a Walmart catalog, I also bought a set of World Books and a full series of the Encyclopedia Britannica soon after. The two sets of reference books served me well in doing deeper research on some complex subjects.

More often than not, I worked seven days a week under the pressure of meeting my end-of-month deadlines. Meeting the deadline in my case bore some unconventional meanings. It referred to a time limit by which I "frequently had to do an extra amount of work," due to the following two reasons:

One, I had an unwritten quota of editorial space to fill each month. The volume of this quota varied according to an increasingly important role Taiwan played in Asian Sources' overall sales of advertisements. Since Taiwan played a leading part in the magazine's advertisement sales, there was a bigger portion of editorial space for me to work on. This meant that I from time to time had to contribute more to the magazine as its Taiwan correspondent. Asian Sources set a strict ratio of advertisement to editorial space during my time, standing at 3 to 1.

How important the role Taiwan played in Asian Sources' overall advertisement sales at the time can be seen from the remarks made by the magazine's co-founder Merle Hinrichs in the previously cited article, memorializing its first 40 years: "By 1972, Dean Wilson's sales team in Taiwan was already a strong and steady earner. In fact, it was the key to the company's survival and growth in the early years. If it hadn't been for Dean Wilson (manager of Asian Sources' sales office in Taiwan at the time), we would not have had a company…We would not have been able to generate the revenue necessary to gain momentum in advertising sales."

In addition to having a growing editorial quota to fulfill, I also had the pressure to build up my output of words each month. I had to write a minimum of 9,000 words (referring to the words that were actually published) to assure me of a comfortable income. The level of income I now earned was higher than I did previously at the China Post. But I needed to get and maintain a much higher salary, considering the fact that Asian Sources provided me no employee benefits at all.

During the three years with Asian Sources, from mid-1972 to mid-1975, I learned a lot from my editor Mr. Bendy. Each month when he mailed me assignments, for example, he would include in his letter a list of questions that he thought I should ask while conducting interviews with corporate executives. Even more importantly, he taught me how to write better English through his correcting of my product and trade reports. Therefore, I would say Mr. Joe Bendy was my trade journalism mentor.

I now have no idea of how many different sorts of export products I covered for Asian Sources during the three-year period. But unquestionably, they ran long in number. I can still remember some of the products which I was assigned to cover early on. They ranged from canned mushrooms and pineapples to wigs, fishing lures, handicrafts, toys of various categories, and ceramic ware.

The scope of export products that I was assigned to cover gradually expanded to include goods requiring higher-level skills to produce. The following are some of those I can still recall: textiles, garments and accessories, footwear, sporting goods, knock-down furniture, pocket-sized calculators, citizens band radios, clock radios, quartz watches, tape recorders, printed circuit boards, and integrated circuits.

Witnessing Taiwan's Early Economic Transformation

The long series of products that I reported on underscored an ongoing transition in Taiwan's export business, from processed farm produce to textiles and clothing, consumer electronics, and high-technology goods. Therefore, it was not an overstatement to say that my three years of experience in reporting on export products for Asian Sources provided me an opportunity to personally witness Taiwan's early stages of economic transformation.

In the course of my covering Taiwan's export products, I acquired a wealth of general industry knowledge. For example, while doing a survey of Taiwan's ceramics-making business, I came to know some important technical skills pertaining to the production of ceramics, which previously were unknown to me.

One industry executive during an interview described to me how there were two main types of kilns adopted in Taiwan to turn out ceramics wares: traditional wood kilns and more advanced electric kilns. The executive explained his company was among a small number of local producers which had recently converted to the use of electric-powered facilities. One important advantage of this producing method he said was that it could allow better control of temperatures, a most important concern in making quality ceramics.

With electric kilns, he continued, you could attain any high temperatures you desired. Furthermore, he added, they allowed you to better control heat rise and fall, while at the same time protecting the wares against the rigors of heat.

In a separate interview with a porcelain specialist working with the Taipei-based National Palace Museum, I discovered that Taiwan lacked deposits of fine clay needed to make quality wares, forcing some producers to rely on foreign sources for the supply of the material. This, however, added to their production costs.

Quoting a survey, the specialist told me there were indeed deposits of high-quality clay in the military-garrisoned offshore island of Kinmen. But developing them would have to obtain the permission of the garrison command there. Since my conversation with the National Palace Museum specialist, I never had a chance to go back and revisit that issue. So I have no idea whether any porcelain producer had successfully filed applications for clay mining in

Kinmen, an ROC-held front-line island opposite the Chinese mainland's southern coastal city of Xiamen.

In the early 1970s, Taiwan's textile and clothing industry grew and expanded rapidly, thanks to manufacturers' success in boosting their competitiveness and developing overseas markets. As a trade magazine, Asian Sources gave almost constant coverage of that industry. Each time when I interviewed a manufacturer or an industry official, I would like to ask them a range of questions. The two most frequently asked questions were about the supply of raw materials and their production costs.

From these interviews, I learned that Taiwan's textile and clothing industry consisted primarily of two broad sectors: cotton fiber and synthetic fiber. Both sectors were highly competitive in world markets. Cheap labor surely was a contributing factor, but not the determining one. Wages in neighboring countries, such as South Korea, were similarly low then, but their manufacturers did not seem to operate as competitively.

Cheap labor aside, Taiwan's textile and clothing industry also enjoyed several other important advantages. Take for example the cotton fiber sector. Many of its leading manufacturers, such as Far East Textile and Tai Yuen Textile, had already been well-established operators before they relocated from Shanghai to Taiwan back in the early post-World War II years. They moved to this island along with their manufacturing facilities and technologies. This meant that these companies had the advantage of technical know-how and experience.

Taiwan's cotton textile companies also benefited from a government-encouraged strategy to integrate their production processes from spindling to weaving, dyeing and finishing, and end-product manufacturing. Such integrated operations made it possible for them to run businesses more efficiently and hence more competitively.

The same strategy of pursuing vertical integration, from downstream to upstream or vice versa, was also applied and implemented in the synthetic fiber sector since the late 1960s--a time when Taiwan began producing its first man-made fiber, called rayon (by the government-invested China Manmade Fiber Corporation). Soon after, another state-supported firm was created to manufacture nylon, the other major type of man-made fiber then. The government encouraged such investments in a policy to expand the supply of man-made fibers, while at the same time reducing the reliance on cotton. Taiwan did not grow significant amounts of cotton.

By the early 1970s when I covered export products for Asian Sources, Taiwan had as many as 16 companies turning out four major types of artificial fibers—polyester and acrylic in addition to nylon and rayon. The bulk of such output was exported to overseas markets, making Taiwan the third largest exporter of synthetic fibers in the world, only after the United States and Japan.

While working hard to develop overseas markets, the various synthetic fiber manufacturers generally followed a guiding principle of the government: Manufacturers who sought to develop overseas markets had to meet domestic demand first. Taiwan's early start in producing synthetic fibers attracted a large number of downstream investors. They set up processing facilities to spindle yarn, weave cloths, and make garments, taking advantage of readily available but less expensive supplies of raw materials.

The limited domestic market, however, forced the downstream investors of synthetic fiber textiles and garments to develop and expand sales in foreign countries--such as the United States and Canada. They followed the same marketing strategy as their counterparts in the traditional cotton fiber branch.

But overseas sales expansions were not without limitations. Manufacturers in both the cotton and artificial fiber textile sectors soon met with strong protectionism in importing countries. The U.S. and Canadian governments, for example, imposed strict import quotas on textiles and garments from Taiwan, forcing local companies to restrain exports.

In the fall of 1974, the Asian Sources company, which I was working for, formally launched its first specialized magazine, Asian Sources Electronics. The nature of this new magazine was in sharp contrast with that of the parent publication, which was and remained a general-interest trade journal.

In the many years that followed, as I recently learned from the article 'First 40 Years of Asian Sources,' the Hong Kong media company also published a series of other specialized trade journals, including Asian Sources Components, Asian Sources Computers, and Asian Sources Hardware.

The sustained effort at publishing various specialized trade magazines underscored the company's realization of an ideal embraced early on by its CEO Merle Hinrichs and Editor Joe Bendy. "Industry specialization is a growing trend worldwide. Therefore, we will need to follow that trend by specializing in our own media in order to better and more effectively serve both of our advertisers and readers," Mr. Bendy revealed to me during a conversation in Taipei months before Asian Sources Electronics' inaugural issue came out."

With the launch of Asian Sources Electronics, also a monthly, I had to do assignments on Taiwan's electronics products as well, in addition to covering general consumer products for the parent publication. This meant, in a certain sense, I also had the chance to interview corporative executives in the electronics industry -- a technology or young business in Taiwan then. I cannot remember, in particular, how many electronics executives I met, while reporting for Asian Sources Electronics.

Some Electronics Execs Behave Arrogantly

But the number of them was surely large enough to allow me to draw a conclusion: There was a marked difference in attitudes between executives in the electronics industry and those from traditional manufacturing businesses. This marked difference, I must admit, however, came merely from my own observations. I cannot back it up with any figures from survey results.

Many electronics corporate executives gave me the impression that they wanted to be recognized as better educated and equipped with a lot more scientific knowledge than their cousins in the conventional manufacturing sector. They, therefore, wanted to be so received and treated by the rest of society. Some even went to such an extent that they could be noticeably seen as displaying an air of arrogance.

I will give an example, one still vivid in my memory, to demonstrate what I described above to be true: Doing a report on Taiwan's quartz watch-making business, I sought to interview a general manager of a leading company in the sector. I can remember neither the name of the executive nor that of the company he represented.

To my disappointment, the general manager refused to receive me, citing his company policy against media coverage. But I was unwilling to give up easily. So I called him again and again, explaining to him that I could not finish my assignment without including a major company like his. At my insistence, he finally granted me my interview request, though still reluctantly.

By the time I arrived at his company, located on Section 5, Nanjing East Road in Taipei, the general manager had been in his office ready to receive me. But before we got down to business, he was quick to express his doubt about my journalistic credibility. The general manager first enquired as to how long I had been in the journalism profession. "A little over 10 years," I replied. He responded with a smile. Then he went further to ask: "Are you familiar with the electronics business?" "A little bit," I answered.

"To be honest," he explained, "I used to not like talking with you journalists for fear that I might be quoted erroneously. Should that kind of thing happen, unfortunately, it would hurt the image of our company."

"Don't worry," I assured him, "I will listen to you very carefully and take notes of everything you tell me in the interview." I also assured him that I would call him back and let him know how his remarks were presented in my report, once I finished my writing. By then, he would be given a chance to add any necessary information to what he had failed to tell me during the face-to-face interview or correct any errors I might make.

The day following the interview, I did call the general manager back, asking him whether it would be okay for me to read my draft article concerning the part of his company over the phone. He agreed. After hearing what I read to him on the phone, he commented that I got all the essence of what he described to me. He then added, "You did the job very much like a tape recorder." To this day, I am still not quite sure whether this comment was a compliment, flattery or something else.

I never really blamed that general manager for the attitude he held toward me. This attitude issue, I knew, had its historical background. During those early post-World War Two years, Taiwan had a severe shortage of skilled manpower needed to develop its economy and industry. To relieve the shortage, the government offered various incentives to encourage overseas Chinese scholars and professionals to come back to Taiwan to either start technology businesses or work for local companies. These professionals once returning to Taiwan were given special treatment and enjoyed higher social status. The above-cited general manager of the quartz watchmaking company was among those overseas returnees.

I have no data that would allow me to say for sure whether that arrogant quartz watch company executive was only a minority or not. But I did meet, from my numerous interviews, many electronics officials who were the complete opposite. They were humble, easily accessible, friendly, and always liked to share their expert views.

One such electronics executive, whom I can still clearly remember to this day, is Mr. Stan Shih, the founder of Acer--a Taiwan company that later would become one of the world's top computer manufacturers and suppliers.

But when I first interviewed him in late 1972 or early 1973, he was merely a junior computer engineer working for a small firm making calculators. I covered him at the time because I was doing an assignment on Taiwan's calculator manufacturing business.

I decided to include Mr. Shih in my survey of the calculator industry because at the time he had already become a noted engineer in the local electronics circles for his success in designing and developing Taiwan's first desktop calculator and in leading a team that designed the world's first pen watch.

My First Interview with Stan Shih

After leaving Asian Sources, I interviewed Mr. Shih several more times. But I can still vividly remember my first interview with him. It was conducted in the late afternoon in his company on Lin Shen North Road in Taipei. When I arrived at his office, he was working on a piece of electronic machinery. From the place where he worked and the way he described his job to me, I got the impression that Mr. Shih was a hard-working young engineer.

After returning home from that interview, I found I failed to get him to provide an overall view of the calculator industry in Taiwan. Moreover, I forgot to bring home a photo which he agreed to give me for use in our Electronics publication. The photo in question showed a desktop calculator model which he designed and developed on his own recently.

So I immediately gave Mr. Shih a ring telling him that I hoped to come back to see him soon for the above-cited two things. Just as I was about to ask him whether it would be convenient for him at the time, I heard him reply to me from the other end of the phone: "OK, I will wait for you in my office." So I rushed back to his workplace. I cannot remember how long my second meeting with him that day lasted. But it was late into the night when I said goodbye to him.

Since then and during the many years that followed, I interviewed Mr. Shih multiple times on various other topics, while working for other news organizations besides Asian Sources. While most of the interviews I had with him were conducted face-to-face, some were carried out over the telephone. Since he was always busy, there were cases when he was not in the office, and I could not reach him. On such occasions, he would always call me back after reading the message I left.

Whenever I left a message asking him to return my phone call, it was usually because I had something urgent and hoped to obtain his views on it as soon as possible. I will cite one such case here.

On a certain day, I was writing a newspaper editorial that involved me examining a newly imposed multinational mechanism for regulating high-tech product exports. I needed to get a well-informed, high-tech industry leader to discuss the matter. So I turned to Mr. Shih for help. But he was not in the office at the time I called. I thus left a message telling him I was writing a commentary on a tech trade regulating regime, as cited above, and that I would like to learn his views on the issue. Mr. Shih called back not long after I left that message.

By this time (in the early 1990s), Acer, the company he founded, had already evolved into a global electronics giant, producing desktop and laptop PCs and a range of other devices. Mr. Shih himself had become a well-known business leader in Taiwan and abroad. As for me at the time, I had left Asian Sources Electronics years earlier and was writing commentaries regularly for two Taipei-based English publications, the China Post and the China Economic News Service.

The multilateral export control mechanism in question, previously known as Coordinating Committee for Multilateral Export Controls, or Co-Com, was a Cold War era product. It was established by Western bloc powers to put an arms embargo on communist countries. In the early 1990s, however, Co-Com was replaced by another similar multilateral export control regime called the Wassenaar Arrangements on Export Controls for Conventional Arms and for Dual-Use and Technologies.

The aim of the multi-government agreement, as Mr. Shih described to me, was to contribute to regional and international security and stability by promoting transparency and greater responsibility in transfers of conventional arms and dual-use goods (civilian as well as military) and technologies.

It was around this time that Taiwan also became a party to the multilateral agreement. Taiwan qualified as an agreement member only after it enacted a series of rules and regulations as required. One was the adoption of a Foreign Trade Act that would provide a legal basis for regulating the trade of strategic high-tech commodities. The other was the passage and promulgation of a list of specific high-tech products and technologies subject to export controls.

The impact that such export controls had on Taiwan's high-tech companies, like Mr. Shih's Acer, was twofold. One was fundamental: Any export controls tended to impede the flow of free trade. The other impact was a practical one: the difficulty faced by companies in complying with the export control rules.

Taiwan companies with components sourced from the United States, as was mostly the case, had to gain consent from the original American suppliers and their judicial authorities before they could export their end products. This meant tremendous legal hassles and delays inherent in the process of obtaining U.S. "re-export" approval.

Any attempt by Taiwan high-tech companies to not use American components in their products to avoid the time-consuming U.S. "re-export" controls would not be that easy. First, Taiwan's economy was just so closely linked to the U.S. at the time that had made it difficult, if not impossible, for local companies to source key components elsewhere. Second or more fundamentally, Taiwan with industry technology lagging far behind simply lacked the capability to design and build the many core components its companies needed to manufacture their own high-tech goods.

My telephone interview with Mr. Shih this time was very long, though I cannot recall exactly how long it was. But from my memory, it was quite an informative interview. I remain grateful to him for his kindness to return my phone call and answer my questions in a timely manner, and for his willingness to share his expert views with me on a subject which I knew very little previously.

While working for Asian Sources, I at times also did some special features examining and analyzing certain big economic changes as they occurred, in addition to writing specific product reports. During the first half of the 1970s, the world experienced a full economic cycle, characterized by an unprecedented boom in 1972-73 that, in turn, triggered a round of hyperinflation in 1973 and 1974, then followed by a severe recession in 1975.

As Asian Sources' Taiwan correspondent from mid-1972 to mid-1975, I witnessed and covered what happened in the middle stage of that economic cycle--commodity price hikes and acute raw material shortages. My coverage focused on the impact these changes had on Taiwan and its economy. For starters, the sharp 1973-74 upward spiral of prices was global, affecting virtually all commodities supplied in world markets. According to some statistics, most rose dramatically to 20-year highs, while many even went to historical highs.

Surveying the Impact of the 1973 Oil Crisis on Taiwan

For Taiwan, according to my memory and my own research, the quadrupling of world oil prices in 1973 hit the island's economy especially hard. Shortly after the Arab petroleum countries imposed their initial price hikes, I received a letter from my editor Joe Bendy. In it, he urged me to examine their possible effects on Taiwan. I, therefore, conducted a survey of economic officials and manufacturers, from sector to sector, to assess how seriously the local economy was affected by the "first oil crisis," as it was later called.

The 1973 oil crisis did serious damage to the Taiwan economy by disrupting its longstanding double-digit annual growth and causing hyperinflation. In the preceding decade since 1961, Taiwan saw its real GNP grow at an annual average of 10.2 percent, while inflation rose at a yearly 2.9 percent at the consumer level.

But, according to some post-crisis studies in 1974, the year after the onslaught of the jump in oil prices, Taiwan's inflation rate rocketed to 40.6 percent, while its economic growth rate dropped to 1.1 percent.

(Note: The above post-1973-oil-crisis economic statistics were quoted from a study entitled Taiwan's Development Experience: Lessons on Roles of Government and Market, edited by Erik Thornback of Cornell University and Henry Van, Jr. also of Cornell University).

However, since a large part of the import oil price increase was absorbed by the government-owned Chinese Petroleum Corporation and Taiwan Power Company, only a small portion of that 40.6

inflation rate that occurred in 1974 could be explained by the hike in the oil price.

This meant that the two resource-rich state companies were left to bear the brunt of the astronomical oil price hikes. Consequently, the actual impact of the oil shock-driven hyperinflation on the private sector— export businesses included—was much less severe than otherwise would have been the case.

Even so, as I learned from my interviews with government officials, industry leaders, and manufacturers, Taiwan was hard hit by the 1973 steep oil price hikes. This was attributed to two particular reasons. One, Taiwan did not produce crude oil itself. Hence, it relied almost entirely on crude imports, making this island especially vulnerable to world market changes.

Two, Taiwan's reliance on crude oil was drastically deepened since the late 1960s when this island began to build and expand a petrochemical industry to produce intermediates, as part of a government-led bid to achieve self-sufficiency in raw materials.

The various kinds of petroleum-based intermediates in turn were supplied to midstream processors to produce synthetic fibers for use by manufacturers making cloths and garments, as well as a wide range of plastic products. However, as Taiwan continued to expand its petrochemical-producing capacities, its reliance on the supply of crude oil deepened accordingly. This fast-growing consumption of petrochemicals explained why Taiwan was hurt so badly in the first worldwide oil crisis.

A paper shortage was among the many other major raw materials scarcities that plagued businesses across the world in 1973. In Taiwan as elsewhere, paper from newsprint to packaging paper products to toilet tissue all became scarce at the time, unable to match market demand. The shortage of newsprint, for example, was so severe that it forced many small newspapers and magazines in Taiwan to suspend publication.

At the request of my Asian Sources editor, I did a story on paper shortages in Taiwan, with emphasis placed on packaging papers and paperboard. For that story, I interviewed companies making paper board and boxes, manufacturers who in turn used such paper materials to package their export products, as well as industry association executives.

I vaguely remember that one of the questions I put to manufacturers of export products was whether their paper packaging materials suppliers had increased their prices because of paper shortages. If so, how would they address the increased costs: absorbing such higher costs themselves or passing them on to overseas customers who bought their exports?

The other question I raised for export manufacturers was whether the current paper shortages had prompted suppliers to use substandard packaging boards (made from low-cost pulp for example), which tended to undermine the ability to safely protect and deliver products to the buyers abroad. Owing to the lack of a copy of that special report, there is no way for me now to cite any direct quotations from that article.

Among other special reports I wrote for Asian Sources was an investigation into the question of how much it would cost a foreign company to set up and operate a purchasing office in Taipei's commercial districts. This became an issue of concern at the time because more and more international buyers were turning to Taiwan for the supply of consumer products.

In recounting this investigative report, I will be able to cite more direct quotations from it. That will be so because somehow I still have an original version of that report. This was very unusual. I had previously written numerous journalistic articles, long and short, but I never saved an original version except for this one.

The office-cost report as mentioned above was written with a typewriter running 15 pages in length. The passing of time had turned all of its pages yellow. Yet after taking a quick glance at the content of the report, I found something bewildering: Several places in the article suggested that it was done around 1983. This finding confused me at the outset because by that time I had already left Asian Sources for some eight years. And during this period and the many years that followed, I had been working for the China Economic News Service (CENS), an English media affiliated with the mass-circulation, Chinese-language United Daily News.

But after combing through my memory, I found I indeed contributed a couple of articles to Asian Sources during the said time period. I vaguely remember I was asked by the editor of Hardware--another spin-off magazine from Asian Sources--not Mr. Joe Bendy--to do a special report for him every month. For each such report, I was paid US$500 (The exchange rate at the time was 40 New Taiwan dollars to one U.S. dollar).

The venue where we met seemed to be a basement bar of the former Hilton Taipei Hotel across from the Main Railway Station. At that place, the Asian Sources Hardware editor (whose name I can no longer remember) and I reached the article-contribution and fee-payment terms over beers. I have no idea who arranged the beer meeting between us two. But it definitely was not an accidental encounter.

My only speculation, a logical one, was that the Asian Sources Hardware editor intended to get me back to work for them. At this time, I had just stepped down as CENS editor-in-chief, a position that I had held for the past seven years. During this long period, I rarely had time to do any writing. But I loved writing. After leaving the editor-in-chief job, I had plenty of free time. So I was eager to get a writing job as a contributor.

But this did not mean that I intended to quit CENS. At this time, I still served as CENS vice president and had a weekly column to write. Moreover, it would make no sense to quit a leading Taiwan newspaper group in favor of going back to work for a trade magazine company. All this seemed to explain why my contributions to Asian Sources lasted for only a few months.

Talking with Three U.S. Buying Agents in Taipei

Back to the report investigating the cost of opening a purchasing office in Taipei by an international company: In this report, I interviewed six people--three resident foreign buying executives, one accountant, one real estate agent, and one interior designer. As can be seen, the investigation covered a representative sample of people each with specialized knowledge about a specific aspect of the subject being examined.

The cost of setting up an office in the commercial districts in Taipei at the time, the report discovered, was fairly reasonable with rents ranging from US$20 to US$30 per ping (one ping equals 36 square feet).

The article also reported that the legal procedure to register a purchasing office by a foreign company was easy. It required only filing a letter of application with a district tax office. Normally a reply of acknowledgment could be expected within two weeks of the application.

As to how much it would cost to maintain and manage a purchasing office in this capital city depended on the scale of the buyer's business operations. The above-cited three foreign buying executives were deliberately chosen for their different sizes: small, medium and large. So what these executives said could provide a representative view on the cost of operating a purchasing mission in Taipei. All of the three executives interviewed were American nationals, as were the companies they represented.

Mr. Richard Hollands, manager of the Taiwan Liaison office of Thomas Radio Corp., said his company set up its own buying office here in 1981, a time "when we decided that purchasing directly from suppliers would be not only more economical but also necessary."

He then explained to me why it was more economical. He took for example 1980, the year before Thomas Radio established its Taipei buying office. "In that year we purchased some US$3 million worth of home stereo products in Taiwan through a local agent and for that, we paid a total US$150,000 in commission."

"Now this year," he compared, "our purchases here will top US$7 million, more than double the 1980 figure, while the operating budget for my office, of four, for this year, is only US$84,000. So the economic benefits of setting up our own buying office are quite obvious."

"What's more," Mr. Hollands continued, "the market has become exacting all the more, demanding better quality merchandise. To meet this demand, we felt it was necessary for us to purchase directly from the suppliers. By purchasing directly from the suppliers, we could better control quality."

As a purchasing representative, Mr. Hollands said he had the following responsibilities to fulfill: "Source new products, negotiate prices, oversee quality control, and monitor delivery schedule."

The other purchasing representative I interviewed was Mr. Gary Melyan of Fuqua World Trade Corp. Fuqua, also a U.S. firm, "currently bought US$30 million worth of goods a year from Taiwan. They included rainwear, inflatable items, golf equipment, motorcycle parts, and accessories."

Mr. Melyan acted as Fuqua Taiwan manager heading a 10-member procurement mission. He and his mission members operated from the fifth floor of a high-rise office building in downtown Taipei. The floor is 3,300 square feet in size and was partitioned into two sample product rooms, one main office, one storage room, and one reception room. "It is a comfortable office building to work in, with good structure, good view, good security, and parking space," Mr.

Melyan said of the general conditions of the office building and its costs.

The entire fifth floor, plus a parking lot, cost Fuqua Taiwan more than US$28,000 a year in rent. Yet the rental accounted for only a small portion of Fuqua Taiwan's annual spending budget, which amounted to US$250,000 in total.

According to Mr. Melyan, payroll accounted for the single largest of all his annual expenses. Salaries he paid his employees then ranged from US$1,500 a month for an experienced local manager to US$170 a month for an office girl. "Employees all get an annual bonus amounting to two months' full pay. In addition, we paid all legally required employee benefits, including medical insurance, accident insurance, a two-week annual leave, and a six-week childbirth leave for female employees," he said.

Fuqua World Trade Corp. set up its Taipei purchasing office in the early 1970s when its purchases from Taiwan reached more than US$1 million a year. "At that time we were moving several new items from Japan to Taiwan for production here because we found this island has a great potential as a supply market for us. So we decided it's time for us to set up a permanent office here to handle purchases by ourselves," Mr. Melyan recalled.

"In my opinion, when a buyer's purchases in a foreign land involved several different product lines, he needs to consider establishing a permanent local buying office for the sake of specialization. On the other hand, if you purchase only a single item it might not be worth such an investment, in that you can appoint a local agent to do that on your behalf. Buying in such a way would be more economical," Mr. Melyan said.

In the same special report, I also interviewed Mr. Sunny C. Shen, chairman of the board of Kmart's Taiwan purchasing mission. In terms of buying amounts, Kmart Taiwan was the largest, compared to the above-cited two trade missions: Fuqua World Trade Corp. and Thomas Radio Corp.

Kmart Taiwan purchased more than US$200 million worth of products -- mainly garments and sundry items -- a year from this island on behalf of its parent company in the United States.

At the time of the interview, Kmart Taiwan had more than 80 people in its employ, with operating expenditure reaching US$1.5 million a year. "The Kmart Taiwan team," as I wrote in the report, "in many ways operates just like a local business concern. Unlike the other two foreign purchasing missions, Kmart Taiwan had its own spacious offices (not rented ones), totaling nearly 20,000 square feet.

"Operating from offices owned by ourselves saved us the trouble of having to move frequently from one place to another, as is the case in the past. Previously, we worked from rented offices and often had to move out and find a new place elsewhere once the lease ran out."

Unlike other international purchasing missions here, according to chairman Shen, Kmart Taiwan was only responsible for supervising production, quality control, and securing long-term suppliers. They did not do any actual purchases, which were performed by its head office in the United States. The head office normally sent purchasing executives to Taiwan twice a year to place orders for garments and sundry items.

"A buying office is cost-effective only if it is able to perform better quality control, make purchasing prices competitive in the selling market, and secure the right long-term suppliers who would always be willing to improve product quality and designs," Mr. Shen said.

"With a sizable staff of more than 80, Kmart Taiwan attached great importance to the hiring and retraining of employees in order to raise operating efficiency while reducing turnover rate. It pays its purchasing executives from US$1,200 to US$2,500 a month according to their performance and seniority. Salaries accounted for about 50 percent of Kmart Taiwan's expenditure. Employee benefits such as labor insurance, accident insurance, annual leave, and childbirth all are provided in accordance with Taiwan's labor laws," I wrote in that special report.

To examine the expenses of opening and running a buying office in Taipei, I also interviewed an accountant, a real estate agent, and an interior designer, asking them to comment on the subject from their respective professions.

The accountant I talked with was Ms. Grace Liu, principal of T.N. Soong & Co., a leading Taiwan accounting firm, which concurrently provided consulting services to foreign companies planning to do business in this country. She replied to me "registering a buying office in Taipei is very easy and simple. It only needed to file an application, accompanied with three documents: a letter of appointment, a copy of the applicant's identity card or a passport, and a duplicate of an office lease." Ms. Liu said, "It would be ideal for the letter of application to be notarized and authenticated by a ROC consulate or trade office in the applying company's home country."

She continued: "The responsible local government agency with which the application is filed is in the tax-collecting office in the district where the proposed buying office is to be located...The purpose of the registration is for record...No tax responsibility is involved since a foreign buying office in Taiwan is not considered by the government authorities as a profit-generating business concern." She added, "Leading local law and accounting companies all offer such registration services, with fees starting from US$400 to US$500, hinging on the size of the applying company."

One real estate agent contacted by me in the survey said: "Renting an office in Taipei these days should not be a problem in terms of availability and cost. The growth in the supply of office building spaces in Taipei now has far exceeded the growth in demand due largely to a building spree in recent years, triggered by a new government policy. The government had declared that all landlords 'must develop their vacant lots' within a prescribed period of time. Failing to do so could result in their undeveloped lands being procured by the government at state-set prices. New high-rise buildings in Taipei's recently developed commercial districts, such as Zhongxiao East Road and Nanjing East Road, ranged in rent from US$20 to US$30 per ping (one ping equals 36 square feet)."

Most local interior design companies charged their clients on a package deal basis. That is, "they charged a covering-all price for doing interior designs, arranging partitions, installing office furniture, and working for lighting, wiring, and plumbing." Mr. Sin Ching-long, a designer of the High Way Interior Design Company, explained that "charges under such a package deal average US$25 per ping. To put it in a more exact way, design service charges go from US$5,000 for a modest office accommodating five workers to US$25,000 for a bigger one accommodating up to 15 people."

Normally, the above-discussed design service price also obligated the design company to clean up the whole office space after it completed design changes, partitions, and all other contracted work, usually within one to four weeks' time. Mr. Sin went on to explain: "Most interior design companies also help to install communications equipment. Landline telephones can be installed within one week with a fee of US$500 each. The monthly basic rate is US$10. A three-minute call to the U.S., person to person, costs about US$13 and US$9 for the station to station, on weekdays. Telex systems take about one month to install. The installation fee is US$550 and its monthly basic rate is US$200."

Asian Sources Job a Rewarding Experience

Now as I look back to the three years—from mid-1972 to mid-1975–working for Asian Sources, I felt they were one of the busiest but rewarding periods in my journalism life. During that three-year period, all I had to do was carry out my monthly assignments covering export products and writing reports, without having to do any administrative chores or non-reporting tasks.

The Asian Sources job benefited me greatly because it allowed me to concentrate my attention and energy all the time on collecting information on export businesses and writing articles about them. Such concentration made it possible for me to steadily improve my writing and news-gathering skills, as well as accumulate economic knowledge.

There was another meaningful aspect of my journalistic tenure at Asian Sources. That was, as I now vividly remember, the feeling of fulfillment I got at the moment when I airmailed my finished assignments to my editor Mr. Bendy in Hong Kong. That moment normally came at the end of every month--the monthly deadline by which I was supposed to have carried out all of my assignments and submitted them to the editor.

With the deadline just met, I felt a huge surge of relief and happiness. Such feelings can be understood only by people who have the same working experiences as I did. Typically, I worked long hours every day, much longer than that spent by those nine-to-five workers. Sundays and holidays were no exception.

I worked long hours and on holidays only to get my "two phases" assignment works done in time to meet the end-of-month deadline. The first phase of my work involved me going out to conduct some two dozen interviews, mostly with manufacturers. After finishing all those interviews, I then began my second phase of work: Sitting at my typewriter day and night struggling to turn all the finished interviews into written reports before the deadlines. Tension and anxiety grew in me with each passing minute, as the cutoff date neared for me to submit my articles.

While meeting deadlines was always stressful, it paid off in several important ways. First, I earned a feeling of achievement at the end of each month -- a moment when I had accomplished all my assignments on time. I felt very happy because I had fulfilled my commitment to meeting the deadline. After all, always finishing your assigned work within a designated time is one of the most important journalism ethics.

Two, I got a sense of relief after putting all of my articles in the airmail box of the Post Office. I felt like a weight had been lifted off my shoulders, though only temporarily. I usually took about two to three days to relax, before starting to work on the assignments for the month ahead. My way to relax was somewhat unusual. It began right after I walked out of the Taipei North Gate General Post Office, from where I airmailed my articles to Hong Kong.

Outside the Post Office, I walked directly to a nearby newsstand to buy a copy of Reader's Digest. I then hailed a taxi to my home in Shih Lin, nearly a one-hour drive north of the Taipei Post Office. In the cab, I immediately opened the American magazine, turned to my favorite column "My Most Unforgettable Character," and started reading it in a relaxed and happy mood.

Once getting home from the Post Office, the first thing I discussed with my wife, Yen-ming, was the subject of where or how we were going to spend a couple of days off. My wife generally lets me make the final decision in this regard. Mostly I used my free time to bring Yen-ming and our two kids Wen-yi, then attending kindergarten, and her younger brother Wen-chieh to visit attractions in and outside Taipei.

In the city, the Children's Amusement Park, Taipei Zoo, New Taipei Park, and the Botanical Garden were the places we visited more often. During the summer days, we also went to some northern Taiwan seaside resorts, such as Pa-Li and Baisha Bay. To save time, we always chose to take a taxi to those beaches, instead of getting a bus.

No matter where we traveled, I myself always brought with me some English-language publications. I did so in the hope that I might be able to read them on the way to, or after arrival at, our tour destination. Sometimes, I liked doing my reading on the grass or in the shade of a tree in particular. Reading in such a way, I felt, was a good way to help me reset and relax.

This reading habit of mine apparently had an effect on my daughter Wen-yi, who was then in kindergarten. Oftentimes she too brought some children's readings with her when we went on an outing. She liked to sit or lie down in the grass beside me doing her reading, just the same way as I did. Her imitating my way of reading often drew admiring glances from passers-by.

Why I Left Asian Sources

If the Asian Sources work was so rewarding, then why didn't I work for the trade magazine longer, rather than three years? Several reasons are given below. By the early second half of 1975 when I left, the Hong Kong trade media company had already launched a second trade monthly, called Asian Sources Electronics.

The publication of the new magazine prompted a significant increase in my workload. Consequently, I was authorized by Mr. Bendy to hire two reporters and a copy editor. With his approval, I also rented an office for me and my editorial team to work in. Previously, I always worked from my home.

What is also worth mentioning was that by this time I had already been promoted as bureau chief from the position of the correspondent. I thus got a pay increase. Although symbolic, it was my first salary raise since I joined the trade media group some three years earlier.

The funding for the above-cited staff increase and office renting as well as my own pay raise did not come easily, however. They were approved only after much hard bargaining with Mr. Bendy. The hard negotiations did cause some bitter feelings between him and me. But such tensions were not the determining factor in my final decision to quit Asian Sources.

Rather it was a number of other concerns that caused me to leave my Asian Sources job. I sometimes felt a lack of job security. From start to end, to give an example, I was never issued a formal employment contract. Surely, I had never taken the initiative to ask for one. But the company, as the employer, had the responsibility to sign a formal hiring document with me from the outset, spelling out its obligations and expectations. The absence of such a document could put me at risk of being arbitrarily fired, in the event that I could not agree with the company over a controversial editorial policy.

During my entire tenure from the summer of 1972 to the summer of 1975, Asian Sources only issued me two media credentials. But these documents were good at only proving my journalistic status, enabling me to gain access to government and private organizations, while performing my information-gathering duties. They could in no way serve as a contract of my employment with Asian Sources.

To this day, I still keep both of those media credentials. The first one was issued on January 1, 1973, about half a year after I joined Asian Sources. It reads as follows: "This is to certify that the bearer of this letter--Mr. Osman C. H. Tseng, is the Taiwan correspondent for Asian Sources magazine. He is charged with the responsibility, and has our full authority, to collect information on trade, economic, and other related matters, as we assign him to, or as he determines on his own initiative…The reports he submits to us will be used to reveal to Western businessmen--our readers, the export capabilities and potential of the Republic of China. We respectfully request that he be granted courtesies due him as a professional journalist, and we are grateful for any cooperation and assistance rendered him in the pursuit of his duties."

The other media credential, dated June 21, 1974, was addressed to the Government Information Office of the ROC Cabinet. It reads, "This is to inform you that Mr. Osman C. H. Tseng, as Taiwan Bureau Chief for Trade Media Ltd., has been authorized by us to hire, instruct and guide journalists, both local and foreign, to carry out assignments related to coverage of the Republic of China as a source market for consumer products for overseas buyers. Our magazines are specialized trade journals that help Western businessmen understand and appreciate the economic growth and potential of various Southeast Asian countries."

Another major concern that led me to depart from Asian Sources was that the company persistently failed to provide employment benefits of any kind: no labor insurance coverage, no annual leave, and no year-end bonus, for example. This was the case despite the fact that Asian Sources performed quite well in Taiwan in terms of advertising revenue, as I understood.

In addition to the lack of a hiring contract and employee benefits, there were some other considerations, which had more to do with me but which prompted me to review whether I ought to continue to stay with Asian Sources. After working with the trade magazine for years, for instance, I came to realize that always covering and reporting consumer products would never make it possible for me to achieve my goal of becoming a full-fledged journalist.

I felt that if I wanted to fulfill that ideal, I had to have the chance to do a diverse range of journalistic work, not just practicing trade journalism as I was doing then. This desire appeared to be reflected in a question, which I put to Asian Sources co-founder Merle A. Hinrichs during a face-to-face conversation with him in Taipei: "Have you ever conceived of the possibility of publishing a general-interest English newspaper in Hong Kong?" I cannot remember how he replied to me. The reason that I recited that question here is that I wanted it to attest to what appeared to be a subconscious desire in me at the time: I hoped to have a chance of working for an English daily of general interest.

Working for Asian Sources in some way, for another instance, was like performing a freelancing job. A freelancer tended to constantly face two emotional problems: loneliness and isolation--problems inherent in this type of occupation. You felt lonely because you worked from home and got a sense of isolation because you had no peers to communicate with. So it can be said that I personally experienced the above two kinds of feelings during the years working for Asian Sources.

In addition, I sometimes also had a sense of not belonging. By "not belonging," I did not mean that I could not fit in with my family members or friends. I had no problem with that. What I meant was that I myself never really felt like a part of Asian Sources, a feeling which I had had from start to finish.

My connection with the magazine, I would say, was limited to a pure working relationship: I submitted my required number of articles to my editor at the end of each month and received my check payments at around the same time, all of which were delivered through airmail.

During my three-year tenure with Asian Sources, I met with my editor Mr. Bendy only a couple of times. All such meetings took place in Taipei during his visit here. Our first meeting, as I already recounted at the beginning of this chapter, occurred when he came to my China Post office and invited me to cover trade and export products in Taiwan for his magazine.

Among the other meetings, which I can still recall, were the ones when Mr. Bendy and I gathered in Taipei to meet with three senior ROC economic officials for exclusive interviews on different occasions. As a resident correspondent, I had arranged the appointments in advance. One of the three interviewees was then chairman of the Council for Economic Development and Planning, Dr. Sun Chen. The other two officials we talked with were the director of the Industrial Development Bureau and the director of the Board of Foreign Trade.

By stating my "not belonging" feelings and describing my interaction with editor Bendy as being limited to a working relationships, I did not mean that I was not given due attention by him.

Nor did I mean the management of Asian Sources did not care much about me and my service.

None of my above speculation was true. I will cite below a significant event to prove why it was not the case. One day (August 7, 1975) toward the end of my third year of work for Asia Sources, I received a letter from the headquarters inviting me to visit Hong Kong for a couple of days. In the letter, Mr. Bendy wrote: "On behalf of Trade Media Lt., I am very pleased to invite you to visit our Hong Kong headquarters. We are happy to cover your transportation costs and the cost of your accommodations for three days and two nights. We leave the date of your visit up to you, but we hope you can get here soon. Please let us know when you think you can break free from duties to join us."

I was grateful to Mr. Bendy and other authorities of the company for their generosity and thoughtfulness in inviting me to visit the head office and its media operations. Also, I took great comfort in the significance of the invitation. In my view, it was a reflection of Asian Sources recognizing the work I had done for it in the past three years. And they, therefore, wanted to reward me for that by treating me to a three-day, Hong Kong visit at the company's expense.

But regrettably, I failed to make the trip in the end. The reason was that way ahead of the arrival of the invitation letter, I had decided in principle to take a job offer from a newly launched English news service created by the Taipei-based United Daily News group. This being the case, I felt it was inappropriate for me to accept the Hong Kong visit invitation.

I agreed to work for the China Economic News Service (CENS), as referred to above, not because they promised me higher pay. No, they did not. Actually, I had been reminded in advance that I would probably earn even less with CENS than I did at Asian Sources.

What prompted me to accept the CENS job was a number of particular considerations that outweighed the salary factor. One of them was that the Taipei-based English-language economic news service was a domestic media affiliated with the United Daily News, one of the two largest media groups in Taiwan then. This was unlike Asian Sources, a trade journal that was owned by American nationals and published outside Taiwan.

Another consideration was that if I joined CENS, it would involve me regularly going to the office to work alongside fellow journalists. This would bring an end to my freelancing life. An end to my freelancing life would wipe out my feelings of "loneness, isolation, and not belonging."

One further consideration that led me to join CENS was a then widely shared observation in the Taiwan media circles: That the Chinese-language United Daily News was likely to branch out into English-language media by publishing a newspaper in that language. Its launch of CENS, or the China Economic News Service, was seen as the first step in that direction.

As a lover of English journalism, I certainly hoped that observation would prove to be accurate. There was reason to be so optimistic, given the United Daily News group's rich resources and its experience in publishing several Chinese-language newspapers of wide circulation.

Chapter 7
Hired as Asian Sources Taiwan Bureau Chief

It was against such a background that I agreed to join CENS. Why the authorities of the United Daily News wanted to hire me was a question not very difficult to answer. Look, by this time, I had already a little more than 10 years of experience in practicing journalism. And the vast majority of this period involved me using English as a tool. Thus they perhaps thought I might be the person they needed to help them organize and run the editorial department of the newly established CENS.

I started working for CENS in May 1975. There I spent the next 15 years playing various journalistic roles. I served first as a writer, then as city editor and editor-in-chief. I held the latter position for as long as seven years. The 15 years working for the China Economic News Service, I would say, were the most challenging and memorable period of my journalism career spanning more than four decades. I always valued my experience in working with the many dozens of colleagues at the CENS editorial department -- all of them hard-working young people, male and female, and local and foreign.

I retired from CENS in 1989 at the age of 55. During the final several years leading up to my retirement, I no longer wore two hats. I performed only as vice president. In that post, I was not as busy. So I could take time out to do the writing. I have always loved writing. During the preceding seven years working as editor-in-chief, I rarely had time to write.

Among the things I wrote was a weekly column for CENS's Economic News Monday Edition. From time to time, I also translated into English some newsworthy articles, carried by the sister newspapers of the United Daily News group, for use in our own publications.

A detailed recollection of my years in the China Economic News Service will be given in the following section, Chapter 8.

Chapter 8
Joining China Economic News Service

Reviewing and editing articles were my primary duty as CENS editor-in-chief.

Working with the Editorial Department

When I joined the China Economic News Service (CENS) in June 1975, the media company was a startup. Its aim was to publish economic and trade news in the English language. CENS in the early stages printed only three English publications--an economic news daily bulletin, an economic newsweekly as well as an overseas trade weekly.

CENS was composed of two departments: editorial and business. I worked with the editorial department from the outset. The time I spent with this section accounted for the vast majority of my entire 15-year tenure at CENS.

In the beginning, I worked as a writer. But after a short time, I was assigned an additional job as a city editor. This meant that I soon wore two hats--city editor and writer. I performed this dual role for some three years until I was promoted to the position of editor-in-chief, a post that I held for about seven years. My last CENS job was as a full-time vice president.

I retired from CENS in 1989 at the age of 55. Legally, I could have continued working for CENS for as long as 10 more years, if I desired to. There was only one single reason why I took early retirement: I wanted to change course and pursue full-time writing as a career. It had long been my goal to become a professional English writer as well as a professional journalist.

But if I remained at CENS as vice president, I would continue to be tied down by administrative work, without being able to do writing only. That I had to leave CENS was because the company could not provide me with a full-time writing job. As such, leaving CENS to pursue my interest elsewhere was my only option.

Since its 1975 founding, CENS grew and expanded fast. In a few years' time, it evolved into a leading English-language publishing company in Taiwan, printing a wide variety of publications and disseminating business and trade information for readers at home and abroad.

The picture shows me (sitting in the middle) discussing publication policies and content with my editors, while serving at CENS.

For domestic audiences, we printed two economic news publications: a daily and a weekly one. Both of the two publications essentially followed a newspaper format. And both were targeted at international companies doing business in Taiwan and locally invested firms conducting export and import businesses.

Unlike those general interest newspapers, the CENS daily bulletin was published only five days a week -- Monday through Friday. It consisted of three major sections, domestic news, international news, and world financial and commodity markets. The news bulletin was well received in the Taiwan business community.

Another domestic market-targeted news publication of CENS was a tabloid format weekly published every Monday. This publication, therefore, also was called by us and many of our readers The Monday Edition or the ME.

The ME was significantly different from some traditional tabloid newspapers seen here in Taiwan and elsewhere. Those tabloids mostly placed emphasis on the use of crime stories, lurid features, and eye-catching headlines to stimulate sales. But we never tried to increase readership with sensationalism.

The ME, like the Daily Bulletin, focused on disseminating economic and trade information. But unlike the Daily Bulletin, the ME with its larger page size allowed us to put in more manpower to enrich its content and enliven its pages, making it more pleasant to read.

I can still remember how we ran the ME. As the editor-in-chief, I operated the ME essentially in line with the key characteristics unique to a weekly newspaper. The primary mission of a weekly newspaper, unlike that of a daily, was not to report news or break it. This was because any current event news, if held up for days until the publication date of a weekly, would have become history, not having news value anymore. This being the case, most weekly newspaper operators, instead, placed great emphasis on investigative and interpretive reporting.

In the same fashion, during my time as CENS chief editor, I always stressed expanding and analyzing news events as a basic editorial policy for operating the Monday Edition. I required that all reporters and copy editors follow this policy in covering news or editing articles for publication in the ME.

I can't remember for what purpose this group photo was taken. But I do recognize the vast majority of the people around me (in blackjacket) were CENS reporters, when I was working there.

Business dinners and after-work drinks were not uncommon events during my time at the CENS editorial department.

News articles printed in the ME came mainly from three sources. The bulk of them, covered and written by our reporters, were exclusives such as special reports and interviews with celebrities. A lesser portion of articles was removed from the Daily Bulletin after they were enriched in content. (The Daily Bulletin was produced by our staff working on the night shift). In addition, we sometimes also carried news stories taken from CENS's sister publications, mainly the Chinese-language Economic Daily News and the United Daily News. All such stories invariably had to go through the fact-checking process, before they were translated into English texts for publication in the ME.

I set out a rule that no matter where the news articles came from, they all had to be presented in a way to meet one essential prerequisite: Reporting what had happened this past week and/or predicting what was likely to happen in the week ahead.

In general, materials printed in the ME were in-depth news articles and features. They, unlike run-of-the-mill stories, contained facts and explanations necessary to provide an overall view of an ongoing complex economic issue or a social phenomenon.

In addition to printing in-depth news stories, the Monday Edition also ran a number of widely read columns. They included, as I recall, a column called "Page Two." This column, written by our senior reporter Philip Liu, explored social, cultural, and other topical events that happened in the past week.

Another feature column, entitled "From the Other Side," was devoted to reflecting opinions by prominent professional women in Taiwan. However, this column sometimes also printed views by some well-known male figures. They included martial arts novelist Chin Jong and world-class historian Yu Ying-shih, for example.

This column was first written by Michelle Pao and then by Fu Li-yeh. Both of the two intelligent female reporters left CENS in succession to pursue advanced studies in the United States. Pao took up residence in the U.S., while Fu returned to Taiwan after getting a doctorate degree. She later taught in several leading universities in Taiwan.

A third column, called Commentary and Analysis, was written by me. The topics I dealt with in this column were wide-ranging, from the economy, finance, and foreign trade, to cross-Taiwan Strait politics and economic exchanges. My contribution to this column continued for many years after I left CENS.

Besides printing the various columns, special reports, and news stories, the ME also featured a special weekly interview. In it, a senior economics official, a business leader, a prominent scholar, or a famous cultural celebrity was asked to share their views on a still developing issue of wide concern.

Despite its rich content, the ME was a fledgling weekly newspaper. By the time I stepped down as the editor-in-chief, it was less than 10 years old. But in this short period of time, the Monday Edition quickly became popular with its subscribers and readers. It gained a reputation as a quality English-language publication in the Taipei metropolitan area.

The ability of the ME to gain fast public recognition, I believe, was due largely to its success in diversifying its content and increasing the depth of its articles. These were the two most important efforts we at the editorial department made to increase the paper's appeal to its expatriate as well as local readers.

But producing good news articles and features that could attract readers was a constant challenge. It required a series of conscientious efforts by the editorial staff. First, you needed to consistently develop well-conceived story ideas. In some news media organizations, story ideas came from the team leader. In our case, they mostly came from me as the editor-in-chief.

The other part of the efforts involved reporting and editing. The two important tasks, as anyone in the journalism profession would know, are performed by reporters and editors respectively. Yet how well they perform their respective tasks depends on the levels of their journalistic skills and personal qualities.

Hiring Reporters & Copy Editors

In light of the above considerations, I paid particular attention to the recruitment of reporters and copy editors. I required that all applicants, whether they were looking for a reporting or copy-editing job, had to take both written and oral tests. At the end of such tests, I would invite senior editors to join me in screening and evaluating the prospective candidates. Test results were the sole factor in reaching an employment decision. A successful candidate for the reporting job had to undergo a three-month trial period before they were formally accepted and employed.

Generally speaking, as I recall, a CENS reporter having passed our entry tests, gone through a three-month trial period, and done the job of coverage and reporting on the ground for two years, was most likely to have attained at least four important journalistic skills: being able to 1) gauge what makes good news, 2) find news topics worth reporting, 3) organize copy content in a logical and objective way, and 4) write clear English.

I personally recruited dozens of talented young reporters, male and female, during my time with the editorial development. Yet most of them left CENS after working for only two to three years. One main reason for this apparently high turnover was the inability of CENS to provide its journalists with clear career prospects if they chose to stay on. Why that was the case will be discussed in later pages.

In general, as I observed, the majority of reporters, who quit CENS to pursue non-journalistic careers elsewhere after working for a couple of years for us, did impressively well in their new fields. Their success seemed to suggest that the experience they got at CENS was useful to them in pursuing their new careers.

If my memory serves me correctly, a half dozen or so former CENS reporters, whom I worked with, left to pursue advanced studies in the United States and obtained their doctoral degrees there. After finishing their academic programs, they all returned to Taiwan and got teaching jobs at major public and private universities.

They included Ms. Fu Li-yeh, who was teaching health and welfare policy at National Yang-ming University as an associate professor at the time of this writing. Another former CENS reporter who also did well academically was Ding Shu-fan. Ding, like Ms. Fu, acquired a doctoral degree in the U.S. and returned to Taiwan to teach at a number of public universities.

There were a number of other reporters, who left CENS but still stayed within the same big family--the United Daily News group. Some of them worked for the flagship United Daily News and others went to join the Economic Daily News, the United Evening News, or the World Journal.

These former CENS reporters all performed quite well in those sister newspapers. Among them was Yen Kuang-you, who deserves special mention for a number of reasons. First, he was among the few reporters who joined CENS at its founding. More significantly, he worked so hard that his English knowledge and writing skills advanced quickly. This made him stand out notably from other reporters. A few years later he was promoted to city editor, taking over from me. This came after I was transferred to the post of editor-in-chief.

Yen Kuang-you, however, worked in the CENS city editor role only briefly. He was reassigned by the Economic Daily News publisher Wang Bi-li to Washington, D. C., as the paper's correspondent in the U.S. capital. The publisher did not consult with me in advance about Yen's transfer to Washington. But even if he had I would have been unable to say no to him because he was also my boss. Mr. Wang at the time was wearing two hats. Besides heading the Economic Daily News, he also acted as the publisher of CENS.

But soon after Mr. Wang did invite me to his office to talk about Yen's reassignment. He explained to me why he decided to dispatch Yen to collect news in the U.S. capital. One main reason was that he wanted to draw on his news covering skills and English knowledge acquired during his years of work for CENS.

I am not sure how long Yen stayed in Washington. But I do remember he was recalled to Taipei later to continue working for the Economic Daily News, first as city editor and then editor in chief. Many years on Yen was transferred to the United Daily News, where he too played a range of important roles, both editorial and administrative.

What impressed me about Yen Kuang-you was his firm adherence to practicing journalism, never taking a job outside this profession. It could be said that Yen was one of a few former CENS reporters who had successfully built themselves up as a career newspaper person.

Several other former CENS reporters left to work for international wire agencies. One of them was Peter Chen, who was hired away by Reuters as one of its Taiwan reporters. Peter Chen had a strong passion for English journalism. This could be demonstrated by the length of his service in that news agency. He continued to work for Reuters until his retirement.

Peter Chen was not the only CENS reporter who was hired away by the international news media. James Peng left his CENS job also after Reuters offered him an opportunity to help cover Taiwan news. Not long after, he transferred to Bloomberg. Later, I heard, he was promoted and became Bloomberg's Taipei bureau chief.

Among other former CENS reporters were Richard Chuang and Chang Cheng-kou. They joined us early and left early. But they impressed me with two particularly interesting interviews--one with Milton Friedman and the other with Peter Drucker.

Richard Chuang, with a background in both finance and law, was often tasked with handling some of the more specialized topics, such as financial and foreign exchange reforms. He also scored some of our better interviews with well-known authorities in these two areas.

A Funny Episode in Interview with Milton Friedman

I recall on one occasion Chuang had an interview with Milton Friedman. The American economist, who received the 1976 Nobel Prize, had been invited to Taiwan by the Central Bank of the Republic of China. Chuang filed a report based on his interview, and we published it prominently in the Monday Edition where we showcased some of our best stories.

When we were editing the story, there was one area which required some clarification. So we checked the text against Chuang's tape recording of the discussion. The problem was quickly sorted out, but we found the wide-ranging interview so interesting that we listened to the rest of the recording.

The interview was conducted over dinner and, at the end of the discussion, Chuang offered to pick up the check for the meal. Friedman, the scholar who famously said "There is no such thing as a free lunch," could be heard saying not to bother, adding: "It's all on the central bank." This led us to conclude that perhaps there was such a thing as "a free dinner." Milton Friedman's "It's all on the central bank," remarks, which contrasted with his "no free lunch" adage, made this one of our more memorable interviews.

The interview with Peter Drucker was interesting in another way. Drucker, widely recognized as the founder of modern management, was one of the most internationally known figures we had ever interviewed in the early days of CENS. But it was the way we interviewed him, which I felt was unusual.

I recall we airmailed a questionnaire to the Austrian-born American management authority while he was in Canada for a speaking engagement ahead of a planned trip to Taiwan. He accepted our interview request and mailed back his written answers just in time for us to get a high-profile scoop. We ran the exclusive interview first in our daily bulletin on the very day Peter Drucker arrived in Taipei. This came before any other local media could get a chance to interview him.

In the above, I have recounted many talented young reporters leaving CENS because of its failure to show them clear career paths. I roughly divided them into three groups. In one group were those who quit CENS in order to pursue advanced studies abroad. Another was made up of those who preferred to transfer to our sister publications, such as the United Daily News and Economic Daily News, to practice journalism in the Chinese language. In the third group were some who were hired by international news agencies to work as one of their resident reporters in Taiwan.

In contrast to the previously cited three groups of reporters who quit CENS for various reasons, there were some who chose to stay with the company until their retirement. As I know, they numbered about half a dozen, me included. They all persevered in practicing English-language journalism. I meant they went to work for other

English news publications after retiring from CENS. It could be said that these former CENS journalists have devoted their entire careers to reporting or writing in the English language.

Besides me, the rest of this fourth group included Kennix Lu, Philip Liu, Stephen Shen, Willis Ke, and Judy Lin. Perhaps because of the fact that we all loved journalism and English writing, we have maintained contact with each other, even long after our departure from CENS.

They, like me, did writing from home. Philip Liu, for example, wrote for the English monthly Taiwan Business Topics, published by the American Chamber of Commerce Taipei, and TrendForce, a high-tech market information medium. He did so without having to go to the office. Stephen Shen and Willis Ke worked for DIGITIMES as their regular contributors. DIGITIMES is an online English publication printed daily to report news on Taiwan's wide-encompassing electronics industry, including for example PCs and telecommunications equipment.

As for me, after my retirement from CENS, I also worked from home, writing editorials for the China Post for the next 18 years, plus one-year doing translation from Chinese into English for an online news bulletin of the China Times.

In the preceding pages, I discussed how I recruited reporters during my years as CENS editor-in-chief. Now I will recollect our copy editor-hiring practices, which were similarly strict. Copy editors played a no less important role in turning out a quality news article, special report, or feature. A CENS copy editor, as I required, had to have a reasonably high level of editing skills and the ability to change or rewrite copy submitted by reporters.

This had to be the case because the job faced by our copy editors was especially challenging. Most of the articles handed in by the reporters needed to be heavily edited or even rewritten. This was so in part because some of our reporters were relatively less experienced in gathering news and writing stories, and in part because English was a non-mother tongue to them.

Specifically, I required that a copy editor needed to be a native English speaker. He or she had to have a bachelor's degree in journalism or English. It was desirable that they had some practical experience in the journalism profession.

I placed particular emphasis on an applicant's organizational skills. They needed the ability to rearrange a poorly organized article in a logical order. They of course needed to possess the basic capability to spot and correct typos, grammatical mistakes, and inaccuracies.

During my years at the CENS editorial department, I had in succession hired no small number of talented young people who met the above-cited standards to work for us as copy editors. The majority of them were American nationals, with some coming from Britain or Australia.

The turnover of our copy editors was similarly high as that of reporters. But the reasons were quite different. The inability of CENS to keep reporters working for long was mainly because of its inability to offer them clear career prospects. For instance, we were unable to create an environment in which they would have opportunities to become a professional English journalist and writer if they decided to stay and continue to work for CENS.

On the other hand, the high turnover of copy editors was an inherent problem. Below is a brief description of that issue: Most of the copy editors we hired were young foreign nationals. They were in Taiwan to learn Chinese or Chinese literature and culture. During their stay, they took time out to work for us, in part to earn some income to help cover their expenses on this island and in part to gain some practical journalism knowledge and skills. Once their stints in Taiwan expired, they had to go back to their home countries to resume their studies or do teaching or other jobs.

Some Ex-CENS Copy Editors Still on My Mind

Although the length of time those foreign copy editors worked for us was brief—mostly a year or two, they contributed greatly to upholding and raising the quality of our English publications. I still remember some of them and the specific editing jobs that I assigned to them.

Charles Hartman was one of our copy editors. I recall he was in Taiwan in the mid to late 1970s to study middle-period Chinese literature and culture, while at the same time teaching as an assistant professor at the Department of Foreign Language, National Taiwan University.

One day Hartman came to me to apply for an editing job. I briefly interviewed him and gave him an English news article. I explained to him the article was raw copy submitted by one of our reporters. It needed to be processed into a clean article ready for publication. I went further to tell him that in the process he could change words and sentences or rewrite the text, partially or wholly. It all depended on his judgment.

Hartman handled the copy well and promptly. He rearranged and rewrote several paragraphs of the text. Additionally, he reworded some sentences and made grammatical changes. The article, after being so revised, was smooth, easy to understand, and more interesting to read.

I passed Hartman's work to our senior associate editors and asked them to make comments. I had set a sort of peer review policy on evaluating news articles edited by candidates applying for the editing job. The results of such a review played an important role in my decision as to whether or not to hire the applicant involved.

All those who vetted Hartman's edited work agreed with the changes he made to the original copy. So I promptly invited him to join our copy-editing staff. One of the main tasks I assigned to Hartman, as our new copy editor, was to edit feature stories meant to be published in the column "From the Other Side" in the Monday Edition.

I asked him to edit feature stories meant to be used in the "From the Other Side" column because I felt he could best do that job. I took into account his educational background, his interests in Chinese literature and culture as well as his writing style. This column mostly carried soft stories, such as interviews with celebrated women, human interest pieces, and discussions about entertainment and the arts. They differed from hard news, such as politics, economics, and crime.

Hartman's subtle editing and rewriting skills added greatly to the appeal of the "From the Other Side" column, noted for being rich in content with well-selected subjects. The column, as I can recollect mow, was written by two CENS female reporters successively, Michelle Pao and Fu Li-yeh.

I cannot remember how long Hartman worked for CENS. We almost completely lost touch with each other since his departure from Taiwan. I last heard him teaching as a professor of Chinese Studies at the University at Albany, State University of New York.

One other copy editor, whom I can also vividly recollect, was Mike O'Connor. O'Connor, also an American national, had no previous journalistic experience. But he was a good English writer. Besides, his knowledge of Chinese was a plus in editing news stories for us. At the time, he had already become a translator of Chinese literature. I have no idea when he left CENS, but I do know his interest in writing has never changed. His relentless writing has led him to become a noted poet and prodigious author. I came to learn about his writing achievements because each time when O'Connor published a new book he would mail me a copy. His eighth book was "When the Tiger Weeps."

O'Connor, who stayed in Taiwan for about 10 years as an American student learning the Chinese language and studying Chinese culture, twice worked for us with an interval of some two years between his first and second tenures.

One of the jobs I assigned to him was to edit "Page Two," another special column of the Monday Edition. The author of "Page Two" was Philip Liu. In this column, Liu liked to explore current economic, political, and social issues, utilizing relevant material already published in the Chinese-language press media in the past week.

I asked O'Connor to edit this column because I thought his Chinese knowledge and his understanding of contemporary Taiwanese society would be a plus in performing that editing job. O'Connor's editing style was somewhat different from that of most other copy editors who worked for us. He seldom rewrote the original copy. But this didn't mean he cared less about quality or that he was unwilling to put more energy into his work.

On the contrary, he worked hard and with care. Before beginning to edit a feature, as I noticed, O'Connor always spent time reading the text carefully from the beginning to the end to gain a thorough understanding of what the author was trying to say. He did so because he viewed it as much easier to edit after grasping the meaning of the whole story.

He rewrote or restructured an article only when he felt it was absolutely necessary. Otherwise, he would avoid doing that. He believed that a copy editor ought to show due respect for the reporters by not readily restructuring their stories. Therefore, he mostly only polished the text by correcting words, sentences, and paragraphs to improve accuracy and readability.

I have no idea how long O'Connor stayed at CENS over his two tenures. But I can surely say that his combined length of service in the company was sufficient for him to develop professional habits that seemed to reflect his journalistic training. I make this claim based on the correspondence he conducted with me in the early years after his departure from Taiwan for his home in Seattle, Washington.

During those years O'Connor wrote me from time to time by sending either a postcard or a formal letter. He would always go out of his way to discuss with me some current news events concerning Taiwan, or its relations with mainland China, the island's biggest political adversary.

On one postcard, for instance, he said "...I study with a Tai Chi Ch'uan master from Beijing, by the way, a Tiananmen Square refugee no less...." He was referring to the bloody June 1989 Tiananmen Square protest and a resulting flight of protesters and others from the Chinese

Osman Tseng Retires

With CENS publisher Wang Pi-ly standing at his side, Osman Tseng (left) gives a farewell speech to his colleagues during the 15th anniversary celebration of CENS.

Osman Tseng, vice president of the China Economic News Service (CENS), announced his retirement on June 1, 1989, ending 15 years' service with the company.

An outstanding professional journalist, Tseng joined CENS in mid-1974. He served as the city editor, deputy editor-in-chief and editor-in-chief before finally being promoted in August 1983 to vice president of CENS.

His many contributions significantly raised the editorial quality of CENS publications, particularly that of the

The Economic News daily bulletin and weekly tabloid. He has written hundreds of editorials, for which our readers have praised his unique and illuminating treatment of contemporary economic and social issues facing Taiwan.

Osman Tseng has retired from CENS but not from the writing he loves. He now continues his career as a free-lance writer, and our readers may still be treated to a well-polished "Commentary and Analysis" in the terse, insightful style of Osman Tseng.

The newspaper clipping shows me giving a farewell speech on the eve of my retirement from CENS in 1989. Standing on my left side is my boss, CENS publisher Wang Bi-li.

mainland to foreign countries to escape arrest.

O'Connor was still working with CENS at the time when the student-led protests happened on the mainland. We watched, reported, and analyzed the event from this side of the Taiwan Strait. Beijing used assault rifles and tanks to crack down on the pro-democracy movement. The military crackdown provoked condemnations from around the world and elicited sympathy and support for the demonstrators.

O'Connor's journalistic professional habits also were displayed in another postcard mailed to me a week and a half ahead of Taiwan's widely watched, politically charged March 23, 1996, presidential election. His decision to write me that card at this juncture showed O'Connor still had not "broken" those habits even many years after he had left his journalistic work with us.

The 1996 ROC presidential campaign drew world attention because it was carried out amid military threats from the People's Liberation Army. The PLA fired three series of live-fire missile tests off Taiwan. The intimidating missile tests were later known as the 1995-1996 Taiwan Strait Crisis.

The first and second series of missile tests were made in July and August of 1995 in a protest against ROC President Lee Teng-hui's U.S. visit to his alma mater, Cornell University. Lee's U.S. visit infuriated Beijing, which accused him of abandoning the one-China principle. The third set of missiles was fired in mid-March of 1996, exactly one week ahead of the presidential election, in which Lee Teng-hui was seeking a new term. Beijing used the missile tests to warn Taiwan's people not to vote for him.

The PRC's missile firings backfired, however. Lee Teng-hui won a landslide victory. But the military and missile threats did cause panic in Taiwan, sparking a flight of capital and scaring away investors. The military tensions in the Taiwan Strait eased and the strained situation on the island stabilized only after U.S. President Clinton ordered the deployment in early March of two aircraft carriers, the USS Independence and the USS Nimitz, to the international waters near

Taiwan. The carriers' deployment was meant to tell the PRC not to intervene in Taiwan's democratic elections.

The following is what O'Connor wrote on a postcard he sent to me 10 days before the election. "Although it's only March 13th here, I'm going ahead and congratulate you on Lee Teng-hui's victory (democratic victory). Here in the States, there is surprisingly strong support for Taiwan. You know this, about our military by its presence, but it's also strikingly solid among the so many ordinary citizens, who do remember Tiananmen Square…I hope by the time this card reaches you, the explosive situation will have cooled & Taiwan can get on with its business -- to develop the country."

John Tjia and Sumner Gerard were two other former CENS copy editors, whom I am going to talk about below. Tjia and Gerard were unlike Mike O'Connor, who focused on poetry and book writing after leaving CENS, and Charles Hartman, who returned to the U.S. to resume his teaching career. Tjia and Gerard chose to work in the financial industry. They later became specialists in the field.

Reunion in Taipei with Several Ex-CENS Editors

John revisited Taipei between December 2018 and January 2019 for the first time since he left CENS four decades earlier. He brought along his two grown-up children. We met at a dinner party organized by William Kazer.

Bill was the most senior copy editor when he left CENS. Thereafter he continued his journalistic work with Reuters and later The Wall Street Journal with a combined length of service exceeding well over three decades. At the reunion dinner, I asked Bill to write a short piece recollecting his own experience at CENS and how we together conducted our editorial business in the early years of CENS. I will include his account of those days in later pages.

Also attending the Taipei party were Sumner Gerard and Yen Kuang-you. Some of us also brought our wives along. It was a rare reunion allowing us to reminisce about our old days. During conversations over dinner, John told me he had been working in the financial industry all those years. From a business card John handed to me, I learned that he once worked for MUFG Union Bank, N.A. as vice president and senior credit trainer for the bank's Department of Credit Training for the Americas.

Tjia specialized in financial modeling. He had authored a book entitled Building Financial Models. The work, published by McGraw Hill, is a guidebook for designing, building, and implementing a sturdy core valuation/projection model.

Soon after returning to the U.S. from his visit to Taiwan, John Tjia sent me an email. Some remarks in that mail evoked my memories of the old days at the CENS editorial department and I quote them below: "It has been a long journey from our days at CENS. I thank you again for our time together then, when you provided a wonderful and memorable experience of working together with a great team. I have been fortunate in finding my niche in financial modeling, and that was possible in part because of what I had gone through as a young editor under your guidance."

I can no longer recall how long John worked for CENS. But I do remember he wore two hats during most of his time at CENS: copy editor and makeup editor. Initially, he was hired to edit news stories. But I assigned him a concurrent role as a makeup editor, soon after I found him to show talents and interest in magazine design and layout.

CENS at the time published more than a half dozen trade magazines, in addition to the Monday Edition and the daily news bulletin as I discussed in the previous pages. How to make the various publications look more attractive and easy to read was a constant effort. This involved skillfully arranging headlines, news stories, and pictures. John contributed significantly in this regard. In his role as a makeup editor, he was never short of fresh ideas for improving our publications' layout and appearance.

John also impressed me with lots of cute and humorous fillers which he wrote from time to time. Back in my time at CENS, most newspapers and magazines were published using manual typesetting. That kind of printing method frequently resulted in a certain column having a few inches of white space needing to be filled up.

Traditionally, newspaper makeup editors, faced with such cases, used short news items left over from the previous day or ready-to-print public service ads to fit into the spaces, usually a few inches in column length. But this was not John's style. Whenever time permitted, he would prefer to write some cute and humorous pieces—being precisely the right number of inches--to fit into the gaps. So John, though a makeup editor, often also created news fillers.

Nowadays, publications, be they newspapers or magazines, rarely have a gap of that kind, because the layout is done completely on computers. Any space left over can be automatically filled by adjusting an image or the size of headlines or adding a subtitle. So writing news fillers today has long become a forgotten art.

During one late night drinks session after work John informed me of his intention to return to the United States. He asked me to find a replacement for him. After failing to convince John to stay on, we hired Sumner Gerard, also an American citizen.

Sumner had been working for China News, a Taipei-based English language daily newspaper before I invited him to join CENS. He was a meticulous copy editor. He paid particular attention to the usage of basic English, such as punctuation, grammar, and sentence structure, whenever editing copy. He never let any such basic errors pass uncorrected.

For a copy editor, paying attention to detail is an essential quality. But being totally inflexible is not necessarily a good thing. I recall a long-drawn-out discussion over the use of the two financial terms of "paid-up capital" and "paid-in capital." He insisted that the two terms carried different meanings, varying with the context in which they were used.

But in actuality, as shown in various financial news reports and credible relevant papers, the two terms are interchangeable. When or where they are interchanged in use is a matter of the author's personal preference. Some prefer to use paid-up capital others may use paid-in capital.

So, both terms have virtually the same meaning: Paid-up capital is the amount of money that a company has raised as funding capital directly from investors in the form of an initial public offering (IPO)--the primary market. More specifically, paid-up capital is the total amount of money shareholders have paid for shares at the initial issuance. It does not include any amount that investors later pay to purchase shares on the open market--the secondary market.

On the other hand, paid-in capital, refers to the same thing as paid-up capital. That said, paid-in capital can be defined in a different way: It refers to the total money contributed to a corporation by investors by purchasing that entity's stock from the primary market, not by the purchase of stock in the open market from other stockholders or the secondary market.

Sumner Gerard, like John Tjia, got a job in the finance industry in New York City after he ended his CENS stint and returned to the United States. He spent the bulk of his finance career working for a major New York money center bank. Years later he was dispatched to Taiwan and mainland China to develop the business as a senior officer. That he was tapped for these assignments, I assume, might have had something to do with his Chinese knowledge and his work experience at CENS in particular.

Sumner and his family settled in Taipei after his retirement. So we had more opportunities to see each other. In face-to-face conversations, I learned further that his long years of work in the finance industry had earned him the prestigious status as a financial expert. Sumner is a CFA charter holder. He obtained this specialist degree in finance only after having completed a Chartered Financial Analyst (CFA) program. This program, internationally recognized, is open only to investment and financial professionals.

Whenever I recall my early years in CENS, the name William Kazer always comes to my mind. This is so for several reasons. One,

Bill joined CENS at almost the same time as I did. He was supposed to serve as a copy editor. But I often gave him assignments to cover the news. I did so in part because of a shortage of reporters in those early days and in part because he liked to go out to do interviews.

What also impressed me about Bill was that he always worked hard, often to the extent of doing overtime. Yet I never heard him complaining about anything. Bill simply liked the CENS work. He rarely declined my proposal to have a late supper together--usually at a small eatery or a roadside stall--when we got the job done at the end of a long workday. Why did I see his willingness to eat supper with me as his enjoyment of the CENS news job? Here is why: Our late-night suppers were always served as a kind of working meal. We customarily used such occasions to talk about the news business.

Besides Bill and me, there was a constant third participant at the post-work meals, which more often than not went with a few drinks. That was Kenneth Liu, who joined CENS in the early days of its operation. After John Tjia joined our editorial staff, he became a fourth regular attendee at our after-work meal and drinking party.

During the eating and drinking, our discussion always revolved around the job done during the day. How to produce quality copy by improving, reporting and editing skills was a must as a discussion topic. Frequently, our conversations were also dominated by big current economic and political events taking place in or outside Taiwan.

Bill worked for CENS for more than four years and was invited by Reuters to join its Taipei Bureau. Bill, an ardent lover of journalism, as I know, is one of the few former CENS journalists who has devoted his entire career to this profession.

He has covered Asian politics and economics for more than 30 years, including, more recently, as a senior correspondent for the Wall Street Journal and Dow Jones News based in Beijing. His longer stint at Reuters involved him being stationed in a wide variety of world metropolises, which included Shanghai, Hong Kong, Taipei, Bangkok, New York as well as Beijing.

Bill and his wife, Audrey, shuttled back and forth between New York and Taipei during the past decade or so. They spent a lot of time in both places. During a gathering in Taipei, I asked Bill to do me a favor by writing something recounting what he can remember about CENS's editorial operations in its early stages. His description of those days, I explained to him, would be included in my autobiography project regarding my tenure at CENS. The following text put in quotation marks was contributed by him in response to my request.

A Contribution from William Kazer

"In 1974, I was studying Mandarin Chinese in Taiwan and working part-time as a freelance journalist. I saw a newspaper advertisement seeking English news editors and I sent a reply to express interest in being considered for the job. It turned out to be one of the best decisions of my life – both personally and professionally. I spent more than four years at the China Economic News Service, or CENS, an

English language news organization in the United Daily News Group....

"The Chinese language United Daily News had the biggest circulation of Taiwan's daily newspapers. It was a quality newspaper. In my opinion, it is still Taiwan's must-read general newspaper, though the paper and its local rivals suffer from the same financial pressures found in other markets around the world...

"I have long felt that those years were particularly rewarding. Few people can say that they truly enjoyed coming to work every day. I count myself as part of that fortunate minority. In those days, I considered a day not spent at the office as a day wasted. I got to work with Osman Tseng, a talented editor, and writer who has long had a keen interest in all things journalistic--from high-minded policy stories to economic and political analyses to amusingly offbeat human interest items. He was the driving force behind the operation and in later years was a writer of editorials for other publications such as the English-language China Post...

"After all these years I still count Osman as one of my closest friends. Osman supervised a small band of energetic and highly motivated reporters and editors, among them Yen Kuang-you, who later rose through the ranks of the United Daily News to top management and editorial positions at the group's flagship publications...

"Other stalwarts of the CENS operation included Richard Chuang, a specialist writer who focused on law and finance; Philip Liu and Shen Hsi-ta, who both covered trade and industry; versatile writer Angela Chang; and Wendell Chang, who later became an editor at Reuters, but unfortunately passed away well before his time....

"Over the years other editors beefed up the staff including Andrew Tanzer, Michael O'Connor, Sumner Gerard, John Tjia, Dennis Engbarth, and Earl Wieman. Another memorable character was Kenneth Liu, known both for his language skills as well as being a bit of a free spirit who was not intimidated by the prospect of missing a deadline...

"The United Daily News Group included a number of other publications, such as the Economic Daily News, Taiwan's most respected Chinese language business paper. The group's English publications focused on Taiwan's fast-growing economy and business developments. CENS was in its very early stages at that time, and it took advantage of the fact that there was little available for the English-speaking audience in Taiwan. There were two small daily newspapers, the China Post and the China News, but they had little to offer as far as economic news was concerned. CENS filled a critical gap in providing timely business information as the island's export-driven economy prospered...

"At the time, there was no internet and the demand for market information was growing rapidly. The daily publication was actually more like a collection of brief stories written in newswire style. It didn't look like much, printed on rough paper with its pages stapled together...

"But it was packed with useful economic statistics, industrial information, foreign exchange rates, and other market-moving news. It also had a solid reputation in the business community. Often when

I was interviewing officials or businessmen, I would spot the publication on the desk of the person I was talking to.

"I was quite proud to be associated with it, though I have to admit that not all of our customers had the same reverence for the publication. I recall making a trip to a neighborhood eatery where I occasionally had breakfast. The owner served up a range of local breakfast items, including the popular "shaobing" and "youtiao"-- a deep-fried stick of dough, wrapped in a baked biscuit. The tasty combination looked something like a meatless hotdog and bun...

"In the mornings, customers would line up for their "shaobing" and "youtiao" along with a bowl of soy milk. One morning as I stood in line, I noticed the boss had discovered that the pages of the CENS daily publication were just the right size to wrap his best-selling product. I was a little taken aback that all our hard work in getting the facts right and reporting them in a clear and concise manner had come to this sad end. But on reflection, I took it as an indication that our publication was still performing a useful economic service even after its contents had long been forgotten...

"There was also the weekly publication, which focused on trade developments. Light industry was king in those days and Taiwan's leading exports were textiles, garments, toys, and shoes. The weekly carried longer stories on these critical export industries. If a foreign trader wanted to know which company supplied a certain product, this was the place to look.

"There was a healthy rivalry with another publication called Trade Winds, which also served this market. One of the staples of these two publications was what was called the Line Report. It told what products were available and who produced them, gave guidance on prices, and described overall trends in the sector. The weekly, which was chock full of advertisements by exporters showcasing their products, was the publication that paid the bills...

But Osman and the other editors always wanted something that had the look and feel -- as well as the gravitas -- of a traditional daily newspaper. For the senior executives at the group that would have been a risky investment proposition in such a small market, but Osman eventually convinced management to back a once-a-week tabloid format which was known as the Monday Edition...

"It combined some of the best elements of all the publications and looked more like a traditional newspaper. Much of the staff's energy was concentrated on this publication. It was never likely to be a money-spinner, but it kept the staff motivated to produce strong copy and it showcased the best stories we could produce. Those included interviews with a long list of movers and shakers such as government officials, top bankers and businessmen, visiting scholars and other interesting personalities. American economist Milton Friedman and Taiwan economist Shirley Kuo -- who later was tapped to become finance minister and served as Taiwan's first woman Cabinet member--were among the interviewees, as was Anna Chennault, the influential Republican operative who was a frequent visitor to Taiwan (until the U.S. recognized Beijing and she saw brighter business prospects elsewhere)...

"Another was W. Edwards Deming, an American engineer, and consultant who years later was awarded the National Medal of Technology by U.S. President Ronald Reagan. In those years, Deming was better known in Asia than in the United States. In Japan, he was viewed as the guru of quality control and was widely credited with helping the nation's drive to upgrade its industrial sector. Taiwan was quick to notice and sought out his sound advice to strengthen its own export sector…

"After the editorial staff finally put these various publications to bed – usually well into the night -- there was always time for a short hike or cab ride to a nearby food stall and watering hole where we would review the key stories of the day. Osman would lead discussions about global politics, economic policy, the merits of certain stories we had published, and numerous suggestions about how to improve the Monday Edition…

"The conversation was aided by a healthy supply of Taiwan beer, a brew that had a robust personality even if it was sometimes a little short on consistency. It was usually accompanied by "lachiao hsiao-yu" – a tiny, dried fish with hot peppers – as well as dried bean curd, braised beef, and stewed salty eggs or 'ludan'…

"Osman had a knack for English writing and editing but in those days, he was a bit shy about speaking English. But that was true only until the beer started flowing; then the shyness gave way to ever greater fluency and confidence. The staff observed this progression until there was a sign-- often reinforced by the first rays of the morning sun – that maybe it was time for us to wrap up our discussions. Having solved so many intractable global problems and assessed the various plans for improving the publications, we would trundle off for a brief rest before it was time to restart the editorial process once again.

Ultimately, the work, discussion, camaraderie, and Taiwan beer, convinced me that my chosen career path was correct."

How I Got Earl Wieman to Work for CENS

Earl Wieman is another former CENS copy editor still vividly in my mind now, as I recount my time working for the news service organization more than three decades ago. Earl's length of service in CENS was the longest of all foreign editors who had worked for the company.

He was an important asset for CENS. His willingness to stay with the company much longer reduced the turnover of our copy-editing staff. He had a strong work ethic, never failing to meet deadlines. And more, Earl's English and Chinese language skills both are excellent.

Earl's job at CENS was not just editing news articles submitted by our reporters; he also served as a translator -- turning texts from Chinese into English. He did so very well and very fast. At the time Earl joined us, in fact, he had already been widely known as one of the best such authorities in Taiwan.

To draw on his excellent linguistic skills, I frequently asked him to translate good news features and commentaries, selected from our media group's Chinese-language United Daily News and Economic Daily News. These translated texts were then used in our CENS English publications.

The long-term practice of us reprinting high-quality news articles and features selected from the above-mentioned sister publications--

after being translated fluently and flawlessly by Earl--went a long way toward enriching the content of CENS publications.

Earl's consummate translation skills made him virtually irreplaceable in that role. I of course could have those Chinese materials translated by reporters and then corrected by other copy editors. But adopting such an indirect approach could have two drawbacks. One, it would take a much longer time to get a translation ready for print, and that was detrimental to meeting deadlines. Two, a Chinese-language article, if translated by a less experienced reporter and corrected by a copy editor with little knowledge of this language, tended to run the risk of losing its original meaning.

Earl liked to spend his leisure time in places outside Taiwan. I often took advantage of his foreign travels by asking him to do some special interviews. To give an example, one day Earl told me he was planning to visit his family in Kentucky. After pondering this briefly, I gave him the assignment of getting an interview with Kentucky Governor Martha Layne Collins. Ms. Collins was the state's first woman governor.

The aim of conducting that interview was to ask Ms. Collins as governor about how to promote bilateral relations between Kentucky and Taiwan. What prompted me to come up with that story idea was that Taiwan at the time was implementing a policy initiative to develop relations with the various U.S. states after the federal government in Washington, D.C., switched diplomatic recognition to Beijing in 1979.

What also impressed me about Earl was his constant effort to meet deadlines. He always returned his assigned tasks on time. It was not rare that he worked overnight to finish rewriting a special report and turn it the next morning just in time to meet the deadline. Many times his meeting-the-deadline efforts meant he was left with just enough time to rush to the airport to catch a flight for his foreign trip.

I felt, and I still feel, it was lucky that CENS could hire a steady and loyal worker like Earl Wieman. The story of how I got him to work for CENS is an interesting one.

I first met Earl at a reception held by a ROC government agency (I am not sure which agency it was, the Ministry of Foreign Affairs or the Government Information Office) in honor of David Dean, who then served as the first chairman of the American Institute in Taiwan. AIT functions as a de facto American embassy in Taipei after Washington shifted political recognition to Beijing in 1979.

Earl was the tallest person in a large group of attendees gathered at a spacious reception hall. The guests included senior ROC government officials, business and civic leaders, as well as representatives from the news media, both local and foreign.

His tall figure quickly drew my attention. I was curious and walked over to him, introducing myself as from the China Economic News Service, a member of the United Daily News group.

After a brief exchange, I went further to ask what he was doing. He replied to me that he was currently working as a freelancer, writing for a number of regional news organizations, including Asian Business. In the journalism profession, when someone told you that they were freelancing, it generally meant that he or she did not have a regular or fixed job. An idea thus immediately came to my mind. I asked whether he would be available to work for us. At the time I was looking for a part-time copy editor. He did not seem interested in my job offer. Our conversation thus ended there.

Days later I got a chance to call Earl at his home to invite him out for a meal and drinks. He accepted my invitation. We met in the evening at a restaurant, called something like Liang's Kitchen located on Dunhua North Road near Taipei's Songshan Airport.

I can no longer remember the content of our lengthy conversation that evening. But I do recall one embarrassing scene that emerged as we ended our meal and drink meeting: Earl and I kept drinking and talking so jovially that we even failed to notice all other guests had gone after finishing their meals. And that waiters were beginning to put chairs upside down on tables--a signal of closing. As we left our table, I found a dozen empty bottles of Taiwanese beer standing on it, meaning we each had consumed a half dozen.

The following morning, Earl Wieman came to report to me for work. From that day on, he was a regular worker at CENS serving in the editorial department. He later became the most senior associate editor with a tenure well exceeding that of almost all other CENS employees, local and foreign alike.

In the previous pages, I have recollected that during my more than half a dozen years heading the CENS editorial department, I recruited many talented young people, local and foreign, to work for CENS as reporters and copy editors. But I have yet to recite some fine men and women hired to serve as proofreaders in the department. They played a pivotal role in upholding the quality of CENS publications by eliminating mistakes in grammar, punctuation, spelling, and the like.

An Excellent Team of Proofreaders

We had an excellent team of half a dozen proofreaders. All of them held either an English or journalism degree. They worked hard, were cooperative, and often sacrificed Saturdays and holidays in order to meet deadlines set for the various economic and trade publications of CENS.

Now, when looking back on those CENS days, I still feel I owe these colleagues a debt of gratitude. Their hard work and consistent efforts to eliminate errors of all kinds in the process of proofreading contributed greatly to raising the quality of our publications.

I can still remember almost all of their faces, but not their names. There are three exceptions, however. They are Angina Chang, Chen Chui-fa, and David Yang. The three performed in succession as heads of the proofreading team. As chief proofreaders, they often came to me with questions about errors they found in the process of reviewing a final version of a certain news article or a feature story.

Proofreading is the last review of news reports and features before they are published. Specifically, it is a step of finding errors, small and large. Specifically, it is a process implemented to ensure consistency and accuracy in things such as grammar, spelling, formatting, page numbers, and headers.

To find these errors, proofreaders must meticulously and patiently compare the proofs with edited copies. Performing such a job requires a considerable amount of concentration and dedication. My CENS colleagues working at the proofreading desk did their job just in that kind of spirit. This was evident in the fact that our publications carried very few grammar mistakes.

When CENS was founded in mid-1974, the entire editorial department had little more than a dozen staff members. They included an editor-in-chief, a city editor, reporters, writers, proofreaders, typists, and an office boy.

But soon after, the size of the CENS editorial staff began making steady growth along with the expansion in advertising sales of the business department. The expansion of advertising came mainly as a result of a shift in the company's operating strategy from reporting economic news to publishing trade magazines. When I stepped down as editor-in-chief at the end of my nearly eight years in that job, the editorial department had a 50-strong workforce, the largest of its kind in Taiwan.

As I discussed earlier in this chapter, CENS in the beginning printed only a daily economic news bulletin and an economic news weekly--or the Monday Edition. The two economic publications were directed at domestic audiences.

CENS expanded fast. We soon launched a trade journal called the Overseas Weekly. This magazine, unlike the Monday Edition and the daily Economic News bulletin, was aimed at disseminating information about Taiwan's export products to foreign business executives looking to import merchandise from this island.

The Overseas Weekly quickly became popular with exporters in Taiwan and buyers abroad. The popularity led to fast growth in demand for advertising space. In response, we had to constantly increase the number of pages of the Overseas Weekly. It shot up to over 50 pages in a short period of time, rising from just over 10.

It's worth mentioning here that we had adopted a policy that called for editorial content to increase along with the growth in advertisement space in a proportional manner. This meant that the editorial department had to continuously add reporting and editing staff to cope with its fast-growing workload.

The Overseas Weekly's rich editorial content and its huge number of advertisements quickly won recognition from the trade authorities of the government, including those of the China External Trade Development Council. The council was a semi-official body created to help manufacturers and exporters develop sales in world markets. Senior officials of the council approached us and suggested that we publish a trade monthly patterned after the Overseas Weekly. By this time, CENS had already earned a reputation as a credible economic news service organization in Taiwan.

The authorities of the trade council even promised to render us a sort of financial support if we printed a new publication as it suggested. In the end, the promise they made turned out to be only nominal. One main reason was that we, as a private media institution, didn't welcome any form of aid from the government. In fact, we, the China Economic News Service, at the time had been preparing to print a trade monthly ourselves.

The monthly, entitled Taiwan Product, was a general-purpose trade journal covering a wide variety of locally manufactured consumer goods, which targeted cross-industry buyers. The monthly sold exceptionally well in terms of both circulation and advertising sales.

Emboldened by the success of Taiwan Product, CENS moved further to publish a new series of trade magazines. At this time, CENS had undergone a far-reaching strategic change--switching from the publishing of general-interest magazines to the printing of specialized, or industry-specific, trade magazines.

An industry-specific trade journal is unlike a general purpose one, which covers a wide range of manufacturing industries and is targeted at buyers engaging in a variety of similar types of businesses. An industry-specific journal, on the other hand, reports only on a particular industry. These journals are directed only at audiences who trade in these same industries.

CENS, when business was at its peak, published about half a dozen specialized trade journals, in addition to the daily news bulletin and the Monday Edition, both of which were oriented toward domestic readers, as explained earlier. The specialized magazines included machinery, hardware, auto parts, electronics, lighting, and furniture.

In publishing these industry-specific magazines, we covered each and every industry in more detail than we did in the general-interest trade publications. This assumed that people who read a specialized trade magazine tended to be professionals in a relevant business. So we always made sure that all the product or line reports that we printed in our specialized trade journals were in-depth studies, providing business information that was of value to these readers.

In line with our policy of specializing in trade publications, CENS adopted a targeted advertising and circulation strategy. Under this strategy, CENS sold advertising space only to manufacturers and traders doing business in the industry involved. Similarly, our specialized magazines were circulated only to people who were interested in the businesses which we covered. So we followed a controlled circulation policy. Under this policy, a subscription was free but was restricted only to potential buyers.

Generally, the various CENS-run specialized trade magazines, be they monthly, bimonthly, or quarterly, were quite successful in terms of circulation and advertisement sales. Copies of these journals were distributed to readers and subscribers all over the world.

A Strong Sales Department

Two primary reasons could be cited for the success of publishing the various trade magazines. One, we had a strong business department that operated directly under the guidance of CENS president Brian Yu, an innovative, journalist-turned-business executive. The department consisted of about six sections each staffed by a half dozen smart salespersons, who knew how to connect with clients and convince them to buy advertising space.

The other reason was that the launch of the many CENS trade publications came at a time when Taiwan's companies were working hard to develop sales abroad. The vast majority of them were small and medium-sized enterprises. They lacked the resources to set up overseas sales networks of their own. This left them to rely on government and privately funded trade organizations to promote their products in world markets. Yet while such efforts were helpful, their beneficial effects were limited, given the fact that there were numerous Taiwan companies striving to sell their products overseas.

So the coming into being of CENS trade-promoting magazines--and its rival publications--provided a much-needed medium for Taiwan's small businesses to promote overseas sales in those times. Here is an example of how successful and helpful our trade magazines had become: There were often cases in which manufacturers spontaneously called in to buy advertising space in our publications. Some clients even told our salespeople that many foreign buyers placed orders with them only after reading our trade magazines.

It's not an overstatement to say that CENS, through the publication of its multiple trade magazines, had played a significant role in promoting Taiwan's exports and, by extension, its industrial and economic development.

Ironically, the success of CENS in publishing so many trade magazines was also attributable to the nonexistence during those days of e-commerce -- the business activity of electronically buying or selling products over the Internet. The unavailability of e-commerce channels made companies reliant on the print medium to promote their merchandise. The demand for advertising space in trade journals, therefore, was always strong. It could be said that running trade magazines were a lucrative business.

Editorial Role Shrinks as Reliance on Ad Sales Grows

In the case of CENS, the vast majority of its annual revenue came from advertisements, with circulation fees accounting for only a fraction of the total amount. This disproportionate revenue structure gave the business department a dominant role to play in the company's direction and policy. Consequently, the editorial department was left with only a supporting part to perform.

From time to time, for instance, the editorial content was designed only to reflect an advertising demographic. There was nothing wrong with this policy. But the question was whether the advertisers that appeared in our publications reflected a whole picture of Taiwan's entire export business. In fact, the advertisers involved did not even represent the industries, in which they were operating.

Professional journalism requires that editorial content needs to be designed to inform, educate and entertain. And that a clear line has to be drawn between editorial content and advertising content. But this line was sometimes blurred under the influence of advertisers, often exerted by our own salespeople or the advertising executives. Of course, we were not alone. Similar situations also existed in our fellow publishing companies. It was an industry-wide problem.

A more fundamental concern for me and my editorial development colleagues--the many young reporters, writers, and copy editors in particular--was that CENS was increasingly focused on running trade magazines with a profit-oriented approach, deviating from its founding policy of operating as an economic news service company.

This policy shift concerned me in particular. I worried that such a deviation would eventually dash my hope that CENS someday would publish an English language daily, drawing on its years of experience in printing a range of economic and trade publications.

The main motivation for me to join CENS at its founding was a desire to help start an English-language newspaper. At the time when CENS was founded, rumors had spread that the United Daily News, one of Taiwan's largest Chinese language newspapers, was likely to make a foray into English language journalism. The new launch of CENS, as many observed, was the first step in that direction.

That observation was plausible. The United Daily News would have a number of advantages if it decided to open a new English newspaper. One, it had the support of abundant financial resources. Strong financial support was crucial to starting a foreign language newspaper--a kind of investment that tended to run the risk of losing money for years before achieving the break-even point.

Two, the founder and chairman of CENS, Wang Tih-wu, was a widely respected veteran newspaper man, who had over the last few decades successfully founded a long list of well-read dailies. They included the flagship United Daily News, the Economic Daily News, Min Sheng Pao daily, the United Evening News, and the World Journal. The latter of which was a news daily appealing to ethnic Chinese communities in New York, San Francisco, Vancouver, Paris, and Bangkok.

However, all of the above-listed newspapers were published in Chinese. So Wang's decision to set up CENS, dedicated to printing economic news and trade publications in the English language, quickly raised speculation in Taiwan media circles. Many speculated that the newspaper tycoon might be attempting to branch out into the English-language media market.

Chapter 8
Joining China Economic News Service

For myself, I too had the conviction that chairman Wang Tih-wu's reported attempt to invest in the establishment of an English newspaper could be true. And I believed that CENS, with the chairman's policy and financial support, would surely be able to successfully run a quality English newspaper.

Why did I hope at the time to see new investment in Taiwan's English journalism industry? I had long held the view that the local English news media, which included a daily and an evening newspaper, needed to bring in new investment to increase competition. Only through competition, I believed, was it possible for this foreign language media sector to raise journalistic standards. It had much room for improvement, as I saw it as both a participant and a reader.

Despite the fact that CENS, driven by increasing commercialization, was steadily moving away from its founding ideals of printing quality economic news publications, somehow I still cherished a dim hope that there would be a reversal of CENS's operating policies.

But even this dim hope was finally crushed during a meeting I had with CENS publisher, Wang Bi-li. I have no idea when that meeting took place. But I do remember it was held in the morning when the publisher called me into his office. After a few exchanges, he told me in the most absolute tone that CENS "has no plan to publish an English-language newspaper either now or in the future."

It was not unusual that I came to the publisher's office to discuss matters about editorial content and operations. But the discussion in question impressed me so deeply that I can still remember some of our conversation.

357

My immediate reaction to the publisher's revelation that CENS had no plan to print an English daily newspaper was "feeling disappointed and to some extent even unhappy." I protested silently why I had been kept out of such a crucial company policy until now. At this time, I had served in the post of editor-in-chief for more than seven years.

The publisher then explained to me that the decision not to invest in the establishment of an English daily was made by chairman Wang Tih-wu, the publisher's father and the founder of the United Daily News group. What prompted the chairman to reach that decision? "Let everyone have a finger in the pie," the publisher quoted chairman Wang as saying.

The above quote from the chairman could be liberally interpreted as a pie-sharing concept--a theory that would let everyone have an opportunity to grow the economy and share its benefits. The publisher went on to elaborate on the chairman's concept.

The chairman was of the view that Taiwan's market for publications printed in the English language was small. If the United Daily News group branched out into the English media industry, it would have a crowding effect on the existing players. Additionally, he said, the chairman did not want to alienate the senior executives of the current English news media companies, because they all were longtime friends.

The decision by the top-level leadership of CENS or the broad United Daily News group not to invest in the establishment of an English newspaper had a direct impact on me as someone who had the responsibility for editorial policy and the well-being of the staff working with him. By now, I had to make a decision of my own as to whether or not to continue working for CENS.

The CENS's policy of not starting an English daily, however, did not pose a question about my continued employment with the company. Legally I could work for the company until I was 65 years old, the retirement age for all employees under the country's labor law. By this time, I was around 52 years old. This meant I could carry on with my CENS work for well over 10 more years.

Why I Decided to Retire from CENS Early

While legally I could stay on, there was a growing sense in me that I had to retire early from the company. More and more I felt it was pointless to continue working for CENS. As the company continued to concentrate its resources on developing its advertisement-focused business, the editorial department helplessly sank to the status of playing only a supporting role. This did not sound right. From the start, the mission of the editorial department was to provide economic news.

With its status degraded, the editorial department was responsible only for the supply of industry or line reports needed to fill all designated editorial space in the various CENS trade journals.

Line reports, unlike news stories and features, all followed the same pattern in terms of reporting and writing. But interviewing manufacturers and writing line reports required no sophisticated journalistic skills. This meant that CENS, despite its role as a news media company, provided no opportunities for its editorial staff members to practice traditional journalism and advance their journalistic careers.

Oftentimes, reporters and copy editors complained to me that they got tired of doing line reports. Some put it even more bluntly that writing line or industry reports was a boring job requiring no thought or creation whatsoever.

In the face of their complaints, I could only feel sorry for failing to create a more favorable environment, in which both traditional journalism and trade journalism had a role to play. But now I realized that building a working environment of that kind would never be possible, after hearing what the publisher personally revealed to me in his office.

The straw that broke the camel's back was Mr. Wang Bi-li's unequivocal statement, as I just mentioned above, that "CENS was not going to print a daily English newspaper." That revelation made me feel it was time for me to go.

So I decided to apply for early retirement rather than waiting until I reached the legally prescribed age of 65. Under the labor law, early retirement was permissible only when the applicant met the following two requirements: 1. Having worked for the same company for at least 15 years. 2. The cumulative length of his or her employment in the labor market had reached a minimum of 25 years. I met both of the two requirements for early retirement.

I retired from CENS in the middle of 1989, about three years after I stepped down from the position of editor-in-chief. Previously, I had worn two hats. Now after leaving the chief editor job, I served only as CENS' vice president, a post which I had held until my retirement.

In the vice president job, I was no longer as busy as before and thus had plenty of time for writing. I regularly wrote a column and translated a feature, from Chinese into English, for the economic news weekly of CENS. At one point, I even worked the night shift to write economic news for the daily bulletin.

As I recall, during the three-year period prior to my 1989 retirement, I sometimes even used weekends and holidays to do English writing. I did so not for the purpose of making extra money. Rather it was because I felt I needed to write more to improve my writing skills. In the previous nearly eight years while working in the editor-in-chief position, I did not have time to do the writing. All of my time was spent reading and editing copy. This kind of task did assist me in developing an eye for what readable writing looks like. But trying to become a full-time English writer, I felt I needed more practice.

Specifically, I planned and sought to make a living as a writer after retirement from CENS. I had to earn enough income to support myself and my family. By "enough income," I meant it had to be no less than what I earned at CENS.

But making a living as a full-time English writer was surely going to be a big challenge for me, no matter what kind of writing I was going to get into. It was a big challenge because the demand for English writers was not all that strong in Taiwan, a place where everyone uses Chinese, their native tongue. This exactly was the reason why I had tried so hard to do more writing during the time prior to my retirement. I believed such hard work would allow me to sharpen my writing skills and thus enhance my competitiveness in the marketplace.

But far beyond my expectations, I got three writing jobs immediately after I left CENS, the China Economic News Service. It could be said that my transfer from retirement to taking on multiple writing jobs was a seamless connection. Also encouragingly, the payments I got from the three separate writing jobs added up to almost the same amount of income as I drew at the time I left CENS.

One of the jobs was offered by publisher Wang Bi-li. Days ahead of my departure I went to the publisher's office to say goodbye to him. He enquired about my post-retirement plan. I told him I was exploring the possibility of doing some writing. He was quick to respond with an offer, asking me to continue to write for a column in the Monday Edition or the Economic News Weekly. I thankfully accepted the offer. It was a "Commentary and Analysis" column, which I had already been writing for some time before I left CENS.

News about my retirement from the United Daily News Group went out way ahead of my scheduled departure (June 1, 1989). A week or so before I departed from CENS, I received a phone call from Richard Vuylsteke, managing editor of the Free China Review. He asked me if I could do a special report each month for the Review. I happily accepted his invitation. Free China Review was a general-purpose magazine, published once a month. It was run by the Government Information Office of the Republic of China with the target audience in foreign countries, which had diplomatic and trade relations with the ROC. Vuylsteke had briefly worked for CENS as an associate editor before he left to join the GIO magazine.

Around the same time I got another call, this time from China Post co-founder and publisher Nancy Yu-Huang -- my former boss and journalism mentor. Over the phone, she invited me out for a lunch at the then Central Restaurant on Zhongshan North Road. I went to meet her at the designated time and place. Over lunch, she sounded me out about coming back to work for the China Post.

At the outset of our conversation, she asked me to help expand the content of the Post's newly opened economic and business section. According to her, she offered me the job in light of my long years of experience working for CENS and Asian Sources. The latter was a Hong Kong-based trade magazine, which I had worked with for years before I joined CENS. I declined Nancy's offer immediately and firmly, citing my current interest in writing. "Editing of any kind was not my option now," I told her.

After learning where my interest lay, she no longer insisted that I edit economic and business news for the Post. Instead, she asked me to write editorials for the paper. She presented this latter job offer, as I saw, more earnestly. "If you agree to write editorials for us," she said, "I would use the opportunity to reshuffle our board of editorial writers." By now I had come to realize that her main purpose in inviting me out for lunch was to persuade me to join her editorial writing board as a member.

"I am looking for a replacement for one of our editorial writers responsible for commenting on economic events and issues," she told me. "The current writer, an economics professor," she continued, "has recently expressed his desire to leave the job for health reasons." She then added, "I think you are a proper replacement, given your economic knowledge and experience in trade journalism."

In addition, Nancy also expressed her wish that I would write some political and diplomatic pieces for the Post as well. The current guest writer dealing with such subject matters was a retired ambassador. But the publisher criticized him in front of me for being unable to respond to news happenings quickly enough. She also viewed his copy as lacking depth.

As we ended our conversations at the Central Restaurant, as I recall, I agreed to write two to three economic and political editorials a week for the China Post. No contract was signed for my service. I worked from my home without having to go to the Post's office. I was paid a fixed rate for each editorial I submitted. Although not bound by any formal contract, my editorial-contributing relationship with the China Post lasted as long as 18 years, without any interruption during the entire length of the said period.

A Watershed Moment in My Journalism Career

I always like to describe the time between my retirement from CENS and my subsequent entry into the field of editorial and commentary writing as a watershed moment in my entire journalism career. The phase preceding the watershed line started in January 1966, when I entered the profession as a reporter, and ended in mid-1989, when I retired from CENS as vice president. The first phase of my journalism career involved me serving as a reporter, city editor, bureau chief, and editor-in-chief. Most of these positions obliged me to perform managerial duties.

The phase that followed the watershed line spanned nearly two decades, during which I wrote editorials for the China Post regularly--to be exact, week after week, month after month, and year after year uninterruptedly. After leaving the editorial writing job at the China Post, I worked for two more years freelancing and translating news articles from Chinese into English. Freelancing and translation were the last two paying jobs I had in my 46 years of journalism and writing.

If I say my journalism career reached its peak at the time when I served as CENS editor-in-chief, then my next 18-year tenure at the China Post as an editorial writer could be defined as the second peak in my career.

The nearly two-decade editorial writing job involved me constantly monitoring and analyzing economic, political, and diplomatic events. All such events happened during the tenures of Taiwan's two former presidents, Lee Teng-hui, and Chen Shui-bian. Many of those events were historically significant. So I will include them in the next two sections--chapter 9 and chapter 10, as I go about recollecting what I had done during my time as an editorial writer.

Before starting to write chapters 9 and 10, I will first finish the current one: Joining the China Economic News Service. By the time I left CENS, I had worked for several different news organizations. But my time with CENS was the longest. The long duration provided me opportunities to serve as a writer, city editor, editor-in-chief, and finally vice president all in the same company. I was grateful that I was given the chance to learn and practice journalism at all levels of this profession, building on my covering, reporting, and writing experiences acquired in the previous more than 10 years.

I served in the position of editor-in-chief much longer -- about seven years--than I did in my other CENS posts. Editor-in-chief was, and still is, a prestigious journalistic role. Having the chance to be ultimately promoted to that post was especially significant for me, given the fact that in my life I have never received any formal education.

But honestly speaking, the CENS chief editor job was the most challenging for me. Anyone in this role was supposed to have a strong command of English. It's true I had already had well over 10 years of experience writing English news stories before I was assigned to the editor-in-chief job. But the problem for me was that English is not my mother tongue and that I began to learn the ABCs in my early 20s.

So I would say I was not well equipped linguistically to perform the chief editor job when I was first promoted to that role. For example, as I recall, it often took me longer than normal time to review an English news feature or correct some grammar mistakes.

What added to the challenge was that I, as editor-in-chief, always had big quantities of unedited and edited copy to review for accuracy and appropriateness. There is no way for me to recall and give an exact number of articles, which I normally had to go over for a given period of time. But the number had to be substantial, considering the fact that CENS, when its business reached its peak, printed more than half a dozen trade and economic publications.

During my stint as CENS chief editor, I built a de facto standard operating procedure (SOP), with the process starting from me. Most of the time I developed story ideas and gave assignments to reporters. They in turn worked on assignments by doing news coverage or conducting interviews and writing them into English stories. They had to finish their assignments and submit them to me no later than the deadlines.

On receiving reporters' finished assignments or stories, I took only a quick look at them for fact-checking. At this time, I also tried to find whether those articles included all the essential information as requested.

After doing such initial checks, I then passed the articles on to copy editors for editing. My decision on whom should I assign a certain editing task to was not entirely based on whether he or she was available at the time. Sometimes, for example, when I found a special report that dealt with a complex topic, such as finance and a controversial public policy, I tended to assign it to a more experienced copy editor or to someone with knowledge of that particular subject.

All reports and features, having gone through the process of revision by copy editors, went back to my desk for final checks by me. I performed the final copy check in a way like this. I carefully read each and every copy editor-revised story that came back to me. I usually did not put too much attention on the language. This was because all of our copy editors were native English speakers and, more importantly, had passed a writing skill test when they applied to us for the editing job.

Instead, I focused on three particular things in reviewing the articles turned in by the copy editors. One was whether he or she had fully grasped the meanings of the authors -- the reporters -- in doing editing or rewriting. This was a matter of concern because none of our reporters were native English speakers. Thus there was the possibility that they might have failed to exactly express their ideas in their articles.

Two, I always read all of the revised articles thoroughly to see whether my copy editors had made errors due to their lack of Chinese knowledge. As the chief editor, I had to make sure that no mistakes would go uncorrected during the final stages of production.

To reduce mistakes introduced in the course of editing, I always encouraged copy editors to go directly to the reporters to talk and check with them, if they had any questions about the content of their reports.

In addition to my efforts at finding and correcting mistakes, I also paid careful attention to the matter of structure, whenever I reviewed edited copy. I wanted to ensure that the finished work was complete, balanced, well focused, and well organized. It was not uncommon that when discovering copy failing to meet any of these standards, I would return it to the relevant copy editor asking him or her to make necessary changes.

In retrospect, I feel my 7-odd years in the post of editor-in-chief led me to develop a lifetime habit of reading articles or any written materials with a critical eye. And I know by instinct what constitutes a good piece of writing, as a result of my long years of reviewing and editing news articles and special features.

The editor-in-chief chief job also benefited me greatly in another important way. It provided me with a constant opportunity to acquire and accumulate economic and general knowledge. This learning experience proved helpful to me in landing an editorial writing job at the China Post right after I left CENS.

As the editor-in-chief, I felt compelled to constantly track the developments of Taiwan's economy, finance, and foreign trade. I did so because I needed to gain a great wealth of economic knowledge to help me perform my duties, like developing story ideas, supervising event coverage, and evaluating news stories.

Another point worth recounting, in particular, is that during my time at the CENS editorial department I had the opportunity to meet and work with a group of fine young people, from reporters to copy editors, proofreaders, and typists. They all were hard-working and cooperative.

Without their devotion and cooperation, it would never have been possible for CENS to steadily and successfully run a long series of trade and economic journals. All CENS publications, whether they were daily, weekly, monthly, or quarterly, appeared on time while maintaining acceptable standards of quality.

To meet the deadlines for the various publications, working overtime among us was commonplace. But all of us had the understanding that overtime was inevitable, given the nature of our publishing business. And despite a high frequency of working overtime, our morale at the workplace was always high. This was due largely to our good fortune: All the people we recruited to work for the editorial department were highly motivated.

The high morale at the workplace, as I now recall, also had something to do with me as a team leader. I often had morale-boosting activities organized. One frequently conducted activity was holding buffet-style dinner parties either in my home or in the homes of married colleagues during the weekends or on holidays. On such occasions, all editorial department members were encouraged to attend.

Aside from holding morale-boosting activities, I would always express, in person or in public, my appreciation and gratitude to whomever for their good performance, like doing an exclusive interview, turning in particularly well-edited copy, or finding a major content error.

I'll always value my 15-year stint at CENS. It's a place where I made many good and lasting friends. And it was there where I learned and practiced English-language journalism in the most extensive manner in my decades of career in this profession.

Here, I must express my deep gratitude to CENS publisher Wang Bi-li and president Brian Yu, my immediate boss, for giving me the opportunity to play multiple journalist roles at CENS. They always respected my news judgment. In the editor-in-chief post, they gave me full freedom to exercise my duties, rarely interfering in my editorial policy.

If there was anything I regretted when I left CENS, it was my failure to win policy support for us to publish an English-language newspaper during my time there. But now when looking back on that matter, I feel it was a blessing in disguise for me.

Had my long-cherished hope of helping to establish an English-language newspaper come true, there would certainly have been a role for me to play at this new newspaper. In such a circumstance, I would not have had any reason to ask for early retirement.

And had I not retired from CENS, it would have been impossible for me to accept the China Post publisher's offer to write editorials for her paper. Writing editorials and commentaries for the English newspaper for the next 18 years enriched my journalism life in a most exciting way.

That 18-year period spanned the terms of two of Taiwan's presidents, Lee Teng-hui, and Chen Shui-bian. This meant that I, as a commentary writer, had the chance to examine the former two leaders' policies, performance, and achievements in a close and critical way.

The following two segments, chapters 9 and 10, will be devoted to recollecting what I wrote then about the two ex-presidents. All such recollections will be based on the numerous opinion pieces, which I wrote, clipped, and kept to this date.

Chapter 9
Switching to Commentary Writing

Examining Lee Teng-hui's Democratic Reforms

Officially, I retired from the China Economic News Service in mid-1989 as vice president, ending my 25-year career in news gathering, reporting, and editing. But in actuality, I did not exit the journalism profession. I soon started a different type of work in journalism as an opinion writer. For the next nearly two decades I wrote simultaneously for a number of English-language publications. They included a daily, the China Post; a weekly, the Economic News; and a monthly, the Free China Review.

But my primary employer was the China Post. I contributed eight to nine editorials a month to the newspaper for the vast majority of that 20-year period. In this long-time, commentary-writing job, I had the opportunity to cover two presidents, Lee Teng-hui and his successor, Chen Shui-bian. Fortunately, I still keep those editorials and analyses from years ago. From these opinion pieces, I will recollect how I evaluated the policies and the performance of these two important political figures.

In this section, chapter 9, I will first examine my editorials and commentaries on former President Lee Teng-hui (1988 to 2000). Under Lee Teng-hui's 12-year leadership, Taiwan transitioned from authoritarian rule to a viable democracy. As an editorial writer, I watched him initiate and push through the various far-reaching reforms from a journalist's perspective.

When Lee Teng-hui succeeded Chiang Ching-kuo in January 1988 as the president of the Republic of China, he also inherited Chiang's unfinished reform policies and, hence, his responsibility to carry them through. Barely six months before his death in 1987, then seriously ill Chiang Ching-kuo had formally ended his father Chiang Kai-shek's authoritarian rule by lifting decades-old martial law, removing the bans on forming political parties, liberalizing investment in newspapers, and easing travel to rival communist China.

"I promise I will do my utmost to carry out political reforms and promote the country's ultimate reunification," pledged Lee Teng-hui, after taking the oath of office. Lee, then 65, was the first Taiwan-born politician to become the president of the ROC. As an agricultural economist, he was invited by Chiang Ching-kuo to serve in the government in the early 1970s. He had since held various senior posts, including mayor of Taipei City. When Chiang died, Lee had been his vice president for years.

Lee Teng-hui gave his first press conference as president only 40 days after his inauguration. I watched the event on TV, listening to him giving his opening remarks and answering press questions. Subsequently, I wrote an article for my weekly Commentary and Analysis column in the Economic News, titled 'President Lee Exhibits Vital Qualities at His First Press Conference.'

In the commentary, I pointed in particular to Lee's replies to the following three questions raised by the press: 1) Whether the government would be willing to return to the Asian Development

Bank under the name of "Taipei, China," if this country could not be admitted under its official national name, 2) What he would do to improve relations with the communist-held Chinese mainland, and 3) Whether he was willing to communicate with opposition leaders face-to-face to ease tensions with them.

Based on the stance and views Lee took in his replies to the above questions, I made a few observations in my column. I said the newly inaugurated president possessed three crucial character traits: flexibility, pragmatism, and a willingness to seek reconciliation. These traits were most important for an ROC president, as he sought to meet the various difficult challenges facing the nation. The leader, for example, needed to adopt a pragmatic approach in carrying out the many political reforms, as he responded to public calls for change. The government also had to follow a flexible foreign policy amid Beijing's increasing efforts to isolate the ROC in the international community.

In conclusion, I called Lee's attention to the leadership style of his predecessor Chiang Ching-kuo. Chiang had long governed through a sort of collective leadership. Specifically, all major government policies were first discussed and passed at a weekly Cabinet meeting. Afterwards, the decisions were submitted to the ruling KMT's powerful Central Standing Committee meeting for ratification. The once-a-week KMT event, attended by top government officials, party heavyweights, and ranking military officers, normally was presided over by Chiang himself in his capacity as president and party chairman.

During such Central Standing Committee meetings, Chiang usually did two things: To settle inter-government department disputes over policies or announce his own reform ideas. In the first case, some attendees might bitterly disagree with one another over a certain policy, but once Chiang ruled against or in favor of that policy, it was final. But Chiang could do so not entirely because of his authority as president or party chairman. Rather it was because of the political influence and prestige he commanded. This was an important leadership asset, something which could not be inherited. It instead had to be cultivated.

So I concluded in the commentary that whether Lee Teng-hui could quickly build his own personal influence and gain party and military support would determine if he was able to win the coming KMT nomination to run in 1990 for a six-year term of his own. Lee currently was performing as an interim president completing the late President Chiang Ching-kuo's unfinished term.

Strictly speaking, Lee Teng-hui did not carry out any of the politically significant reforms he promised during his first more than two years in office. One main reason for the failure was that he was busy consolidating power. Another reason was that he as an interim president lacked a popular mandate that could allow him to legitimately conduct any serious changes without endangering stability.

Lee started to push for reforms only after he was elected in March 1990 to a six-year term of his own. He won the election against a background of widespread discontent among the public at the failure of the KMT-led government to carry out political and democratic reforms fast enough.

I wrote an editorial for the China Post on the night of his win that appeared in the newspaper the following day, carrying the title: 'President Lee Elected to a Six-Year Term.' In it, I pointed out that the newly elected president needed to give first priority to political reforms, changes which he had failed to deal with in the past more than two years as an interim leader.

The editorial read in part "Among the most pressing issues will be political reform. This issue has been brought to the fore by the many thousands of students from colleges and universities around Taiwan, who have been staging a sit-in demonstration on the grounds of the Chiang Kai-shek Memorial Hall in Taipei since last week...

"The students are demanding President Lee undertake sweeping reforms and set a timetable showing how and when their required changes will be accomplished. The student sit-in demonstration gained sympathy and support from all sectors of society...Essentially the people of the country are calling for the government to overhaul parliament, open the office of president and other ranking government positions to direct popular elections, and abolish the suffocating 'Temporary Provisions Effective During the Period of Communist Rebellion.'

"Political reforms such as those cited above are urgent. As Taiwan moves toward an increasingly plural society, more and more people are pushing for political participation and greater democracy...The failure of the government to tackle these and other important changes have been the primary source of increasing social and political tensions in Taiwan in recent years."

At the end of the March 22, 1990 editorial, I pointed out that "a most difficult challenge facing President Lee Teng-hui was how to rally the support of the nearly 700 national assemblymen for his pro-democracy reforms. The assemblymen, who just elected Lee to a new term of office, also had the authority to revise the constitution. This is to say that any important political reforms would become impossible without their support and final ratification...

"Already some of them have expressed their opposition to growing public calls for dissolving the National Assembly. The assembly had failed to undergo reelections since it was first chosen in the 1940s on the Chinese mainland. Now if these long-serving assemblymen support the reform call, it would amount to voting themselves out of jobs, threatening their vested interests. Therefore, President Lee Teng-hui, in pressing for his pro-democracy programs, had to leverage his presidential authority as well as the current nationwide reform movement..."

President Lee Teng-hui assumed his six-year term of office on May 20, 1990. In his inaugural speech, Lee announced a wide-ranging reform program. But I picked only one single point from it for discussion in my editorial, which appeared in the China Post the following day: The point in question was that Lee stated he would declare the termination of the 'Period of National Mobilization for Suppression of Communist Rebellion' in the shortest possible time.

Plan to End 'Emergency Period Provisions'

I focused on that point because I believed that ending the more than 40 years of "emergency period" decree was a fundamental step for Taiwan to achieve greater democracy and, in addition, to break the longstanding political standoff with the communist-controlled Chinese mainland. I went on to analyze:

"Ending the 'emergency period for suppression of communist rebellion' is of particular importance for two reasons. One, it would mean that Taipei will no longer treat the communist government in Beijing as a rebel regime, as it had in the past. This was also to say that Taipei would accept Beijing's rule of the mainland as the reality. At the same time, the termination of the special law may also indicate that the Taipei government has come to acknowledge the political fact that its effective judicial rule is now limited only to Taiwan, Penghu, and the offshore islands of Kinmen and Matsu, not all of China...

"Lee Teng-hui's plan to abolish the Communist Rebellion law could be seen as a revolutionary change in the ROC's long-established anti-communist policy. He proves himself to be a down-to-earth leader willing to accommodate political realities and realize the importance for Taiwan to improve relations with the Chinese mainland.

In his announcement, Lee Teng-hui also pointed out 'that normalization of relations with the mainland must be based on the premise that the communist authorities implement democracy and market economy, renounce the use of force against Taiwan, and not interfere with our efforts to develop foreign relations. Then will we be willing to establish channels of communication, and fully open up academic, cultural, economic, trade, scientific, and technological exchanges with the mainland....I believe such bilateral exchanges could pave the way for the two sides to ultimately discuss the matter of our national unification. No less important, unification has to be founded on the common will of the Chinese people on both sides of the Taiwan Strait...

The law on the "Period of Mobilization for the Suppression of the Communist Rebellion" needed to be revoked, I editorialized, also because its existence and enforcement had blocked Taiwan's progress toward greater democracy in two important ways. "One is that the special law and its provisions have imposed a freeze on reelections of all central representative bodies, including the National Assembly, the Legislative Yuan, and the Control Yuan. The freeze has allowed hundreds of deputies elected four decades ago on the Chinese mainland to continue to exercise their duties without having to stand for reelections. But this denied Taiwan citizens the opportunity to run for public office. Two, the special provisions stipulated that the president of the ROC may be reelected without being subject to a maximum two-term limit, as provided for in the constitution."

In conclusion, Lee Teng-hui said: "In view of the people's growing demand for democratic rule, it is necessary to suspend the emergency provisions and bring the constitution into full play. At the same time the constitution, which was adopted in 1947 for implementation in all of China, needs to be carefully revised to meet Taiwan's present and future needs...''

I wrote the following: "Throughout his 20-minute inaugural address, Lee displayed a high degree of confidence and optimism. He said he believed that through his six years of active reforms, he would be able to bring Taiwan to a new level of development, politically, socially, and economically."

Lee Teng-hui did not declare an end to the Emergency Law until his first anniversary in office in May 1991, however. That was because he needed time to communicate with the many influential national assemblymen and gain their endorsement in advance.

Lee had a high level of political savvy. He knew how to acquire support for himself and his reform ideals. Almost immediately after Lee assumed his six-year term, he called a National Affairs Conference. The event was attended by some 140 delegates invited from the ruling Kuomintang, the opposition Democratic Progressive Party, and civil organizations. By convening such a national conference, Lee hoped to invite public views on his reform initiatives. He believed that reform proposals hammered out in such a way would have better chances of success, in that they had the support of the general public.

Any resolutions that were reached at the meeting would not be legally binding. But Lee in his opening address pledged that "The government will translate the National Affairs Conference's resolutions into policies and carry them out even if this might mean having to overcome considerable difficulties." Lee's remarks, as I saw, were also targeted at his party's conservatives, reminding them of his determination to push through his reforms…

At the end of the six-day National Affairs Conference, I wrote another commentary, dated July 5, 1990, examining the resolutions of the meeting. Major conference conclusions, together with my own analyses of them, are summarized below.

Salient National Conference Resolutions

"The delegates agreed that:

---The president of the Republic of China should be elected directly by a popular vote. And that the existing law, calling for the national leader to be selected indirectly by the National Assembly, needs to be revoked...

---The governor of Taiwan Province and the mayors of Taipei and Kaohsiung should be chosen by their respective citizens, instead of being appointed by the central government, as now is the case.

---Taiwan's mainland policy must be based on two fundamental principles: One, Taiwan's own security. Two, equal government-to-government relations with the Chinese mainland...

"Despite the three agreements as cited above, the delegates to the conference failed to agree on two other vital issues: constitutional reform and the presidential election system. The failure came as a result of sharply different political ideologies held by the ruling KMT and the main opposition DPP...

"On the issue of constitutional reform: The DPP insisted that the existing ROC constitution be frozen and that a new one be adopted to meet Taiwan's actual needs. And any new constitution will have to be approved by the people on the island through a referendum. The KMT, on the other hand, favored revising the constitution. Thus it proposed to pass only supplementary articles added to the end of the current basic law without changing the text of its main body. Failing to reach a consensus on how to revise the constitution, the KMT and the DPP finally were forced to agree to disagree with each other on the constitutional reform issue...

"On the subject of the presidential election system, the DPP insisted that the president should be elected directly by all eligible voters in Taiwan. In the view of the DPP, a direct presidential election system could better suit its independence ideology. But the KMT opposed such a presidential election system for two reasons. One, if the president were to be elected directly by the people without going through the National Assembly, it would result in the dissolution of the electoral college, and by extension the need to drastically overhaul the ROC Constitution. Two, a president elected by the people throughout Taiwan without voting by some specially chosen national delegates would be seen as the president of Taiwan. This could have political implications for relations with the mainland."

At the end of my opinion piece, I urged that the governing and the opposition parties arrive at a consensus on the two undecided but crucial issues at the nearest possible future if they really wanted to carry out reforms.

In the wake of the National Affairs Conference, Lee appointed a constitutional reform planning panel within the ruling KMT. The aim of this panel was to map out enforcement measures to carry out the various resolutions reached at the just concluded conference.

on the other hand, favored revising the constitution. Thus it proposed to pass only supplementary articles added to the end of the current basic law without changing the text of its main body. Failing to reach a consensus on how to revise the constitution, the KMT and the DPP finally were forced to agree to disagree with each other on the constitutional reform issue...

"On the subject of the presidential election system, the DPP insisted that the president should be elected directly by all eligible voters in Taiwan. In the view of the DPP, a direct presidential election system could better suit its independence ideology. But the KMT opposed such a presidential election system for two reasons. One, if the president were to be elected directly by the people without going through the National Assembly, it would result in the dissolution of the electoral college, and by extension the need to drastically overhaul the ROC Constitution. Two, a president elected by the people throughout Taiwan without voting by some specially chosen national delegates would be seen as the president of Taiwan. This could have political implications for relations with the mainland."

At the end of my opinion piece, I urged that the governing and the opposition parties arrive at a consensus on the two undecided but crucial issues at the nearest possible future if they really wanted to carry out reforms.

In the wake of the National Affairs Conference, Lee appointed a constitutional reform planning panel within the ruling KMT. The aim of this panel was to map out enforcement measures to carry out the various resolutions reached at the just concluded conference.

382

Additionally, the panel would also tackle the many nonconclusive issues left by the delegates.

Soon afterwards, I wrote another editorial about the constitutional reform planning panel. In it, I opined that the panel ought to pay particular attention to the following two things. One, "The KMT reform planning panel had to heed the resistance from the party's conservatives. These conservatives worried that the proposed reforms could threaten their vested interests. Their concerns, therefore, needed to be properly addressed, while pushing ahead any reforms concerning them."

The other important point, I raised, was that "President Lee should use his influence to build a dialogue between the KMT reform planning panel and the leadership of the main opposition DPP. Inviting the views from the opposition was necessary to ensure that any formal reform proposals were bipartisan efforts."

After nearly 10 months of study and discussion, the KMT panel came up with a number of reform proposals and submitted them to the National Assembly for enactment. The panel proposals took the form of a reform supplement meant to be added to the existing Constitution. This suggested that the KMT panel, as with the National Conference, also disagreed with the DPP over its stance on freezing the Constitution in favor of writing a new one.

In April 1991, the National Assembly approved the KMT panel's proposed constitutional supplement following weeks of deliberation and debate. The supplement, as in its final form, empowered the government to take on the various proposed reforms within the next two years.

In another analysis written to examine the content of the newly passed constitutional supplement, I focused on three particular reform provisions contained in the new document, which I considered were most important. I now quote them in part below:

"One of them stipulated that the government suspend the 'Period of Mobilization for the Suppression of Communist 'Rebellion ' as soon as possible. Instead, a special law is created to administer civil relations with the mainland, with the aim of paving the way for the normalization of ties between the two sides...

"Another significant point of the newly adopted constitutional supplement is that it provides the government with the authority to fully reelect all of the three parliamentary bodies—The National Assembly, the Legislative Yuan, and the Control Yuan...This is significant because Taiwan would soon for the first time have all of its parliamentary deputies elected by its citizens. This will end the present decades-old, unrealistic situation, where the vast majority of seats have been occupied by deputies elected on the mainland before the KMT-led government retreated to Taiwan in 1949...

"The third and most important point of the supplement states that new national assemblymen must be elected before December 31 this year (1991) with the mission to reform the Constitution, a task which has been scheduled for completion by May 1992."

At the end of this analysis, I offered my opinion essentially like this: Now that a legal basis had been established for reelecting the National Assembly, the Legislative Yuan, and the Control Yuan, the next crucial step forward should be to pass a set of rules that would ensure free and fair competition among candidates running for seats in the three representative bodies.

With the backing of the new constitutional supplement, Lee Teng-hui began to carry out the various stipulated democratic reforms. They included full reelections of the Legislative Yuan and the other two representative organs, opening the positions of Taiwan provincial governor, Taipei and Kaohsiung mayors to popular elections, and changing the presidential election system from indirect (by the National Assembly) to direct election (by popular vote) methods. All these drastic changes were completed within Lee Teng-hui's two terms, spanning from mid-1990 to mid-2000.

Each of these big changes brought about immediate, far-reaching effects on Taiwan's democratic development. The full reelections of the three central representative bodies in 1992, which allowed wider political participation, for example, gave the DPP opportunities to win a large increase in the number of its seats. The seat increase in turn enabled the party to become a stronger opposition force.

The opening up of the three provincial and municipal leadership positions to free election gave 45-year-old DPP politician Chen Shui-bian the opportunity to participate in the 1994 election for Taipei mayor and win. His victory made him a rising political star. As a consequence, he was nominated four years later by the DPP to run in the 2000 presidential election. In that race, Chen defeated his opponents from the ruling KMT and became the first ROC president elected from an opposition party.

The third salient item on Lee Teng-hui's democratic reform agenda was implementing the change of the presidential election system from the electoral college to the popular vote following the recent revision of the constitution. The revision was passed in time for ruling and opposition politicians to run for president in 1996 under the direct election system. Incumbent Lee, nominated by his party, the KMT, ran for reelection and won by a landslide. The presidential term was shortened to four years under the new election system. The reelected Lee served his second presidency from mid-1996 to mid-2000.

Lee Teng-hui's reelection carried two special meanings. One, he was the first ROC president elected directly by the people, not indirectly by the National Assembly as in the past. Two, for the people of Taiwan, this was the first time that they were given the right to choose their president in a direct way.

In terms of democratic development, the 1996 direct presidential election meant that Taiwan by now had evolved into a full democracy. From township to county, provincial and municipal, to central government leaders and council members in Taiwan all were elected by eligible voters.

For relations with the Chinese mainland, Taiwan's 1996 direct presidential election sent an inspiring message to Beijing's leaders that this small island had been further elevated to the status of a fully democratically developed society, while they, in sharp contrast, were still continuing to stick with their undemocratic communist rule, which denied the people basic civil and political rights.

Abolishing the Provincial Government

Lee Teng-hui launched a new round of political reform in his second term. This time he downsized the Taiwan provincial government. As a result of the reform, the provincial level of government was virtually eliminated in December 1998. With the streamlining of the administrative structure, Taiwan's governing layers were reduced from the previous four to the present three: central, county and municipal, and township. The aim of the change was to raise governing efficiency.

When a draft plan to abolish the provincial-level government was first announced, it immediately sparked strong opposition from the incumbent Taiwan provincial governor James Soong, though not surprisingly. He submitted his resignation to President Lee in protest against the reform plan. Many provincial assemblymen, with vested interests threatened, vowed to boycott any attempt to downsize the provincial government.

The provincial governor and assembly were not alone in opposing the plan to do away with the Taiwan provincial layer of government. The New Party, a splinter political group from the ruling KMT, and other opponents even jointly formed an alliance with the aim of blocking the reform proposal from being enacted. They alleged that the proposal was nothing more than a "disguised scheme between the KMT and the main opposition DPP to push Taiwan down the road to independence."

There were also some who saw a conspiracy behind the move to downsize the provincial government. They claimed the reform plan was "a downright power struggle waged by the newly elected Governor Soong's enemies in the top KMT leadership to weaken the powers of the party's rising political star."

Lee Teng-hui, the chief driver of the province-abolishing program, refused to accept Governor Soong's resignation, telling the press that he would "never allow him to leave his post." In a face-to-face conversation, as I noted in an editorial then, Lee explained to the governor that his agreement to downsize the provincial government came in response to a majority consensus that was reached at the previously mentioned National Affairs Conference. Most attendees to the conference called for the government to overhaul its structure in favor of raising efficiency; It was not something directed at the governor himself.

But Governor Soong remained unconvinced by Lee's explanations. At a subsequent high-level KMT meeting following his talk with President Lee, who also served as chairman of the ruling party, Soong issued a solemn statement to his fellow KMT politicians, urging that the KMT "must stick to its basic anti-communist and anti-Taiwan independence stances." He added that "while there is nothing wrong with the KMT engaging in cooperation with the opposition, it must not do so by sacrificing the core values of the party."

Governor Soong surely had strong reasons to protest against the plan to downsize or abolish, to be exact, the Taiwan provincial government. "But for all the reasons to curtail the size of the provincial government," I wrote in a China Post editorial, "the backlash from Governor Soong is understandable. The proposed curtailment has made him appear as a target of reform all of a sudden.

This is unfair to him if just considering his devotion and his performance on the job. The governor's approval rating has continued to remain high since he won that office by a landslide two years ago. Many believe that if he decides to run for a second term when his current tenure expires two years from now, it would be easy for him to get reelected.... What also presumably concerns him was that, as the central government proceeds with its campaign to marginalize the provincial administration, it has already made Soong look like a lame duck governor undermining his efforts to carry out his duties and deliver his election promises."

The plan to downsize the Taiwan provincial government was finally approved by the National Assembly following nearly a year-long process of soliciting public opinions via hearings, and group discussions held at a specially convened National Development Conference.

As the reform plan went through each of the three law-enacting processes, I kept making comments as an editorial writer on the pros and cons of the issue. Basically, I supported the initiative to downsize the provincial government. My stance can be seen from the following passages contained in a January 1997 China Post editorial:

"...The proposal to freeze the gubernatorial and provincial assembly elections is the desire of a majority of the public. Why the public favors a freeze of the provincial government is clear: We have a cumbersome governing system, extending from central to provincial, county, and town. This chain of governance is longer than that in many far larger countries. Taiwan has a population of only 21 million people and an area of 35,961 square kilometers. So legal action must be taken to shorten the layers of the government. And if only one layer is needed to go or be marginalized, it is obviously the provincial level, not the central government, nor either of the county and town governments...

"Beyond the need to abolish the level of the provincial government in favor of efficiency, many people who support the reform also raised some politically sensitive issues: One, the vast majority of the governor's constituents overlap with those of the ROC president. And as now is the case, the governor is legally empowered to head 80% of the population of Taiwan, with jurisdiction over nearly 90% of its land...

"Additionally, with vast powers wielded by the governor, it tends to encourage him or her to rebel against the central government, whenever they feel it necessary to do so to gain concessions on whatever issues from the premier or even the president. The chances for such rebellion could be even greater in the event that the central government is in the hands of a rival party..."

In another editorial published in July 1997, I wrote: "Now that the bill to marginalize the Taiwan provincial government has won approval by the National Assembly, authorities should begin to work on measures to implement the newly adopted constitutional provisions, which call for the freezing of both gubernatorial and councilor elections and the streamlining of the provincial administration. The latter part of this will be a tremendous and complicated task. Any such measures must gain final passage of the Legislative Yuan. And they have to be completed in time for implementation on December 20, 1998, when the terms of both the incumbent governor James Soong and the Provincial Assembly run out, as the new constitutional provisions call for...

"The streamlining work is considerable and complex simply because it will first require a comprehensive review of the provincial administration's over 1,000 agencies. Together these agencies have an estimated 250,000 employees in total. Among the agencies were some 30 banking institutions, utility companies, and manufacturing businesses. Also needed to be reviewed were the numerous laws and regulations in place to govern the operations of the province and its relations with the central government."

Lee Teng-hui's Cross-Strait Policy

Former President Lee Teng-hui's contribution to Taiwan went beyond his far-reaching democratic reforms. During his 12 years in office, Lee also attained considerable achievements in easing a longstanding political standoff with the communist-ruled Chinese mainland. The easing of the political standoff made it possible for Taiwan to expand its trade, travel, and other civil exchanges with the mainland rapidly.

But ironically, Lee Teng-hui, the leader who adopted both executive and legal steps to normalize cross-strait relations, twice brought Taiwan to the brink of war with the mainland. The first such crisis was triggered by his visit to the United States in mid-1995. The U.S. has maintained no diplomatic relations with the Republic of China since its switch of recognition to the PRC in 1979. Thus Lee Teng-hui's U.S. visit was seen as an attempt to create two Chinas.

Beijing protested the journey with a series of missile tests in the waters off Taiwan. The other one happened in 1999, less than one year before he left office. This time Lee angered Beijing with his controversial description of 'Taiwan-mainland relations as those between two states."

Lee's "two-states" theory was a sharp departure from his established one-China policy. During almost all of his 12 years in office, Lee had maintained that Taiwan and the mainland both belonged to China and that the two sides had to be unified ultimately.

The list of his initiatives to improve cross-strait relations was long, and some are worth citing here. In October 1990, Lee Teng-hui created a National Unification Council with himself serving as chairman. The council was entrusted with the task of "guiding Taiwan's relations with the Chinese mainland and promoting an eventual unification of the two sides."

At the inauguration of the council, Lee said that "seeking national unification to maintain the integrity of sovereignty is a responsibility that he cannot shirk as the president of the Republic of China." He noted that "the most serious barrier existing between Taiwan and the mainland are the differences in sociopolitical systems and the mutual misunderstandings that they brought about."

As I wrote in an opinion piece, "the ideological differences are the underlying problems that have blocked the fundamental improvement of relations across the Taiwan Strait. During the last 40 years, Beijing has imposed communism and enforced a centralized economy on the mainland. Beijing has persisted in its adherence to those systems, despite the fact that their implementation has plunged the mainland into extreme poverty. Taiwan, on the other hand, has been following a market-based economic system and carrying out democratic politics during the same period. Both of these systems have proved successful and won worldwide acclaim for Taiwan. Thus if the mainland and Taiwan ought to narrow their ideological differences for the sake of unification, it is obviously the former that needs to revise its systems, not the other way around...

"Surely this is something easier said than done. But the leaders of the two sides could adopt a pragmatic approach to improving bilateral relations," I pointed out. "They should put aside their political differences in favor of promoting trade and economic exchanges, which until recent years have been totally disrupted by decades of the political divide. Taiwan, for example, still bans official contact with the mainland. Restrictions on bilateral relations at the civil level, though, have been lessened lately. But all mainland-bound travel, trade and investments still have to be carried out indirectly, via third areas such as Hong Kong and Singapore."

I concluded in the same commentary that the newly created "National Unification Council should move quickly to work out a set of guiding principles that would allow freer trade and travel exchanges with the mainland so long as they would not endanger Taiwan's security."

Four months later in February 1991, the newly established National Unification Council indeed adopted a package of guidelines meant to serve as the government's basic principles for addressing relations with the mainland.

The guidelines called for unification with the communist Chinese mainland to be carried out through a three-stage process: institutionalizing bilateral exchanges, entering into mutual cooperation, and opening unification talks.

"But for bilateral relations to normalize in the way as the guidelines call for," I commented, "it will require that the mainland side interact positively and reciprocally with Taiwan. Without reciprocation from the mainland, normalizing relations would never be possible...

"Take for example the guidelines' short-term goal. To achieve this goal, the guidelines propose that both sides end the decades-old state of hostility toward each other and recognize each other as a political entity in the absence of formal ties to pave the way for institutionalizing bilateral exchanges...

"In this regard, Taipei is preparing to recognize Beijing and its rule of the mainland by ending a decades-old law, the Period of Mobilization for Suppression of the Communist Rebellion, in May this year...

"A positive reaction to this overture would be for Beijing to renounce the threat of using force against Taiwan and recognize it as an equal political entity, instead of treating it as a subordinate provincial government. Unless Beijing is willing to make the above policy changes, Taipei will remain hesitant in normalizing relations with the mainland for security considerations...

"Only when Taiwan feels no security threat from the mainland will this island be willing to expand bilateral exchanges and enter into the second stage of normalization as set forth in the guidelines. During the second stage, Taipei will lift the bans on direct trade and post, air, and sea links with the mainland...

"The third and last phase of normalization will be the time for Taiwan and the mainland to enter into negotiations for unification...In this respect, the guidelines stress that unification must proceed based on the wishes of the people on both sides of the Taiwan Strait."

A Systematic Approach to Improving Beijing Ties

As I observed firsthand as a journalist, the way that Lee Teng-hui followed in improving Taiwan's relations with the mainland was a systematic approach. He first created the National Unification Council (a presidential advisory body) and adopted a set of unification guidelines in its wake. He then moved further to set up a Mainland Affairs Commission under the Cabinet. This ministerial-level agency was charged with the responsibility of addressing mainland affairs. This included setting policies and regulating private sector exchanges across the Taiwan Strait.

At almost the same time, the legislature passed a bill to establish a semi-official agency responsible for handling private or non-government exchanges with the mainland. The Strait Exchange Foundation (SEF) got most of its funding from the government, but it performed as a quasi-official body. Such arrangements were made because of a lack of official links between the two sides.

Seeking to administer economic, travel, and other civil exchanges with the mainland through a semi-official agency was the only but practical way, given the non-recognition policy each side adopted toward the other. During those times, Taipei still treated Beijing as a rebel regime and maintained a principle of "three no's" -- no contact, no negotiations, and no compromise. Beijing, on the other hand, has refused to recognize Taipei, claiming that the 1912-founded Republic of China it represents had disappeared after the communist People's Republic of China was established in 1949.

The SEF, short for Taiwan Strait Exchange Foundation, is accountable to the newly created Mainland Affairs Commission. It was delegated with the authority to administer commercial, travel, and cultural exchanges as well as handle matters about bilateral trade disputes and the repatriation of illegal immigrants and criminal suspects.

Many in the public, however, had remained skeptical of the viability of the semi-official agency all the way from the planning stage to its enactment. The main concern was whether or not Beijing would recognize the agency and respond positively by setting up a counterpart body to perform similar functions on its behalf. Such a positive response was essential because any effort to effectively promote and regulate exchanges needed the backing and cooperation of each other.

But despite public skepticism, I took an optimistic view of the process of the exchange foundation's enactment. I wrote a series of three commentaries. In them, I consistently stressed the need for the government to establish the foundation and expressed my belief that Beijing would eventually reciprocate Taipei's exchange-promoting initiative. There was no reason that Beijing would not reciprocate, I said.

In an editorial published in November 1989, one year before the organization came into being, I raised the following cross-strait exchange data to support my optimistic views.

"Following the easing of political tensions across the strait in recent years, indirect trade between this island and the mainland has continued to grow at a fast pace, rising to more than US$2 billion in the first seven months of this year (1989). Taiwan's approved cumulative investment in mainland China reached some US$600 million as of the end of last year. The amounts of investment remitted from Taiwan to the mainland without being registered with the government were estimated to be far larger than the above figure...

"On travel, some 370,000 Taiwan citizens visited the mainland from January to August this year, a 45 percent increase over the same period last year. The number of mainland citizens visiting Taiwan is also on the increase following Taipei's relaxation of rules on such visits...

"Trade, investment and travel aside, the two sides also need to cooperate in cracking down on increasingly serious smuggling activities in the Taiwan Strait. Mainland China-produced firearms, for example, were smuggled into Taiwan in growing numbers, posing a threat to the island's social security."

At the end of my analysis, I concluded that "In short, the need for both Taiwan and the mainland to form government-backed private representative agencies to facilitate and regulate civil relations is obvious and pressing. So the two sides must bury their political differences and work together to address the issues of mutual interest in a realistic manner."

Taipei's consistent effort to improve ties with the mainland was not lost on Beijing. In December 1991, exactly one year after the administration of Lee Teng-hui established the SEF, Beijing set up a similar semi-official organization called the Association for Relations Across the Taiwan Strait (ARATS).

At an inaugural ceremony, the association's chairman Wang Daohan, a former Shanghai mayor, announced that the aim of ARATS was to facilitate exchanges across the Taiwan Strait, promote bilateral relations and ultimately achieve the goal of unification. "The willingness of Beijing to set up a corresponding exchange body," I commented, "reflected a welcome change in its Taiwan policy. Beijing, like Taipei, is becoming more pragmatic now. They are willing to put aside their political differences in favor of promoting civil exchanges with this island."

Prompted by their shared pragmatism, Taipei and Beijing began to contact and talk with each other through their respective SEF and ARATS officials. Initially, all such contacts and talks were held in third areas like Hong Kong and Singapore. With easing political relations, commercial and civil exchanges between the two sides underwent fast growth.

The Underlying Cross-Strait Difference

However, the one-China dispute remained the fundamental difference between the two sides. It blocked the settlement of any bilateral issues concerning sovereignty and government power.

At the time Beijing and Taipei both followed a one-China policy. But they differed sharply with each other about the meaning of "China." For Taipei, China is the Republic of China. But for Beijing, it means the People's Republic of China. This fundamental disagreement continued to trouble Taiwan and the mainland until 1992 when they finally agreed to put aside the thorny political issue in favor of moving forward in non-political areas.

Late that year delegates from Taiwan's SEF and the mainland's ARATS held a landmark meeting in Hong Kong. At that meeting, the mainland accepted the Taiwan delegation's proposal, which called for both sides to stick to the one-China principle but allowed each other to interpret the meaning of one China. This pragmatic approach later came to be known as "one China, two interpretations" or "the 1992 consensus." The breakthrough in the longstanding political standoff made it possible for Taiwan and the mainland to extensively expand their bilateral exchanges thereafter.

In April the following year, Taiwan's SEF head Koo Chen-fu and the mainland's ARATS head Wang Daohan held a three-day conference in Singapore to negotiate exchange issues, with each side leading a large delegation to the historic event. The 1993 Koo-Wang conference marked the first time that Taiwan and the mainland had conducted top-level negotiations through their semiofficial representative bodies since 1949 when a civil war divided the two sides.

During the three-day Singapore meeting, I wrote a series of commentaries for the Post from its opening to closing, using information based on news dispatches transmitted back by Taiwan journalists sent to the site to cover the event. Among the main issues discussed on the opening day was a request by Taiwan for the mainland to strengthen the protection of its investments, and a counter request raised by the mainland was urging this island to ease controls on mainland imports and investments. The two sides failed to reach any agreement on their first day of discussion.

In this editorial, I opined that "both the mainland and Taiwan had strong reasons to positively respond to each other's requests. To begin with, the one raised by the Taiwan delegation called for the mainland to enact a special law to effectively protect Taiwan companies' investments. They reasoned that the mainland's existing '22-point regulation' in place to serve that purpose was an executive order adopted by the State Council, thus having no binding effect. They quoted Taiwan investors as saying that this regulation was not strictly observed by the various local governments...

"Beijing as the host government," I wrote, "has the responsibility and obligations to adequately protect Taiwan's investors. Their investments now standing at a cumulative US$9 billion have played a major role in the development of the mainland economy over the years. By providing effective protections, the mainland could bring in more capital and technology from Taiwan to help deepen its economic reforms...

"By the same token," I continued, "Taiwan's reluctance to liberalize restrictions on mainland imports and investments is unreasonable. Bilateral trade between any two trading partners must be carried out in a mutually favorable manner. Over the years, Taiwan has continued to run a large trade surplus with the mainland, which last year topped US$5 billion, due mainly to strict government restrictions imposed on mainland imports..."

At the conclusion of their unprecedented top-level Singapore negotiations, Taiwan and the Chinese mainland still failed to resolve their differences on the two vital investment and trade issues. However, the two sides in a joint statement issued afterward did agree to leave their unresolved differences to be addressed in future meetings.

Besides issuing a joint statement, the two chief delegates, Koo Chen-fu of Taiwan and Wang Daohan of the mainland, signed three separate agreements. One of them called for rendering document certification services. Another one concerned the handling of registered mail. The third agreement provided for regular exchanges of visits by personnel from the two semi-official bodies.

Generally speaking, the 1993 Koo-Wang talks in Singapore were successful with each side declaring they have achieved most of their desired aims. For Taiwan, it came to the talks with "the goal of winning the mainland's commitments to institutionalize civil exchanges and to jointly tackle maritime crimes, illegal immigration, and fishery disputes. From this angle, the three accords signed by the two chief delegates at the end of the meeting apparently were designed to serve those purposes." For the mainland side, "Its primary aim was to get Taipei to the negotiating table and establish official contacts with it, in hopes of paving the way for eventual unification talks."

In short, the long series of executive and legal actions that Lee Teng-hui had taken to improve mainland relations during his 12-year presidency from late 1988 to mid-2000 went a long way toward the normalization of ties between the two longtime political rivals. Improved relations were most evident in the areas of semi-official contacts, cultural and academic exchanges, and travel, trade, and investment interflows.

But at the same time, Lee Teng-hui persistently followed a cautious approach, unwilling to fully open the Taiwan economy to the mainland throughout the entire length of his presidency. He adopted regulations requiring that cross-strait exchanges of trade, investment, travel, and transport service be conducted indirectly, via third places like Hong Kong and Singapore. He maintained that unrestrained opening to the mainland before the two sides settled their deep-rooted political differences [under the principle of one China] could weaken Taiwan's economy and endanger its security.

The impact of the one-China dispute was reflected not just in cross-strait trade and economic relations. It also seriously impacted Taiwan's effort to develop foreign ties. Beijing constantly used its political clout to prevent foreign governments and international organizations from recognizing Taipei, or the ROC. It claimed that Taipei's policy on international relations violated the one-China principle. The battle for international recognition between the two sides has, in fact, never ceased since 1949 when the ROC government retreated to Taiwan. If anything, it has become ever tenser.

At the center of the diplomatic battle was that the mainland insisted "There is only one China in the world and that Beijing is the sole legitimate government of China. Taiwan is but a province of China and therefore has no right to pursue diplomatic recognition."

On the other hand, Taipei has never accepted Beijing's sovereignty claim. In an April 1996 commentary written for the Economic News, I said that Taiwan and the mainland needed to mend their political differences in the interest of bilateral economic and trade exchanges.

In this opinion piece, I analyzed Taipei's one-China position: "For Taipei, the idea that there is only one China in the world is not a question at all. The real question is about the definition of the term China. For Beijing, China refers to the People's Republic of China or the PRC which was founded in 1949 after the communists defeated the then KMT-led Republic of China government in a civil war and drove it to Taiwan...

"But Taipei maintains that the PRC and China are not one and the same thing. The China that Taiwan identifies with is the ROC, the country that was established in 1912 following the overthrow of the Manchu government in a revolution led by Dr. Sun Yat-sen."

Reflecting on the government policies of the two sides, the one-China dispute meant persistent refusal to recognize each other. Beijing refused to recognize Taipei's status as the ROC government and banned official contact with it and its officials. Taiwan adopted the same stance toward Beijing. Yet the mutual non-recognition, as I observed, caused the two sides to miss out on several golden opportunities to break their political impasse during the course of President Lee Teng-hui's 12 years in office.

An Attempt to End the State of Hostility

In 1993 -- in the middle of Lee's first elected term as president -- Beijing made calls, through its state media, for Taiwan and the mainland to negotiate a "non-aggression agreement" to end decades of hostility toward each other. But it insisted that any such peace treaty had to be concluded under the principle of one China. Not surprisingly, Lee Teng-hui was unmoved by the offer, because he was unwilling to accept Beijing's one-China position as the precondition for negotiations.

In early 1995, Taiwan's chief negotiator Chiao Jen-ho, secretary general of the semi-official SEF, met with his mainland counterpart Tang Shubei in Beijing for their third round of talks on illegal immigrants and fishery disputes. In the Beijing talks, the mainland delegation expressed a desire for making arrangements for a summit meeting between Presidents Lee Teng-hui and Jiang Zemin. But the proposed summit failed to materialize. One main reason was that the mainland side insisted that any Lee-Jiang meeting had to be conducted in a "private capacity." Beijing insisted on the "private capacity" prerequisite because it refused to recognize Lee's official title as the President of the ROC.

In February 1998, Lee Teng-hui, while addressing a meeting of the National Unification Council, made a conciliatory overture to Beijing, but he received no positive response. He said, "Taiwan and the Chinese mainland should negotiate and sign a peace agreement to end the state of hostility in accordance with the reality of a divided China and based on the principles of equality and mutual respect."

(Lee's remarks were taken from an editorial that I wrote for the China Post then.)

In that same address, Lee also cited Taiwan's successful experience in economic and democratic achievements. "We are willing to share this development experience with our mainland compatriots in hopes of jointly creating a free, democratic, and economically prosperous China."

The reason why Beijing did not positively respond to Lee Teng-hui's peace overture, according to the state media of the mainland, was that it disagreed with his reference to "a divided China" and his proposed unification formula. But the truth was that from day one, Beijing had refused to recognize Taipei's political status as the ROC government. It insisted that Taiwan had to be unified with the mainland under its imposed "one country, two systems" model.

In addition, Beijing was also firmly opposed to Lee Teng-hui visiting foreign countries and his efforts to win wider diplomatic recognition, including his applications for admission to the United Nations. Beijing branded these activities as attempts to create "two Chinas" or "one China, one Taiwan" in the international arena.

But Lee called his efforts to build relations with foreign governments and join international organizations a matter of "survival and development" for Taiwan.

President Lee did not overstate why Taiwan needed to expand foreign relations. In an editorial on this issue, I wrote in part: "...Taiwan is sending abroad billions of U.S. dollars in investment capital annually, conducting two-way trade worth US$130 billion a year. Additionally, this island is becoming an increasingly important tourism source and destination with outgoing and incoming visitors totaling more than four million a year. If just for the reason of helping administer and facilitate the above-cited economic and travel exchanges, there is a need for Taiwan to expand official links with as many foreign countries as possible, and participate in as many international bodies as it could…"

Pragmatic Diplomacy

To break Beijing's constant practices of isolating Taiwan in the international community, Lee Teng-hui worked out a sort of pragmatic diplomacy. This policy in essence advised the agencies of his administration to place substantive benefits above politics in promoting foreign relations. The following three instances (taken from my commentaries) are given to provide a brief look at how this pragmatic foreign policy was actually applied.

First, whenever Taiwan was barred from joining a certain international body under the name ROC due to Beijing's opposition, Lee Teng-hui would adopt a flexible stance in such cases. He would not insist on using the national name of the country to apply for admission.

He decided to be so flexible because past experiences showed that insistence on using the ROC title to apply for admission always ended up in failure. In view of this, he was willing to accept some less politically sensitive names that could circumvent Beijing's intervention and therefore enhance the chances of success.

It was the exercise of his pragmatic attitude that made it possible for Taiwan to join the Asian Development Bank and the Asian Pacific Economic Forum under the name "Chinese Taipei."

There was another high-profile case in which Taiwan's willingness to accept a universally acceptable name, other than the ROC, opened the door for Taiwan to join the World Trade Organization. Taiwan was admitted to the WTO under the title of a "separate customs territory."

Second, Lee's pragmatic diplomacy was also successfully applied to developing relations with other countries that were reluctant to recognize Taiwan diplomatically for fear of angering Beijing.

In such situations, Taipei instead adopted the second-best approach, meaning it would be willing to establish semi-official ties with these countries in the form of representative offices. These offices would be responsible for addressing bilateral economic, trade, travel, and cultural exchanges. Taipei during the 12-year administration of Lee Teng-hui had opened semi-official representative offices in numerous countries around the world.

And third, Lee also applied his pragmatic diplomacy to his foreign travel. During his first term from 1990 to 1996, he visited more than half a dozen countries in a private capacity, instead of using his official title as the president of the Republic of China. He avoided using his presidential title because Taipei maintained no diplomatic relations with any of the countries he visited. The countries he traveled to as a private citizen included Indonesia, Thailand, Singapore, the Philippines, Jordan, the United Arab Emirates, and the United States.

Lee's overseas visits helped greatly boost Taiwan's global visibility. But his overseas travels always invited strong protests from Beijing. The mainland leaders routinely attacked his travels as activities conducted to "create two Chinas" or "one China, one Taiwan." But they never responded as strongly as they did to his June 1995 visit to the United States. The People's Liberation Army retaliated militarily by launching three rounds of missile firings off Taiwan in the period from July 1995 to mid-March 1996. The PLA suspended its missile tests only days before Taiwan's presidential election, in which Lee Teng-hui was running for a second term.

The 1995-1996 Missile Crisis

The months-old military crisis in the Taiwan Strait calmed down without escalating into a hot conflict only after intervention by the United States. President Bill Clinton dispatched two aircraft carriers, the USS Independence and the USS Nimitz, to the waters off Taiwan days ahead of the March 23 election. The Clinton administration made it clear that the deployment of the two aircraft carriers near Taiwan was intended to achieve two purposes. One was to help defend this island against PRC invasion, as called for in the Taiwan Relations Act. The other purpose was to block the PRC from intervening in the island's democratic elections.

The mainland made no secret that its missile firings were intended to achieve the following two goals. One was to let Washington understand the serious consequences of its decision to grant Lee Teng-hui a travel visa to the U.S.-- a country with which the

PRC maintains diplomatic relations. The other was to intimidate the people of Taiwan into not voting for Lee Teng-hui.

But Beijing failed to achieve either of the two aims. Washington was not deterred by the retaliatory missile firings. Nor were the people of Taiwan intimidated by the missile threat. They overwhelmingly reelected Lee Teng-hui for a second term.

As an opinion writer, I made commentary and analysis on every turn of events during Lee Teng-hui's high-profile six-day U.S. visit from start to end. In an editorial appearing in the May 5, 1995 edition of the China Post, one month before Lee's U.S. visit, I observed that the Clinton administration was most likely to revise U.S. policy to grant a travel visa to Lee Teng-hui. I analyzed there was no reason not to do so.

"The Clinton administration, faced with mounting pressure from Congress, is most likely to change its rigid policy at the last minute in favor of allowing a visit to the United States by the ROC President Lee Teng-hui...The U.S. House of Representatives days ago had passed 396-0 a resolution urging the executive branch to reverse its position and issue a travel visa to President Lee, permitting him to visit his alma mater Cornell University in New York. A similar resolution is expected to pass the U.S. Senate soon, judging from the ongoing public opinion in the United States...

"The State Department has banned President Lee from traveling to the U.S. on grounds that granting such a visit would be inconsistent with America's unofficial ties to Taiwan and would not be in its best interests... These State Department positions, however, appear to be irrelevant in the proposed Lee Teng-hui visit. First, the invitations for

Lee to visit America were extended by private U.S. institutions, and Lee, if given entry, will make the trip in a private capacity and undertake no official activities in the U.S. So giving President Lee entry permission does not run counter to the American policy of maintaining only unofficial relations with Taiwan...

"Allowing President Lee to visit the U.S. would mean America's recognition of Taiwan, as in the words of the House resolution, as a model emerging democracy with a free press, free elections, stable democratic institutions, and human rights protection. The U.S. has no reason not to respect these achievements. These are the values that have been respected in the United States. And Washington has long made the promotion of democracy, freedom and human rights protection around the world important goals of its foreign policy."

One month after I wrote the above China Post editorial reasoning that Washington ought to allow Lee Teng-hui to visit the United States, the State Department finally issued the ROC president an entry visa. On the eve of Lee's departure for his U.S. visit, I wrote another opinion piece, this time for my weekly column in the CENS Economic News.

In it, I examined the significance of Lee's upcoming U.S. visit. The following is a summary of that column: "When Lee Teng-hui stops in Los Angeles on June 7, en route to his alma mater Cornell University in Ithaca, New York, for a reunion event, he will be the first top ROC official to visit the United States since 1979, when Washington switched diplomatic recognition from the ROC to the People's Republic of China...

"President Bill Clinton finally decided to issue a visitor's visa to President Lee Teng-hui only because he faced mounting pressure from Congress, which unanimously adopted a resolution urging that the Taiwan leader be allowed to travel to the U.S., and from influential American newspapers, which questioned the wisdom of the administration's opposition to the Lee trip. The widespread Congressional and public opinion support for Lee to visit America illustrated one encouraging thing: Taiwan and the U.S. still maintain strong substantive relations despite the lack of political ties...

"Also significantly, President Lee is visiting the United States in a private capacity conforming to U.S. policy requirements. The State Department, in announcing Lee's visit, said 'President Bill Clinton has decided to permit Lee Teng-hui to make a private trip to the United States in June for the express purpose of participating in an alumni reunion event at Cornell University as a distinguished alumnus...

"Lee's agreement to travel to the United States as a private citizen as a condition for gaining an entry visit is another successful exercise of his pragmatic diplomacy--one which places substantive benefits above formality. Had he insisted on visiting the United States in his role as the President of the ROC, he would not have had the chance to visit the United States to promote relations with a superpower of great importance to Taiwan. Further, Lee's success in traveling to the U.S. in a private capacity once again proved that his strategy to advance foreign relations in a low-key manner is the most effective way to surmount Beijing's strategy of isolating Taiwan...

"One more thing worth noting is that the recent liberal rule changes by the Clinton administration that made it possible for

President Lee Teng-hui to visit the U.S. appear likely to apply to other top-level ROC officials in the future, if and when they need to visit the United States for one reason or another...

"This can be seen from the announcement made by State Department spokesman Nicholas Burns. He said 'The action follows a revision of administration guidelines to permit occasional private visits by distinguished leaders of Taiwan, including President Lee.'

"Since cutting off diplomatic relations with Taipei in 1979, Washington has banned senior ROC officials from visiting the U.S. on the grounds that the two sides no longer maintained political ties. Moreover, if the U.S. government violated the travel restrictions, it could invite protests from Beijing."

After President Lee returned from his six-day visit to the United States, I wrote a third piece assessing what he had achieved on the trip and, at the same time, analyzing why Beijing had gotten so furious at Lee's U.S. journey that it even threatened to respond militarily. What I wrote in that article is summarized below:

"Mainland China's attacks on President Lee Teng-hui's recent six-day private visit to the United States have not abated with his return to Taipei. The People's Daily, Xinhua News Agency, and some Hong Kong-based communist-owned newspapers last week all carried articles attacking President Lee. These media even foretold that the mainland might likely retaliate by taking military action against Taiwan...

"Many people wondered why Beijing was getting so angry at Lee's visit to his New York State-located alma mater Cornell University. First, Lee flew to that state mainly to attend a reunion event as a distinguished alumnus. And he has repeatedly denied Beijing's accusation that the trip was aimed at promoting 'two Chinas' or 'one China, one Taiwan.'

"Vincent Siew, chairman of the Mainland Affairs Council--an agency in charge of regulating relations with the mainland--provided a good answer to the above question the other day. The chairman, in a report before a Cabinet meeting, said: 'The reason that Beijing's reaction was becoming stronger and fiercer was that President Lee's U.S. trip had proved to be far more successful than expected...

"Truly, Lee's American visit went a long way toward strengthening Taiwan's crucial relations with the United States, a superpower with which this island has maintained defense and other strong substantive links, despite a lack of diplomatic ties. The Lee visit itself had profound symbolic significance for Taiwan. He was the first ROC leader to set foot on American soil since the U.S. government switched diplomatic recognition to Beijing in 1979...

"Lee's U.S. visit and his Cornell speech received unexpectedly extensive press coverage by the media outlets from around the world, in addition to those from the host country. The worldwide media coverage has undoubtedly raised the understanding of the ROC in Taiwan and its international profile...

"In the Cornell speech, Lee personally introduced Taiwan's experience in economic and political developments. In the economic field, he pointed out, the island has over the last few decades evolved from a primarily agricultural economy to a leading industrial player, despite its lack of natural resources...

"Politically, he continued, Taiwan has peacefully transformed itself into a democracy in the last 10 years. As a result, free elections now prevail, human rights are fully respected and protected, and the freedom of speech is enjoyed by all...

"Yet despite Taiwan's successful economic and political reforms and its willingness to fulfill more international obligations, Lee pointed out, the ROC does not receive the rightful share of diplomatic recognition it deserves from the international community. This is not fair to the ROC and its 21 million people, he complained...

"However, Beijing sees Lee's visit to the U.S. and the widespread media coverage he received along the way as a serious setback for its longstanding policy of isolating Taiwan. Moreover, Lee's success in traveling to the U.S., a country with which Beijing maintains official relations, was seen by the mainland as an infringement of its diplomatic interests. All this explained why Beijing has become so angry with President Lee's U.S. trip, and why the mainland leaders have vowed to retaliate militarily (a threat which they carried out soon after in the form of three rounds of live missile tests, as discussed in previous pages.)"

Lee Teng-hui's 'Two States' Statement

President Lee Teng-hui angered Beijing again in July 1999--a time when his term of office was to expire in less than a year--with his "two states" statements. In an interview with the German radio station Deutsche Welle, Lee characterized mainland China-Taiwan relations as those between two countries. President Lee was responding to a question put to him by the German radio station about Beijing's long-held claim that Taiwan is a province of China. In reply, Lee angrily refuted Beijing's claim. He went on to elaborate his argument: "The association between the mainland and Taiwan was state to state, or at least special state to state, relations, not as ties between a central government and a local government within the framework of one China."

Beijing reacted promptly and strongly to Lee's characterization of Taiwan-mainland relations. It condemned Lee Teng-hui for "flagrantly advocating his 'two states' theory, which Beijing said completely exposed his political nature of splitting the country." It demanded Lee "retract his 'two states' remarks and stop his activities to split up China." The mainland backed up its condemnation of Lee by staging multiple military exercises along its southeastern coast opposite Taiwan. At the same time, the PRC government required the United States to "scrupulously abide by its commitment to one-China policy and refrain from making any remarks or moves that would encourage Taiwan independence activities."

Lee Teng-hui's "two states" theory also alienated Taiwan's most important defense ally, the United States. Washington moved quickly to urge Lee to clarify his remarks. The U.S. government outrightly blamed the Taiwan leader for provoking Beijing and stirring up tensions across the Taiwan Strait. Almost at the same time, President Bill Clinton personally called his Chinese counterpart Jiang Zemin to reaffirm America's longstanding commitment to the "one-China" policy. In the telephone conversation, Clinton also reassured Jiang that the U.S. policy on Taiwan had remained unchanged.

There was economic fallout from the new cross-strait political and military tensions; Taiwan's stock market plunged as investors scrambled to unload their holdings. In the manufacturing sector, exporters were worried that overseas buyers might shift orders elsewhere fearing that a cross-strait conflict could disrupt supplies from Taiwan.

During the weeks-long cross-strait tension I wrote multiple editorials discussing Lee Teng-hui's inflammatory "two states" theory and the impact it had on Taiwan and its economy. In one of them, entitled 'Continuing Tension Hurts the Economy,' I urged that something had to be done to ease the statehood controversy, if just for the sake of saving the economy from collapsing.

I wrote that both Taiwan and the mainland, the latter of which was also feeling the economic effects of the escalating cross-strait tensions, needed to come up with a mutually acceptable way to settle the political wrangle. "Actually, there is already such a way if the two sides are willing to reembrace the '92 consensus' reached between the two sides back in 1992 in Singapore. This consensus, a bilateral tacit agreement, obliges Taiwan and the mainland to acknowledge that there is only one China, but that it allows each side to interpret the meaning of that one China," I continued.

Under pressure from both within and abroad, Lee Teng-hui finally rephrased his controversial "two states" remarks during a meeting with a group of visiting overseas Chinese. They read roughly like this: "While one China is a goal to be achieved in the future, there currently are the Republic of China and the People's Republic of China." He also used the occasion to deny he used the terms "two states" in the interview with Deutsche Welle. He went further to reiterate his government's longstanding commitment to eventual national reunification.

Lee Teng-hui remained a controversial political leader throughout his 12 years in office. Lee's opponents and critics constantly questioned his political intentions. In mainland China, Beijing leaders from almost day one of Lee's presidency labeled him a "closet separatist," seeking Taiwan's secession from China. In Taiwan itself, he faced similar accusations from within and outside his party, the KMT. They accused him of quietly and steadily advocating an independent Taiwan.

But the irony was that Lee Teng-hui in fact was the first ROC president who enacted and implemented a coherent policy on improving relations with mainland China. He established guidelines on Taiwan's unification with the mainland, he passed legislation to promote civil and economic exchanges across the strait, and he set up institutions dedicated to implementing laws and rules governing mainland affairs. All this was a drastic departure from the conservative policy of his mentor and predecessor Chiang Ching-kuo. Chiang insisted on a "three-no's" rule: "No contact, no negotiation, and no compromise with the Chinese communists."

But despite Lee's efforts to promote cross-strait exchanges, his critics constantly accused him of supporting Taiwan's independence movement. They cited his localization policy and his pursuit of a Taiwan identity separate from China. But Lee's proponents saw things differently. They contended that the policy of promoting Taiwanization, as the policy was also known, was essential for the

KMT to compete with the opposition DPP, a party founded mainly by native Taiwanese politicians.

The KMT, which has its roots in mainland China, had been labeled by the DPP as an "alien" party. In terms of electoral politics, therefore, the KMT had a "legitimacy" problem to overcome. That was to say that the KMT had to identify with Taiwan and solicit the support of its citizens through democratic elections if it wanted to win public office or retain power.

Lee, as president and KMT chairman, had the need and responsibility to lead his party to win elections at central and local levels amid increasingly strong competition from the DPP. Thus it was logical and natural that he had to adopt government policies and election platforms appealing to Taiwan voters, reversing the past tradition of often considering things from a mainland China perspective.

In other words, the KMT needed to make localization its basic policy to win the support of the voters. Examined from this angle, it was appropriate to say that for the KMT the policy of promoting localization or Taiwanization was an inevitable development in the process of Taiwan's democratization.

Lee's critics also accused him of advancing Taiwan independence by promoting a separate political identity for this island, making it virtually independent of mainland China. But again such an accusation did not seem to be quite justified. Proponents reasoned that Lee's effort to create a separate political identity was aimed, in essence, at breaking out of longstanding diplomatic isolation imposed by Beijing.

Beijing always treats Taiwan as part of China, preventing it from joining international organizations. And this one-China position was almost universally accepted. As a result, world bodies mostly refused to admit the ROC or Taiwan. But Taiwan, as a leading economic player and trader needed to have a representation in vital international bodies, like the World Bank.

Reversal from Pro-Unification to Pro-Independence

Having said all that, there was no denying the fact that Lee Teng-hui did make an overt about-face on his cross-strait policy--from pro-unification to pro-independence--in his final months in office. July 1999—less than one year before his term expired--was a watershed. In that month, Lee for the first time openly espoused the concept of Taiwan and the Chinese mainland being two separate states, as discussed previously.

But until then Lee Teng-hui had been sticking to a one-China position, maintaining that Taiwan and the mainland had to be eventually reunified under the framework of a democratic China. Lee had held such political views as late as mid-1998, a year before he came up with his two-state theory. This can be seen in a speech that Lee Teng-hui gave before the National Unification Council in July of that year. I covered that speech in my Post editorial. In it, I quoted him as saying "Taiwan is a sovereign political entity, a fact which must not be denied by Beijing. While there is only one China, this country has been divided for the last half a century, with Taiwan and the Chinese mainland being ruled by two separate governments…China has to be reunified. But reunification must be achieved under a democratic system, not the communist system--one which he said has proved a failure worldwide...Before reunification, the people of the Republic of China on Taiwan must have the right to fully defend themselves. And before reunification, the ROC must have the right to participate in international activities. This is a matter of survival and development for us."

But no one had ever thought that Lee Teng-hui would abandon his basically "one-China, pro-unification" policy in favor of promoting a two-states theory barely one year later. It's hard to ascertain exactly what prompted the ex-president to make such a drastic turn, while he had less than a year in office. Some saw Lee Teng-hui's "two states" remarks as a sudden burst of his pent-up anger at Beijing over its unrelenting diplomatic isolation of and sustained military threat to Taiwan.

If that was the case, then Lee's deep dissatisfaction with Beijing had to be traced back to his reelection in March 1996. In the months leading to the election, the People's Liberation Army, as previously recounted, launched three series of missile firings near Taiwan in a bid to intimidate people on this island into not voting for him. Such military intimidation and intervention were obviously indelibly imprinted on his mind.

This unhappy memory was clearly reflected in the way Lee addressed mainland relations in his second term. He adopted a more cautious approach. He maintained bans on direct cross-strait airline and shipping services. He imposed ceilings on investments in mainland China. Mainland-bound investors and cross-strait transport service operators all were urged to follow a restrictive guideline called "avoid haste, be patient."

This guideline sparked widespread criticism. But he defended it by stating "The restrictive policy must be maintained to counter Beijing's hostile behavior toward Taiwan...They stepped up efforts to isolate Taiwan diplomatically, build military pressure on Taiwan, and make this island dependent on the mainland economically. Beijing has not eased its hostile behaviors because of the efforts Taipei has made to increase mutual exchanges over the years. Taiwan now is an important source of tourism for the mainland, with tourist visits now totaling 1.8 million a year. And Taiwan is the second largest foreign investor in mainland China, with cumulative contract investments now exceeding US$38 billion."

Truly, Beijing's ever more severe political and diplomatic suppression hurt Taiwan immeasurably and ought to be responded to strongly. But any attempt to retaliate by redefining Taiwan's political relationship with the mainland as country-to-country relations, as Lee did, would go beyond the realm of logic and could invite strong responses from the mainland.

Examined from this angle, Lee Teng-hui's "two states" remarks were unlikely to be a mere expression of his dissatisfaction with Beijing. Rather they appeared to have more to do with his political leanings. Officially, Lee had throughout his two terms followed a one-China policy and maintained that Taiwan and the mainland had to be unified. But in actuality, he adopted and implemented pro-independence programs all the way.

His "localization" policy, for example, was enacted outwardly as an effort to help the KMT take root in Taiwan. But in fact, this policy had increasingly become a tool to advance the Taiwan independence movement by steadily cutting its political and cultural links with the Chinese mainland. This was why Lee was constantly accused by his critics of being a "closet separatist."

Lee's independence leanings were more clearly displayed after his retirement. He retired in May 2000 at the end of his tenure. The long-ruling KMT, which Lee headed during the past 12 years, also lost power after being defeated by Chen Shui-bian and his pro-independence Democratic Progressive Party (DPP) in the presidential election two months earlier.

Observing Lee Teng-hui's Return to Politics

Lee Teng-hui reentered politics a year and a month after handing power over to his successor Chen Shui-bian. But the purpose of his return was not to help his KMT to regain power by using his influence as a former party chairman and a former president. Rather he switched allegiance to a radical political group actively advocating the establishment of a Taiwan state.

I made some comments on Lee Teng-hui's reentering politics in a China Post editorial, dated June 20, 2001. I now will quote part of my observations from that editorial below to give a brief account of his pro-independence remarks and activities, which he made shortly after his departure as president.

"…President Lee Teng-hui delivered a politically charged speech this week, one of the few he has ever made in public since he handed power to President Chen Shui-bian a year ago. In it, he called on all citizens who care about the future of Taiwan to participate in the birth of a 'New Taiwan.' The creation of a new Taiwan, he said, was necessary to ensure that this island will not deviate from its 'correct course'. He apparently was referring to his KMT chair successor Lien Chan. Lien recently openly abandoned the 'localization policy,' one which the former president initiated and pursued in office. Lee did not specify his 'New Taiwan' idea. But one could not but take it to mean a call for an independent Taiwan.

"Consider, Taiwan has already undergone a most important political rebirth: a successful transformation from authoritarian rule to a dynamic democracy. Lee himself must get all the credit, as almost all of such political transformation was achieved during his two terms. So Lee's New Taiwan must refer, logically, to an independent Taiwan. In retrospect, Lee's independence leanings became increasingly more manifest in the various policies he successfully carried out during his presidency. Most noticeable were his push for localization or Taiwanization, his ardent pursuit of a Taiwan identity, and his public description of the Taiwan-mainland China relationship as being state-to-state relations…

"What was also unusual was Lee's public appearance at a ceremony marking the establishment of the 'North Society.' The Society was a political forum organized by a group of scholars and political activists who advocated that Taiwan split from mainland

China. His presence at the ceremony suggested that the former ROC president was sympathetic to the cause of the North Society...

"Also worth noting was the event organizers' arrangement for Lee to appear together with President Chen Shui-bian on the occasion. Chen has been a staunch political opponent of Lee and his KMT party. The deliberately arranged coincidences seemed to symbolize the formation of a new alliance between the former and the current presidents in the interest of the independence movement..."

Another high-profile action that Lee Teng-hui took after his return to politics was the former ROC leader's open endorsement of the formation of a new political party, the Taiwan Solidarity Union. The Solidarity Union advocated Taiwan's independence and campaigned for the creation of a de jure Republic of Taiwan. The party was founded in time for it to run in the December 2001 legislative elections. In the lead up to the year-end elections, Lee even traveled around the island to stump for the party's candidates.

In an editorial I wrote for the China Post on August 22, 2001, I called former President Lee Teng-hui's close association with the Taiwan Solidarity Union and his unreserved support for it a "risky game." In reply to a question by the press, Lee said he supported the TSU because "the party upholds ideals consistent with what he had pursued during his presidency." He went further to say that he believed the new political group "will assume a role in restoring political stability."

"To that end, however," I wrote, "it will first require the TSU to win a significantly large number of seats in the coming December legislative elections to effectively help the pro-independence DPP attain a majority in the lawmaking body, thus reversing its current role as a minority government. But few believe that the TSU could even win a minimum of 10 seats necessary to play that supporting role, given the fact that most of the 39 candidates it has fielded are those who were eliminated by the opposition KMT and ruling DPP during their respective primaries..."

"By campaigning for the TSU, Lee hopes that the party will pursue his political ideals and establish itself as a stabilizing force. But his hopes may prove unrealistic. No party with 10 or so legislative seats could push its causes in a forceful way...Finally, Lee's open and unreserved support for the TSU could eventually lead him to be humiliatingly expelled by the KMT. The party has so far been reluctant to do so in part out of respect for the former chairman."

As widely predicted, Lee Teng-hui was finally expelled by the KMT ahead of the December 2001 legislative elections, a highly contested race. The disciplinary committee of the KMT said Lee had "maliciously harmed" the party by campaigning for a rival political grouping. What was also humiliating for Lee Teng-hui was that the TSU's performance fell below expectations in the poll. It won only nine seats in the 225-member lawmaking body, failing to gain enough votes to be eligible for government funding.

Interestingly, Lee Teng-hui never formally participated in the TSU. But he was hailed by the party as its "spiritual leader."

In the above, I have recounted what I, as a commentary writer, wrote about former President Lee Teng-hui's democratic reforms and his overt embrace of Taiwan's independence in his final years in office. During my nearly two decades in that writing job, I also wrote extensively about his successor Chen Shui-bian (2000 to 2008), regarding his governing practices and reform programs. In the following segment, chapter 10, I will examine some of those writings, all based on my editorials and commentaries which I have kept to this day.

Chapter 10
How I Assess Ex-President Chen Shui-bian

Disappointing First Year in Office

In the previous pages, I have examined my opinion pieces about Lee Teng-hui's political and democratic reforms, which he carried out during his 12 years in office from 1988 to 2000. I wrote these as a columnist who regularly contributed to the China Post, a daily, and the Economic News, a weekly. Since my column-writing job lasted for nearly 20 years, I also had a chance to cover Lee's successor President Chen Shui-bian. Chen also served two terms spanning eight years until May 2008.

My account of what I wrote about President Chen will be focused on the following areas: a short honeymoon period; suffering from the impact of a minority government; Chen's unstable leadership; a bad decision to halt the ongoing construction of a multi-billion-dollar nuclear power plant; failing to improve vital mainland China relations; delivering a disappointing first-year report; the economy got even worse in the remaining three years of his first presidency; and a turbulent second term.

Chen Shui-bian made history when he, as an opposition politician, defeated ruling KMT candidate Lien Chan and won the March 2000 presidential election. His win brought an end to the KMT's 50-year rule of Taiwan and ushered in a viable two-party system in the country's politics.

Also significantly, Chen and his Democratic Progressive Party (DPP) had long advanced independence for Taiwan in the past. Hence, his election in some sense meant that the people in Taiwan now had an option to vote for the island's political future. This was unlike in the past when the KMT was single-handedly ruling Taiwan, Voters then had only one choice: Taiwan had to reunify with the communist-ruled Chinese mainland ultimately.

Chen Shui-bian's 2000 election victory drew widespread attention in the Western media. He was praised by some American and European newspapers as a democratic icon in Taiwan. Domestically, Chen enjoyed high popularity in the post-March 2000 election days. This was so despite the fact that the mandate he got was a weak one in terms of voter support.

Chen Shui-bian's honeymoon period was short, however. He finished his first 30 days in office with approval ratings reaching as high as more than 80%. But his popularity soon entered a downward spiral. By the time Chen marked the first anniversary of his presidency, his approval ratings had dropped well below 50%. I wrote editorials on both occasions. The opinion pieces provided some indications of why Chen's honeymoon was so short and why his popularity plunged fast and steeply thereafter.

The first piece on Chen's first month in power was titled "President Chen displays vital presidential attributes." This editorial appeared in the China Post on June 21, 2000. Some parts of that article are given below:

"President Chen Shui-bian, during a press conference given yesterday on the occasion of his first month in office, exhibited a number of qualities essential for a top government leader....First, he reiterated his determination to honor his promise to be a president for all the people. That meant he would not just serve the 39% of the population that voted for him in the March 18, 2000 presidential election. This is also to say that Chen would take into account the interests of the entire populace in adopting major policies, not merely those of his supporters and his pro-independence Democratic Progressive Party...

"Beyond reiterating his commitment to be a leader for all the people, Chen also emphasized the point that he is the president of the Republic of China. By going out of his way to cite the national name, the pro-independence president obviously intended to tell everyone that he was willing to show loyalty to the ROC, observe its laws and adhere to its basic values, just as his KMT predecessors had...

"That Chen decided to use the occasion of his first month in power to once again define his office as the president of the ROC appeared also aimed at easing ongoing concerns among the public about his political leanings. Truly, there are still doubts here and abroad about his political intentions, given his past ardent advocacy of Taiwan independence and the pro-independence DPP he stands for...

"President Chen also made a friendly gesture to the two opposition leaders, Lien Chan of the KMT and James Soong of the People First Party, inviting them to his office to discuss issues of national concern. The president's willingness to meet with Soong and Lien suggested his desire to promote reconciliation with them. Relations with the two former fellow candidates were damaged in the bitterly contested three-way race. In fact, President Chen has to repair relations with the two leaders, if he wants to win their cooperation in the opposition-dominated legislature…

"Relations with Beijing accounted for a great deal of the president's meeting with the press…Chen for the first time publicly expressed a willingness to honor all the accords and understandings the former KMT government had concluded with Beijing. This apparently was a response to the mainland government's repeated calls since his election for him to return to the 1992 consensus for the resumption of bilateral talks. The consensus referred to was a tacit agreement signed with Beijing in 1992 to address the longstanding one-China dispute. The agreement was widely seen as a cornerstone of stable relations across the Taiwan Strait…

"But President Chen was quick to add that, as he understood, the two sides never reached a bilateral accord on the definition of one China. If there indeed was a consensus, it was one to 'agree to disagree.' However, Chen still promised that he would be willing to make any effort with the mainland to work out a realistic one-China definition that would be acceptable to both sides of the Taiwan Strait…

"Chen throughout the news conference gave the impression of being confident about his new job. Obviously, Chen's confidence came in part from public recognition of his performance since taking office. Fresh opinion polls showed his approval ratings being as high as more than 80%. Yet it remains to be seen as to how long his presidential honeymoon will last. It could quickly come to an end if and when the people find that the new leader is slow in introducing major reform programs, or unable to deliver on his campaign promises."

The honeymoon period for the Chen administration indeed was short. One month after he took office, his popularity began to fall and since followed a downward spiral. According to a commentary I wrote in late February 2001--nine months into his first presidency, Chen's approval rating fell to 34%, the lowest since he took office in May 2000. The finding came from a survey conducted by the cable television company TVBS. The same survey also discovered nearly 64% of respondents expressed dissatisfaction with his Cabinet. They cited a weakening economy, rising unemployment, and a widespread feeling of uncertainty about the future of Taiwan.

By the time Chen marked the first anniversary of his presidency, his approval ratings had plummeted to their lowest levels. Days ahead of the occasion, I wrote another editorial entitled "Chen Fails to Deliver in His First Year." In it, I examined Chen's popularity plunge and analyzed what contributed to the decline. Below are excerpts taken from that article.

"On May 20 last year when Chen Shui-bian assumed the presidency, he promised to bring a better and happier tomorrow for the country's 23 million people in his four-year term. But he has so far not made any noticeable progress in fulfilling that promise. On the contrary, most people found their lives have become harsher in the past year, with many saying they were deeply disappointed with Chen and his administration. A survey conducted this week by the United Daily News showed that eight out of 10 people across the country gave a negative reply when asked 'whether they are better off than a year earlier.

"In a separate survey carried out by the Chinese-language newspaper China Times at around the same time, Chen received a disapproval rating of 45%, only one percentage point lower than the ratio of respondents who rated him positively. The same China Times poll also discovered that more than half, 52%, of the people said they were dissatisfied with Chen's governing team, while only 35% gave it a positive rating.

"Looking back to the year since last May, it will be easy to find out why President Chen and his administration have performed so poorly and disappointingly. One, the administration failed to set policy priorities leaving the various government agencies to hastily come up with bills to fulfill the president's campaign promises. Yet many of such bills were so controversial that they caused the administration to be mired in stormy debates with opposition lawmakers in the golden first few months...

"Two, the Cabinet's sudden announcement of abandoning an already one-third completed nuclear power project was particularly damaging. It prompted the three opposition parties to form a united front against the administration over the move. For four months until the power project was revived, the whole society of Taiwan was thrown into bitter pro- and anti-nuclear debates, wasting a considerable amount of valuable production time. Moreover, the decision to scrap the multi-billion-dollar construction project raised serious investor concerns about the supply of electricity and the continuity of government policy. Such concerns served to accelerate the pace of Taiwan's capital outflows, primarily to mainland China, a market which has become increasingly important for Taiwan..."

"And three, many top DPP politicians, most of them hardline supporters of independence, often dragged President Chen from trying to move to the center on a number of divisive issues, such as national identity and relations with mainland China. This thwarted any effort to heal the political divide after a bitter election."

Inability to Create a Stable Governing Team

The failure of President Chen Shui-bian to deliver in his first year in office also had much to do with his inability to move fast to establish a strong and stable governing team, a problem inherent in a weak mandate. Chen won only 39% of the vote in the March 20, 2000, presidential election, while his party, the DPP, held only one-third of the seats in the Legislative Yuan--the lawmaking body. This made it difficult for DPP lawmakers to effectively defend Chen and his administration.

In Western democracies, a president or a premier-elect, faced with political difficulties like this, normally would remedy them by inviting another political party, or parties, to form a coalition to ensure stable and effective governance. But Chen Shui-bian paid no attention to such foreign governing experiences. He refused to form a coalition government as urged by many, apparently because he was unwilling to share power with the opposition parties.

Instead, he established a so-called "government for all the people." He touted this policy as a government that transcended party lines. Judging by the composition of the Cabinet he formed, it indeed was a government going beyond party lines. "Of the 38 senior Cabinet positions, as many as 12 were filled by politicians enlisted from the main opposition KMT. Only about the same number of those posts were given to politicians coming from Chen's own party, the DPP. The remainder were filled by people recruited from academia, the business community and independents."

His "government for all the people" strategy, however, failed to help him achieve his desired results of establishing a stable and efficient government. But rather it brought about a host of governing problems. Among them was a controversial but serious question: Was the incoming administration a DPP government, or a bipartisan government as billed by President-elect Chen Shui-bian?

To Lin I-hsiung, chairman of the president's DPP party, the former was the case. Chairman Lin made the above assertion in an interview with the press shortly after President-elect Chen announced the formation of his party-transcending government. He continued that "since the new government is a DPP administration, its policies must not run counter to the DPP's platform and positions."

In an analysis written for the Economic News, I said, "...But Lin's claim raised two major questions. One, they contradicted President-elect Chen Shui-bian's promise that his government, in enacting laws and policies, would take into account the interests of the entire population, not just those of his party and its supporters. Also, the DPP chairman's remarks would disappoint the many non-DPP appointees, who agreed to join the new government in response to

President Chen's call for the formation of a government that would put national interests above those of any particular political party...

"But unfortunately the chairman's recent remarks already have had an impact on the new administration to be sworn in within two weeks from now. Economics Minister-designate Lin Hsin-yi has ordered the halting of a nuclear power plant already 30% complete. He wanted a review of the multi-billion-dollar plant simply because anti-nuclear power was one of the DPP's core values...

"The incoming economics minister's order to halt the nuclear power project has raised doubts about President-elect Chen Shui-bian's commitment that his government would follow a middle-of-the-road approach in governance. A middle-of-the-road approach must mean restraining from going to extremes. A new survey found that only 27% of the people polled supported stopping the nuclear project, while as many as 42% were against it..."

The third problem with President Chen's "government for all the people" formula was that it made things difficult for his premier, Tang Fei, to exercise his duties. Specifically, Premier Tang governed without a real ruling party throwing support behind him. The DPP, which held a mere 12% of senior positions in the Cabinet, saw itself as a governing party in name only. So many DPP lawmakers were not eager to defend the premier and his policy in the opposition-dominated Legislative Yuan. In fact, they sometimes were far more critical of the premier's policy than were opposition politicians.

Wu Nai-jen, the DPP's secretary-general, for example, time and again accused Premier Tang of being slow to usher in reforms and of ignoring the wishes of their party. The premier got more isolated in his job after he publicly expressed his support for finishing the construction of the nuclear plant. His pro-nuclear position, however, was in direct contradiction to the policy of the DPP, which wanted the US$5.4 billion power project to be scrapped. The premier could not get the support of his boss either. President Chen while repeatedly vowing to serve as a bipartisan leader now openly announced that he would like to stop the nuclear project.

In addition, President Chen Shui-bian's own leadership style also posed a problem for Premier Tang. The president "often overruled the Cabinet's policies despite the fact that by law the premier was the head of the executive branch." It's true that the premier was directly appointed by the president. But what is also true is that the premier constitutionally is accountable to the Legislative Yuan. This meant that the premier had to respect the lawmaking body's views and resolutions on making or changing major policies and events.

"Premier Tang, for his part, was becoming increasingly unhappy with President Chen's 'unjustified' interference in his conduct of business, making it difficult for him to carry out his duties. The president's practices of overruling the premier's policy and the latter's complaints of unjustified interventions by the former inevitably resulted in a heightening tension between the two top leaders. Worse, when the president and the premier did not see eye to eye, it tended to cause a crucial compliance problem among the many Cabinet ministers as to whose opinion--that of the president or that of the premier-- they should take as the guiding principle in policy making."

Tang Fei resigned in early October 2000 less than five months after he took over the premier's job. He announced his resignation after meeting with President Chen Shui-bian. Tang cited poor health. But many in the public believed he stepped down under mounting pressure, particularly from the DPP, the president's party.

The premier's resignation came days after DPP Secretary General Wu Nai-jen publicly expressed his dissatisfaction with the performance of the Tang-headed Cabinet for the second time in as many days. More recently he went further to call for President Chen to reshuffle the governing team and nominate a senior DPP politician to assume the premier's position. This, he said, would allow the DPP to play the governing role de jure and de facto. (Note, Tang was a member of the main opposition KMT and a retired air force general before he was tapped by President Chen to head the Cabinet.)

After accepting Tang Fei's resignation, President Chen moved quickly to name Tang's Vice Premier Chang Chung-hsiung to be his replacement. Chang, a top DPP politician, was at the same time authorized by the president to form a new governing team.

President Chen's nomination of a person from his own party to serve as his premier, however, marked an outright retreat from his campaign promise that he, if elected, would form and operate a government that would transcend party lines. Many in the public had taken that promise seriously, believing it was a commitment by the pro-independence leader to follow a middle-of-the-road approach to governing the country.

Shifting Back to Minority Rule

By appointing a fellow DPP politician to the premier's post, Chen appeared determined to enforce minority rule. But an administration, headed by a president winning well below half, 39%, of the vote, with his party holding just one-third of the legislative seats, was bound to face constant hostile boycotts from opposition lawmakers, who dominated the legislative agenda.

Before Chen reshuffled his Cabinet, many opinion leaders had called for him to invite opposition parties to form a coalition government. They believed that a multi-party-based government could reduce partisanship and ease ongoing political tensions. Political instability had continued to hurt the economy by eroding consumer confidence and scaring away investors, local and foreign.

Chen Shui-bian ignored the calls. But the problem was that the DPP-based minority Cabinet which he formed was also short-lived. It lasted for just a little more than one year, or only about five months longer than the previous Tang Fei-led governing team. The reason that Chen's new Cabinet lasted for only such a short time was due primarily to its failure to reverse a declining economy.

Chang Chung-hsiung, the premier who replaced Tang Fei, had to deal with a host of economic woes during his one year and three months on the job (from October 2000 to late 2001). Some of them were inherited from the previous Cabinet. Some were new stemming from unwise government policies and adverse changes in world markets.

As a commentary writer, I had the chance to examine and analyze in my columns the various economic problems which the Chen administration faced and the way it tackled them. The following are excerpts taken from some of the editorials and commentaries I wrote then. These extracts I feel could provide a brief view of how Chen and his government addressed the economic problems during his first four-year term.

In one of these opinion pieces, entitled 'Restoring Confidence Is Key to Averting Economic Slump' and published in the China Post on November 3, 2000, I wrote in part: "What has gone wrong with the Taiwan economy? The underlying problem is a loss of public confidence in the new government. This can be seen simply from investors' reluctance to buy shares and increase spending on new plants and equipment.

"What caused the public to lose confidence in the Chen government is not because its leaders are inexperienced. This problem alone would not matter much. People are sympathetic to them and willing to give them time to learn on the job. What is really worrying the public and investors, in particular, are a number of fatal shortcomings in the leadership of the administration…

"The first is its inability to handle relations with the opposition-controlled lawmaking body, a failure which has led to lingering political chaos. Another ruinous shortcoming is that the Chen administration has given the public the impression that it is carrying out an anti-business agenda. Specifically, they were troubled by a series of policy initiatives advocated by the new government: Shortening work hours, abandoning a dam project, discouraging private investments in two huge petrochemical plants, and scrapping the fourth nuclear plant--a project already one-third built with billions of dollars spent...

"A third damaging problem with the DPP-led administration has been the party's dogged adherence to the cause of Taiwan independence. This prompted the DPP to antagonize the main opposition KMT and two smaller parties, all of which are opposed to Taiwan splitting from China. The net result of such antagonism has been constant, bitter wrangling over the two divisive issues of national identity and Taiwan's relations with mainland China."

Another editorial that I authored and appeared in the same English-language newspaper on December 6, 2000, carried the headline: "How the Gov't Has Been Mishandling the Economy." In this piece, I wrote in part: "The administration of Chen Shui-bian must move quickly to change course and seek to ward off a potential financial and economic crisis. The new administration has been mishandling the economy from almost the very moment it took power in the middle of this year...

"Most unwise is the way the administration has been addressing the falling stock market and its liberal policy of encouraging banks to provide debt relief to financially troubled companies in the industrial and commercial sector. Also, the Ministry of Finance in the past more than six months has rarely had a day without entering the stock market in the form of purchases by the various government-supported banks and funds, including the 'National Stabilization Fund'...

"When share prices go up or down, they reflect investors' responses to changes in economic fundamentals, business climate as well as politics and government policies. The government's role is to improve the health of the market and allow market mechanisms to be in full play…However, these basic market norms have been entirely ignored. In fact, the funds' continued purchases of shares have only caused huge losses for the government, while doing little to reverse the plunges of the bourse…

"When industrial companies in growing numbers ran into financial problems, the Ministry of Finance responded with ever more debt-relief measures. Never mind that such measures would not help companies cure their ills, but only prolong them. And never mind that such interventions could even aggravate the problem of already high overdue loans plaguing most banks…What is more, the Finance Ministry, instead of adopting more active steps to prompt banks to dispose of their mounting nonperforming loans, recently even offered to allow them to take up to 10 years to write off any losses from stock market investments. This was in total violation of international banking norms on addressing questionable loans…

"As with the Finance Ministry, the Ministry of Economic Affairs has failed to properly play its role. Economics Minister Lin Hsin-yi has from the very beginning of the new administration devoted almost all of his time and energy to the cause of scrapping the fourth nuclear power plant, as pushed for by the ruling DPP. He forgot that his primary duty is to provide leadership in the development of the broad economy…"

A third editorial, dated December 26, 2001, carried the headline "The Need to Win Back Investors." I started this China Post commentary with the following question. "If a global economic upturn does materialize toward the middle of 2002, as is widely predicted now, will Taiwan be able to recover in sync with the anticipated worldwide revival and, moreover, regain its competitive edge in a post-recession era?

"The answer to that question, discouragingly, is not positive. The main concern is that Taiwan appears to have lost its appeal as a place to attract direct investment, especially in the manufacturing sector. This kind of investment matters more for two reasons. One, if investors are willing to increase spending on plants and equipment, it will help boost demand for products and services and, thus, can fuel a broad-based economic recovery. Also importantly, equipment spending can best increase productivity and competitiveness."

"According to the latest statistics, Taiwan's investments in the manufacturing business fell 24% in the first nine months from a year earlier. Not only that, while the island's domestic capital spending contracted, its outward fund flows followed an opposite trend in the same period, increasing drastically to a combined total of US$5.4 billion. The same pattern was also true with foreign investment in Taiwan. In the January-September period, capital brought in by foreign firms for investment in Taiwan's non-financial sectors was down by 28% to US$4 billion.

"On the other hand, such offshore fund flows to many neighboring economies, particularly mainland China, showed significant increases during the same months of this year. In the final analysis, when the investors, local and foreign alike, decided to reduce investment in Taiwan while proceeding with their commitments for places outside this island, it went beyond reflecting the effect of the ongoing economic recession. It also reflected that many investors have chosen to bypass Taiwan in favor of investing elsewhere in the region, attracted by more favorable business conditions...

"It's not too difficult to find out why Taiwan is losing its attraction as a leading location for direct investment. First, Taiwan fails to offer new promising investment opportunities. For many years, this island has absorbed huge amounts of capital in high-tech sectors, especially in semiconductor production. But this latter segment has lost its allure because of excess capacity here and abroad amid a global slowdown in demand...

"Nor do Taiwan's traditional industries provide as many profitable investment opportunities as they used to. With wages and land prices far exceeding the levels in other countries around the region, it has become very difficult for many traditional businesses to operate completely in Taiwan any longer...

"That Taiwan has lost its battle for investment also has much to do with the sweeping restrictions the government has imposed on the movement of cargo, capital, and personnel to the Chinese mainland, the single largest offshore destination for Taiwan investors. To overcome these business restrictions, more and more local companies are moving their production facilities to the mainland to eliminate the need to transport their goods and raw materials to and from the mainland through third countries. Similarly, many multinational corporations with businesses in Taiwan or originally having plans to come here found it more appropriate for them to switch their production bases or regional headquarters to the mainland, as shown in various data on cross-strait business activities...

"A third major reason for Taiwan's drastic slowdown in corporate spending has been a failure of the government to maintain political stability. Fighting between the administration of President Chen Shui-bian and the opposition-dominated lawmaking body has never really eased since he assumed office two years ago."

Third Cabinet Reshuffle in 18 Months

By the end of 2001, Taiwan's economy still showed no signs of recovery. This prompted Chen Shui-bian to reshuffle his governing team again, the third time and the largest in size in his 18-month-old presidency. He had to. As I pointed out then, "the economy under the management of the Chen presidency has deteriorated to its worst level in recent history, with record unemployment, a steep downturn in business investment, and a severe contraction in GDP output…Chen's decision to refocus effort on the economy at this point apparently has taken into consideration the presidential election in 2004. He understood that if he failed to bring the Taiwan economy back on a growth track and reduce unemployment, there would be little chance for him to get reelected."

Heading the latest reorganized Cabinet, which Chen billed as a "Combat Cabinet," was his former Secretary General Yu Shyi-kun. Yu, also a senior DPP politician, had considerable administrative experience, including eight years as a two-term magistrate. So the public pinned high hopes on the new premier in raising governing efficiency and fulfilling the president's promises to the people.

But that hope didn't come true. The "Combat Cabinet" still failed to restore public confidence in the Chen Shui-bian administration as a whole and did not make life easier for the people. This can be seen in an editorial I wrote one year after Yu Shyi-kun's appointment to the premier's post. In this December 25, 2002 piece, I wrote "President Chen Shui-bian's own approval ratings, for one thing, have plummeted to well below 40%, as more and more people have doubts about his ability to lead the country. Similar skepticism also comes from within his ruling Democratic Progressive Party. Fellow DPP politicians in growing numbers are dissatisfied with his leadership style..."

"Chen came to power with a promise to pursue a 'new middle-of-the-road' policy, but now -- two years and one month into his presidency -- he is losing the support of centrist voters. This was strikingly evident in the December 7, 2002 mayoral election in the capital city Taipei, in which the ruling party lost the election to the opposition KMT by a margin of more than 380,000 ballots, mostly believed to be swing votes..."

"In fact, people discontented with his administration's policies now come from all walks of life. The last few months have seen mass demonstrations staged by farmers, teachers as well as blue-collar workers, and the disadvantaged. The latter two categories of people had traditionally voted for the DPP, the governing party. They had done so in the belief that the party could best advance their interests...

"The widespread dissatisfaction with President Chen and his government has arisen, not least because of serious economic weaknesses. Unemployment has remained painfully high. Sustained stock price plunges have considerably diminished the wealth of companies and individuals. Taiwan has become miserably poor in a matter of just two years, with everybody now feeling the pinch of poverty."

Following three consecutive years of a slowdown, Taiwan's economy finally began showing clear signs of an upturn in late 2003 along with a global rebound. For President Chen Shui-bian, this obviously was particularly encouraging news. At this time, he was already on the campaign trail to run for a second term in the coming March 2004 presidential election.

I wrote a couple of pieces examining the state of Taiwan's economic recovery. One of which, dated September 5, 2003, read in part: "Most business indicators from export orders to share prices, home sales, and money supply, all show clear signs that the local economy is gaining momentum for a stronger rebound ahead. The government was so optimistic that it raised its growth forecast to 3.8% for 2004, up from the previously predicted 3.1%...

"A closer look at the overall performance of the economy, however, points to some concerns. Up to this point, the recovery was led mainly by a pickup in exports. Business investments and consumer spending have yet to improve significantly. Without meaningful improvements in the two vital sectors, the pace of growth cannot possibly accelerate...

"Yet the biggest uncertainty facing the economy is about the March 2004 presidential election. No matter who finally wins the race, Chen, or the joint ticket of the opposition alliance, there could be a post-election period of uneasiness among businessmen. If Chen gets a second term, he may need time to convince businesses that he can better manage the economy during his second term...

"On the other hand, if KMT chairman Lien Chan and his running mate of PFP James Soong capture power, they too need time to persuade the DPP and its supporters that their promise to improve relations with Beijing will not be carried out in a way that would hurt Taiwan's crucial interests including its political sovereignty."

On the Campaign Trail

Chen Shui-bian launched his unannounced reelection campaign in the middle of 2003. After that my focus of coverage as an editorial writer and commentator shifted to the March 2004 presidential election. I scrutinized everything the candidates said and did on the campaign trail. The following are excerpts taken from some of the editorials that which I wrote about the campaign, mostly concerning the incumbent president. The excerpts are presented in order of publication date. Such information is given in parentheses or inserted in suitable places in the relevant text.

In one editorial (dated June 25, 2003), I pointed out that "President Chen Shui-bian is playing a game of brinksmanship by pushing ahead with a plan to hold a nationwide referendum despite the strong disapproval of the United States--Taiwan's most important defense ally, and mainland China, the biggest adversary of this island, as well as firm objections from the two domestic opposition parties...

"Chen on Sunday rebuffed Washington's concern over his referendum plan by responding with a stinging remark that 'Taiwan is not a state of any country.' His response to Beijing, which was said to have privately urged the Bush administration to intervene, was a similar rebuke: 'Taiwan is an independent state, not a subordinate province of any country'...

"Many took President Chen's referendum plan as a central reelection strategy designed to shore up his popularity ratings ahead of the March 2004 presidential election...Recent opinion polls consistently showed him lagging by more than 10 percentage points behind the opposition Lien-Soong ticket...

"By this time (July 2003), Chen Shui-bian has not yet formally announced his candidacy for a second term. But the president has since late May raised a series of high-profile issues. They ranged from a call to hold a referendum on Taiwan's entry into the World Health Organization; a popular vote to decide whether or not to complete a nuclear power plant; and a projection of a tougher line on Beijing. While public responses were mostly negative, these issues did help Chen build momentum for his campaign...

In an August 18, 2003 editorial, I said this: "Increasingly, President Chen Shui-bian appears to be steering the campaign for the coming March presidential poll into a vote on the advocacy of an independent Taiwan versus the support of a one-China policy, after gaining high ground in the recent sovereignty debate...

"With his recent characterization of Taiwan-Chinese mainland relations as 'one side, one country,' and his renewed support for a string of pro-independence policies resonating well with the public, Chen was emboldened to shift completely away from his once hyped 'middle of the road path' to extreme independence fundamentalism...

"In talks with senior DPP politicians and his grassroots friends during this past week, Chen defended his advocacy of 'one side, one country' or 'one country on each side.' He described such advocacy as part of the ruling DPP's core values. Chen this week went further to say that he, as the leader of the country, must have a sense of mission. At the same time, he reiterated his refusal to accept Beijing's 'one-China' principle...

"By highlighting these political views, Chen wanted to call public attention to a position he first raised weeks ago that the coming presidential election will be a vote to make a choice between a candidate who would pursue a pro-independence agenda and one, who would be more willing to promote better relations with Beijing...

"Besides manipulating the pro-independence versus pro-unification issue, President Chen Shui-bian recently also gave overt support for a campaign to change the country's national name Republic of China." In an editorial (dated September 5, 2003), I noted: "A proposed 100,000-strong mass rally, organized to promote changing the country's name to Taiwan from the ROC, is to be held in the capital city of Taipei tomorrow with the blessing of President Chen Shui-bian and his governing party...

"The mass rally in itself is not drawing particular public attention. The event's organizers, which include a minor political party, the Taiwan Solidarity Union, and several independence fundamentalist groups, are long known staunch advocates of having the nation's moniker changed...

"In their opinion, the nearly century-old ROC as a country has long been defunct since the KMT government lost its control of the

Chinese mainland in late 1949 and, therefore, it is unrealistic to continue to use the ROC as the national name. To these fundamentalists, a change of the title ROC is a crucial step in achieving their goal of building a new state called Taiwan, one which they think can more accurately reflect the political status of this island...

"They naively believe that establishing an independent Taiwan state will make it possible for the 23 million people of this island to reject Beijing's sovereignty claim and, therefore, enable Taiwan to pursue broader international recognition and thus break its longstanding diplomatic isolation...

"Yet what is attracting special attention is the unreserved support President Chen has given to the coming mass rally. Under his instructions, the ruling party was reportedly mobilizing tens of thousands of their supporters to the capital city from all over Taiwan to participate in the demonstration...

"Many people are concerned that why Chen, who as the president has the constitutional obligation to defend the ROC against any form of security threat, should have decided to support a political movement seeking to eliminate it. Also, Chen's open embrace of nation-building contradicts his 2000 inauguration pledge to neither declare independence nor push for a change of the national name. These pledges have since served as the cornerstone of stable relations with mainland China and as a commitment to secure continued defense assistance from the United States..."

A Taiwan State Building Agenda

'Chen Clarifies His Agenda for a Taiwan Nation' was the title of another commentary that I wrote, published on October 8, 2003. Below are the main parts of that text: "Now President Chen Shui-bian has drawn up a clearer independence timetable. He wants to build a Taiwan state through the enacting of a new constitution by 2006. According to him, such a draft basic law would be adopted directly by an island-wide referendum. This meant that the new constitution enacting procedure would bypass the Legislative Yuan to go around a high threshold. The current legislative rule requires a three-fourth vote by the lawmaking body for any constitutional changes...

"Judging by Chen's intensifying rhetoric, his push for the writing of a new constitution can no longer be viewed merely as an election gambit intended to prompt harsh Beijing responses that, in turn, would alienate Taiwan's voters ahead of the March presidential poll. The beneficiary of any such response would be Chen Shui-bian, the pro-independence DPP candidate...

"Chen's new constitution plan may go even deeper. He wants to use a string of his political remarks and advocacies to achieve two other purposes: One, he intends to promote a wide public awareness of the need to write a new constitution for Taiwan. Two, he hopes to use his campaign to instill in the minds of the 23 million people of Taiwan that they have the inherent right to determine the political future of Taiwan..."

In a November 21, 2003 editorial, entitled A U.S. Warning Signal for Chen, I wrote the following: "While President Chen Shui-bian is still basking in the success of his recent high-profile transit visit to New York, where he overtly publicized his plan to write a new constitution for Taiwan, the United States issued the Taiwan leader a sober warning alerting him to the possible political implications that his constitution initiative may have...

"In a just-released report to the US Senate, the State Department assessed that should Taiwan omit the mention of the ROC name from the existing constitution because of a revision or rewriting of the basic law, it runs the risk of inviting an armed attack from Beijing...

"That assessment is valid. Writing a new constitution with the name Taiwan replacing the ROC as the national title, as being pushed for by the independence activists, would amount to laying a legal foundation for the birth of a Taiwan nation. Beijing has gone on record that it would not hesitate to invade this island should it declare independence...

"At the same time of the State Department release, Washington reiterated that it remained concerned about Chen's ongoing constitution and referendum plans. It clarified that the reception and treatment the US gave to Chen during his recent stopover in New York by no means represented agreement with his policy....

"Yet many in Taipei were wondering why the U.S. authorities had failed to make that clarification earlier. When the news about the explanation reached Taiwan, it had already been 10 days after Chen Shui-bian registered a hefty popularity surge in opinion polls, thanks to his successful New York transit visit, which was billed by the president and his administration as an 'important diplomatic breakthrough.'"

A Rebuke from George W. Bush

"A Rebuke from George W. Bush" was one of the many topics I dealt with in tracking the Chen Shui-bian campaign in the 2004 presidential election. In a commentary piece, dated December 12, 2003, I examined Washington's dissatisfaction with Chen's controversial referendum plan. The parts of this article: "President Chen Shui-bian now must make a difficult decision as to whether or not to push ahead with his 'defensive referendum plan,' after George W. Bush, the 43rd President of the United States, recently issued a verbal statement condemning the provocative policy...

"Bush, in the face of visiting mainland Chinese Premier Wen Jiabao in his office, said 'The comments and actions made by the leader of Taiwan indicate that he may be willing to make decisions unilaterally to change the status quo, which we oppose.' In response, Chen and his senior aides said that Taipei will continue to communicate with Washington. Presumably, Taipei will try again to convince the U.S. government that President Chen's push for a defense referendum, scheduled to coincide with the March 2004 presidential election, will have nothing to do with the issue of promoting independence for Taiwan.

"But this reassurance might not work. A State Department spokesman in a subsequent press conference singled out Chen's defensive vote for criticism. U.S. authorities believed that designating a "particular day" for a referendum on a "political subject" was a political action aiming to 'move in a particular direction.' Therefore, the spokesman said, the referendum plan will not have the support of the United States…"

In a February 11, 2004 editorial, I pointed to Beijing's frustration being unable to use America's influence to block President Chen from conducting his controversial referendum. Some passages of the editorial are given below:

"Beijing now seemed desperate after failing to secure a commitment from the U.S. to prevent Chen Shui-bian from holding a referendum scheduled for March 20, 2004, alongside the presidential election in which he was running for a second term. Whether the PRC government will thus resort to using military action against Taiwan is a matter of concern for this island...

"Beijing, which sees Chen's proposed referendum as part of his action plan to split Taiwan from the Chinese mainland, might be worried that should Chen get reelected on a pro-independence agenda, he would have a strong mandate to carry out his campaign promise to write a new constitution for Taiwan. Note, he had already set a schedule for the task: "To draw up a new constitution, have it approved by the people of Taiwan through a popular vote before 2006, and bring it into force by 2008, if he wins a second term. Many saw the planned series of actions as a timetable for building a Taiwan nation...

"Such worries among PRC leaders could prompt them to make strong responses, according to Deputy Assistant Secretary of State Randall Schriver. He said late last week 'Washington had the impression that Beijing, deeply concerned about the March referendum, was considering certain countermeasures.'

"How actually the PRC government will react will depend on how Chen is going to promote the referendum to the voters in the final weeks of the campaign. Recently Chen did reword the content of the referendum. The toned-down version would ask voters two questions. One, should mainland China refuse to remove the missiles it has targeted at Taiwan, would you agree that our government should acquire more advanced anti-missile weapons to strengthen Taiwan's self-defense capabilities?...

"The second question asks "Would you agree that our government should engage in negotiation with mainland China on the establishment of a 'peace and stability framework for cross-strait interactions?'... In the end, both of the above referendum proposals were rejected due to insufficient turnout. A newly enacted law stipulates a voter turnout of 50% was required for a referendum to pass...

"With election day less than 40 days off and Chen Shui-bian's poll ratings still lagging behind his main challenger Lien Chan of the KMT, the incumbent president has the incentive to rachet up the sovereignty issue to energize pro-independence voters and broaden his political base."

President Chen, since announcing his bid for a second term in mid-2003, had resorted to using a range of pro-independence policies and mass rallies to drum up support and build momentum for his campaign. This strategy, while frequently prompting tensions with Beijing and Washington, worked well for him by distracting public attention from his challenger Lien Chan of the KMT. The reason was clear. As public attention continued to focus on Chen's campaign issues and activities and the controversies they brought about, it naturally contributed to his poll rating improvements, allowing him to gradually bridge his gap with Lien Chan.

A Spectacular 500km Human Chain

Among the various mass rallies which Chen Shui-bian had held in his second term campaign was a spectacular 500km human chain, which proved to be a turning point in his reelection. On February 28, 2004, three weeks ahead of the March 20 presidential election, Chen and his supporters organized a high-profile mass demonstration. The event featured two million people joining hands to form a human chain along the 500 km west coast of Taiwan. On the surface, the day-long activity was held to oppose mainland China's deployment of some 500 missiles targeting Taiwan. But in actuality, it was an activity designed to exhibit President Chen's courage to openly protest against Beijing's military threat to Taiwan, with the ultimate aim of winning domestic support for him.

Furthermore, by holding the demonstration on that particular day February 28, Chen also intended to draw the attention of voters to past atrocities of the KMT, the party his challenger Lien Chan represented. This date was a national holiday devoted to remembering the many victims killed in a military suppression of civilian protesters executed by the KMT-led government a half-century ago. Most of the victims were native Taiwanese.

Three days after the February 28 demonstration, I wrote a piece on the event and its implications for the presidential race. Below are parts of this article: "Opposition presidential candidate Lien Chan faces the most serious challenge of his campaign. His long-running lead over the incumbent Chen Shui-bian has for the first time narrowed down to levels near or within the margin of error in most recent polls at a time when election day is only two and a half weeks off...

"Lien's recent rating slip came due largely to President Chen and his strategists' success in rallying close to two million people on Saturday in the form of an impressive 500-kilometer hand-in-hand chain along Taiwan's west coast. This impressive rally, as many have observed, has substantially built momentum for Chen's reelection campaign...

"Through the rally's call for solidarity against Beijing's missile and military threats, along with its slogan of saying 'yes' to Taiwan and 'no' to China, Chen has noticeably raised a sense of Taiwanese nationalism and, in addition, built a reputation for him as the brave leader advocating a separate political identity for this island...

"Not only that, but Chen has also used the mass rally to effectively publicize his plan to hold a defensive referendum on March 20, alongside the presidential election, as the best democratic weapon to safeguard Taiwan against aggression from China...

"These successes have enabled Chen to claim the high ground on the two issues in the campaign of national identity and democratic reform, greatly boosting his appeal to centrist voters as well as his and his party's core constituents—those who want to pursue permanent independence for Taiwan."

Reelected by a Thin Margin of 0.2%

At the end of Election Day, March 20, 2004, as the final batches of ballot tallies came in, Chen Shui-bian was shown to have won a second term by a razor-thin margin of 0.2%, or less than 30,000 votes out of 12.9 million ballots cast. The narrow-margin win prompted the supporters of KMT candidate Lien Chan to challenge the legitimacy of the election results.

The legitimacy question was further complicated by an election-eve assassination attempt on Chen and his running mate Vice President Annette Lu. The shooting incident was believed by many to have won some sympathy votes for Chen, the incumbent president. Lien Chan's supporters speculated that the attempted assassination was deliberately staged by the Chen campaign.

Little wonder that the defeated candidate Lien Chan and his running mate James Soong immediately contested the election results. They filed a lawsuit to invalidate the poll results and call for a vote recount. A vote recount request aside, Lien and his supporters also demanded an independent investigation into the election-eve shooting, which slightly wounded Chen and his vice presidential candidate Lu.

Days after the election, President Chen finally agreed to Lien's ballot recount request. At the end of the lengthy recounting process, some defects were indeed found in some of the election districts. But they were not serious enough to change the election results.

Yet unlike the ballot recount issue, the case of probing the election eve's mysterious shooting was far more complicated, posing formidable challenges to judicial and legislative investigations launched after the March 20 poll.

The shooting incident occurred in the early afternoon of March 19, 2004—the final day of the presidential campaign. At the time President Chen and Vice President Lu were campaigning in his hometown of Tainan. They were escorted by nine police motorcyclists but were not wearing bullet-proof vests. Chen and Lu were standing and waving at supporters from an open-top vehicle.

Soon after the shooting, Chen and Lu were taken to the nearby Chi-Mei hospital for medical checks and treatment. Doctors at the hospital announced, a few hours later at 5:45 p.m., that the president had suffered a gash 11 centimeters (4.3 inches) long and 2 centimeters (0.79 inches) wide across his abdomen.

According to the police, two bullets were fired at the vehicle around 1:45 p.m. One bullet, fired from the side of the vehicle, grazed Chen's stomach, traveled through his jacket, and lodged in the rear of the jacket. The other one penetrated the windshield of the car and hit Lu in the right knee. No suspect was arrested at the scene.

At around 9:00 p.m. the president was released and returned to his official residence. The leader, in a video released to the public at the same time, urged the people of Taiwan to remain calm and stated that neither his health nor the security of Taiwan was threatened.

Hours after the incident, police authorities announced they were certain that the shooting was not politically motivated, and that mainland China was not involved as alleged by some. But the failed assassination attempt sparked shock and unease in Taipei's political circles as well as among the general public.

A series of politically significant events happened in the hours that immediately followed the shooting. At 3:30 pm, the spokesperson for the president, Chiou I-jen, declared that the "National Security Mechanism" had been activated and many police officers and servicemen were recalled to duty to deal with the emergency.

By 5:30 pm, the opposition candidate Lien Chan announced that they had ceased all campaigning activities scheduled for the rest of the day. But the presidential election slated for the following day, March 20, was not postponed as a result of the election campaign being disrupted by the shooting case.

At one time Lien Chan and his campaign manager Wang Jin-pyng tried to visit Chen on the night of the incident but were not received on the grounds that the president was resting. Chen appeared in public the next day, as he went to the polls to cast his vote. At the time, he showed no signs of suffering any gunshot injuries.

An Independent Probe into the Shooting Case Demanded

Lien's supporters and many independents believed the election eve shooting was set up by Chen and his campaign to win sympathy votes. Most opinion polls conducted ahead of election day had consistently shown him trailing his challenger Lien Chan by about 5%. The noticeable difference between the pre-election poll ratings and the election results reinforced that belief. This explained why Lien Chan demanded an independent probe into the mysterious shooting immediately after the Central Election Commission declared the results of the election.

Three days after the March 20 election I wrote a commentary with the title 'Opposition Lawsuits Challenge Legitimacy of Chen's Victory.' In this article, I said that President Chen "has a crucial role to play in the investigation of the election eve's shooting. He must not shirk the responsibility on the grounds that the investigation is a matter needing to be handled by the judicial authorities. That is only partly true. The judicial institutions cannot address all of Lien Chan's complaints, some of which go beyond their authority and require the involvement of the president...

"For example, KMT Lien Chan's request that an independent panel of experts in various related fields is created to probe into the shooting case must be assisted by the president. Only the president has the authority to appropriate funds needed to support the operations of the panel once it is established. Further, only the president can mandate his Cabinet members to cooperate with panel investigators by, for example, giving testimonies or providing material evidence, whenever are so requested..."

Theoretically speaking, President Chen should have positively responded to the request. If he did, he would have won the opposition's agreement to end their ongoing mass demonstrations staged in front of the presidential office since the election night. The marathon protests had caused political unrest and impacted the stock market, which plunged continuously after the presidential polls. Similarly, a prompt positive embrace of the opposition's calls for an independent probe into the election eve's shooting would have gone a long way in demonstrating the willingness of the president to help find the truth behind the assassination attempt.

But the opposite was true. President Chen Shui-bian and his administration took every possible measure to block each and every investigative action launched by Lien Chan and his supporters in the wake of the election. Below are some of those obstructing measures, as covered and examined in a series of editorials that I wrote to track the gunshot-probing case and the controversies surrounding it.

In an April 21, 2004 editorial, headlined 'Election Win Has Fed Arrogance among Officials,' I expressed my views about how rudely the newly reelected President Chen treated opposition leaders, and how defiantly his administration officials refused to cooperate with lawmakers in the investigating of the shooting incident. The following are excerpts taken from that editorial:

"With his reelection victory last month, President Chen Shui-bian and his administration officials have become extremely haughty and overbearing in dealing with the opposition parties...Over the weekend, Chen repeated his harsh criticism of KMT chairman Lien Chan and PFP leader James Soong—the two opponents whom he narrowly defeated in the March poll. He criticized that Lien and Soong refused to concede the defeat, and are irresponsible and unwilling to step down from their party leadership positions...

"Haughty arrogance was also displayed by many Chen administration officials following Chen's March election victory. They refused, for instance, to appear before legislative committee meetings to answer questions about the shooting and related issues....

"The lawmakers from the opposition parties, in this instance, wanted to understand the actual circumstances, in which the Chen administration declared a state of emergency immediately after the shooting. Opposition lawmakers questioned the justification of the decree. They charged that the order was utilized by authorities to restrain large numbers of military and security personnel from returning home to cast votes...

"What's more, by refusing to attend the legislative hearings, these officials were also showing contempt for the lawmaking body. In addition, they also violated relevant constitutional provisions, which stipulate that government leaders have the duty to testify before the legislature and that they must place themselves under parliamentary scrutiny..."

Protesters Chant: No Truth, No President

In another piece, published on June 2, 2004, and dealing with the same subject matter, I noted "The legislature yesterday continued to challenge the legitimacy of President Chen Shui-bian's March 20 reelection. Lawmakers from the main opposition KMT and the PFP jointly blocked Premier Yu Shyi-kun from delivering his report before the lawmaking body. They formed a human chain to prevent the premier from proceeding to the podium while chanting slogans of "No Truth, No President.'

"The opposition's persistent refusal to recognize the validity of President Chen and his administration was understandable. More than two months after the election-eve shooting incident, in which Chen and his vice president Lu were slightly wounded, there were still no clues as to who did it and what were the motives behind it...

"The opposition's persistent demands that the president appoints an independent commission to probe the event and the controversies surrounding it were ignored. And the requests made by lawmakers and the members of the Control Yuan (a government watchdog body) to subpoena senior national security officials and the minutes of their meetings were flatly rejected."

'A Constitutional Crisis Is Brewing in Taiwan' was one other China Post editorial that I wrote in mid-October of 2004 about the shooting of President Chen Shui-bian, nearly seven months after the incident occurred. This article discussed how an opposition-driven piece of legislation, aimed at investigating the truth of the March 19 shooting, triggered a string of constitutional confrontations among the three branches of government--legislative, executive, and judicial. Below are passages excerpted from the mid-October opinion piece:

"...For starters, the legislature, disappointed at the progress of the executive branch's investigation into the election-eve assassination attempt, last month passed a law called the 'Statute of the March 19, 2004 Shooting Truth Investigation Special Committee. The background was that opposition lawmakers were suspicious about the shooting, which slightly wounded President Chen Shui-bian, but believably earned him sympathy votes enabling him to retain the presidency...

"After failing to veto the passage of the statute, President Chen took another blocking measure by refusing to ascertain confirmation of investigators appointed under the special legislation...Lawmakers had foreseen the problem. They included in the law a clause stipulating that the appointments of investigators would become effective automatically, in the event that they failed to acquire presidential confirmation...However, this counter-boycott regulation did not work, as the president continued to challenge the legitimacy of the investigators, unwilling to cooperate with them...

"This week the Chen administration even launched a campaign to implement a full-scale boycott of the investigating committee. Already in force were administrative orders banning appropriation of funds needed by the body to finance its operations and loan of judicial personnel necessary to aid investigation work, as well as a call for all administrative agencies to carry out a non-compliance practice....

"Chen and his ruling party have insisted the investigation law is unconstitutional. But whether it is constitutional or not is a question that should be left to the Council of Grand Justices to judge. And since the administration has already asked the Grand Justices for interpretation of the special law, it should wait for their judgment. Until then, the Chen administration must obey the law and cooperate with the newly appointed investigators in performing their duties...

"On the other hand, the Legislative Yuan has declined an invitation by the Council of Grand Justices to dispatch representatives to a hearing scheduled for next week. The objective of the hearing is to decide whether or not to issue a restraining order against the law and the investigating committee, as requested by the administration...

"The reason cited by the lawmaking body is that the council's decision to hold such a hearing is in violation of the constitution. It argued that the judicial body is only empowered to interpret constitutional and other crucial policy disputes, having no right to give an injunction of any kind...

"At risk is that should the Grand Council finally decide to grant a restraining order against the law and the investigating committee in the absence of legislative representation, the legislature will most likely refuse to accept the decision. Should such a conflict between the legislature and the Grand Council happen, there will not be a legally eligible third institution to mediate the constitutional disagreement...

"In a democratic country, the judicial authorities must act as the guardians of justice. But the credibility of our grand Justices has been damaged by widespread allegations that they have failed to maintain independence in handling the legislative-executive quarrel."

Because of the executive branch's obstruction, the March 19 Shooting Investigation Committee of the Legislative Yuan never came up with a conclusive report.

Probe Report Reads Like a Dime Store Novel

The executive branch for its part did come up with an official report after a year-long investigation into the March 19, 2004 shooting incident. But it lacked credibility. Most people in the country were doubtful about the findings contained in the document. The New York Times even described the investigation report as "spinning the sort of story once found in dime-store novels."

In August 2005, top police officers, including Hou Yu-ih, then commissioner of the Criminal Investigation Bureau, formally announced the closure of the presidential election eve shooting case, accompanied by a report on the results of the investigation. But some key findings in it were accepted with a high degree of skepticism among many in the public. They were unconvinced that the government investigators had truly solved the two main questions: Who committed the shooting and what was the motive behind the action?

In a newspaper analysis that I wrote then, I raised my own doubts about the credibility of some parts of the content presented in the police report. Below are excerpts taken from that analytical piece of mine:

"...Investigators identified Chen Yi-Hsiung, a mid-aged man who formerly worked as a wrestling coach, as the lone suspect. Chen, who lived in a neighborhood near the scene of the shooting, allegedly fired the shots that wounded President Chen and Vice President Lu. However, the lone suspect was found dead in a nearby harbor nine days after the incident occurred...

"Investigators claimed that Chen Yi-Hsiung committed suicide by drowning himself. They said Chen Yi-Hsiung did so for fear of being caught by the police. But the investigators failed to provide any solid data to prove that it was the case. This led many to speculate that the suspect's death might be a case of homicide instead of suicide...

"Henry Lee, a noted U.S.-based forensic scientist who was invited to Taiwan to help probe the incident and the cause of Chen Yi-Hsiung's death, concluded there was no way to determine whether the suspect had died in the water or before. This was because his body was cremated almost immediately after his death. Thus, how or in what circumstances the alleged shooter died has become a mystery itself...

"The investigators' conclusion that Chen Yi-Hsiung was the person who attempted to assassinate President Chen Shui-bian was also questionable. It was questionable because investigators might never have had a chance to interview the suspect, given the fact that they even did not know who he was before his drowning. If that was true, the investigators should have been unable to provide any direct evidence needed to support their claims...

"Instead, all the confessions cited in the report were obtained from the suspect's wife, Mrs. Chen Yi-Hsiung. She confessed that her husband had disclosed to her and their children that he was the one who shot at the president. But Mrs. Chen later contradicted that confession, when she told the press 'It was not done by my husband.' Mrs. Chen also told investigators that her husband had left three suicide notes. But Mrs. Chen was quick to add that she had burned all those notes before the arrival of investigators...

"The report also gave the reason why the suspect attempted to assassinate President Chen Shui-bian: He suffered from depression and blamed the president for Taiwan's struggling economy. However, Chen Yi-Hsiung's neighbors, when interviewed by TV reporters, all felt surprised. They did not believe he had committed such a crime. The suspect's elder sister called the police report just incredible. She pointed out that her brother had always behaved well since his childhood and, therefore, he could not possibly have shot at the president."

Most residents in Taiwan expressed disbelief in the police findings when surveyed for their views by two leading Chinese-language newspapers following the announcement of the "319 shooting" investigation results. In the survey by the China Times, only 26% of the respondents believed Chen Yi-Hsiung was the shooter, while 51% replied they were doubtful. The survey by the United Daily News found that 46% did not believe Chen Yi-Hsiung was the gunman, while only 20% said they believed he was.

KMT supporters and many others even called for reactivating the probe into the election-eve shooting. Those who supported reopening the investigation notably included Vice President Annette Lu. The vice president was riding in the same campaign car with President Chen Shui-bian when the incident occurred. She suffered a knee wound in the shooting.

The above two newspaper surveys also found that by this time-- more than a year into Chen Shui-bian's second presidency, there was still a majority of the population having doubts about the legitimacy of his reelection victory. But the legitimacy question posed no problems at all for him in playing his presidential role and exercising his power and duties.

During the vast majority of Chen Shui-bian's second term, I still kept writing editorials and commentaries regularly for the China Post and Economic News. Hence, I continued to have chances to examine and assess his policies and political advocacies, as I did during his first term. I will select a few from among the numerous such writings here. The selected pieces will tell a lot about what President Chen Shui-bian said and did during his renewed tenure from 2004 to 2008, as well as what reactions and controversies his words and deeds generated at home and abroad.

Overstating His New Mandate

"When President Chen Shui-bian recently declared that his reelection underscored a crucial point that most of the people in Taiwan agreed with his political beliefs, he was overstating his popular support base...The win he attained in the March 20, 2004 election could hardly allow him to claim to have the support of a real or any significant majority of the people. Consider: Chen defeated his challenger Lien Chan by only a razor-thin margin of 0.2% of the total ballots cast, even though he garnered 50.1% of the vote...

"The concern is that if President Chen really saw his 0.2% win over his challenger Lien Chan as an absolute majority, he could be led to pushing a radical pro-independence agenda in his next four years in office. Should this be the case, it could have serious political implications for Taiwan and its relations with mainland China...

"In less than three weeks since his reelection, Chen has on several occasions expressed his determination to make good on a high-profile campaign promise--to write a new constitution for Taiwan. A rough schedule has already been set for completing the task: To adopt such a new basic law in 2006 by a popular referendum, and to proclaim it for implementation in mid-2008, a time when he leaves office...

"But should Chen really push ahead with his new constitution plan as scheduled, Taiwan could face endless political turmoil and social unrest. The two main opposition parties have vowed to block the plan, arguing it was a timetable for Taiwan's independence. The

KMT and the PFP combined to account for half of the political landscape in Taiwan, as shown in the recent presidential poll...

"Chen's overstating of his new mandate was also reflected in a claim that his reelection was an unequivocal message that the 'vast majority of the people in Taiwan' back his antagonizing stance toward Beijing,' as well as his political viewpoint that Taiwan and the Chinese mainland are two separate countries...

"Far from what he claimed, the prevailing public opinion, as shown in recent surveys, preferred to put aside the sovereignty dispute with Beijing in favor of building closer trade and economic relations between the two sides. So Chen's statement that his mainland China stance has the support of most voters is misleading too...

"But if President Chen Shui-bian insisted that his advocacy of Taiwan and the mainland being two separate countries had now become the mainstream political view and that he had an obligation to have it reflected in his future cross-strait relations, it would certainly spark a new wave of confrontation with Beijing."

A Stern Warning from Beijing

"President Chen Shui-bian was left little room to maneuver, after Beijing issued him a stern warning on the eve of his May 20, 2004 inauguration as a new four-year term as the president of the ROC. In a strongly worded statement, Beijing urged him to make a choice between pursuing independence for Taiwan and embracing the principle of one China.

"Beijing said that there are only two roads lying ahead of Chen: One is to rein in the horse before the cliff by suspending separatist activities and accept the position that both sides of the Taiwan Strait belong to one China. The other road is to persist in the pursuit of independence to split Taiwan from China. The choice of this latter road is to play with fire and will, in the end, lead to self-destruction...

"The reason that the mainland chose to issue the warning three days ahead of Chen Shui-bian's assumption of his second term is clear: It attempted to influence his widely watched inaugural speech at the last minute by adopting a 'carrot and stick' approach...

"To put it briefly, Beijing wanted Chen to reiterate in his May 20 speech the 'four no's and one without' pledges, which included no declaration of Taiwan independence. He made the pledges four years ago when he assumed his first term. But the mainland charged that Chen had since continued to act in a way contradicting those pledges...Beijing also wanted him not to declare in his address, any plan to write a new constitution that might work to change Taiwan's status of de facto independence to a legal fact...

"Beijing in the statement also dangled hopes before Taiwan of better cross-strait relations in several crucial ways if it accepted the one-China concept and suspended independence activities. They included promises to resume talks, end the state of hostilities, and set up a confidence-building mechanism. Also, negotiations would be conducted to work out ways for Taiwan to gain diplomatic recognition appropriate to its status. Additionally, arrangements would be made for Taiwan and the mainland to promote closer economic cooperation, including broader market access for Taiwan's agricultural produce."

Differing PRC, U.S. Stances on Taiwan Come to the Fore

"President Chen Shui-bian got completely different reactions from Washington and Beijing over his May 20, 2004, inaugural speech--an instance which once again illustrated the disparate policy and interests the two big powers have had in addressing relations with Taiwan...

"Washington, unlike Beijing, responded positively to Chen's two high-profile inaugural promises: One, he will not touch on the sovereignty issue, while pushing for an overhaul of the constitution. Two, he will stick to the 'four no's and one without' commitment, which he had made four years earlier in 2000 when he began his first term. The U.S. government saw the two promises as 'responsible and constructive, thus opening up an opportunity for the resumption of talks with the Chinese mainland.'

"Beijing, on the other hand, viewed Chen Shui-bian's concessions of excluding the territory and independence vs. unification themes from his planned new constitution as 'vague and deceptive.' It pointed out that Chen's decision to leave out these issues only because a majority consensus has yet to be reached in Taiwan. Beijing also critically pointed to Chen's persistent refusal to accept the principle of one China...

"Beijing, therefore, concluded that the source of tensions in the Taiwan Strait has not yet been eliminated and that the menace affecting the peace and stability in the Asian-Pacific region still exists. The PRC government went further to warn that whether a war will erupt in the Taiwan Strait will depend on Chen's attitude...

"Why the U.S. and the PRC responded to President Chen's 2004 inaugural speech so differently was clear: The two powers have, as mentioned previously, fundamentally different interests in Taiwan. For Washington, as long as Chen pledged not to take moves to unilaterally change the status quo of Taiwan during his new term, it will be in line with America's strategic interests. While Washington has made it clear not to support Taiwan's independence, it was only willing to go to the extent of seeing this island preserve its status quo. As to whether or not Chen Shui-bian was willing to embrace Beijing's one-China principle, is not a matter of vital importance to the US...

"But Beijing has more to be concerned about in its policy toward Taiwan. Seeking to prevent this island from splitting from China is only a part of that policy. More fundamentally, Beijing wants Taiwan to accept its one-China policy and, ultimately, to integrate with the Chinese mainland."

Beijing Enacts Taiwan-Aimed Anti-Secession Law

As discussed above, when Chen Shui-bian assumed his second presidential term on May 20. 2004, he pledged in his inaugural address that he would not declare Taiwan independence or change its constitutionally defined sovereignty during the next four years. But the ink was barely dry on that address when he intensified his pro-independence and anti-China rhetoric, so much that it prompted Beijing to enact an anti-secession law targeted at Taiwan. I wrote commentaries about the PRC legislation on two occasions: One when it was submitted to the standing committee of the National People's

Congress of the PRC, and one when it was about to be officially adopted by the Congress.

The first piece, published on December 22, 2004, was entitled "Beijing's 'Anti-Secession' Bill Will Further Alienate Taiwan." This one is excerpted as below:

"The opposition coalition of the Kuomintang and the People First Party, which was just granted by the voters a fresh majority in the Legislative Yuan, has the responsibility to present a strong voice against Beijing's motion to enact an anti-secession law, said to be aimed mainly at Taiwan...

"Most of the people on this island do not support independence despite the fact that the radical cause has now been embraced and advanced by President Chen Shui-bian and his administration as a major political agenda. But they are deeply worried about the possible impact the proposed law will have on Taiwan and their well-being...

"At the same time, the opposition should use their newly enhanced legislative powers to provide a stronger check on President Chen and his fellow party leaders, forcing them to abandon their bids to hold a referendum in 2006 on a new constitution and other pro-independence policies...

"The reason for Beijing to introduce legislation against secession is obviously the result of a series of provocative actions by President Chen. He passionately called for the enactment of a new constitution, which was seen as a move to pursue de jure independence. He also launched a name-rectification campaign to get rid of any symbols that refer to China. And he overtly and repeatedly described China as a 'foreign country, an enemy country.'

"By passing the law, Beijing wants to show to Taiwan, as well as the United States, the island's most important defense supporter, that the Chinese government will resolutely take military actions against Taiwan, if and when it sees its prescribed red lines crossed by the Taipei government…

"But the mainland leaders must understand that their plan to create a legal basis for taking harsh measures against Taiwan will have grave consequences. It will radicalize public opinion in Taiwan and prompt even greater popular support for the independence cause. This in turn would make it more difficult for long-stalled bilateral relations to move forward. In the worst-case scenario, an escalation of political and military tensions could lead the two sides to a mutually destructive conflict, an unfortunate outcome neither side would want to see."

My second opinion piece analyzing the "anti-secession" bill was published a couple of days before it was formally adopted by the tenth National People's Congress on March 14, 2006, in Beijing. Major concerns which I raised in this article are given below:

"Beijing yesterday unveiled an outline of a draft 'anti-secession' law, which, if passed in its present form, would authorize the People's Liberation Army to use 'non-peaceful' means to suppress Taiwan, in the event it was seen as seeking 'virtual independence' or engendering any 'grave events' that aim to split this island from China….

"The legislative move is highly regrettable…Most disturbing are the two conditions, which, as set forth in the draft law, are so vague that could allow Beijing to arbitrarily use force against Taiwan. By 'virtual independence,' for example, what do the mainland leaders exactly mean? Taiwan as the Republic of China has for the last six decades been performing as a de facto independent country: electing its own government, maintaining its own army, and conducting foreign relations on its own…

"Now if Taiwan wants to continue to its current self-rule systems and preserve its lifestyle and refuses to accept Beijing's 'one country, two systems' formula for unification with the communist mainland, will this be interpreted as perpetuating de facto independence and justify an invasion by the Chinese People's Liberation Army?

"In addition, suppose Beijing maintains its military threats against Taiwan by, for example, deploying more missiles opposite this island, as it has been doing now. And that Taiwan is eventually forced to enter into a military alliance with Japan and the United States as a strategy to boost the protection of its security and stability. Will such a move be taken by Beijing as a 'grave event' intended to break away from China and warrant a military intervention by the People's Liberation Army?…

"What is more, the proposed law may work in a way that would give Beijing the authority to unilaterally interpret cross-strait relations. Or by extension Beijing in the future will have the right to decide what Taiwan can do and what it cannot…

"So Beijing's move to create the 'anti-secession' law will be sure to further alienate the 23 million people on this island and certain to increase the difficulty for the government here to take any bolder measures to improve relations with the mainland."

Dropping a Series of Political Bombshells in 2006

President Chen Shui-bian first announced a politically sensitive action plan in his 2006 New Year message, as he was entering his final two years in office. The announcement provoked strong responses from both the U.S. and the PRC. Washington immediately demanded the Taiwan leader clarify his policy. In the weeks that followed Washington continued to exert pressure on the president to retract his remarks. U.S. authorities insisted that President Chen had to do so to ward off a potential conflict with the PRC.

As a commentator, I covered Chen's contentious action plan as well as several other perceived political provocations that he created in the wake of his New Year address. The following sections were excerpted from three separate editorials, which I wrote for the English-language China Post and were published in the period from late January and early February of 2006:

"President Chen Shui-bian's 2006 New Year speech has provoked a strong backlash in Washington. In the speech, Chen declared that he would push for the drafting of a new constitution this year and put it to an island-wide referendum the following year. U.S. officials were alarmed by the declaration. They worried that President Chen might be pressing for de jure independence for Taiwan, shifting away from his past position. Previously he had time and again promised that his planned constitutional reforms would not involve any sovereignty changes…

"A new constitution, he strongly suggested, must redefine the sovereignty and territory set forth in the current constitution of the

ROC. He put it: 'Taiwan is our country. It has a land area of 36,000 square kilometers with 23 million people. The sovereignty of Taiwan resides with its people and is not subject to the justification of Beijing...

"Upon learning of Chen Shui-bian's New Year message, U.S. authorities quickly contacted Taipei and that began a series of bilateral discussions. In such discussions, they urged him not to make provocations. Washington at the same time made clear its longstanding position on cross-strait relations: The U.S. does not support Taiwan independence and opposes either side of the Taiwan Strait trying to unilaterally change the status quo of their relations...

"U.S. concerns about Chen's political intentions have not eased because of his repeated policy assurances in the past. The Bush administration reportedly is still watching closely what Chen will do next. Beijing, for its part, has already warned that the tension in the Taiwan Strait is resurging, referring to Chen's New Year address..."

In another editorial dated February 3, 2006, I criticized President Chen for dropping another bombshell in Taiwan's relations with mainland China. In a new statement, the president declared that 'it's time for Taiwan to abolish the symbolically significant National Unification Council and Guidelines for National Unification.' The declaration came barely one month after he announced his provocative Taiwan constitution plan.

"...This is a dangerous idea," I wrote. "By proposing to abolish the council and the guidelines, Chen is in effect moving to break one of his five pledges, which he made in both his 2000 and 2004 inaugural speeches. These pledges oblige him not to push for independence or change Taiwan's relations with the Chinese mainland…

"The Unification Council and Guidelines, though not binding legislatively, carry crucial political meanings. Their existence represents a formal recognition by Taiwan or reminds its political leaders that this island and the Chinese mainland are two divided parts of China and that it is the ultimate goal for the two sides to be reunited."

Chen's proposed abolition of the Unification Guidelines, as well as his earlier call to write a new constitution, fiercely angered Beijing. The mainland leaders took Chen's political remarks as an indication that the "separatist forces in Taiwan have yet to suspend their activities in spite of the rapidly improving cross-strait relations in the last year. They, therefore, saw the need to step up their 'anti-independence' struggles…

"However, Beijing still seemed to be trying to steer clear of a head-on confrontation with Taipei for fear of spoiling the newly improved commercial ties between the two sides, while waiting to see how the U.S., as well as Taiwan's domestic opposition forces, will respond to Chen's new provocative rhetoric…

"Washington indeed has swiftly expressed its concerns over Chen's political remarks, saying that his call for the abolition of the Unification Guidelines and his renewed push for a new constitution as well as his plan to join the United Nations under the name of Taiwan all are moves intended to change the political status quo. After expressing its concerns, the U.S. reiterated its position that it opposes any moves by either side of the Taiwan Strait to alter the political standing."

Bush Urges Chen to Reaffirm His Commitments

President Chen's new tensions with Washington, which were triggered by his New Year call to enact a pro-independence constitution and his attempt to scrap a basic policy on Taiwan's mainland China relations--continued into the following February. The prolonged tension prompted me to write a third piece to follow the ongoing Taipei-Washington political clashes. That opinion piece reads in part:

"The Bush administration remained firm that the pro-independence Taipei government must publicly reaffirm its 'four no's and one without' commitments, which included a promise to keep Taiwan's decades-old National Unification Council and National Unification Guidelines...

"Two weeks after President Chen surprised Washington by announcing that he was considering abolishing the unification council and guidelines, the latter of which is a set of rules enacted by the previous KMT government under President Lee Teng-hui with the aim of securing stable relations with mainland China, the U.S. government still refused to accept Taipei's explanations...

"The reason that Washington wanted to get tough with Chen is clear: U.S. officials were alarmed by Chen Shui-bian's recent series of inflammatory remarks. They worried that the president was deviating from his commitments to neither declare independence nor pursue a formal separate political identity, commitments which he had made in both his first and second inaugural speeches...

"In the course of their recent negotiations with Taipei, Washington officials made crystal clear American policy of not supporting Taiwan independence. To ensure that no vagueness was left, they publicly commented that the sovereignty of Taiwan must not be defined by Taipei unilaterally. And that Taiwan's differences with Beijing need to be settled in a manner acceptable to the people on both sides of the Taiwan Strait. The latter part of the above sentence was a refutation of Chen's persistent claim in the past that the future of Taiwan can only be decided by the 23 million people on this island...

"Beijing in its first public response made two days earlier to Chen's recent string of provocative statements branded Chen Shui-bian both a 'troublemaker and saboteur,' posing a threat to the peace and stability in the Asian-Pacific region by challenging the principle of one China...

"Domestically, President Chen's renewed adventurism did not earn him much public sympathy either, except for the various fundamentalist independence groups, which rendered firm support for him. More cruelly, Chen received even harsher criticisms from within his own party. Some senior DPP lawmakers considered some of Chen's recent radical statements as reckless, doing nothing good for Taiwan."

A Premature Lame Duck President

Chen Shui-bian assumed his second four-year presidential term in May 2004. But his authority and influence quickly began to slide into lame duck status, so quickly that he barely had time to celebrate the first anniversary of his new term. In politics worldwide, this was a rare phenomenon. Normally, when we call a leader a lame duck, it refers to someone in office during the brief period between an election and the inauguration of a successor.

Signs of his lame duck status cropped up noticeably as of May 2005--exactly one year after his second inauguration. The key contributing factors were his frequent vacillation on key issues and a long series of corruption allegations implicating his wife Wu Shu-Chen, his son-in-law Chao Chien-ming, and his top aides past and present.

As a column writer, I covered all the major events that could mark President Chen's worsening lame duck status and analyzed them in my articles. Below are passages excerpted from those articles covering the period from mid-May 2005 to the second half of 2006. They are presented in accordance with the sequence of time, at which they were published. Also, they bore the same titles as the original versions. The excerpts:

---Rebellion from Within His Own Ranks (dated May 6, 2005)

"The most urgent task facing President Chen Shui-bian is how to defuse what appears to be the biggest-ever rebellion from within his own party, the DPP. Leading the rebellion against him are his party lawmakers. Some of whom were scathing about Chen's leadership style. One of them bluntly complained, 'No president behaves in such a way.' In my opinion, grumbled another, 'the president is simply not acting as a president.'

"Chen's perceived betrayal of the independence cause of the ruling party is perhaps the main source of the dissatisfaction with him.

One hardline DPP lawmaker said, for example, Chen may consider 'quitting the party should he believe the independence cause has become a liability for him to perform his presidential duties.'

"The recent outbreak of anger among DPP politicians and rank-and-file members was triggered by his flip-flops on an 'ice-breaking' Beijing visit by the chairman of the opposition KMT, Lien Chan. The eight-day Lien visit to Beijing significantly eased longstanding hostility in cross-strait political relations, paving the way for benign interactions. But the newfound relationship improvement with Beijing has sparked fears in Taiwan of a China-leaning trend among independence supporters...

"The president altered his position on Lien's mainland visit four times. At the outset, Chen attempted to intimidate Lien into canceling his trip by warning him not to betray Taiwan in his embrace of China. After finding the KMT leader undaunted by his remarks, Chen quickly dropped his opposing stance and even gave him his blessings on the eve of Lien Chan's departure...But he vacillated again after Lien met with China's most powerful leader Hu Jintao and reached with him a non-binding four-point consensus on relations between Taiwan and the Chinese mainland. Chen suggested that Lien's mainland behavior may have broken Taiwan law...

"However, when his administration officials and party lawmakers joined him in his renewed attack on Lien, the president changed his stance once again, this time by coming out to commend Lien's performance. He said the opposition leader has abided by the law on his mainland trip without overstepping the authority of the government...

"But the president's position flip-flops alone would not have brought about the recent eruption of public anger, as people in the country have long become accustomed to Chen's volatile leadership style. What is causing particular indignation among DPP politicians and his grassroots supporters is an unsubstantiated rumor associated with Chen's latest position shift on the Lien visit...

"The rumor was that Chen's final decision to take a positive view of Lien's China visit was because he wanted to leave room for him to adjust his own mostly anti-China stance. What was true was that Chen himself has recently shown signs of wanting to pay a visit to Beijing and meet with Hu Jintao. This led many to speculate that President Chen might attempt to bring about a rapprochement with Beijing so that he could build a reputation as the real peacemaker in cross-strait relations...

"Many DPP hardliners and supporters had already become impatient with Chen over a string of high-profile remarks and moves he has made in recent months. Among them was his public admission that there will be no way for him to achieve the goal of formal independence for Taiwan by writing a new constitution and dropping all the references to China in the names of government institutions...

"His move to form a political alliance with the People First Party, a known staunch opponent of Taiwan independence, was another major irritant contributing to the latest outburst of anger at the president among his supporters. They criticized Chen's policy of forming a coalition with an anti-independence and pro-China party that ran counter to the core values of their own party, the DPP. They were also angry with President Chen for publicly embracing the ROC as the highest common denominator. In their eyes, Chen's willingness to embrace the ROC contradicted the DPP's basic policy. The party's ultimate goal was to eliminate the ROC and build a Taiwan country…

"It remains to be seen whether President Chen Shui-bian will be able to survive the rebellion from his own party and reverse his plummeting popularity without being rendered a lame duck leader at a time when his presidency has three more years to run."

---Ceding Power Leaves Chen a Weak President (dated June 7, 2006)

"President Chen appears to have weathered a rebellion from within his own ruling party and stabilized his leadership role after he decided last week to cede some of his powers to his subordinate, Premier Su Tseng-chang. But the move, as it seems now, has left him a weak president…

"In some sense, the decision to relinquish power, even if he really meant it, not an attention-diverting scheme, was an open admission: That he has in the past wielded too much of government power, overstepping the bounds of the authority given to the president under the constitution of the Republic of China…

"Yet the willingness of Chen to de-concentrate power did little to help ease public outrage, sparked this time by a range of corruption allegations that implicated his wife Wu Shu-Chen, his son-in-law Chao Chien-ming, and a couple of aides past and present. Calls for him to step down to take responsibility continued to grow from various sectors of society...

"The two opposition parties, the KMT and the PFP, for example, have decided to jointly push a recall bill at an extraordinary session of the Legislative Yuan. The KMT is also seeking to launch an island-wide campaign against President Chen, with the slogans 'Down with Chen, Clean government protects Taiwan.' This indicates that the opposition parties are attempting to expand their protests from the legislative floor to the streets...

"On the other hand, President Chen's move to de-concentrate power has achieved both positive and negative results for him. On the positive side, his power-yielding action has quickly silenced his critics in the DPP, with top party politicians coming forward to publicly defend him. They, for example, attacked the opposition's campaign to recall the president as a political struggle with the aim of creating social unrest in order to reap partisan interests...

"The largest beneficiary of Chen's move to cede part of his powers was his premier Su Tseng-chang. As a result of this move, the premier would no longer be obliged to perform as the president's 'chief executive officer.' Premier Su was quick to amass both administrative and party powers in his hands. Days earlier the premier called an unprecedented meeting with the participation of DPP chairman Yu Shyi-kun and its legislative caucus convener Ker Chien-ming. The premier explained subsequently he wanted to use the opportunity to hear Ker and Yu's views on how to respond to 'public expectations' and restore 'political stability'...

"All this suggested that a 'new power center' was shaping up with Premier Su playing the dominating role, reversing a six-year tradition when President Chen Shui-bian retained a grip on both the executive branch and the party machine...That said, it would be unlawful should the new power center work to undermine the president's constitutionally stipulated authority to make final decisions on cross-strait, defense, and foreign relations...

"It remains to be seen whether President Chen's power surrender could help him to survive the mounting public pressure for him to resign from office. The pressure was intensified recently by the detention of his son-in-law Chao Chien-ming on charges of insider trading and a half dozen other alleged crimes. The Chao case is especially harmful to the president because it happened at a time when he had already been mired in several other unlawful allegations involving the people around him, including his wife Wu Shu-Chen."

---Political Unease amid Campaign to Recall President (dated June 14, 2006)

In mid-June of 2006, the opposition-dominated Legislative Yuan formally adopted a bill to recall President Chen Shui-bian over a string of corruption allegations. The recall bill came after the leader had made a high-profile concession a week earlier to yield some of his powers to Premier Su Tseng-chang and party leaders. I examined the politically charged recall bill in my editorial. The following passages are excerpted from that article:

"With the adoption yesterday of an opposition-sponsored motion aiming to recall President Chen Shui-bian, the legislature has begun a two-week debate on the question of whether or not the president should be removed from office. A full legislative session has been scheduled for June 27 to vote on the bill. Yet even if the bill wins approval, the legislative action alone won't have the authority to oust Chen. It will still have to obtain the support of more than half of the eligible voters in a popular vote slated for September 26 of this year...

"The immediate challenge Chen faces as the legislature proceeds to deliberate the bill in the weeks ahead is how to conduct his defense. The lawmaking body has given him seven days until June 20 to do so. He could choose to present his defense in writing. It is challenging because Chen will have to come up with more convincing arguments over the various corruption allegations that involve first lady Wu Shu-Chen, his son-in-law Chao Chien-ming, and other family relatives, as well as two former top aides...

"In the past, Chen has repeatedly denied such charges. He refuted them as baseless and maintained that neither he nor Mrs. Chen was involved in any offenses. But most public members did not believe the president told the truth. The recent detention of his son-in-law for insider trading and a range of other alleged crimes reinforced their suspicion of the various other wrongdoings reportedly committed by the people around him...

"The KMT and the PFP have stressed that their decision to introduce the recall bill was a response to raging public anger at the president over his failure to prevent the practice of 'nepotism' and 'favoritism' by the people surrounding him, and to growing public demand that he step down to take responsibility...

"But the challenge facing the two opposition parties will be very serious as their lawmakers proceed to debate Chen's removal. They must substantiate their allegations and prove that their recall demands are justifiable, not a 'power struggle' as charged by President Chen and his DPP party politicians...

"In this regard, KMT chairman Ma Ying-jeou has raised a good reason for the recall of President Chen. He said recently: The people--such as his wife, his son-in-law, and his two ex-deputy secretaries who were suspected of committing crimes in one way or another--were able to do so, because they have the advantage of access to the president, but failed to be restrained from improperly using their influence...

"Another difficult challenge confronting the two parties is that they will have to get the support of two-thirds of legislators to pass the bill before it can be submitted for approval by the people. Holding only a thin majority, they need an additional 14 votes by defections from the ruling camp to meet the passage threshold. But the DPP and its ally, the Taiwan Solidarity Union, have threatened to boycott the vote."

---Report to People Won't Help Defuse Crisis (June 21, 2006)

"President Chen Shui-bian delivered a televised speech directly to the people refuting the various wrongdoing allegations against him and his family members yesterday in his first formal response to a legislative bill to recall him. By doing so, however, the president bypassed the legislature, which had invited him to give testimony. His refusal to testify before the lawmaking body ran the risk of being charged with contempt and violating the rules of democracy...

"The legislature had given Chen seven days until yesterday to testify either in person or in writing... Instead, he spent the past week seeking to galvanize his traditional supporters by urging them to safeguard his so-called 'native government,' playing the divisive ethnic card. He also smeared opposition leaders by attacking their recall motion as an attempt to 'seize power'...

"From Chen's standpoint, it's a wise idea for him to bring his case directly to the people and solicit their support. But unfortunately, he devoted a considerable amount of time in his nearly two-hour-long report to slamming the opposition for 'amplifying judicial cases' and 'making up accusations against him and his family.'

"He denied any involvement by his wife in the widely reported ownership battle among the board directors of the private Sogo department store. But he stopped short of explaining, for example, why many business executives serving at government and private companies had in the past found it necessary to pay visits to the first lady for her support in business negotiations...

"He also used the occasion to refute charges that his wife had received free Sogo vouchers. But he failed to rationalize the many contradicting comments made by him and his staff on the voucher issue. And he didn't explain why his family physician Huang Fang-yen has consistently refused to answer prosecutor subpoenas to testify for his alleged intermediary role in the voucher-giving case...

"President Chen also touched on his son-in-law Chao Chien-ming's implication in an insider trading case. But he quickly excused himself by arguing that Chao had committed all the alleged crimes without his knowledge. But he ignored the point that Chao was able to peddle influence because of his role as the president's son-in-law. In all, the president left many important questions unanswered.

"What is also inconceivable was that President Chen presented his TV speech like an authoritarian leader addressing his subjects--only allowing them to listen to his propagandist views or one-sided story while taking no questions from the dozens of local and foreign reporters present to cover the event. The attitude suggests that the president is still unwilling to honestly face the people and come clean about the various alleged wrongdoings against him and his relatives."

---Putting Self-Interest above Fighting Corruption (July 26, 2006)

"The ruling Democratic Progressive Party recently opened its national party congress in Taipei under two grand slogans: 'To engage in sincere self-examination' and 'To boldly bear responsibility.' But in reality, the two-day event ended with nothing corresponding to the two proclamations. If anything, it served more like a venue where party factions competed for power and control over policy and political resources...

"The DPP has been in the doldrums ever since its humiliating defeats in the December 2005 elections of local governments. Popular support for the party has since continued to decline. But the drop deepened further more recently, burdened by its morally tainted leader President Chen Shui-bian...

"Against such a background, the convention of the congress should have been seen by the leaders of the DPP as a good opportunity for them to rebuild the party's image and restore public faith in it by introducing and carrying out crucial reform programs, including how to address the party's relations with President Chen...

"But the DPP disappointed the public. No motion was ever raised at the two-day conference to discuss Chen's role in a variety of alleged corruption scandals involving his wife Wu Shu-Chen, his son-in-law Chao Chien-ming, and a former top aide Chen Che-nan...

"On the contrary, delegates to the meeting unanimously voted to defend Chen by adopting a 'common stance' that the president 'needs not step down.' They contended that he was not directly involved in any of those reported scandals. But this party's position runs counter to the prevailing public opinion. The vast majority of the people maintained that Chen must resign to take both political and moral responsibility, even if he is proved innocent of the various alleged crimes....

"The congress delegates did pass a new anti-corruption resolution, which would authorize an internal investigation into bribery allegations committed by party members regardless of their political status. But there was no mention anywhere in the resolution as to whether the new anti-corruption rule will apply to President and Mrs. Chen. And if the answer is yes, when will such probes be carried out, and by whom? Or will any such investigating team include members from outside the DPP? This is necessary to play an objective and unbiased role in conducting interviews and gathering evidence?

"The DPP needs to translate its 'stiffened' anti-corruption rule into action. Unless this is to be the case, the party will risk being accused of hypocrisy. On the one hand, the party tried to show the people a determination to clamp down on law violations. But on the other hand, it was unwilling to condemn Chen and join public calls for his resignation for tolerating bribery and money politics taking place right under his nose."

---A Disastrous Second Four-Year Term

It's not an exaggeration to say that Chen Shui-bian's second administration was disastrous. Since late 2005 one and a half years into his second four-year term, his DPP party had lost three elections from local to central, all under his watch. An election defeat or win always reflects people's desire for change. But Chen Shui-bian and the DPP entirely ignored this rule. Take for example the 2005 county and mayoral elections. Had Chen and his fellow DPP leaders heeded the message sent by the voters in this poll, they might not have lost the subsequent legislative and presidential elections--held in January and March of 2008 respectively. Or even if they did, the results might not have been as humiliating.

In the 2005 local elections, the DPP was the biggest loser, while the KMT and two other smaller opposition parties won hugely, gaining control of 16 of the 23 counties and cities. The results conformed to pre-election media surveys and analyses. Newspapers and TV stations cited economic failure and corruption scandals as the two main factors in the DPP's heavy losses in the elections of local governments.

Before the December 3, 2005 mayoral and county leader elections, I wrote two commentaries analyzing the impending polls. The first of the two articles carried the title 'Scandals Likely to Take Heavy Tolls on DPP in Polls,' dated November 16, 2005. It read in part:

"...The ruling Democratic Progressive Party is most likely to experience sweeping setbacks in the December 3 polls of local governments...Currently, DPP candidates have been trailing in most districts. The reason for that is not much about the performances of the individual DPP candidates. Many of them, in fact, are strong in terms of both capability and character...

"But they are burdened by a DPP-led central administration. The DPP candidate must face large numbers of people who have become disenchanted with the government's persistent failure to improve the economy. Few people are better off than they were five years ago when President Chen first came to power. A lot more are getting even poorer these days...

"Yet what is hurting the DPP's candidates even more were the recent outbursts of a string of corruption scandals involving senior administration officials, party politicians, and First Family members…It is truly ironic that a political party, which captured power on an anti-corruption and pro-reform platform, has now found itself mired in a wide variety of scandals."

The other article I wrote about the December 3 election was headlined 'Sunday's Elections May Prove Discouraging for DPP.' It was published days before election day. Some passages of this commentary are given below:

"With only three days to go before the December 3 magistrate and mayoral elections across Taiwan, many observers, including some from the international community, have begun to assess the possible impact that a crushing defeat for the governing DPP will have on the island's political trends and its economic development…

"Despite the fact that the impending elections will affect only the leaders of local governments, the race has actually turned into a party-level contest between the ruling DPP and main opposition KMT. So which of the two parties, the DPP or the KMT, emerges from the race as the biggest winner or loser will surely have an impact on Taiwan's politics and economic policy…

"Taiwan's local elections this time drew keen attention from world media and research institutions, including Business Week of the United States and multinational institution Merrill Lynch…

"Business Week rightly saw Taiwan's local elections this time as a popular vote on the performance of President Chen Shui-bian and his administration. That is so because rarely have policies and issues concerning the counties and cities been brought up for debate between the ruling and opposition candidates. In these local elections, however, the whole campaign has seen President Chen and his fellow party leaders smearing the KMT by raking over its past wrongdoings. In return, the KMT chairman Ma Ying-jeou and his lawmakers have focused their criticisms on the Chen administration's recently exposed scandals and its failure to carry out reforms…

"This being the case, it is natural that Saturday's event will become something like a midterm election test of the popularity of the DPP and the KMT. In other words, if one side comes out as the loser, it must mean that the accusations made by the other side are justifiable and have the support of the majority of the people…

"The assessment made by Merrill Lynch, contained in a report on Taiwan issued for the reference of its investor clients, was more direct and blunt. The brokerage firm believed that a setback in the polls for the DPP would be positive news for investors, predicting that such a blow would prompt the ruling party to launch major policy reforms and further liberalize restrictions on doing business with Taiwan's crucial trading partner China…

"Theoretically, the Merrill Lynch assumption is correct. If the DPP indeed ends up losing several seats to the KMT, it will be an unmistakable message that the governing party must move swiftly to address widespread discontent by revitalizing the economy and pursuing changes, if it is to win the more important subsequent legislative and presidential elections in early 2008…"

But President Chen and his DPP politicians did not see things that way. The party's huge losses in the 2005 local elections failed to stimulate them to carry out economic and political changes. For example, they still stuck to their anti-China stance despite the fact that the Chinese mainland now is the most important market for Taiwan. In January 2006, one month after the December 2005 magistrate and mayoral elections, Chen Shui-bian announced a set of new measures to tighten control over Taiwan's investment in mainland China. The move immediately raised concerns in Washington. In an opinion piece (published on January 13, 2006), I wrote:

"U.S. officials said that such new investment restrictions not only run counter to Taiwan's own economic interests but also threaten to hurt that of American companies which have been doing business with both sides of the Taiwan Strait...

"They even questioned the logic behind Taipei's decision to impose tighter mainland investment restrictions. They just didn't understand why the government here wanted to place stricter restrictions on cross-strait economic exchanges at a time when world economies are becoming increasingly interdependent and when China has grown into a very important economic player in the region."

Chen and his party also failed to learn a lesson from the 2005 election defeats. Had they done so, they would have adopted stricter measures to combat and prevent government corruption. Quite the contrary, many top DPP politicians continued to defend President Chen when he faced corruption charges and judicial investigations.

Nor did Chen and his DPP change their traditional election strategy. They still resorted to running a series of political issues, as they launched their campaign for the 2008 legislative and presidential elections. They included playing the ethnic card, like calling for voters to safeguard the "native" government. Another program advanced by the DPP was to push for transitional justice programs aimed at raking over the KMT's past wrongdoings. A third controversial theme campaigned for by the ruling party was pitching a referendum calling for Taiwan to join the U.N. under the name "Taiwan." It was controversial because the U.N. requires statehood for membership. Taiwan is not an independent country. Chen's U.N. entry referendum hence was seen by Beijing and Washington as an attempt to change Taiwan's political status.

In the end, the voters made their choices. The DPP lost the legislative elections in January 2008 and the presidential race in March two months later, both in a humiliating way. The opposition KMT was the biggest winner in both races. It clinched a more than two-thirds majority of total legislative seats. Its presidential candidate Ma Ying-jeou won an overwhelming 58.45% of the votes cast, while his DPP opponent Frank Hsieh garnered only 41.55% of the ballot.

A post-presidential election survey found that the DPP's approval ratings had dropped to a pathetic 18% in the wake of its devastating defeat in the 2008 legislative and presidential elections. The outgoing ruling party was actually in tatters now. President Chen Shui-bian, subject to a two-term limit, did not run for the presidency himself this time. But he, as DPP president, led his party to a series of three crushing defeats from local to central during his second four years of presidency. It could be said that the DPP's political fortunes were closely linked to Chen's.

In 2000 when Chen Shui-bian rose to power after defeating the long-ruling KMT, the DPP, as the party of the president, was elevated to governing status as a result. Chen's 2000 election victory was so impressive that its earned him praise as being Taiwan's democratic icon. But in his final years in office, Chen became a political liability for the DPP, due mainly to his poor governing performance and his involvement in a spate of corruption scandals. So heavy was the liability that it caused the DPP to lose both the legislative and presidential elections in 2008, relegating it to the status of an opposition party for the next eight years.

For Chen Shui-bian himself, things turned terribly bad at the end of his presidency: He ended up in jail. Chen was escorted directly to a Taipei detention center for investigation almost immediately after he handed over power to his successor, the KMT's Ma Ying-jeou, and lost presidential immunity. He later was convicted in bribery and money laundering cases and was sentenced to lengthy prison terms. He was granted medical parole in 2015 after serving more than six years of a combined 20-year sentence for the various offenses he committed in office.

I had no chance of monitoring former President Chen Shui-bian's final days in office as a commentary writer. It was around the time when Taiwan's March 2008 presidential election drew to a close, that I had left the China Post, no longer writing editorials for the newspaper. Leaving that editorial-writing job also marked my full retirement from a journalism career that spanned more than four decades. By this time I was in my early to mid-70s. But I didn't quit writing altogether. After a short time, I began writing books. I already finished my first one, which deals with former President Chen Shui-bian. My second or current one recounting my own life and career is now in the final process of completion.

Afterword

A Self-Made Man--the story of my life and career--took me four years to complete. In the course of writing this autobiography, I sometimes wondered whether I could live long enough to finish it, given the fact that I am 90 years old now (2022). But as it happens, I am still alive, energetic, and able to think clearly. Emboldened by my current state of health, I am beginning to ponder what to write next, after getting this 120,000-word work published.

The idea of A Self-Made Man was formed in response to suggestions made by some of my former colleagues and longtime friends. They suggested that I ought to write something to recount my own life and long journalistic career. Such an account, they believed, would be of interest to journalists and non-journalists alike.

At first, I was hesitant to include some of the commentaries that I wrote on the reform programs of former President Lee Teng-hui and his successor President Chen Shui-bian in my autobiography. But I soon realized there was nothing wrong with me doing so. Consider: Some of the programs that the two leaders carried out during their years in office had far-reaching effects and some were highly controversial. As an opinion writer, how I saw those events then obviously was something worth recalling.

As I was writing the afterword for A Self-Made Man, I had a feeling of being fulfilled in my life. Some striking examples: Writing two English-language books after retirement had long been my dream. Now with the finishing of my autobiography, I will soon have attained that goal. Four years earlier in 2017, I had already completed my first book manuscript, which deals with Taiwan's former President Chen Shui-bian. Back in mid-1966 when I first joined the journalism profession, I aspired to become a professional journalist. In the more than four decades that followed, I played all key journalistic roles. In the course, I never neglected my obligation to follow the rules of journalistic ethics. Then even earlier when I was still serving in the army, I taught myself English intending to use it to help find a new job. This aim was achieved a decade later when I passed a China Post examination and was hired as a reporter by the English-language newspaper.